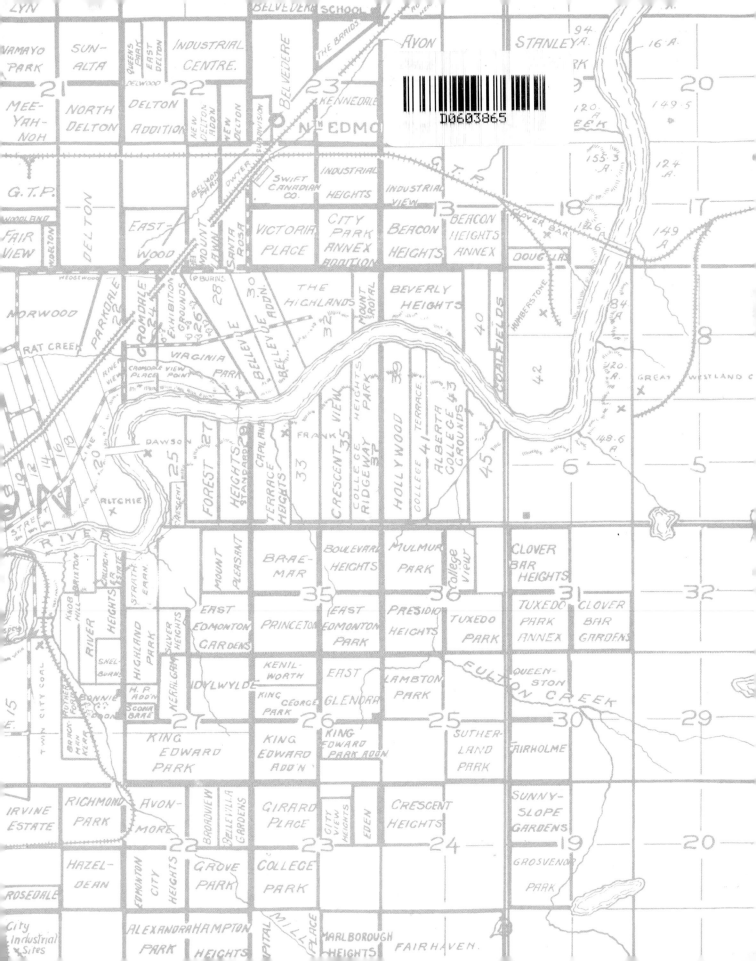

Naming Edmonton

From Ada to Zoie

Naming Edmonton

From Ada to Zoie

CITY OF EDMONTON

The University of Alberta Press

Developed and Compiled by Heritage Sites Committee, Edmonton Historical Board

Merrily Aubrey
Marie-Louise Brugeyroux
Kim Christie-Milley
Dorothy Field
Enid Fitzsimonds
June Honey
Bruce Ibsen
Helen LaRose
Leslie Latta-Guthrie
David Leaker
Marie Lesoway
Enid Liddell
Leonard Liddell
George Milner
Lois Porter
John Walter

Editorial Panel

Merrily Aubrey
Dorothy Field
Bruce Ibsen
Helen LaRose
Leslie Latta-Guthrie

Writer/Copy Editor

Carol Berger

Researchers

Glynys Smith Hohmann
Susan Stanton

Published by

The University of Alberta Press
Ring House 2
Edmonton, Alberta, Canada T6G 2E1

Copyright © The City of Edmonton 2004
ISBN 0-88864-423-X

Library and Archives Canada Cataloguing in Publication

Naming Edmonton : from Ada to Zoie / City of Edmonton,
developed and compiled by Historic Sites Committee, Edmonton
Historical Board.

Includes bibliographical references and index.
ISBN 0-88864-423-X

1. Streets—Alberta—Edmonton. 2. Edmonton (Alta.)—
History. I. Edmonton (Alta.) II. Edmonton Historical Board.
Historic Sites Committee.

FC3696.67.N35 2004   971.23'34   C2004-903388-3

Printed and bound in Canada by Friesens, Altona, Manitoba.
First edition, second printing, 2005

The University of Alberta Press gratefully acknowledges the
support received for its publishing program from The Canada
Council for the Arts. The University of Alberta Press also gratefully acknowledges the financial support of the Government of
Canada through the Book Publishing Industry Development
Program (BPDIP) and from the Alberta Foundation for the Arts
for our publishing activities.

The Edmonton Historical Board and the City of Edmonton
acknowledge the support of the Community Initiatives Program,
Alberta Lottery Fund, Alberta Gaming and the Alberta Historical
Resources Foundation.

Title page photograph: Jasper Avenue looking east, circa 1927.
(CEA EA-10-206)
Map on page xiii by Wendy Johnson.
Photograph page 361: Firemen in Market Square, 1929.
(CEA EA-10-2595)
Endpaper map: Mundy's Map of Edmonton District No. 2, circa 1920s.
(CEA EAM226)

*Respectfully and affectionately dedicated to three
who were the collective soul of the Edmonton
Place Names Project—*

Marie-Louise Brugeyroux, June Honey and Lois Porter

Contents

Foreword

WHAT MAKES A GREAT CITY? There are many possible answers, but one way to find out is to look at a city's history. Edmonton's centennial year is a good time to reflect on the rich and varied threads from the city's past that help create this exciting place we call home. Many historical threads are woven into the names of the places in Edmonton that create a rich tapestry of the city's history.

Naming Edmonton: From Ada to Zoie provides readers with the opportunity to learn the "how and why" of Edmonton place names—names derived from nature, historical places and events, and from other cultures. Place names also acknowledge the contributions of many persons who, in diverse ways, created a vibrant, thriving community here on the banks of the North Saskatchewan River and, for their efforts, were honoured in the naming of streets, bridges, neighbourhoods and parks.

Why produce a book of names? Behind the street signs, pictures and names on a map is the history of Edmonton writ large. Some place names acknowledge historical events important to those who made this city their home. Many newcomers are happy to have a naming link to their faraway birthplaces. Pioneers, early inhabitants and present-day citizens are represented in many place names, recognizing their contributions through programs, facilities and a truly remarkable spirit of volunteer cooperation. Edmontonians and visitors enjoy the benefits of the far-sighted dreams of the people who have inhabited our community and walked our streets.

As Edmonton celebrates its 100th anniversary as a city in 2004, it is only fitting that this book provides a touchstone to our city's history. *Naming Edmonton: From Ada to Zoie* gives us a glimpse as to what goes into the creation of a community. It is a fascinating read about the ideas, the energies, and the experiences of citizens who helped build Edmonton.

It is vitally important to recognize and acknowledge the tremendous dedication and amount of work that has gone into the writing of this book. When the Edmonton Place Names Project began over ten years ago, few dreamt of the perseverance and countless hours of volunteer work that would follow. Sincerest thanks and words of appreciation are offered to the members of the Heritage Sites Committee of the Edmonton Historical Board, and others who, through their heroic efforts over the years, have seen their work come to fruition. What a beautiful tapestry we have woven showing the history of the City of Edmonton! Congratulations to all contributors. Your dedicated efforts will do much to enhance the understanding that Edmontonians and visitors have of this city's remarkable history. Your work will ensure that we have a fine book worthy of pride that will serve as a legacy for future citizens.

It is with a great sense of accomplishment that the Edmonton Historical Board presents the publication of *Naming Edmonton: From Ada to Zoie* as our official contribution on the occasion of Edmonton's 100th anniversary.

CATHERINE GARVEY, PhD
Chair, Edmonton Historical Board

Preface

AS PART OF the City of Edmonton's centennial, the Heritage Sites Committee of the Edmonton Historical Board undertook a project to look at the city's history through its names. Names reflect our history from the ground up. As we name our children with pride and care, so too do we name our surroundings. Names are a reflection of our past and our aspirations for the future. Yet often these place names become so much a part of our daily lives that we cease to think about them. *Naming Edmonton: From Ada to Zoie* helps change that. It provides the reader with an appreciation of the people and events that helped the city become what it is today. The project, a decade in the making, was accomplished by a number of hard-working souls who tirelessly volunteered their time to see it to its completion. Some are no longer with us. Each had a strong tie to the city. All had a deep love for its history.

Edmonton is one of the oldest areas of European settlement in present-day Alberta. Originally located at the mouth of the Sturgeon River, across from today's Fort Saskatchewan, Edmonton House was established in 1795 as a fur trade post of the Hudson's Bay Company. The final site of Fort Edmonton was built atop the high bank of the North Saskatchewan in 1830. It was such an auspicious site that the newly created province of Alberta decided in 1906 to locate its Legislature Buildings just above the old fort.

With the influx of settlers in the late 1800s, and the city's historical significance as a "gateway to the north," Edmonton prospered. By 1892 it was erected as a town, and by October 1904 it was chartered as a city. Because of its geographically centred location, and other factors such as politics and transportation connections, Edmonton became the capital of the new province of Alberta in September 1905.

As we approach Edmonton's centennial, the city and the province as a whole are experiencing a period of tremendous growth. Some old neighbourhoods have faded and even disappeared, while others are in the process of renewal. New neighbourhoods are being built and new names are being added to the history of Edmonton's place names. Each generation of naming brings with it the sensibilities of its time. *Naming Edmonton*, by its very nature, can be only a snapshot from the time of its writing. Edmontonians of today and the future can learn more about their city's history in its pages.

MERRILY K. AUBREY
Provincial Toponymist

Acknowledgements

NAMING EDMONTON: From Ada to Zoie could not have been produced without the hard work of many people. To begin, it is important to note that the nine-member Edmonton Historical Board is comprised primarily of volunteers. They are appointed by Edmonton City Council, and its Heritage Sites Committee is chaired by a board member. The board includes six citizens-at-large, two representatives of the Northern Alberta Pioneers' and Descendants' Association and a representative of the Edmonton Chapter of the Historical Society of Alberta. Current board members are Catherine Garvey, Chair; Marianne Fedori, Vice-Chair; Linda Affolder; Percy Connell; Enid Fitzsimonds; Joe Friedel; Jean Mucha; John Walter; and Bert Yeudall.

Current members of the Heritage Sites Committee are Enid Fitzsimonds, Chair; Merrily Aubrey, Head, Alberta Geographic Names Program and Project Historian, Alberta Community Development; Dorothy Field, Head, Heritage Survey Program, Alberta Community Development; Helen LaRose, City Archivist Emeritus; Leslie Latta-Guthrie, City Archivist; David Leaker; George Milner; and John Walter. Former members of the committee include Marie-Louise Brugeyroux; Kim Christie-Milley, Acting City Archivist; Bob Gaetz; James Goebel; June Honey, City Archives; Bruce Ibsen, Past City Archivist; Rod Keith, City of Edmonton Parks and Recreation (now known as Community Services); Marie Lesoway; Enid Liddell; Leonard Liddell; Lois Porter; Braj Prasad, City of Edmonton Parks and Recreation (now known as Community Services); and Karen Russell, City of Edmonton Planning and Development.

Naming Edmonton: From Ada to Zoie is the result of the dedicated efforts of volunteers. In the course of the project, eight volunteers and staff put in over 10,000 hours of research at the City of Edmonton Archives. Among these were Marie-Louise Brugeyroux, Dorothy Field, June Honey, Bruce Ibsen, Helen LaRose, David Leaker, George Milner and Lois Porter.

Many partners have played a large role in the Edmonton Names Project, including:

- the City of Edmonton Archives, providing staff and volunteer time and overall administrative support;
- the City of Edmonton Community Services Department, providing management support through Linda Cochrane, Branch Manager, Recreation Facility Services Branch; Carol Watson, Past Director, Heritage Facilities; and Bryan Monaghan, Director, Programs and Events;
- the City of Edmonton's Planning and Development Department; and
- the Cultural Facilities and Historical Resources Division of Alberta Community Development.

Naming Edmonton: From Ada to Zoie received generous grants from the Alberta Historical Resources Foundation and the Edmonton Community Lottery Board to hire two researchers, over the period of 1997 to 2001, to complete the research begun by volunteers in 1994. A final grant from the Community Initiatives Program in 2002 allowed the hiring of Carol Berger as Writer/Copyeditor and the production of the book.

The University of Alberta Press wishes to thank Keith Stotyn for his detailed readings of the manuscript. We would also like to thank Sharon Budnarchuk of Audrey's Books for helping shape the book. Thanks also to Sima Khorrami, Richard Siemens and Alan Brownoff who photographed the letters opening each section. Mike Clark at Colorfast scanned the photographs. Mary Mahoncy-Robson managed, edited and proofed the project, Peter Midgley provided a final reading, and Alethea Adair helped on the appendices and index. Alan Brownoff did the book and cover design, the duotones and the layout of the book. Denise Ahlefeldt assisted in page layout. Wendy Johnson provided cartographic assistance on the maps. Cathie Crooks and Laraine Coates provided marketing and promotion for the project. We also wish to thank the coordinators of this project, Merrily Aubrey, Dorothy Field and Leslie Latta-Guthrie, who have been a pleasure to work with.

Big Bear, no date. (CEA EA-10-1023) ← **Photograph caption**

Official place name

Information on the origin of the name

Description of the location

Big Bear Park

1312–109 Street ←

This 1.74-ha. park in the Bearspaw neighbourhood honours the life of Plains Cree Chief Mistahimaskwa "Big Bear" (c. 1825–1888). By the 1870s, Big Bear, who had been born in what is now Saskatchewan, was a leader of his people. In 1876 he refused to sign Treaty No. 6 because he believed it would destroy his people's way of life. By 1882, however, the threat of starvation finally forced him to submit to the treaty, and with it, to accept the forced relocation of Aboriginal people onto reserves. He was later blamed for the Frog Lake Massacre of 1885. Despite his innocence, Big Bear surrendered at Fort Carleton and faced treason charges. He was found guilty and sentenced to three years at Stony Mountain Penitentiary. Big Bear served two years of his term before being released because of ill health. He returned to the Poundmaker Reserve where he died the following year.

→ **Park 1986 SW 1:A1** ←

Feature type

These types include Area, Bridge, Cemetery, City, Creek, Lake, Neighbourhood, Park, Ravine, River, Road, Subdivision, Underpass and Walkway. Often the same name is used for more than one entry, so the type of feature is very important in using cross-references.

Year the name was approved

Most place names are officially approved by the Names Advisory Committee (NAC) of the city's Planning and Development Department (PDD). CU indicates that no date can be attached to the origin of a name, since it has become recognized through "common usage", rather than by the official process.

Map sheet reference

The city is divided into 12 map sheets. These are in the City of Edmonton Reference Maps section, starting on page xxxiii. In this sample entry, Big Bear Park is on City of Edmonton Reference Map 1 on page xxxiv at coordinates A1. The maps are at a scale of 1:35 000 (one centimetre on the map represents 300 metres on the ground. Any map sheet reference followed by an asterisk (*) has not been labelled on the map.

General location of the feature

To make it easier to locate a place name, the city has been divided into five general areas: SW (Southwest), SE (Southeast), NW (Northwest), NE (Northeast) and C (Central). See map on page xiii.

How To Use This Book

NAMING EDMONTON: *From Ada to Zoie* offers a comprehensive guide to the names of the city's streets, parks, neighbourhoods, subdivisions and other features, including bridges, walkways, cemeteries, ravines and waterways. By exploring the background of the people, the events and the natural features that inspired Edmonton's place names, readers can learn about the development and growth of the city's neighbourhoods, parks and roadways.

Introductory sections look at the history of the Edmonton's Place Names Project and the history of the City of Edmonton on its centennial. A Timeline of the City of Edmonton outlines major events in the past, starting with 1795 when the first Edmonton House was built north of Fort Saskatchewan to present-day events. Historic maps of Edmonton show the growth and development of the city.

The place name entries include all the official names within the current boundaries of Edmonton up to and including the year 2002. Each entry includes a description of the location of the named feature and information about the origin of the place name. At the bottom of the entry the following information is listed: the type of feature; the year the name was officially approved by the Names Advisory Committee; the area of the city the feature is located in; and the location on the City of Edmonton Reference Maps. The Reference Maps section includes an index map to the twelve separate maps of the city that are listed in the place name entries. These colour maps have been compiled by the City of Edmonton, and are based on the official mapping data of the city. The maps are at an approximate scale of 1:35000.

The place names are arranged alphabetically, word by word, as they are officially recorded in the public record. Many places are listed under the first name of the person the place is named after. For example, **William Hawrelak Park** will be found in the W section under William, although most people know it simply as Hawrelak Park. The Index by Surnames of Entries will assist readers with finding the full names of well-

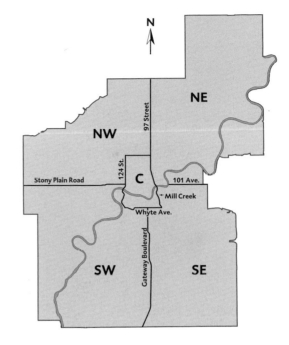

known and some not so well-known people whose names grace the city. As well, names starting with abbreviations, for example, Dr. and St. will be found alphabetically where the full word would be, i.e., Doctor (**Dr. Anne Anderson Park** follows the **Dickinsfield** entry) and Saint (**St. Albert Trail** follows the **Saddleback Road** entry).

Feature stories on well-known Edmonton places complement the alphabetical entries. Although not official place names, there are feature stories on **The Rat Hole** and the **Coal Fields**. Features on **Fort Road** and **St. Albert Trail** tell of the earliest roads in the region. Famous and not so famous Edmontonians are also highlighted, ranging from **Ada Boulevard's** Ada Magrath to the park named in honour of Violet "Zoie" Gardner.

Often place names reflect prominent and honoured contributors to local development and growth. For example, **Mayfield** was named in honour of Wilfrid R. "Wop" May, a WWI pilot and pioneer of Edmonton's civilian aviation scene. Developers held a naming

Looking east through an arch over Jasper Avenue at 97 Street, celebrating the coronation of King Edward VII, 1901. (CEA EA–10–2809)

contest in 1954 and awarded Peggy Stewart a prize of fifteen dollars for her submission. Other names reflect growth of local business. **Central McDougall** was named for John Alexander McDougall (1854–1928), an early Edmonton businessman and mayor of Edmonton.

Edmonton's place names also reflect commemorative events and prominent physical characteristics that make neighbourhoods unique within the context of the city. **Kingsway** commemorates the June 2, 1939 visit of King George VI and Queen Elizabeth to Edmonton. **Mill Creek** is named for the flour mill that William Bird operated from 1871 to1874 beside the creek that ran through his property (River Lot 19). **Aspen Gardens** is named for the abundant aspen trees in the neighbourhood.

Over the years, many of Edmonton's natural features have changed and an annotated map in the appendices highlights where and when Edmonton's waterways were lost.

The extensive listings in the Lost Names appendix document names that are no longer in use in Edmonton. Many historic names were "lost" when the city went to numbering streets and avenues in 1914.

Historic place names no longer in use, such as Blatchford Field and John Ducey Park, will always have a place in Edmonton's collective memory and many places no longer physically exist, such as the Rat Hole. Other names have still not fallen out of common usage, although Calgary Trail North has been replaced officially by **Gateway Boulevard** and the Capilano Drive by **Wayne Gretzky Drive**. Some of these lost names are making unofficial comebacks, as the numbered streets and avenues in the designated Heritage section of Groat Estates have the original names preserved in the sidewalks.

A multitude of sources were used in compiling this reference work. In addition to hours spent in the City of Edmonton Archives, researchers used many books, publications and websites to trace Edmonton's place names. A list of the Sources used includes resources for further research on Edmonton's history.

Finally, the Index by Surnames of Entries will assist the reader in finding the entries for places named after people, which are commonly listed under the first name or even honorific (Dr.) of the person being honoured by the City.

Abbreviations

A&GW	Alberta & Great Waterways Railway
AMA	Alberta Motor Association
BA	Bachelor of Arts
BC	British Columbia
BD	Bachelor of Divinity
BSc	Bachelor of Science
CCF	Co-operative Commonwealth Federation
CEF	Canadian Expeditionary Force
CFB	Canadian Forces Base
CFL	Canadian Football League
CNIB	Canadian National Institute for the Blind
CNoR	Canadian Northern Railway
CNR	Canadian National Railways
CPR	Canadian Pacific Railway
CU	Common Usage
DEW	Distant Early Warning
DSO	Distinguished Service Order
ED&BC	Edmonton, Dunvegan & British Columbia Railway
EHB	Edmonton Historical Board
EHS	Edmonton Historical Society
EHS	Edmonton Horticultural Society
EPSB	Edmonton Public School Board
EY&P	Edmonton, Yukon & Pacific Railway
GTP	Grand Trunk Pacific Railway
HBC	Hudson's Bay Company
IAAF	International Amateur Athletics Federation
IODE	Imperial Order Daughters of the Empire
LRT	Light Rail Transit
MA	Master of Arts
MBA	Master of Business Administration
MLA	Member of the Legislative Assembly (Provincial)
MSc	Master of Science
MP	Member of Parliament (Federal)
NAC	Names Advisory Committee
NAR	Northern Alberta Railways
NDP	New Democratic Party
NHL	National Hockey League
NWC	North West Company
NWMP	North West Mounted Police
PDD	Planning and Development Department
PEI	Prince Edward Island
PhD	Doctor of Philosophy
RCAF	Royal Canadian Air Force
RCMP	Royal Canadian Mounted Police
RNWMP	Royal North West Mounted Police
SIS	Secret Intelligence Service
SPARE	Society for the Protection of Architectural Resources in Edmonton
UFA	United Farmers of Alberta
US	United States
WCTU	Woman's Christian Temperance Union
WWI	World War I (1914–1918)
WWII	World War II (1939–1945)
YMCA	Young Men's Christian Association
YWCA	Young Women's Christian Association

High Level Bridge under construction, 1911. (CEA EA-134-1)

Edmonton's Official Place Names

HOW WELL DO YOU KNOW EDMONTON? Do you know the stories behind the names of the streets? The neighbourhoods? The parks? Maybe you have learned about Edmonton through the history of your own family. My husband, Rick, born in the late 1950s, is proud to be a third-generation Edmontonian. Perhaps his family's story is not unlike yours. His mother's family immigrated to Canada from England in 1952, settling in the Strathearn neighbourhood. As a young child, his family lived in the Boyle Street neighbourhood with his paternal grandparents. There, he heard stories of his grandmother's childhood in McCauley and his grandfather's adventures building the High Level Bridge. When his grandfather passed on, his grandmother moved north to the neighbourhood of Alberta Avenue. Rick remembers being a north-side boy who travelled by bus to go to movies with a south-side friend in Garneau. Later he explored the south side while living in the Strathcona and Mill Creek neighbourhoods, finally ending up back in Strathearn. With his family, he returned to his original roots in the city centre and we now call Norwood our home. Like many who live in Edmonton, Rick wonders about the origins of the names of the streets, communities, parks and other parts of the city he has grown to love.

THE YEAR 2004 marks the 100th anniversary of Edmonton's incorporation as a city. As part of the celebration, the Edmonton Historical Board—through the facilitation of and a decade of hard work by its Heritage Sites Committee—has created *Naming Edmonton: From Ada to Zoie.* This book chronicles the background of the names given to the city's streets, communities and parks. It is an illustrated work using a wonderful selection of archival photographs, largely from the City of Edmonton Archives, as well as detailed maps of Edmonton.

Naming Edmonton provides a window on the history of the origins and meanings behind the nearly 1,300 official Edmonton names. The book focuses on names that were approved by the Names Advisory Committee (NAC) of the city's Planning and Development Department (PDD) and are still in use. The names included fall within the current boundaries of Edmonton and represent the city's naming history up to and including the year 2002.

Naming Edmonton creates benefits that reach far beyond its immediate goal of celebrating and commemorating the centenary of Edmonton's creation as a city in 1904. The book makes available a wide range of historical information to the citizens of Edmonton that will enhance their awareness and appreciation of Edmonton's heritage. It tells the stories of the everyday people who have made an impact on the life of the city, and provides genealogists with a good source of family history. The book also provides visitors with an easy entry to the history of the city.

Naming Edmonton will be used in Edmonton's schools, libraries, heritage sites and other community centres throughout the province to provide Albertans with insights into our city's history. It is an excellent resource for land developers and realtors who want a quick and easy source of information on the background of communities and existing names, as well as how these names have developed. A ready reference will be at hand to provide businesses and private individuals with background information previously available only after extensive archival research. The book will enhance a greater appreciation and understanding of, and foster pride in, Edmonton as a community.

Looking at Edmonton's History Through Place Names

Place names provide a unique way of looking at our history. Names reflect the culture and sensibilities of the age in which they are introduced. Previously, the only written documentation on Edmonton names were two pamphlets: one produced by the Edmonton Regional Planning Commission in 1964, and the other by the city's Planning and Development Department in 1974. *Naming Edmonton: From Ada to Zoie* brings the knowledge of the origins of Edmonton's names up to date and reflects both the century-long history of the city and its growth in the latter part of the twentieth century and the beginning of the twenty-first.

The place names of Edmonton are an important expression of the city's cultural heritage. The study of place names, known as toponymy, provides a view of the past from the ground up. Toponymic research is primarily concerned with the origins and meanings of place names. Geographical names unlock a valuable store of information, not only as the key components of reliable maps, but they also reflect cultural heritage and provide clues to the groups and individuals who have had an impact on the city.

Naming related to the development of cities involves the concept of boosterism. Names in new urban developments often reflect aspirations, or try to create an ambience or character for the city. Parks, in particular, and sometimes neighbourhoods, streets and bridges provide an opportunity to honour the movers and shakers in the city's history. The types of names used are also a reflection of the times. Since the 1970s, a great number of places have been named after women. This is in contrast to the city's early history, when place names almost exclusively honoured prominent men. Also, recent decades have seen the use of non-Anglo-Saxon names, reflecting the changing ethnic makeup of Edmonton.

The Names Advisory Committee

Who officially names the places in Edmonton? The City of Edmonton's PDD formed the District Names Advisory Committee in 1956. It was created by Bylaw No. 1754 to establish suitable names for subdivisions, neighbourhood unit areas, highways, parks and other public places as well as public buildings and structures. The committee's first task was to help avoid confusion over similar subdivision names such as King Edward and King Edward Park.

Members of that first committee, in 1956–1957, included Alderman J. F. Falconer, Chairman; Miss C. McGrath, Edmonton Separate School Board representative; Mrs. F. C. Butterworth, Edmonton Public

District Names Advisory Committee, 1956.
(CEA EA–10–2379)

School Board representative; Mr. W. R. Brown, town planner; Mr. G. Kyle, Secretary; and one representative of the Archives and Landmarks Committee, now known as the Edmonton Historical Board (EHB).

Today, the NAC is appointed by City Council. The committee's job is to recommend names for municipal facilities, new neighbourhoods, parks and roads to the Executive Committee of City Council. The NAC has five members: two citizens-at-large, one representative of the EHB and one representative from each of the Edmonton School Boards. The Planning and Policy Services Branch of the PDD provides administrative services to the NAC, including researching names; maintaining an inventory of names for future use; receiving requests from the public for names to be honoured; creating and providing agendas to the committee; and making presentations at Executive Committee.

How to Suggest an Official Name
The PDD, on behalf of the NAC, receives naming requests from citizens-at-large, organizations and civic departments. The "Naming Application and Requirements" form can be accessed online within the PDD's section of the City of Edmonton web site

(www.edmonton.ca). The NAC reviews a request in consultation with the applicant, civic departments, homeowners' associations and community leagues, as necessary.

The NAC submits a recommendation of support or nonsupport to the Executive Committee of City Council. The Executive Committee then receives the recommendation and makes a final decision. The PDD, on behalf of the NAC, notifies the applicant, as well as affected civic departments and other agencies.

Making and Preserving Edmonton's History

Naming Edmonton: From Ada to Zoie is the result of the courage, leadership and exceptional effort of the Heritage Sites Committee of the Edmonton Historical Board.

The EHB was created to address concerns over the loss of Edmonton's heritage and traces its origins to 1938. Known then as the Archives and Landmarks Committee, it began to identify and acquire historical documents and artifacts. The committee's work was scaled back during WWII. In 1947, the Archives and Landmarks Committee bylaw was approved and the committee's work continued. Throughout the ensuing years, the committee, which officially became the EHB in 1966, has been involved in numerous activities. It currently operates under Bylaw 10794.

The purpose of the EHB is to advise City Council on matters relating to the history of the City of Edmonton. By providing advice to Council, the board helps that body achieve its goal of supporting the process of democratic governance in the City of Edmonton. The board's duties and responsibilities are divided among several committees. On an annual basis, the Recognition Awards Committee raises an awareness of significant contributions by local individuals and organizations involved in making or preserving Edmonton's history, while the Plaques Committee identifies and distinguishes historical sites and buildings in Edmonton with commemorative markers. The Historic Resources Review Panel works in association with the PDD to oversee the Register of Historic Resources in Edmonton. Another board committee is the Heritage Sites Committee.

Meeting of the Edmonton Historical Board, 1966. (PAA BL. 2598)

The Heritage Sites Selection Committee was established in 1975. Its original mandate included assessing requests for building and site preservation; evaluating other buildings and sites for their historic, aesthetic and associative value; and making recommendations to the EHB on all such matters. Over the years, activities of the committee have included: producing a booklet called *Edmonton's Threatened Heritage* (1980); evaluating and making recommendations for a list of buildings to be included on the heritage list of the Downtown Area Redevelopment Plan bylaw (1981); producing a booklet called *Edmonton's Lost Heritage* (1982); and evaluating the historical significance of the Boyle Street/McCauley neighbourhood (1989). In later years, evaluations also were completed for the Scona East, Highlands, Rossdale, Garneau, Queen Alexandra (partial), Northlands (including Cromdale, Parkdale and Bellevue), Strathcona, Westmount/Inglewood and Riverdale neighbourhoods.

In 1994, the committee's name was changed to the Heritage Sites Committee. From 1994 to 1996, volunteers, all members of the Heritage Sites Committee, researched and compiled data about the origins of named streets, districts, parks and other local features for the Edmonton Place Names Project. This work began by committee member Lois Porter taking information provided on sheets compiled by former NAC

The Edmonton to Strathcona Ferry, Alberta.

600,267

Ferry at night—Edmonton to Strathcona, circa 1900. (CEA EA-10-1226)

secretary Nancy Diettrich and transposing the information onto index cards. From 1997 to late 1998, Susan Stanton was hired to research and uncover further details about the names provided by the committee's research. Glynys Smith (Hohmann) was hired in 2001 and completed the project, providing details about the names from S to Z and locating relevant maps and photographs.

The individuals involved in the development and production of *Naming Edmonton: Ada to Zoie* consider it a fitting tribute to Edmonton's centennial in 2004 and an excellent source of information for new generations of Edmontonians.

We would be grateful to hear from people who can provide additional information related to Edmonton names. Anyone who has history to share should contact:

City of Edmonton Archives
Prince of Wales Armouries Heritage Centre
10440–108 Avenue
Edmonton, Alberta   T5H 3Z9
Telephone: (780) 496-8711
Fax: (780) 496-8732
Email: CMS.Archives@edmonton.ca

LESLIE LATTA-GUTHRIE
City Archivist

From Trails and River Lots to Modern Edmonton

Edmonton's Early Trails and Settlement

THE HISTORIC TRAILS that the Aboriginal people, fur traders and early settlers used played an essential role in the creation of modern Edmonton. Fort Assiniboine Trail, used by fur traders since the 1820s, was a hazardous 80-mile (129-km) portage linking Fort Edmonton with Fort Assiniboine on the Athabasca River (near present-day Whitecourt). In the mid-1800s, Carlton Trail stretched from Fort Garry, Manitoba, through to Edmonton. Fort Road, part of the Carlton Trail, wound northeast from Jasper Avenue to Fort Saskatchewan. One of Edmonton's busiest thoroughfares today, St. Albert Trail is one of the oldest trails in Alberta, dating back to the 1820s. The Athabasca Landing Trail was developed around 1877 as a portage between the North Saskatchewan River at Fort Edmonton and the elbow of the Athabasca River. The Calgary-Edmonton Trail was an important conduit of communication and movement between the open prairie and Fort Edmonton. The Telegraph Trail originally ended at Hay Lakes but was extended to Edmonton via Leduc along the Calgary-Edmonton Trail in 1879. Even today, many of these original trails are recognizable as part of the major roadway network of Edmonton and northern Alberta.

The foundation of modern Edmonton began in 1869–1870, when the Dominion of Canada purchased Rupert's Land from the Hudson's Bay Company (HBC). In 1872, the HBC sent surveyors to Fort Edmonton to measure and mark out the boundary of the company's land around the old fort. The terms of the agreement allowed the HBC control of 3,000 acres (1,214 ha.). Known as the Hudson's Bay Reserve, the area stretched from present-day 101 Street in the east to 121 Street in the west, and from the river north to approximately 125 Avenue. Eleven years later, the government completed its own survey, delineating large lots on the northern and southern banks of the North Saskatchewan River. This system of surveying was called a river lot survey.

City Directories

In the early 1880s the Henderson Directory Company, based in Winnipeg, began to produce an annual gazetteer and directory for use in western Canada. The 1893 edition of Henderson's *Manitoba and Northwest Territories Gazetteer and Directory* included classified business information for the towns of Edmonton and Strathcona. It was noted that the company intended "to publish this work annually, corrected and revised to date of publication, keeping up with the rapid development of the country."

Similar directories covering the Edmonton area were published in the years that followed. The *Edmonton District Directory* for the year 1895 contained "full and authentic information, statistics, tables, maps" and a guide to northern Alberta. In his introduction, editor and publisher J.B. Spurr stated, "No more complete history and directory of the district has ever been printed." Spurr used census information collected by the North West Mounted Police in 1894 to complete the directory. It was noted that the directory's advertisements would "acquaint the reader with the industries and business houses of the district and…prove mutually advantageous."

The *Lowe's Directory of the Edmonton District* was first published in 1899. It contained information about towns, villages and country districts, as well as schools and churches, extending beyond the Edmonton district as far south as Red Deer. The publisher believed that, with the exception of the 1895 Spurr work, this was the first Alberta directory that "attempted to deal with the names and locations of settlers throughout the district." Another volume, the *Edmonton City Directory*, was compiled and published by John Aitken in 1905–1906 and printed by the Edmonton Printing and Publishing Co. Ltd., located on Howard Avenue (100 A Street).

The most influential of the directories, however, remains the Henderson's *Directory*. Annual editions of Henderson's *Edmonton City Directory*, dating back to

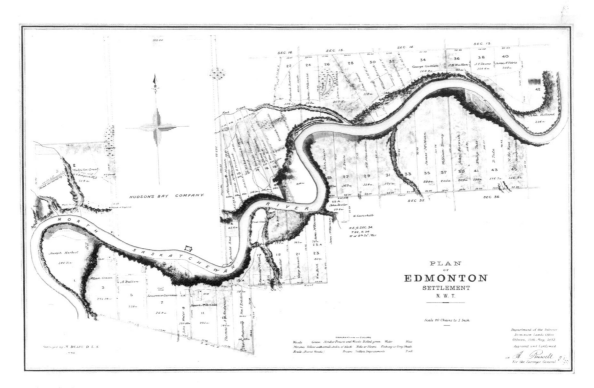

Plan of Edmonton Settlement, NWT, 1882. (CEA EAM 84)

1904, provide extremely interesting reading and are full of historical tidbits and advertising gems. The 1907 edition noted: "Every home and business house has been visited to secure the names of every person who makes this city his or her home, together with information concerning occupation, business address and private address." The 1915 edition recorded Edmonton's population at 63,400, provided a translation for addresses effected by the city's move from named to numbered streets in 1914, and made serious note of the effect WWI was having on Canadians. No directory was produced in 1918, due to the Spanish Influenza epidemic. The 1919 edition provided information on Greater Edmonton, "comprising the City proper, South Edmonton (formerly Strathcona), North Edmonton, Calder, Beverly, and all adjoining subdivisions, suburbs and environs" and noted the city's population at 66,231.

Today, Henderson's Directories provide an invaluable resource for those looking to research the history of their homes. They comprise "a street directory of the city, an alphabetically arranged list of business firms and companies, professional men and private citizens." Henderson's Directories provide listings of home and building occupants, spouse and occupation. Though not always accurate, these directories can indicate who has owned or lived in a particular home, suggest roughly when the home was built, and may provide a hint of if or when a structure was demolished. The City of Edmonton Archives has volumes spanning 80 years—from 1907 to 1987—within its collection.

The Street Grid System

Even before Edmonton became a city in 1904, the town adopted a grid system of street alignment and established 101 Street and 101 (Jasper) Avenue as the central axes of the system. Thereafter, the development of the city was based on this grid system superimposed on the original river lot system. This made for an easy

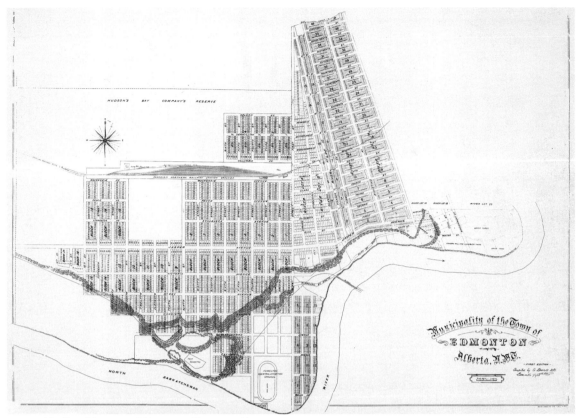

Municipality of the Town of Edmonton, Alberta, NWT, 1903. (CEA EAM 52)

division of the land into rectangular lots. It also facilitated a more convenient laying down of water mains and sewers, the erection of telephone poles and easier access to buildings in case of fire.

With the arrival of the Calgary and Edmonton Railway in Strathcona in 1891 and in the Canadian Northern Railway in Edmonton in 1905, settlers began flooding into the area. From 1904 to 1914, Edmonton's population grew from 8,300 to 72,500. Evidence of the 1905–1914 boom is still visible in many Edmonton neighbourhoods today. During that time the HBC subdivided most of the 3,000 acres received in their land settlement. However, the real estate market in western Canada had collapsed by 1913, and the HBC lots sold in 1912 were virtually worthless. Residents were soon forfeiting ownership of their properties because of nonpayment of taxes; the city became the majority owner of residential lots in Edmonton.

From Street Names to Numbers

Edmonton and Strathcona were originally independent cities using totally unrelated street naming and numbering systems. Their amalgamation in 1912 enhanced the city's growth, as realtors developed new subdivisions. The naming of streets was left entirely to the discretion of realtors, there being no control on street naming. Not surprisingly, this resulted in a haphazard, confusing and often repetitive system of street identification. By 1913 it was apparent that an overall street-numbering system had to be created for the entire city.

To resolve the matter, City Council launched a contest to select the best naming system. The one-hundred-dollar prize went to the "Edmonscona Plan," which proposed an alphabetical model. However, it was never adopted as City Council decided on the all-numbering system proposed by Mayor William Short. Before many of the familiar street signs (including

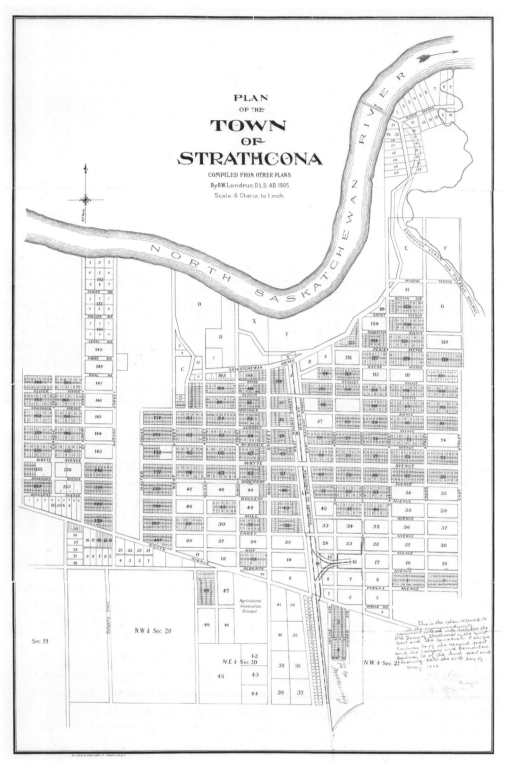

Plan of the Town of Strathcona, 1905. (CEA EAM 241)

Snow on Fort Trail, now Fort Road, 1932. (CEA EA-160-542)

Hardisty Street–98 Avenue, Sinclair Street–95A Street, Rice Street–101A Avenue, Alberta Avenue–118 Avenue) were torn down, a court action was launched by a citizen who was opposed to the move. The entire matter was held up until a plebiscite was called. It was not until 1914 that the complete changeover came into effect.

Until the adoption of the street numbering system in 1914, the city was developed primarily with a grid street pattern so there was little difficulty in street and avenue numbering. After 1950, however, with the advent of innovative subdivision designs, the rigid grid street pattern was abandoned in favour of a more flexible system called a modified grid. This included culs-de-sac, curvilinear streets and even diagonal streets, all of which necessitated modifications to the street numbering system. More named streets were introduced and, in 1956, the PDD formed the NAC.

The continued expansion of the city and the subsequent need for new subdivision names has ensured a heavy workload for the committee ever since.

Edmonton's Neighbourhood Development

Building construction between the two world wars was at times stagnant, at other times slow but steady, but nowhere near the pre-1914 levels. During WWII, Edmonton became a hub of activity with the Alaska Highway and Canol pipeline construction, as well as the British Commonwealth Air Training Plan. Without any major construction in over 25 years, Edmonton's housing was no longer adequate for the numbers of people needing homes—the city was jammed full. The city aggressively and successfully lobbied the Dominion government for funding for wartime housing.

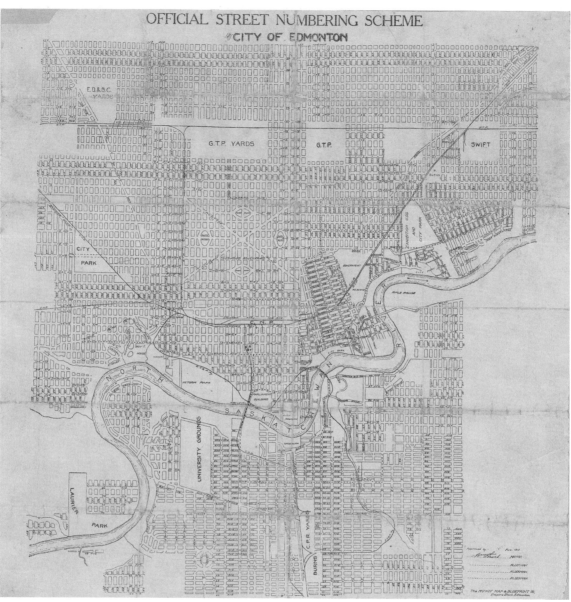

Official Street Numbering Scheme, 1913. (CEA EAM 73)

Aerial view of Mayfield neighbourhood, looking south, 1961 (CEA EA 75-559)

With the discovery of oil in nearby Leduc in 1947, Edmonton's growth rate started to rise to pre-1914 levels. Neighbourhoods surveyed, plotted and laid out in 1912 were now being developed and the housing market boomed. Since then, Edmonton's housing market has continued to expand.

Up until 1947, Edmonton used the grid street system. The introduction of British influence within the city planning staff brought Edmonton crescents, curves and neighbourhoods that were so complex the fire department often had trouble locating the scene of a blaze. Above all else, this influence brought the city traffic circles. Constructed throughout the city in the mid-1950s, traffic circles were designed to ease the flow of traffic through intersections. Although controversial from the start, it was argued that traffic circles were a good way to hold land in the name of the city until such time as the construction of intersections was justified.

The building of Mill Woods and Castle Downs was initially just as controversial as traffic circles. Castle Downs was seen as the positive result of innovative neighbourhood planning by the city administration, but many citizens did not like the new direction that moved dramatically away from the familiar grid pattern. It was first designed in 1969, documented the next year and approved for development by City Council in 1972. Construction began shortly thereafter. Several unique neighbourhoods were incorporated into the design, each consisting of 250 to 350 acres. Most of the Castle Downs neighbourhoods are named after famous castles, illustrating a move by the city's NAC to choose names along a certain theme. Some attempt was made to revise the traditional grid pattern with neighbourhoods such as Mill Woods. Since then, numbers have been all but forsaken in favour of names.

Edmonton Today

New Edmonton subdivisions continue to be isolated by topography and distance from older, numbered streets and avenues. Culs-de-sac and scenic loops continue to be a trend in new neighbourhoods and developers continue to prefer named roads to numbered ones because of their marketability.

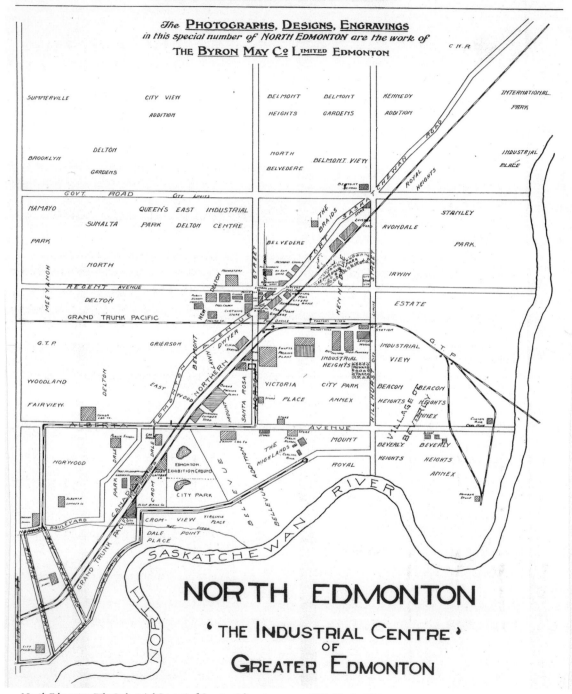

North Edmonton 'The Industrial Centre' of Greater Edmonton, 1913. (CEA Clipping File)

A Timeline of the City of Edmonton

1795   First Edmonton House is established across the North Saskatchewan River north of Fort Saskatchewan.

1830   Edmonton House moves to its final site below the present-day Legislative Buildings and continues its role as one of the most important depots in the North West.

1840   Arrival of Methodist minister Robert Rundle.

1842   Arrival of Roman Catholic priest Father Thibault.

1870   The Government of Canada purchases the vast area of Rupert's Land from the Hudson's Bay Company bringing the North-West Territories under Dominion government control.

1871   First log building outside the fort is built— McDougall Methodist Church.

1874   Arrival of the North West Mounted Police.

1875   Arrival of the first stern-wheeler, the *Northcote*.
Edmonton's first hospital is built by the Church of England under Canon Newton.

1876   Donald Ross builds the first hotel.

1878   First post office opens, with Richard Hardisty as postmaster.

1879   Telegraph line extends to Edmonton.
First Agricultural Show and Fair is held at Fort Edmonton.

1880   Frank Oliver and Alex Taylor's *Edmonton Bulletin* is first published.
First school is built outside Fort Edmonton.

1882   Edmonton Settlement is first surveyed by the Dominion Lands Surveys.

1883   Canadian Pacific Railway reaches Calgary.

1885   First telephone service.

1888   First Roman Catholic School is opened by the Sisters, Faithful Companions of Jesus.

1889   Edmonton Board of Trade is established.

1891   Calgary and Edmonton Railway is completed to the south side of the North Saskatchewan leading to the establishment and growth of South Edmonton.
Alex Taylor establishes the first electric light plant.

1892   Edmonton incorporates as a town on January 9.

1893   First fireworks display is held in the town for Dominion Day.

1898   First women's hockey team is established in Edmonton.

1899   South Edmonton incorporates as a town and is renamed Strathcona.

1900   Low Level Bridge opens.

1902   First train crosses the Low Level Bridge.
The Edmonton, Yukon and Pacific Railway, connecting with the Canadian Pacific Railway station, is built.

1903 *Edmonton Journal* is first published.
First automobile in Edmonton is purchased by Joseph H. Morris.
Alberta Hotel, the first four-storey building is erected in Edmonton.
First pipe organ in Edmonton is installed in McDougall Methodist Church.

1904 Edmonton incorporates as a city on October 8. The first mayor of the newly created city is Kenneth W. MacKenzie.

1905 The Province of Alberta is proclaimed on September 1.
Liberals under Alexander Rutherford are elected as Alberta's first government.
Canadian Northern Railway reaches Edmonton.

1906 Edmonton is confirmed as the capital city of the province.
First session of the Alberta Legislature is held in McKay Avenue School.

1907 Strathcona incorporates as a city.
First paving blocks to be laid in the city on McDougall Avenue, now 101 Street.
First rotary-dial telephone system in Canada is established in Edmonton.

1908 Edmonton Street Railway is established, the first in the prairie provinces.
First convocation at the University of Alberta is held on March 18.
First Alberta Music Festival is held in Edmonton on May 4.
Bijou Theatre, the first in Edmonton, opens on May 24.

1909 Grand Trunk Pacific Railway enters Edmonton.

1910 North Edmonton and West Edmonton incorporate as villages.
First newsreel in Edmonton is shown at the Bijou Theatre. It features the funeral of King Edward VII.
First rodeo is held in Strathcona.
Located on the south side of 105 Avenue and 102 Street, the first service station opens. Gas is sold in square cans packed two to a wooden box.

1911 First meeting of the Edmonton branch of the Women's Canadian Club.
Alberta Legislature is in session in the new Legislature Building for the first time.

1912 Edmonton and Strathcona amalgamate, and North Edmonton is annexed by Edmonton.
Hudson's Bay Company land sale is held.
Alberta Legislature building officially is opened by the governor g eneral of Canada, the Duke of Connaught on September 3.
Dawson Bridge opens.

1913 First door to door mail delivery.
High Level and 105th Street (now Walterdale) Bridges open.
Strathcona Library opens March 13.
Edmonton Technical School opens.

1914 WWI begins.
Town of Beverly is proclaimed.
City streets and avenues are numbered.

1915 Princess Theatre opens on March 8.
River floods the flats.
Fort Edmonton is demolished.

1916 Women obtain the right to vote in provincial elections in Alberta.

1917	City annexes West Edmonton (Calder area). Crestwood Community League, the first in Edmonton is established. (It was also known as the 142 Street District Community League and it served the old Jasper Place district between 142 Street and 149 Street, south of Stony Plain Road.)
1918	WWI ends. First airmail in Canada is delivered by Katherine Stinson who piloted a plane from Calgary to Edmonton. Women obtain the right to vote in federal elections.
1921	The United Farmers of Alberta are elected as the province's second government.
1922	Edmonton's first radio station, CJCA, begins operation.
1926	Edmonton Air Harbour is established. In 1927 it is named Blatchford Field.
1928	First neon sign in Edmonton is installed at Darling's Drug Store at Jasper Avenue and 102 Street.
1929	Women obtain the right to sit in the Senate, having been declared "persons".
1933	First traffic light in Edmonton at the corner of 101 Street and Jasper Avenue is in operation. First baseball game is played at Renfrew Park.
1935	The Social Credit Party is elected as the province's third government.

1939	WWII begins. First drive-in restaurant opens at 10022–109 Street on June 15. First night football game is held August 25.
1942	Alaska Highway is constructed.
1945	WWII ends.
1947	Leduc oil field comes under production.
1948	First oil refinery in operation in Clover Bar.
1949	Jasper Place incorporates as a village. Starlite Drive-In Theatre, first in the city, opens.
1953	Clover Bar Bridge opens.
1954	First telecast in Edmonton by CFRN-TV, Channel 3 is broadcast on October 17.
1955	Groat Bridge opens. Westmount Shoppers' Park opens, the first shopping mall in Edmonton.
1957	Construction of Edmonton International Airport starts. New city hall building opens.
1960	Queen Elizabeth Planetarium opens.
1964	Great Canadian Oil Sands begins production in Fort McMurray.
1968	Quesnell Bridge opens.
1969	Capilano Bridge opens. 911 emergency service begins on March 8.

1971 James McDonald Bridge opens.
The Conservative Party is elected as the province's fourth government.
Mill Woods and Castle Downs/Lake District is annexed to the city, 6,099 ha.

1972 Beverly Bridge opens.

1974 Beginning of the economic boom that leads to growth in south-east and north-east Edmonton.

1976 First Heritage Days festival is held.

1978 LRT system opens.
Edmonton Sun newspaper is first published.
Commonwealth Games is held in the summer.
First Edmonton Folk Music Festival is held in the summer.

1982 36,948 ha. of land is acquired on all sides of the city in this most recent major annexation.
Edmonton's International Fringe Theatre Festival is staged for the first time.

1983 Universiad (World University Games) is held at the University of Alberta.
The world's largest shopping complex, West Edmonton Mall opens.

1984 First of five Stanley Cups is won by the Edmonton Oilers.
Pope John Paul II visits the city.

1987 A tornado sweeps through the southeastern portion of the city on July 31. Twenty-seven people are killed, and over three hundred million dollars in property damage occurs.

1988 The slogan "City of Champions" first appears on signs in the city.

1989 Jan Reimer, Edmonton's first woman mayor, is elected.

1991 The LRT system is extended south across the North Saskatchewan River to the University of Alberta campus.

1992 Current city hall opens on Churchill Square.

1996 World Figure Skating Championships are held in the city.

1997 The world-class Francis Winspear Centre for Music opens.

2001 8th International Association of Athletic Federations (IAAF) games are held in Edmonton on August 8–12, the first time the games are held in North America.

2004 The City of Edmonton celebrates its 100th anniversary.

Sources

Edmonton, Alberta. City of Edmonton Archives. A number of entries are from a list of "firsts" compiled by archives staff.
MacGregor, J.G. *Edmonton, A history,* 2nd ed. (Abridged and appended.) Edmonton: Hurtig Publishers, 1975.

City of Edmonton Reference Maps

Index Map

Note

Neighbourhoods are in bold capital letters.

Parks are in red type.

Street names are in all capital letters.

Water features are in blue.

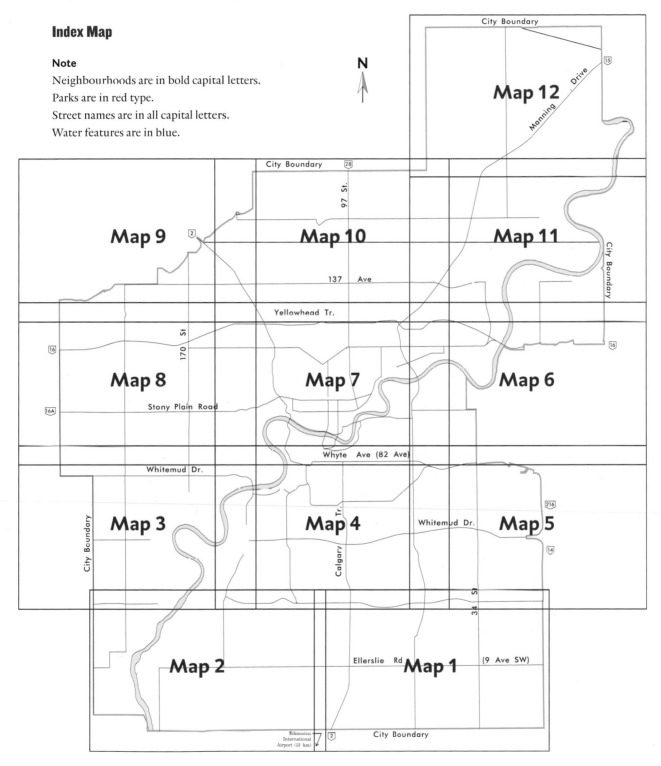

N

Map 12

City Boundary

Manning Drive

15

City Boundary

City Boundary 28

97 St.

Map 9

2

Map 10

Map 11

137 Ave

Yellowhead Tr.

170 St

16

Map 8

Map 7

Map 6

16

16A

Stony Plain Road

Whyte Ave (82 Ave)

Whitemud Dr.

City Boundary

Map 3

Map 4

Calgary Tr.

Whitemud Dr.

Map 5

216

14

34 St

Ellerslie Rd **Map 1** (9 Ave SW)

Map 2

Edmonton International Airport (13 km)

2

City Boundary

Map 1

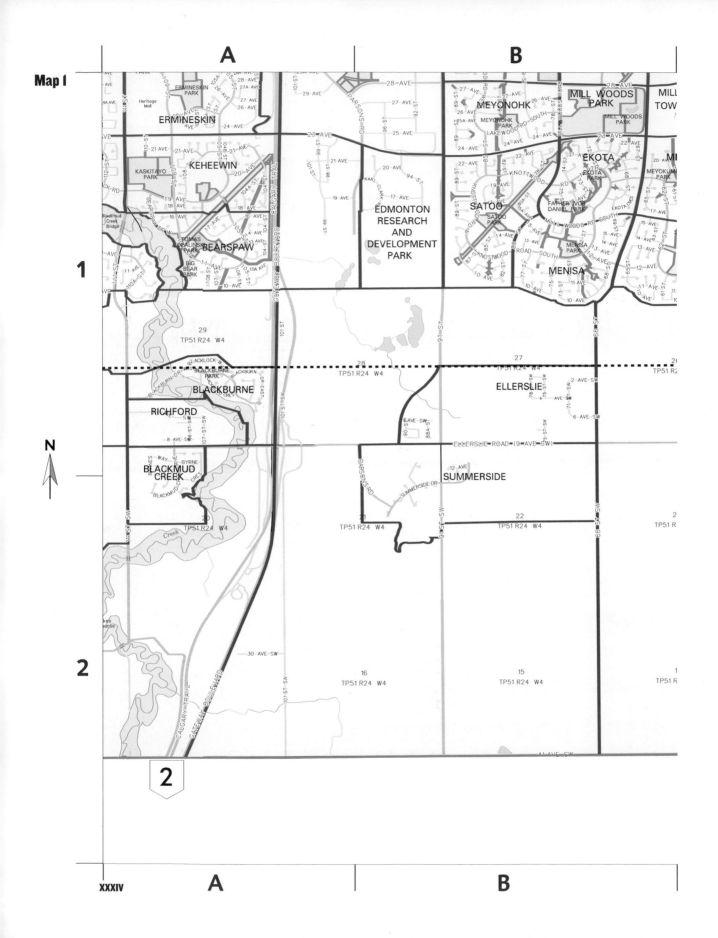

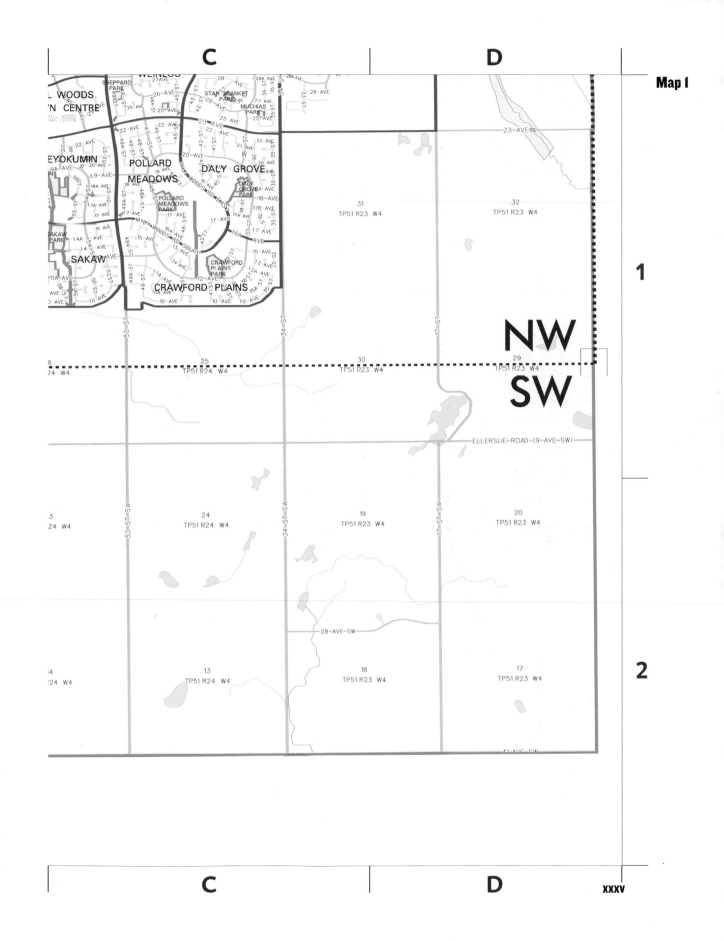

Map 1

C   D

WEINLOS

L WOODS
N CENTRE

SHEPPARD
PARK

STAR BLANKET
PARK

MUCHIAS
PARK

EYOKUMIN

POLLARD
MEADOWS

DALY GROVE

DALY
GROVE
PARK

POLLARD
MEADOWS
PARK

SAKAW
PARK

CRAWFORD
PLAINS
PARK

SAKAW

CRAWFORD PLAINS

31
TP51 R23 W4

32
TP51 R23 W4

23 AVE

NW

SW

1

25
TP51 R24 W4

30
TP51 R23 W4

29
TP51 R23 W4

ELLERSLIE ROAD (9 AVE SW)

24
TP51 R24 W4

19
TP51 R23 W4

20
TP51 R23 W4

28 AVE SW

13
TP51 R24 W4

18
TP51 R23 W4

17
TP51 R23 W4

2

41 AVE SW

C   D

Map 2

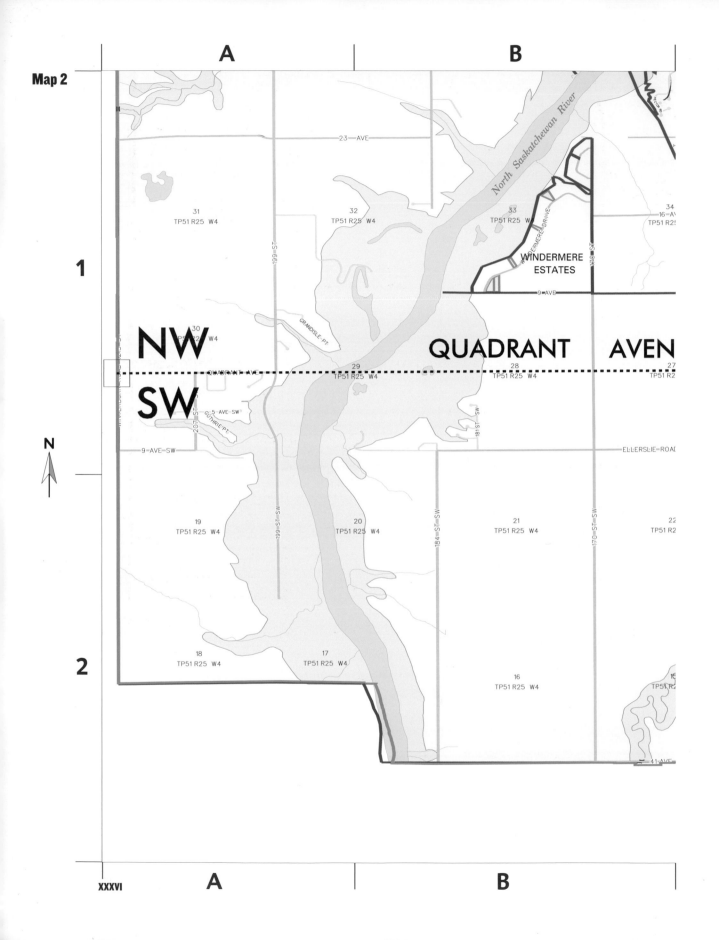

Map 2

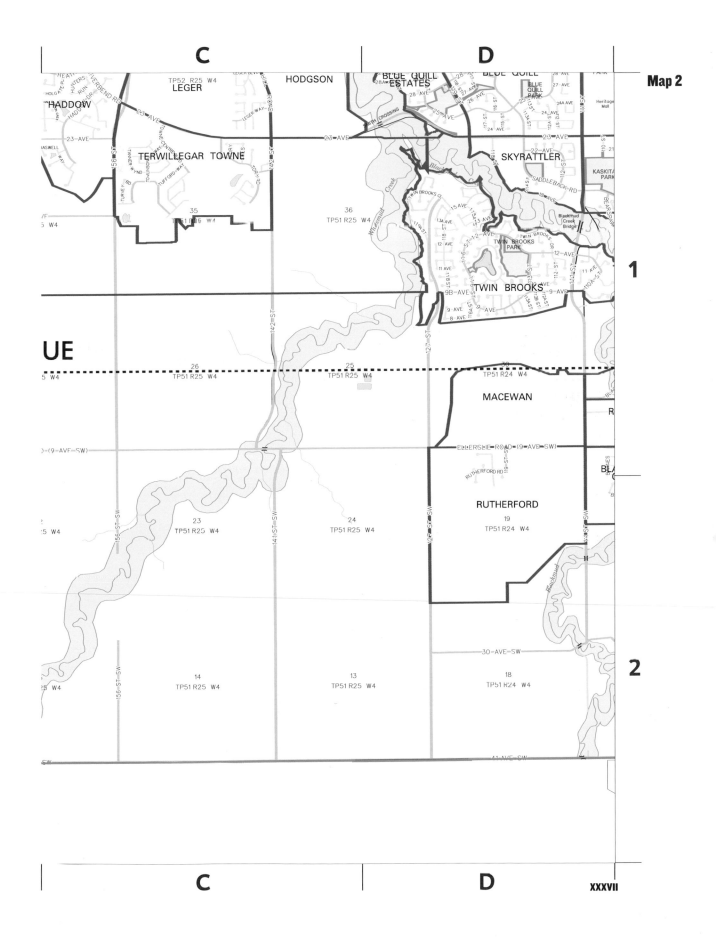

Map 3

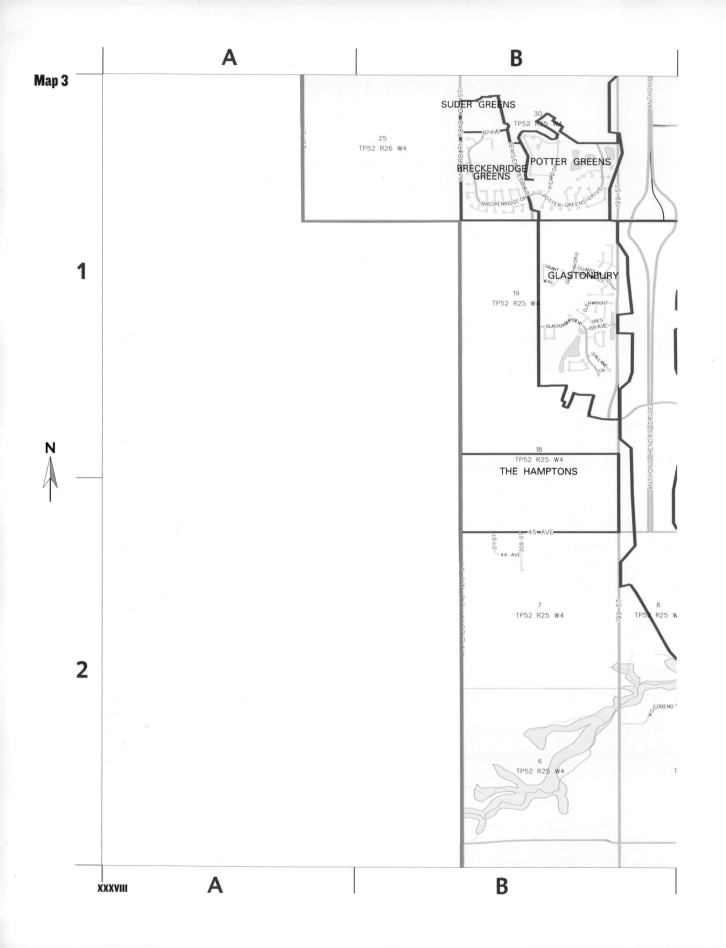

Map 3

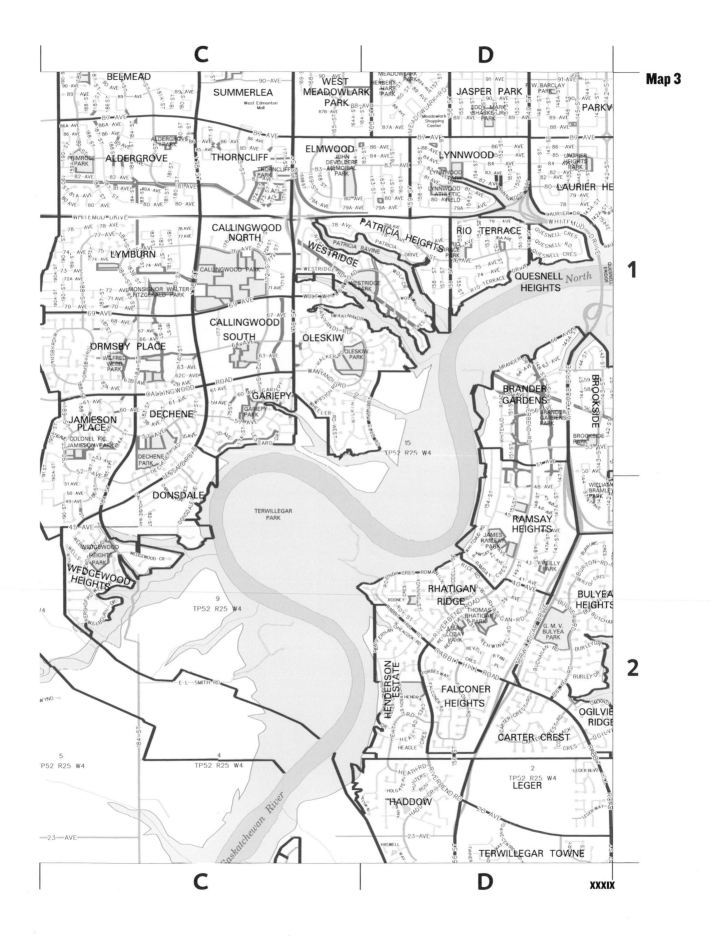

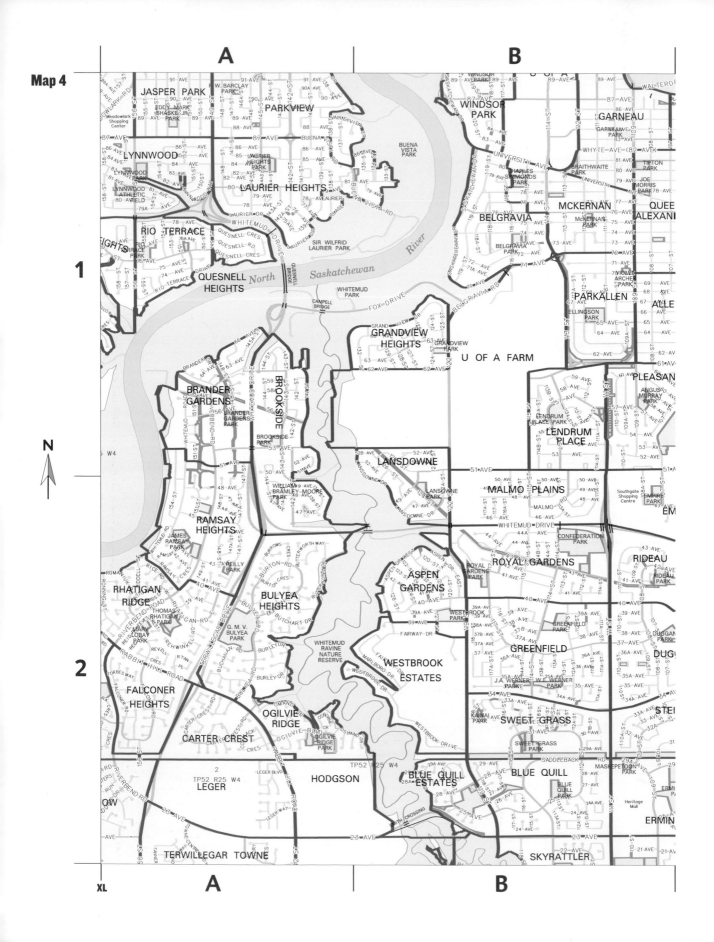

Map 4

Map 4

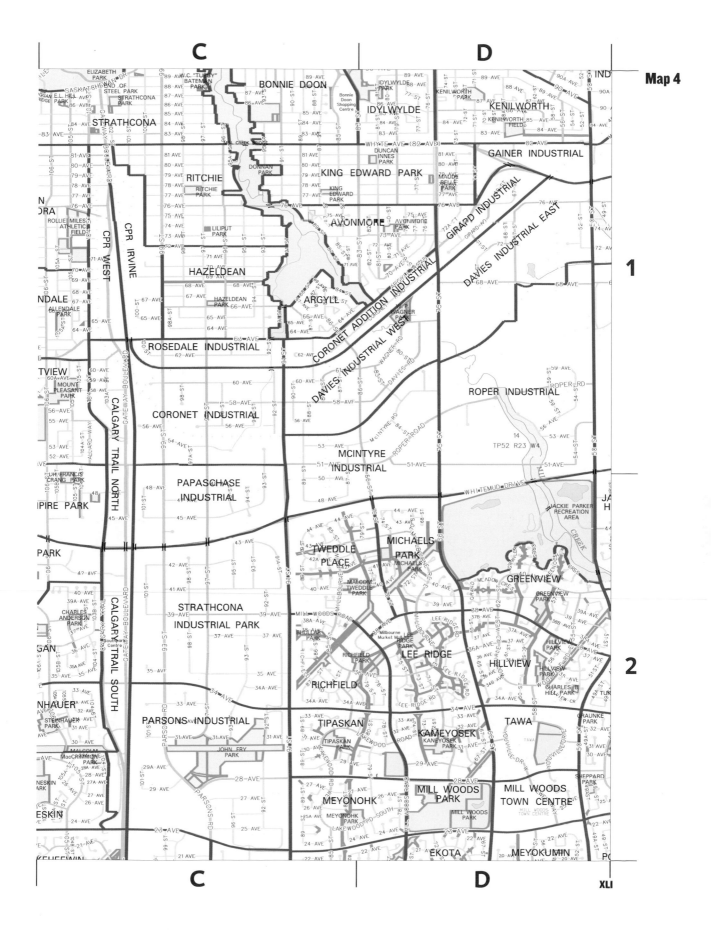

1

2

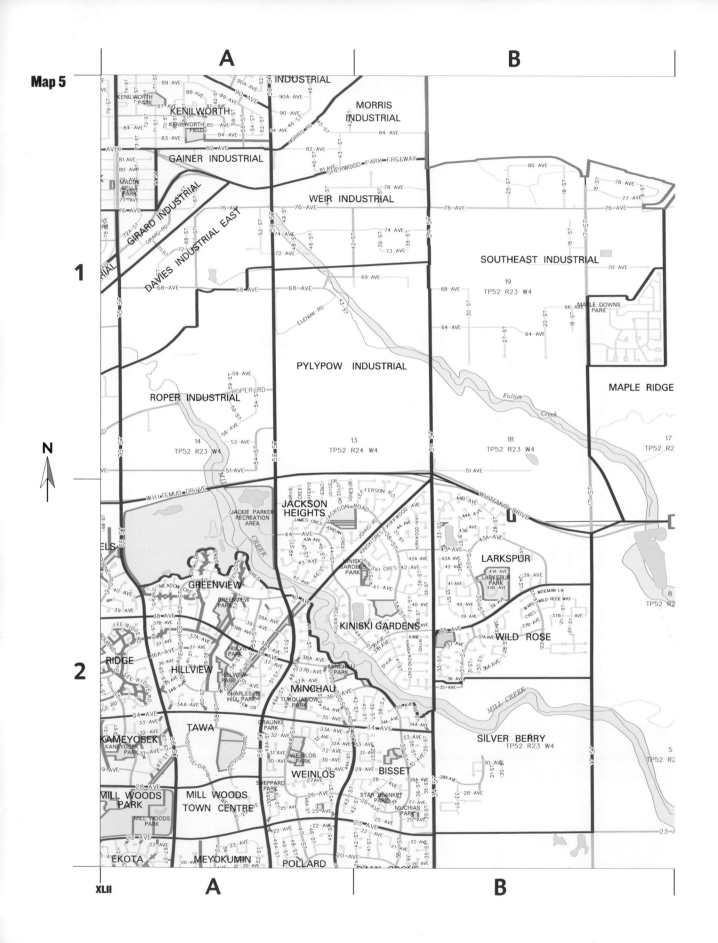

Map 5

A

B

INDUSTRIAL

MORRIS
INDUSTRIAL

KENILWORTH
PARK

KENILWORTH

KENILWORTH
FIELD

GAINER INDUSTRIAL

MAPLE
BELLE
PARK

GIRARD INDUSTRIAL

WEIR INDUSTRIAL

SHERWOOD PARK FREEWAY

DAVIES INDUSTRIAL EAST

80 AVE

78 AVE

76 AVE

77 AVE

SOUTHEAST INDUSTRIAL

1

DAVIES INDUSTRIAL

68 AVE

ELENIAK RD

19
TP52 R23 W4

MAPLE DOWNS
PARK

PYLYPOW INDUSTRIAL

MAPLE RIDGE

ROPER INDUSTRIAL

ROPER RD

Fulton

Creek

14
TP52 R23 W4

13
TP52 R24 W4

18
TP52 R23 W4

17
TP52 R2

51 AVE

WHITEMUD DRIVE

JACKSON HEIGHTS

JACKIE PARKER
RECREATION
AREA

JACKSON ROAD

WHITEMUD DRIVE

EELS

LARKSPUR

LARKSPUR
PARK

8
TP52 R2

GREENVIEW

GREENVIEW
PARK

KINISKI
GARDENS
PARK

WILD ROSE WAY

KINISKI GARDENS

WILD ROSE

RIDGE

HILLVIEW
PARK

HILLVIEW

2

LEE RIDGE RD

HILLVIEW
PARK

MINCHAU
PARK

MINCHAU

CHARLES B
HILL PARK

TURQUANOW
PARK

SILVER BERRY
TP52 R23 W4

5
TP52 R2

TAWA

GRAUNKE
PARK

KAMEYOSEK

KAMEYOSEK
PARK

WEINLOS
PARK

WEINLOS

BISSET

SHEPPARD
PARK

STAR BLANKET
PARK

MUCHIAS
PARK

MILL WOODS
PARK

MILL WOODS
TOWN CENTRE

MILL WOODS
PARK

EKOTA

MEYOKUMIN

POLLARD

A

B

Map 5

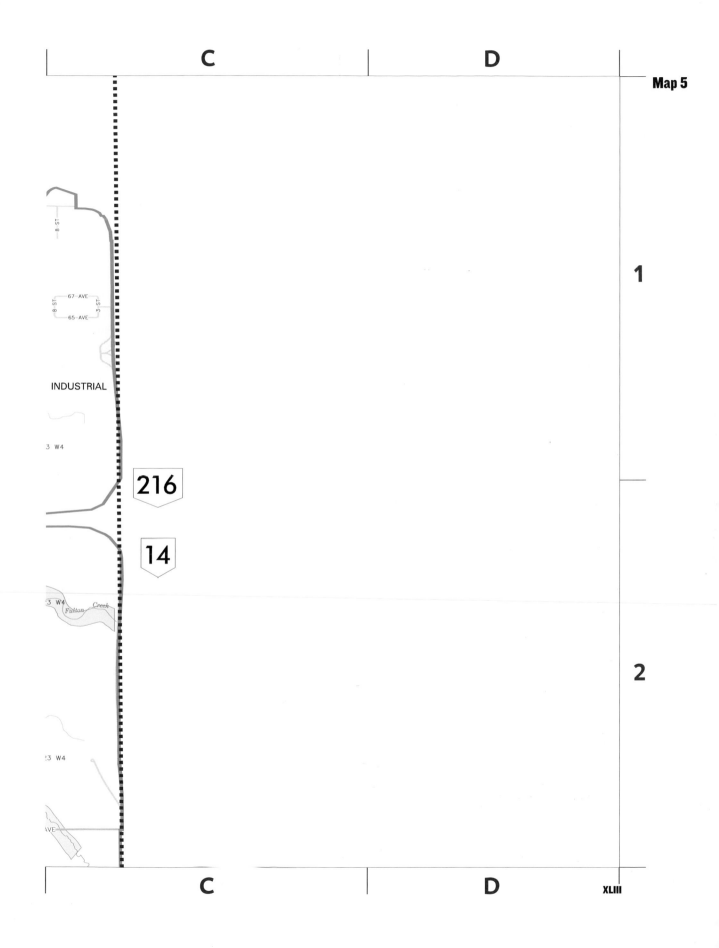

C

D

1

8 ST

67 AVE

8 ST   3 ST

65 AVE

INDUSTRIAL

3 W4

216

14

:3 W4   *Fulton Creek*

2

:3 W4

AVE

Map 6

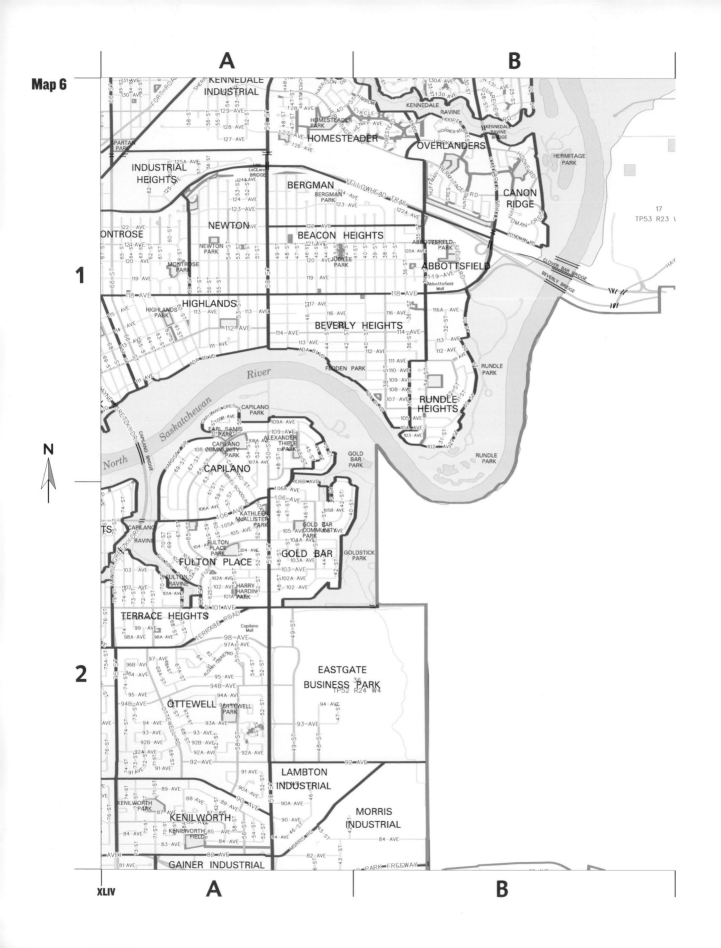

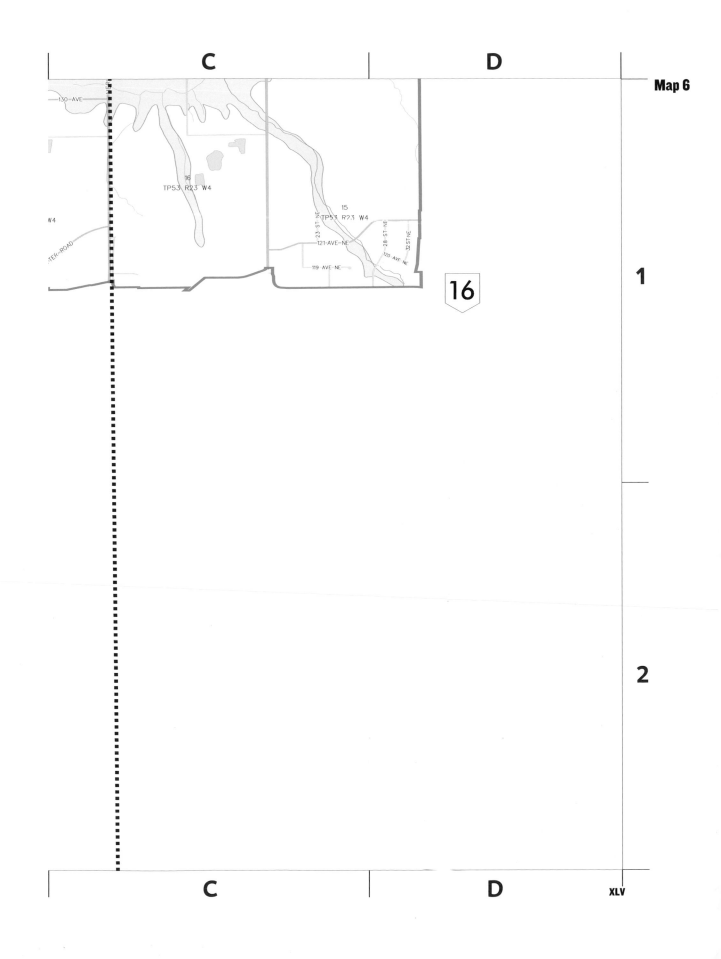

130-AVE

16
TP53 R23 W4

N4

15
23-ST-NE—TP53 R23 W4

TER-ROAD

121-AVE-NE

28-ST-NE

32-ST-NE

120-AVE-NE

119-AVE-NE

16

1

2

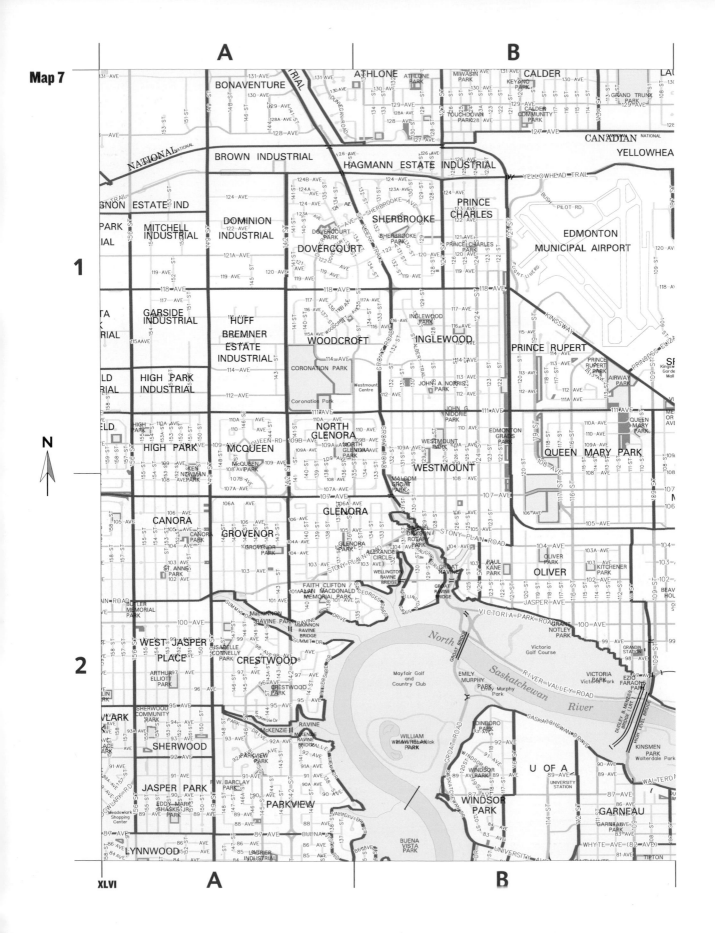

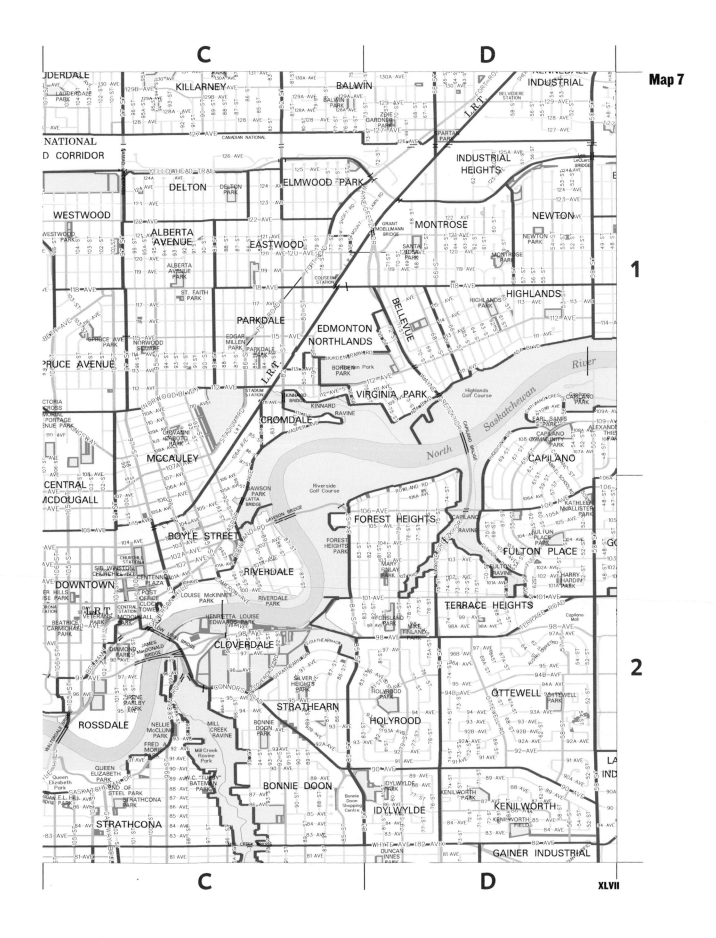

Map 7

Map 8

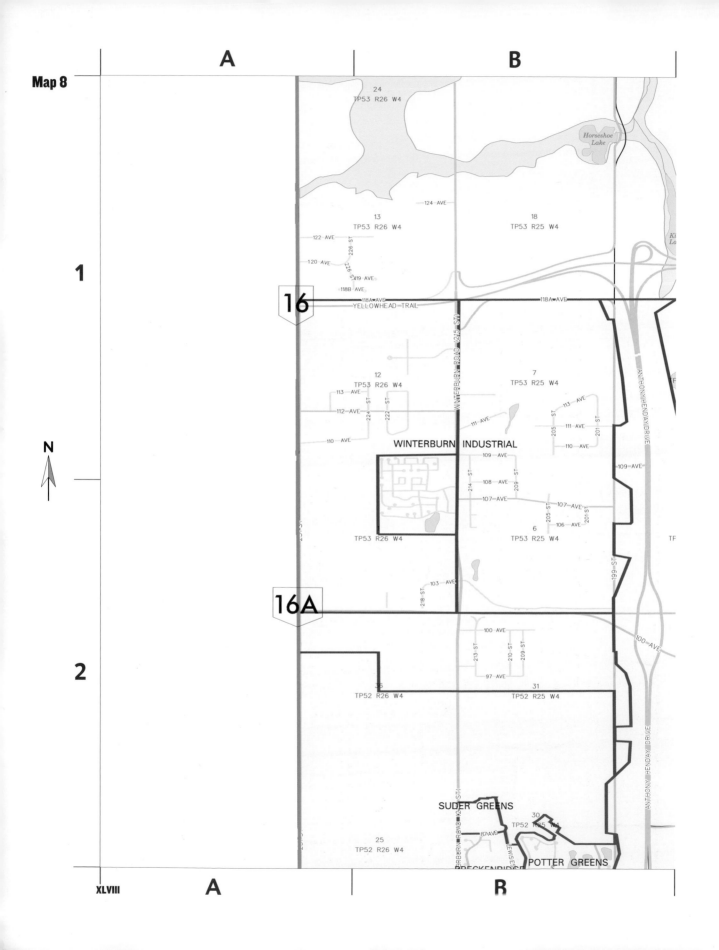

A   B

1

N

16

16A

2

24
TP53 R26 W4

Horseshoe
Lake

124 AVE

13
TP53 R26 W4

18
TP53 R25 W4

122 AVE

120 AVE

226 ST

119 AVE

118B AVE

118A AVE
YELLOWHEAD TRAIL

118A AVE

WINTERBURN ROAD / 215 ST

ANTHONY HENDAY DRIVE

12
TP53 R26 W4

7
TP53 R25 W4

113 AVE

113 AVE

224 ST

222 ST

112 AVE

205 ST

111 AVE

201 ST

110 AVE

111 AVE

110 AVE

WINTERBURN INDUSTRIAL

109 AVE

109 AVE

214 ST

108 AVE

209 ST

107 AVE

107 AVE

205 ST

201 ST

106 AVE

6
TP53 R25 W4

TP53 R26 W4

TP53 R25 W4

218 ST

103 AVE

199 ST

100 AVE

100 AVE

213 ST

210 ST

209 ST

97 AVE

36
TP52 R26 W4

31
TP52 R25 W4

ANTHONY HENDAY DRIVE

SUDER GREENS

30
TP52 R25 W4

87 AVE

25
TP52 R26 W4

WINTERBURN ROAD / 215 ST

BRECKENRIDGE

POTTER GREENS

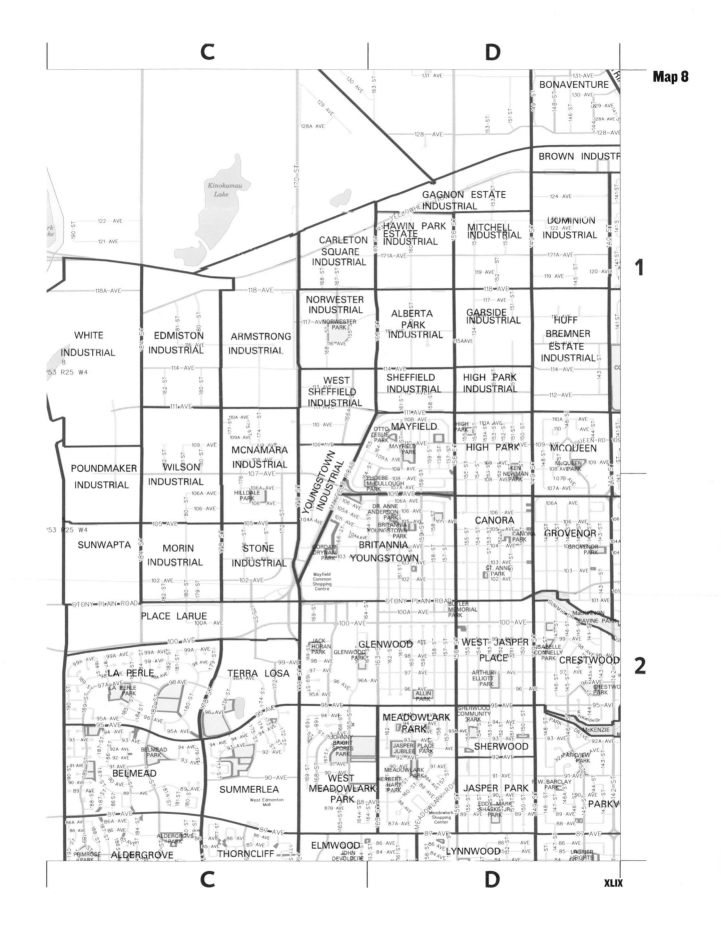

Map 8

C

D

BONAVENTURE

130 AVE

131 AVE

130 AVE

BROWN INDUSTRIAL

GAGNON ESTATE
INDUSTRIAL

124 AVE

128 AVE

128 AVE

DOMINION
INDUSTRIAL

122 AVE

Kinokamau
Lake

122 AVE

121 AVE

CARLETON
SQUARE
INDUSTRIAL

HAWIN PARK
ESTATE
INDUSTRIAL

MITCHELL
INDUSTRIAL

121A AVE

119 AVE

119 AVE

120 AVE

1

118A AVE

118 AVE

118 AVE

NORWESTER
INDUSTRIAL

117 AV NORWESTER
PARK

ALBERTA
PARK
INDUSTRIAL

GARSIDE
INDUSTRIAL

HUFF
BREMNER
ESTATE
INDUSTRIAL

WHITE
INDUSTRIAL
8
'53 R25 W4

EDMISTON
INDUSTRIAL

116 AVE

ARMSTRONG
INDUSTRIAL

116 AVE

114 AVE

WEST
SHEFFIELD
INDUSTRIAL

SHEFFIELD
INDUSTRIAL

HIGH PARK
INDUSTRIAL

114 AVE

112 AVE

111 AVE

110A AVE

109A AVE

110 AVE

110 AVE

110B AVE

MAYFIELD

HIGH
PARK

110A AVE

110A AVE

POUNDMAKER
INDUSTRIAL

WILSON
INDUSTRIAL

MCNAMARA
INDUSTRIAL

107 AVE

OTTO
LESLIE
PARK

MAYFIELD
PARK

HIGH PARK

KEN
NEWMAN
PARK

108 AVE PARK

107B AVE

MCQUEEN

McQUEEN
109 AVE
PARK

107A AVE

106A AVE

HILLDALE
PARK

106 AVE

106A AVE

PHOEBE 108
McCULLOUGH
PARK

DR. ANNE
ANDERSON
PARK

BRITANNIA
YOUNGSTOWN
PARK

106 AVE

106A AVE

CANORA

CANORA
PARK

106 AVE

106A AVE

GROVENOR

GROVENOR
PARK

106 AVE

104A

SUNWAPTA

MORIN
INDUSTRIAL

STONE
INDUSTRIAL

YOUNGSTOWN INDUSTRIAL

105 AVE

105 AVE

104A AVE

GORDAN
DRYNAN
PARK

BRITANNIA
YOUNGSTOWN

ST. ANNE
PARK

103 AVE

104 AVE

102 AVE

'53 R25 W4

105 AVE

102 AVE

102 AVE

103 AVE

Mayfield
Common
Shopping
Centre

STONY PLAIN ROAD

BUTLER
MEMORIAL
PARK

STONY PLAIN ROAD

101 AVE

MacKINNON
RAVINE PARK

PLACE LARUE

100A AVE

100A AVE

100 AVE

100A AVE

WEST JASPER
PLACE

100 AVE

ISABELLE
CONNELLY
PARK

CRESTWOOD

2

LA PERLE

LA PERLE
PARK

99A AVE

99A AVE

99A AVE

99 AVE

TERRA LOSA

JACK
HORAN
PARK

GLENWOOD
PARK

GLENWOOD

97 AVE

ARTHUR
ELLIOTT
PARK

96 AVE

CRESTWO
PARK

98 AVE

97 AVE

97 AVE

96 AVE

96A AVE

96 AVE

95A AVE

95 AVE

95A AVE

94 AVE

JOHNNY
BRIGHT
SPORTS
PARK

MEADOWLARK
PARK

SHERWOOD
COMMUNITY
PARK

95 AVE

McKENZIE

BELMEAD
PARK

93 AVE

94 AVE

92 AVE

93 AVE

JASPER PLACE
JUBILEE PARK

SHERWOOD

94 AVE

93 AVE

PARKVIEW
PARK

92 AVE

BELMEAD

91 AVE

90 AVE

SUMMERLEA

West Edmonton
Mall

WEST
MEADOWLARK
PARK

MEADOWLARK
PARK

HERBERT
HART
PARK

91 AVE

90 AVE

JASPER PARK

EDDY MARK
SHASKE JR
PARK

F.W. BARCLAY
PARK

91 AVE

PARKV

ALDERGROVE
PARK

87 AVE

Meadowlark
Shopping
Center

89 AVE

88 AVE

87 AVE

PRIMROSE
PARK

ALDERGROVE

THORNCLIFF

ELMWOOD

JOHN
DEVOLDENE

86 AVE

LYNNWOOD

86 AVE

85 AVE

87 AVE

86 AVE

LAURIER
HEIGHTS

84 AVE

C

D

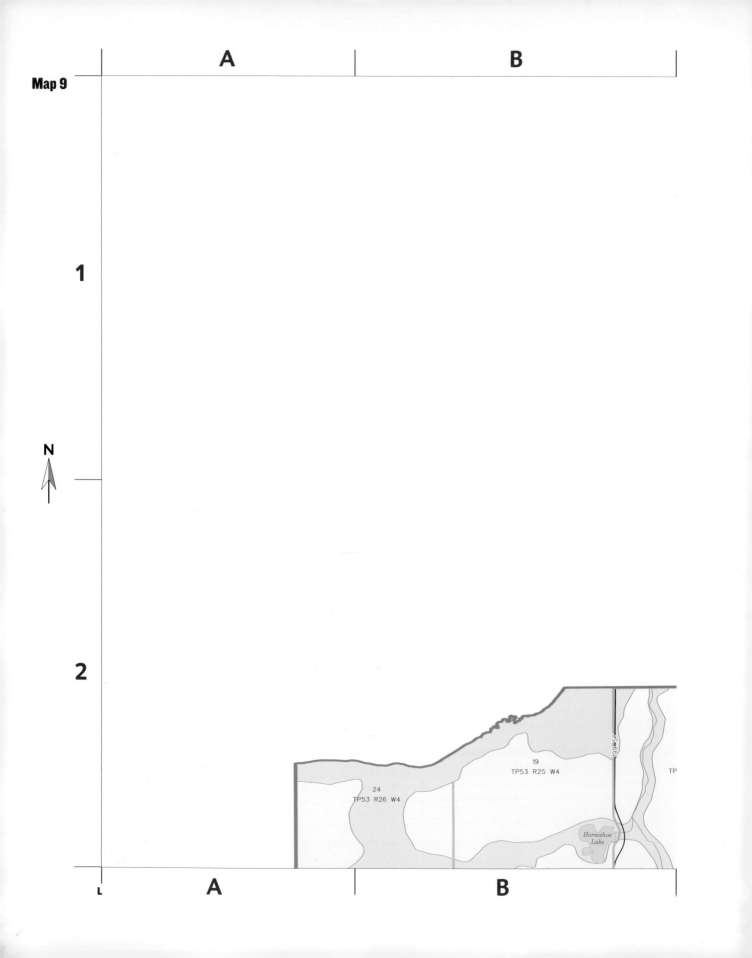

Map 9

A

B

N

1

2

L

A

B

24
TP53 R26 W4

19
TP53 R25 W4

Horseshoe
Lake

TP

Map 9

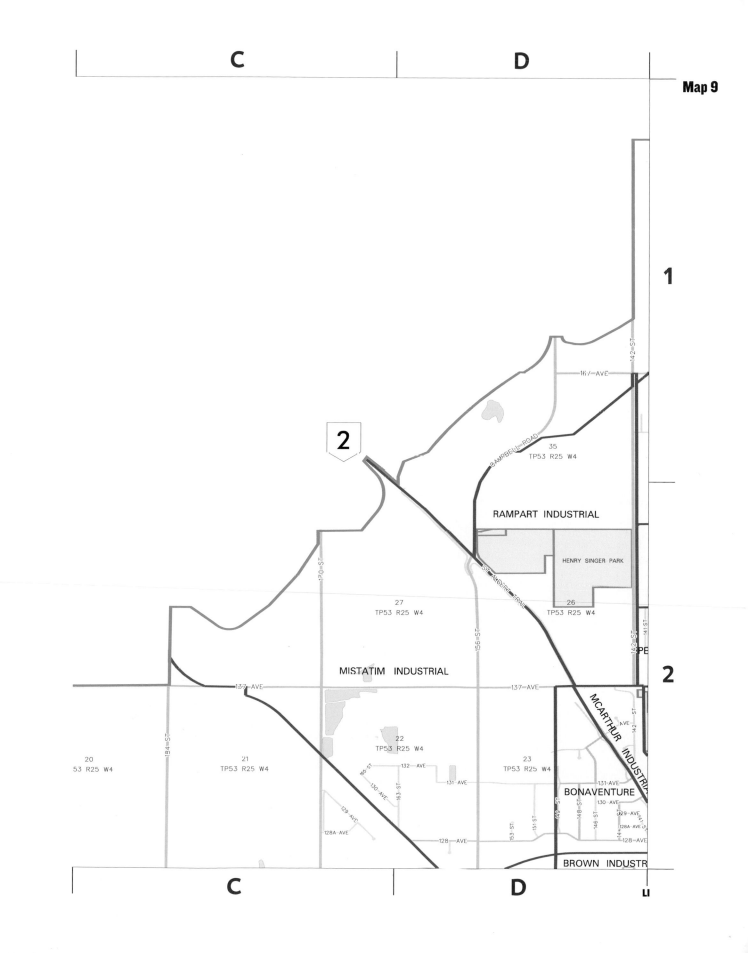

C

D

1

2

167 AVE

142 ST

CAMPBELL ROAD

35
TP53 R25 W4

RAMPART INDUSTRIAL

HENRY SINGER PARK

STEAMBRIE TRAIL

26
TP53 R25 W4

27
TP53 R25 W4

170 ST

156 ST

141 ST

142 ST

PE

MISTATIM INDUSTRIAL

2

137 AVE

137 AVE

MCARTHUR INDUSTRIAL

142 ST

184 ST

22
TP53 R25 W4

132 AVE

23
TP53 R25 W4

131 AVE

131 AVE

BONAVENTURE

20
53 R25 W4

21
TP53 R25 W4

165 ST

130 AVE

163 ST

131 AVE

130 AVE

149 ST

148 ST

146 ST

129 AVE

128A AVE S

142 ST

141

129 AVE

128A AVE

128 AVE

153 ST

151 ST

128 AVE

128 AVE

BROWN INDUSTR

C

D

LI

Map 10

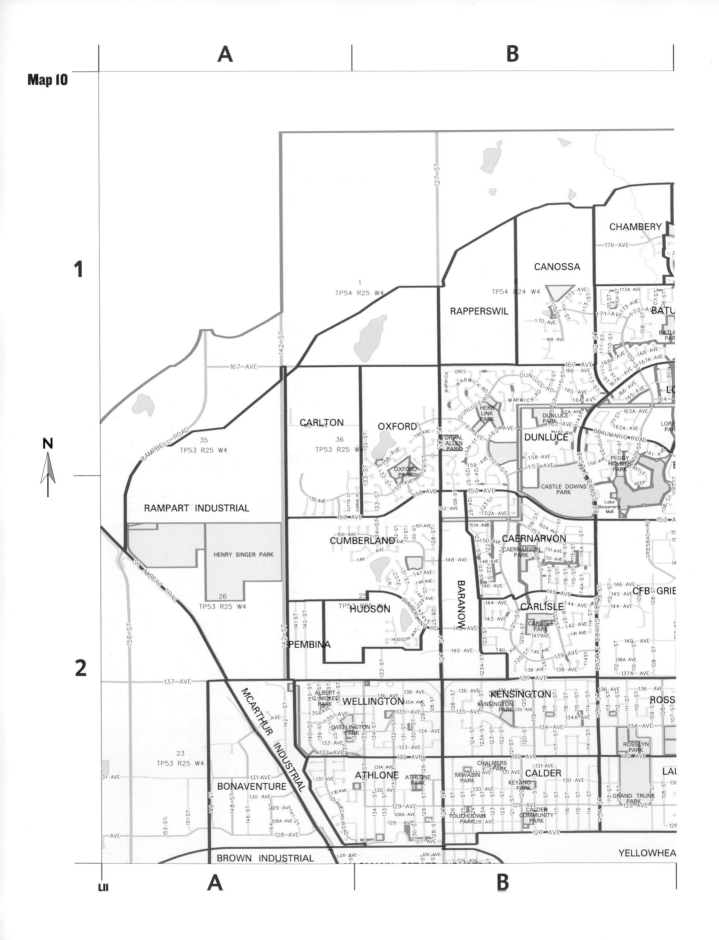

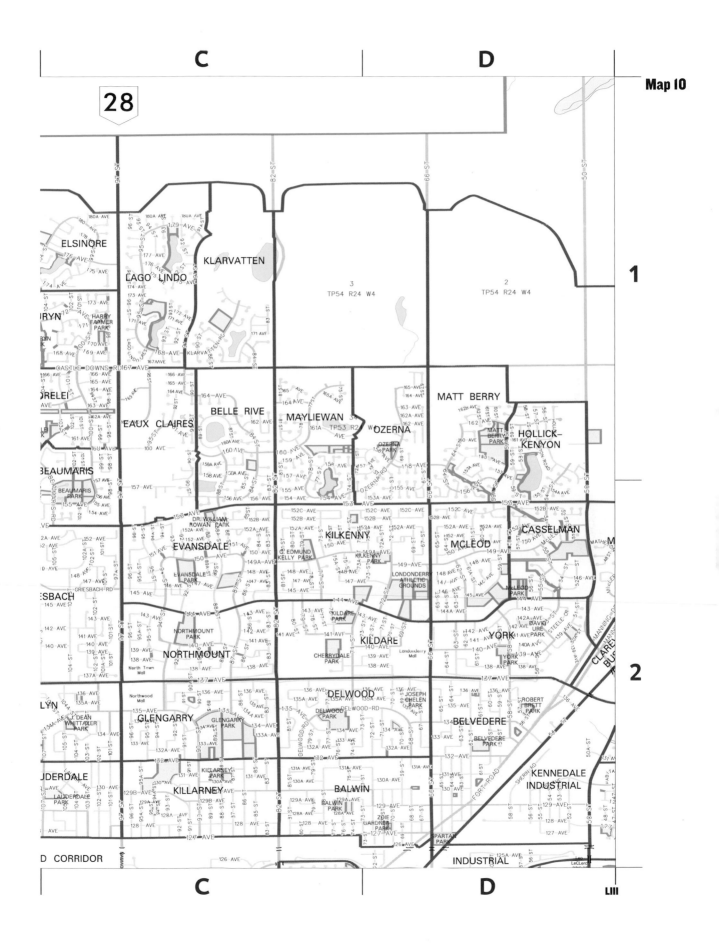

Map 10

28

C

D

1

2

ELSINORE

KLARVATTEN

LAGO LINDO

3
TP54 R24 W4

2
TP54 R24 W4

BELLE RIVE

MAYLIEWAN

OZERNA

MATT BERRY

HOLLICK-
KENYON

EAUX CLAIRES

BEAUMARIS

EVANSDALE

KILKENNY

MCLEOD

CASSELMAN

NORTHMOUNT

KILDARE

YORK

DELWOOD

GLENGARRY

BELVEDERE

KILLARNEY

BALWIN

KENNEDALE
INDUSTRIAL

INDUSTRIAL

C

D

LIII

Map 11

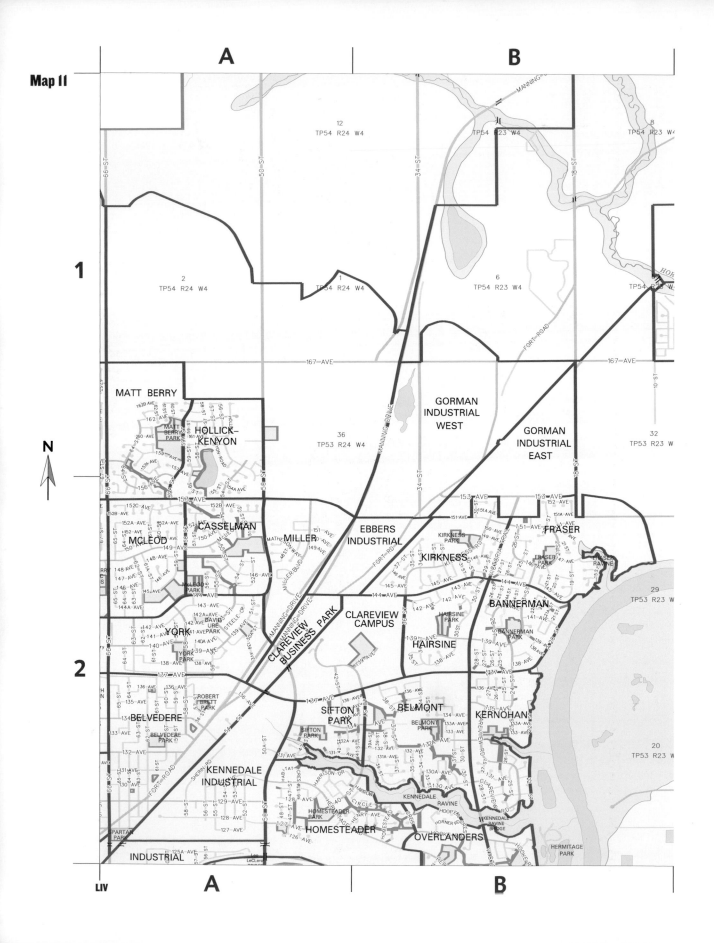

A

B

N

1

2

LIV

A

B

12
TP54 R24 W4

TP54 R23 W4

8
TP54 R23 W4

1
TP54 R24 W4

6
TP54 R23 W4

TP54 R23 W4

2
TP54 R24 W4

167-AVE

167-AVE

MATT BERRY

HOLLICK–
KENYON

MATT
BERRY
PARK

GORMAN
INDUSTRIAL
WEST

GORMAN
INDUSTRIAL
EAST

36
TP53 R24 W4

32
TP53 R23 W4

153-AVE

153-AVE

153-AVE

151-AVE

152-AVE

151A-AVE

151A-AVE

CASSELMAN

MILLER

EBBERS
INDUSTRIAL

FRASER

KIRKNESS
PARK

MCLEOD

KIRKNESS

FRASER
RAVINE

FRASER
PARK

McLEOD
PARK

144-AVE

144-AVE

BANNERMAN

29
TP53 R23 W4

HAIRSINE
PARK

YORK

DAVID
URE
PARK

CLAREVIEW
CAMPUS

BANNERMAN
PARK

YORK
PARK

HAIRSINE

137-AVE

CLAREVIEW
BUSINESS PARK

137-AVE

137-AVE

BELVEDERE

ROBERT
BRETT
PARK

SIFTON
PARK

BELMONT

KERNOHAN

20
TP53 R23 W4

BELVEDERE
PARK

SIFTON
PARK

BELMONT
PARK

KENNEDALE
INDUSTRIAL

KENNEDALE
RAVINE

HOMESTEADER
PARK

KENNEDALE
RAVINE
BRIDGE

HERMITAGE
PARK

SPARTAN
PARK

HOMESTEADER

OVERLANDERS

INDUSTRIAL

Leo
LeClerc
Arena

Map 11

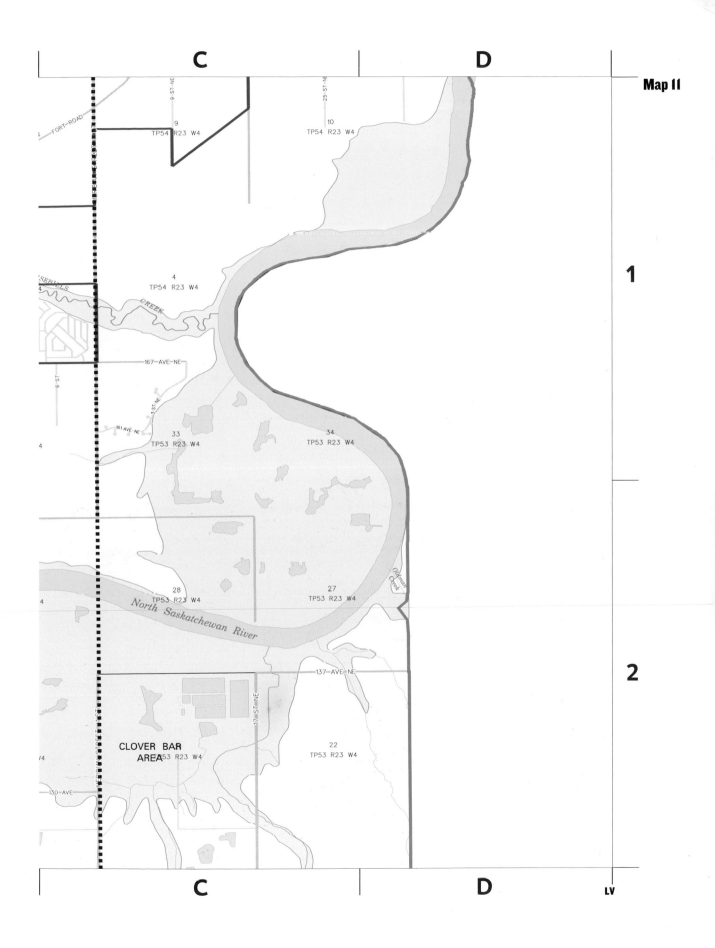

FORT ROAD

9 ST NE

25 ST NE

9
TP54 R23 W4

10
TP54 R23 W4

SCHOOLS

4
TP54 R23 W4

CREEK

167 AVE NE

6 ST

3 ST NE

161 AVE NE

33
TP53 R23 W4

34
TP53 R23 W4

Oldman Creek

28
TP53 R23 W4

27
TP53 R23 W4

North Saskatchewan River

137 AVE NE

17 ST NE

CLOVER BAR
AREA   53 R23 W4

22
TP53 R23 W4

130 AVE

Map 12

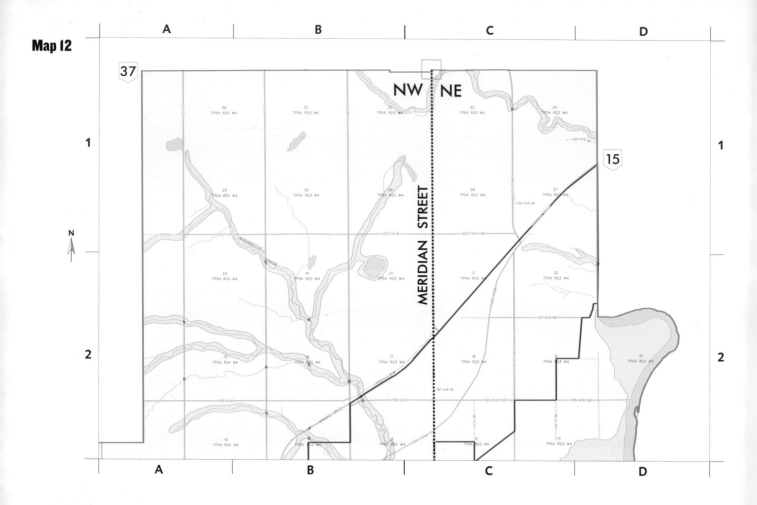

Map 12

A   B   C   D

37

NW   NE

36
TP54 R24 W4

31
TP54 R23 W4

32
TP54 R23 W4

33
TP54 R23 W4

34
TP54 R23 W4

1   1

15

25
TP54 R24 W4

30
TP54 R23 W4

29
TP54 R23 W4

28
TP54 R23 W4

27
TP54 R23 W4

N

24
TP54 R24 W4

19
TP54 R23 W4

20
TP54 R23 W4

21
TP54 R23 W4

22
TP54 R23 W4

13
TP54 R24 W4

18
TP54 R23 W4

17
TP54 R23 W4

16
TP54 R23 W4

15
TP54 R23 W4

14
TP54 R23 W4

2   2

12
TP54 R24 W4

11
TP54 R23 W4

8
TP54 R23 W4

9
TP54 R23 W4

10
TP54 R23 W4

A   B   C   D

MERIDIAN STREET

A.J. Cressey Place

South of 4 Avenue, west of 181 Street

A.J. "Jack" Cressey (1928–1994) was a prominent member of the Edmonton business community and served as chairman of the Edmonton Chamber of Commerce in 1990. Born in Saskatchewan, he served in the Royal Canadian Navy and graduated from university before moving to Edmonton. Cressey became a dynamic, high-profile member of the oil industry, working in Alberta and around the world constructing oil pipelines. He was chairman of Edmonton Power from 1992 until his death.

Road   1994   SW   2:B1 *

Abbottsfield

118 Avenue north to CNR railway tracks, Victoria Trail west to 34 Street

This northeast neighbourhood's name was derived by extending the name of Abbott School, which was named for WWI veteran Abe Abbott. After moving to Beverly in 1912, Abbott was the care-taker of Beverly School from 1922 to 1958. Abbott School was opened in 1960 as an Edmonton Public elementary school.

Neighbourhood   1964   NE   6:B1

Abbottsfield Park

12000 Abbottsfield Road

Located in the Abbottsfield neighbourhood in the northeast part of the city, this park has an area of 1.99 ha. *See* Abbottsfield.

Park   1984   NE   6:B1

Abbottsfield Road

Continuation of 121 Avenue lying east of 34 Street and to 118 Avenue

See Abbottsfield.

Road   1972   NE   6:B1

Alan Brown, first on left, at Edmonton Historical Board's First Annual Recognition Awards with Mary Lobay and William Hawrelak, 1975. (CEA EA-258-15)

Ada Boulevard

Follows crest of North Saskatchewan River Valley between 48 Street and 75 Street

See feature story, page 3.

Road   CU   NE   6:A1

Airport Road

Between Kingsway and the Edmonton City Centre Airport

This road serves as the access and service road to the Edmonton City Centre Airport.

Road   1963   NW   7:B1

Airway Park

11245–113 Street

Located across from the Edmonton City Centre Airport to the south, this 5.0 ha. Park with athletic grounds allows people to watch the planes fly over.

Park   1964   NW   7:B1

Ada Boulevard

ADA THIRSEE MAGRATH (1863–1941), wife of pioneer real-estate developer and entrepreneur William J. Magrath (1870–1920), is the namesake of Ada Boulevard. The road runs past the spectacular Magrath mansion, along the north bank of the North Saskatchewan River in the city's east end. William Magrath is best known for the development, with his partner Bidwell Holgate, of the Highlands neighbourhood. The suburb, along with Glenora, was aimed at housing the wealthy.

Ada Lake was born in Tamworth, Ontario, and married William Magrath in 1894. In 1905 they moved to Edmonton, taking the first Canadian Northern train west from Battleford. They had one son, Adrian. Ada was on the first board of directors of the Edmonton YWCA and was active in the Highlands, Wesley and McDougall United churches.

The 14-room, red-brick Magrath home, at 6249 Ada Boulevard, was built in 1911 and is today recognized as a historic site. The three-storey house was designed by the architect E.W. Morehouse and cost $85,000 to build. Considered one of Edmonton's most beautiful homes, there was a ballroom and a billiards room on the top floor and a swimming pool in the basement. No expense was spared in its construction; the luxurious interior included bathroom fixtures imported from Paris and marble tile from Rome. The family's residency in the grand home was to be short-lived. William Magrath died at the age of 51 in 1920. This misfortune, combined with the 1929 stock market crash and the Great Depression, ruined the family's fortunes. In 1931 the city took possession of the house for nonpayment of taxes.

Now in private hands, the Magrath mansion was, for many years, the residence of the Ukrainian Catholic bishop of the Edmonton diocese. The oak-lined dining room was used as a chapel and the pool served as storage for the church's records.

A six-block portion of Jasper Avenue formally became Ada Boulevard in 1949. However, the name had been in use from shortly after the Magraths built their home there decades before. In 1970 Ada Boulevard was extended to include the portion of 113 Avenue lying between 48 Street and 50 Street.

Ada Boulevard—Magrath Mansion, circa 1912.
(CEA EA-302-17)

Alan Brown Bridge

Spanning the Kinnaird Ravine at 78 Street and 111 Avenue

This foot-bridge in the Cromdale neighbourhood is named after Alan Brown, son of the well-known photographer Ernest Brown. Born in the Cromdale district, Alan Brown devoted many years of service to the community, including 12 years as treasurer for the Cromdale Community League.

Bridge 1982 NE 7:C1 *

Albert G. Nickel Park

13531–139 Street

Albert G. "Bert" Nickel (1904–1984) dedicated years of service to the Wellington community. Born in Saskatchewan, Nickel moved to the Wellington neighbourhood in 1959. He later served as president of the community league and as a director. Nickel received the Wellington Community Honorary Award in 1966, the Area #1 Outstanding Service Award in 1973 and the Federation of Community Leagues' Service Award in 1982. The Albert G. Nickel Park is in the Wellington neighbourhood and has an area of 0.38 ha.

Park 1985 NW 10:A2

Alberta Avenue

Norwood Boulevard north to 122 Avenue, 89 Street to 97 Street

The name of this neighbourhood was adopted from the historic name for 118 Avenue. The community has used the name Alberta Avenue since at least 1922, as the Alberta Avenue Community League was formed that year. That part of the Alberta Avenue neighbourhood between Norwood Boulevard and 118 Avenue was formerly known as Norwood. A portion, from 118 Avenue to 121 Avenue, was once called West Delton. *See* Alberta Avenue *road.*

Neighbourhood CU NE 7:C1

Aerial view of Alberta Avenue neighbourhood, 1924. (CEA Vol. 3, Row 2–9)

Alberta Avenue

118 Avenue

Alberta Avenue first appeared as a road name around 1904 and was probably derived from the provisional district of Alberta. In 1914 the name was changed to 118 Avenue. However, on December 13, 1994, the Names Advisory Committee renamed it 118 Avenue (Alberta Avenue).

The Marquess of Lorne, governor general of Canada from 1878 to 1883, suggested that the provisional district of Alberta be named after his wife, HRH Princess Louise Caroline Alberta (1848–1939), the fourth daughter of Queen Victoria. Princess Louise was considered a strong, independent woman. She studied art and was an accomplished sculptor. The choice of name was not universally welcomed. The *Edmonton Bulletin*, on July 1, 1882, wrote: "Surely in a region having such

118 Avenue (Alberta Avenue) at 88 Street looking west, 1960s. (CEA EA–275–21)

grand and varied features as this, some natural characteristic could be found that could give an appropriate and pleasant sounding name to the whole." Alberta was created as a provisional district in 1882 and became a province in 1905.

Road   CU   NE   7:C1

Alberta Avenue Park

9210–118 Avenue

This Alberta Avenue neighbourhood park is located on 118 Avenue (Alberta Avenue) and has an area of 1.53 ha. *See* Alberta Avenue *road.*

Park   1983   NE   7:C1

Alberta Park Industrial

114 Avenue to 118 Avenue, 156 Street to 163 Street

The neighbourhood of Alberta Park Industrial has existed since at least 1912. *See* Alberta Avenue *road.*

Neighbourhood   CU   NW   8:D1

Aldergrove

79 Avenue to 87 Avenue, 178 Street to 190 Street

This neighbourhood is located in the Primrose subdivision. It is likely named for the local alder trees. The most common species of alder in Canada is the speckled alder.

Neighbourhood   1970   SW   3:C1

Aldergrove Park

8532–182 Street

Located in the Aldergrove neighbourhood, this park has an area of 0.82 ha. *See* Aldergrove.

Park   1981   SW   3:C1

Alex Taylor Road

Connects Jasper Avenue to Rowland Road at 93 Street

See feature story, page 6.

Road   1958   C   7:C2

Alex Taylor Road

A SCHOOL AND A ROAD are named in honour of Alex Taylor (1854–1916), the founder of many of Edmonton's earliest institutions. He was a pioneer newspaperman and businessman who, among many other enterprises, owned the city's first telephone company. Alex Taylor School (built in 1908) is located immediately west of Alex Taylor road.

In 1879 Taylor came west from Ottawa to take the position of telegraph operator at Hay Lakes, more than 30 kilometres east of Fort Edmonton. This was the closest station to the fort at the time. By 1880, Taylor and other local entrepreneurs had extended the line to John Walter's property, located directly across the North Saskatchewan River from the fort. Over this line, he took down news bulletins that went into the *Edmonton Bulletin*, the city's first newspaper, which Taylor founded with Frank Oliver in 1881.

In 1884 he brought the first telephone to Edmonton and, on November 1, 1887, made the first long-distance telephone call, to Battleford, 480 kilometres away. Within a year, there were twelve telephones in Edmonton, all made possible by Taylor's early telephone company, later incorporated as The Edmonton District Telephone Company. Taylor was a majority stockholder in the Edmonton Electric Light Company, established in 1891, the postmaster from 1893 to 1896, and from 1886 to 1915 the clerk of the Supreme Court of Alberta. From 1899 to 1909, Taylor was also chairman of the Edmonton School Board.

Alex Taylor, circa 1880. (CEA EA–10–689.23)
Inset: Alex Taylor Road, also showing Valley Vista Apartments, circa 1968. (CEA EA–20–2420)

Alexander Circle, 1963. (CEA EA–33–300)

Alexander Circle

13222–103 Avenue

Property owners who donated part of the costs involved in developing this park requested that it be named for Earl Alexander of Tunis, governor general of Canada from 1946 to 1952. Alexander Circle Park, with its ornate fountain, is well known in the neighbourhood. Homeowners first attempted to have the road name changed to Alexander Circle in 1958–1959. The motion was defeated by City Council but a later request was approved. This 0.26-ha. circular park is located in the Glenora neighbourhood.

Park 1968 NW 7:B2

Alexander Circle

133 Street and 103 Avenue

See Alexander Circle *park*.

Road 1968 NW 7:B2

Alexander Thiele Park

4611–109 Avenue

Alexander Harold Thiele (1920–1981) was an Edmonton lawyer who contributed years of service to the German-Canadian community. Thiele was born in Germany and moved to Edmonton in 1953 to attend the University of Alberta. He was active in cultural and charity organizations, as well as numerous clubs and associations. In 1977 he was the recipient of an achievement award from the minister of culture on behalf of the government of Alberta. The Alexander Thiele Park is in the Capilano neighbourhood and has an area of 1.46 ha.

Park 1982 SE 6:A1

Allan Stein Park

10025–87 Street

This 1.79-ha. park, located in the Riverdale neighbourhood, is named after the award-winning filmmaker, broadcaster and musician Allan Stein (1948–1994). The Ontario-born Stein produced and directed the 1987 film *Shooting Stars: The Amazing*

Story of the Edmonton Grads. It chronicled the history of the world-renowned women's basketball team, which won dozens of national and international championships. Stein served as president of the Alberta Motion Picture Industries Association and the Alberta Union of Students, and was a member of the Worth Commission on Education. He was also a founding member of Film West Associates. In 1990, Stein turned his talents to radio broadcasting, hosting "Edmonton PM," CBC radio's weekday afternoon program.

Park   1996   SE   7:C2 *

Allard Way

104 Street between 51 Avenue and 55 Avenue

Dr. Charles A. Allard (1919–1991) was a well-known Edmonton surgeon and successful businessman. A native of Edmonton, Allard graduated from the University of Alberta in 1943. After postgraduate studies he returned to Edmonton to start his medical practice in 1948. He was surgeon and then chief surgeon at the General Hospital in Edmonton between 1955 and 1969. In addition to his medical responsibilities, Allard founded Allarcom Developments, one of Canada's largest real estate companies, sold to Carma Developers of Calgary in 1980, and was involved in finance, life assurance and media. He established Allarcom Broadcasting, which owned Edmonton's ITV station and western Canada's Super-Channel.

Road   1991   SW   4:C1

Allendale

61 Avenue to 70 Avenue, Calgary Trail west to 109 Street

Irishman Thomas Allen (1847–1920) and his wife Elizabeth (1860–1939) had farmed here until the turn of the 20th century, when they sold their land. Allendale, then a rural neighbourhood, was annexed by the City of Strathcona in 1907. It

became part of Edmonton in 1912 when Strathcona and Edmonton amalgamated. The majority of its development occurred in the 1950s.

Neighbourhood   CU   SW   4:B1

Allendale Park

6305–105A Street

Allendale Park is in the Allendale neighbourhood and has an area of 1.17 ha. *See* Allendale.

Park   1982   SW   4:C1

Allendale Road

Joining 61 Avenue to 63 Avenue, cutting across 104 Street to 106 Street

See Allendale.

Road   1958   SW   4:C1 *

Allin Park

15919–96 Avenue

The Ontario-born brothers, Dr. Norman G. Allin (1879–1957) and Dr. Edgar W. Allin (1875–1933) were pioneer Edmonton doctors. Edgar Allin received his medical training in Ontario before coming to Edmonton in 1909. The following year he became a member of the Royal College of Surgeons of England. One of the leading surgeons in western Canada, Edgar Allin became a fellow of the American College of Surgeons in 1913, was vice-president in 1916, and also served as president of the Edmonton Academy of Medicine and Canadian Medical Association, Alberta Division.

Norman Allin also received his medical training in Ontario. In about 1912, he joined his brother in Edmonton and began practising medicine. He was a member of the medical staff at the Royal Alexandra Hospital for many years, until his retirement in 1947. Allin Park is in the Glenwood neighbourhood and has an area of 1.82 ha.

Park   1987   SW   8:D2

Anthony Henday Drive

ANTHONY HENDAY, an English-born fur trader
with the Hudson's Bay Company, is believed to have
been the first person of European descent to make
contact with Aboriginal people in today's southern
Alberta. Henday, with a party of Cree guides, travelled
west from York Factory by canoe and foot in 1754–55,
reaching the prairies in the fall of 1754. In the spring
of 1755 he camped along the North Saskatchewan
River, where he met with people from the Cree and
Blackfoot nations. Whether or not he was also the first
to see the majestic, snow-capped Rocky Mountains,
however, remains a matter of dispute. While four copies
of Henday's original journal exist, they are contradic-
tory and the identification of quoted place names with
contemporary geography has proven problematic.

Employed as a labourer for the Hudson's Bay
Company at York Factory, in what is now Manitoba,
Henday volunteered to travel west as part of the
company's program of expanding its contact with
Aboriginal trading partners. Just southeast of present-
day Red Deer, Henday met with the chief of the
"Archithinue" people (believed to be the Blackfoot).
He failed, however, to convince the chief of the
benefits of trading with the Hudson's Bay Company
and returned to York Factory. A second trip west, in
1759, was also unsuccessful. Henday left the Hudson's
Bay Company in 1762 and is believed to have returned
to England.

Anthony Henday Drive forms a portion of a
staged, long-term roadway plan that has been part of
Edmonton's and Alberta's transportation network for
more than 30 years. It is also an important link in the
provincial north-south trade corridor. The ongoing
project will extend Anthony Henday Drive from
Yellowhead Trail in northwest Edmonton to Calgary
Trail in the south. The project's western segment,
Yellowhead Trail south to 45 Avenue and connecting
to Whitemud Drive, was completed in 2001. The
eastern segment, to follow the former Highways 14
and 14X, is in the preliminary design phase. The southwest segment, to Highway 2 in the south, is scheduled
for completion in 2005 and will complete the bypass of
the city.

*Anthony Henday Drive, Whitemud Drive to Stony Plain
Road, 2001. (Photo courtesy of Edmonton Transportation and
Streets Department)*

Argyll looking northwest, circa 1956. (CEA EA–33–198)

Angus Murray Park

5719–109 Street

This 1.88-ha. park, located in the Pleasantview neighbourhood, was named in honour of Angus A. Murray (b. 1916), an outstanding member of the community. Born in Saskatchewan, Murray came to Edmonton after serving in WWII. He joined the Lions Club in 1966 and introduced pee-wee baseball to his community. He also sponsored and supported Pleasantview hockey teams.

Park 1992 SW 4:B1

Annie B. Jackson Park

1011 Jackson Road

This 3.55-ha. park is in the Jackson Heights neighbourhood. *See* Jackson Heights.

Park 1992 SE 5:A2 *

Anthony Henday Drive

Ring road encircling the City of Edmonton

See feature story, page 9.

Road 1988 SW 3:B2

Argyll

63 Avenue and Argyll Road north to Mill Creek Ravine Park and Argyll Park

This land was subdivided in 1912, just prior to annexation by the City of Edmonton in 1913. The land remained largely undeveloped until the 1950s, when it was replotted. Originally called Edmonton City Heights, the neighbourhood was renamed Argyll in honour of Sir John Douglas Sutherland Campbell, the ninth Duke of Argyll and Marquess of Lorne. He was the husband of Queen Victoria's daughter, Princess Louise Caroline Alberta, after whom Alberta was named. The Marquess was governor general of Canada from 1878 to 1883, and founded the Royal Society of Canada in 1882 and the Royal Canadian Academy of Arts, a precursor to the National Gallery, in 1880. In 1881, he was the first vice-regal to tour western Canada.

Neighbourhood 1954 SE 4:C1

Argyll Road

63 Avenue and 91 Street northeast to the Sherwood Park Freeway

Named after the existing neighbourhood, Argyll Road was extended from 75 Street to Sherwood Park Freeway in 1965. *See* Argyll.

Road   1956   SE   4:D1

Argyll Sports Centre Park

6750–88 Street

This Argyll neighbourhood park has an area of 13.84 ha. *See* Argyll.

Park   1967   SE   4:C1 *

Armstrong Industrial

111 Avenue north to CN railway tracks, 170 Street to 178 Street

This neighbourhood is named in recognition of the contributions of businessman and politician George S. Armstrong (1867–1947). Born in Ontario, he came to Edmonton in 1905, where he established a drugstore. Armstrong served as an alderman from 1908 to 1910, mayor of Edmonton from 1911 to 1912 and was appointed Edmonton's postmaster in 1913.

Neighbourhood   1975   NW   8:C1

Arrowhead Trail

From 76 Avenue to 87 Avenue west of 172 Street

The name of this trail, a major walkway in the Thorncliff neighbourhood, reflects the theme of most of Edmonton's walkways, which are named for prominent Aboriginal people or bear a relationship with Aboriginal heritage. Arrowheads, the pointed part of arrows, were made separately from the shaft and were often made from flint. Arrowhead Trail is one of a number of trail names approved between 1969 and 1971.

Walkway   1969   SW   3:C1 *

George Armstrong, circa 1911. (CEA EA-10-1470)

Arthur Elliott Park

9620–152 Street

This 1.46-ha. park, located in the West Jasper Place neighbourhood, was named in honour of Arthur Harold Elliott (1881–1966). Elliott was born in Washington State and came to Alberta in 1905. He served on the Jasper Place town council in 1951 and 1952, and held the post of town welfare officer for six years.

Park   1988   SW   8:D2

Aspen Drive

North of Fairway Drive, west of 119 Street

See Aspen Gardens.

Road   1963   SW   4:B2

Aspen Gardens

39 Avenue and Fairway Drive north and 119 Street west to Aspen Drive West

Aspen, a deciduous softwood, is the most prevalent type of tree in the aspen parkland of western Canada.

Neighbourhood   1962   SW   4:B2

Athlone

127 Avenue to 132 Avenue, 127 Street to 139 Street

The Earl of Athlone, also known as Sir Alexander Augustus Frederick William Alfred George Cambridge, Prince Alexander of Teck (1874–1957), served as governor general of Canada from 1940 to 1946. He was the brother of Queen Mary, great-uncle of Queen Elizabeth II, and was married to Princess Alice, grand-daughter of Queen Victoria. The Athlone neighbourhood is part of a large parcel of land that was annexed to Edmonton in 1913. Most of the neighbourhood's development occurred a decade after the Earl's residency in Canada. This neighbourhood includes the former Dunvegan area.

Neighbourhood   1956   NW   10:B2

Athlone Park

13010–129 Street

This park, located in the Athlone neighbourhood, has an area of 0.91 ha. *See* Athlone.

Park   1982   NW   10:B2

Austin O'Brien Road

North of 95 Avenue west of 57 Street

Austin O'Brien (1896–1972) was superintendent of the separate school board for 37 years. He was born in Prince Edward Island and taught there and in Alberta before being named superintendent in 1924. He retired in 1961.

Road   1959   SE   6:A2

Athlone—looking east on 127 Avenue to the Canadian Government Elevator, circa 1968. (CEA EA-20-1333)

Avonmore

Argyll Road north to 76 Avenue, 75 Street west to Mill Creek Ravine Park

Algernon William Yelverton, Viscount Avonmore was an Irish peer and adventurer who stopped in Edmonton en route to his 1897 expedition to the Klondike Gold Rush. During the mid-1950s, parts of Avonmore were also called the Avonmore Addition.

Neighbourhood   1954   SE   4:C1

Avonmore Park

7902–73 Avenue

This Avonmore neighbourhood park has an area of 0.85 ha. *See* Avonmore.

Park   1967   SE   4:D1

Bailey Court

South of Blackmud Creek Drive and encircled by Blackmud Creek Crescent

Percy Simpson Bailey (1883–1975) was a teacher with the Edmonton Public School Board from 1909 to 1946, and was active in many local organizations. Bailey was born in New Brunswick, gained a BA degree from Mount Allison University, and then taught in his native province and in Saskatchewan before arriving in Edmonton in 1909. His teaching career in Edmonton spanned 37 years, including 11 years as principal of the Edmonton Technical School. Bailey had many other interests. He served as director of the Edmonton Exhibition Association, was past master of the Unity Masonic Lodge, and president of the Edmonton Schoolmen's Club. He was also secretary of the United Empire Loyalists Association, on the vestry of the All Saints Cathedral, a member of the Alpine Club of Canada and of the Mayfair Golf and Country Club.

Road 2001 SW 1:A2 *

Bainbridge Crescent

North of Whitemud Drive, west of Winterburn Road

Rev. Joseph William Bainbridge served as a Methodist, then United Church minister for 50 years. Born in England, Bainbridge came to Canada in 1911. During WWI he served with the Princess Patricia's Canadian Light Infantry and the Royal Air Force and was awarded the Military Medal. Bainbridge was a graduate of Alberta College and the University of Alberta. He was ordained in 1921, and served at Edmonton churches until 1966 when he and his family moved to Calgary. Bainbridge died in 1976 at the age of 87.

Road 1992 SW 3:B1 *

Baker Close

North of Blackmud Creek Drive, east of Barnes Way

This road in the Blackmud Creek neighbourhood was named for Yorkshire-born Herbert Baker (1866–1941). Baker emigrated to Canada in 1882 and found work with Massey Manufacturing (later Massey Harris Co. Ltd.), manufacturers of farm equipment. By 1904, he had been promoted to manager at the company's Winnipeg office. In 1910, he became the northern Alberta manager and was posted to Edmonton. In addition to his involvement in the Chamber of Commerce and community affairs of the Highland district, where he lived, Baker served on City Council as an alderman from 1927 to 1933.

Road 2000 SW 1:A2 *

Balfour Crescent

North of Whitemud Drive, east of Winterburn Road

Harry Ezra Balfour (b. 1893) was a provincial government director of school administration. Born in Ontario, he came to Alberta in 1911 and served in WWI from 1915, returning to Alberta in 1919. He taught at Victoria High School until 1929, then joined the provincial government inspection staff. In 1940 Balfour rejoined the army for WWII, serving overseas in 1943. In 1945 he was appointed director of school administration with the Department of Education. Balfour retired in 1958.

Road 1992 SW 3:B1 *

Ball Cove

South of Ellerslie Road, east of Blackmud Creek Drive

William Robinson Ball (1855–1951) was one of the founders of the United Farmers of Alberta and the Alberta Wheat Pool. Born in Prince Edward Island,

Ball moved to the United States in his youth. In 1895, he came back to Canada and travelled by prairie schooner to Hillsdale, Alberta, settling on a homestead 22 kilometres from Edmonton. Shortly before WWI, Ball moved to Edmonton and was employed as a wood-turner and upholsterer. After two years, however, he returned to farming. In 1923, he retired and moved to Edmonton. Ball Cove is in the Blackmud Creek neighbourhood.

Road 1999 SW 1:A1 *

Balwin

127 Avenue to 132 Avenue, 66 Street to 82 Street

The name of this neighbourhood is a combination of the names of two early property owners, Frank Ball and Luke Winterburn. Previously part of the Village of North Edmonton, Balwin was annexed to Edmonton in 1912. In the early part of the twentieth century it was known as Packingtown. The name stemmed from the fact that most of the families living in Balwin worked at the nearby meat-packing plants. The eastern portion of the neighbourhood was subdivided in the years around WWI while the western portion was subdivided in the late 1950s. In 1956 council replaced the existing subdivision names of Balwin and Balwin Addition with the single neighbourhood name of Balwin.

Neighbourhood 1956 NE 10:C2

Balwin Park

12904–74 Street

This park is in the Balwin neighbourhood and has an area of 2.32 ha. *See* Balwin.

Park 1983 NE 7:C1

Bancroft Close

North of Whitemud Drive, east of Winterburn Road

The musician and composer Hugh Henry Bancroft (1904–1988) was born in England and came to

Canada in 1929, moving to Edmonton in 1958. He was an accomplished church organist and a composer of international repute. For 22 years, until his retirement in 1980, Bancroft was the organist at All Saints Anglican Cathedral. During his career he worked in Canada, Australia, the United States and the Bahamas. In 1977 the Archbishop of Canterbury awarded Bancroft Britain's highest honour for organists, the Lambeth Degree. In 1980 Bancroft received an honorary Doctor of Laws from the University of Alberta. Bancroft Close is in the Breckenridge Greens neighbourhood.

Road 1992 SW 3:B1 *

Bannerman

137 Avenue to 144 Avenue, 20 Street west to Victoria Trail

Like other neighbourhoods in the Clareview subdivision, Bannerman is named for an Edmonton pioneer. Hugh Bannerman (d. 1891) was an early Edmonton businessman who settled in what is now the Belmont neighbourhood in 1883. He was a partner in J.A. MacDougall's general merchandising business from 1883 to 1885, and was one of the original directors of the Edmonton Cemetery Co. In 1887 he opened Alberta Boot & Shoe.

Neighbourhood 1978 NE 11:B2

Bannerman Park

13988–23 Street

This park is in the Bannerman neighbourhood and has an area of 2.83 ha. *See* Bannerman.

Park 1984 NE 11:B2

Baranow

*137 Avenue to 153 Avenue, 123 Street to
127 Street*

Baranow, like all the neighbourhoods and subdivisions in the Castle Downs area, is named for a famous castle. The Baranow castle is located in eastern Poland and was built between 1591 to 1606. Designed in the late-renaissance style, the castle has an arcaded courtyard and turrets. The castle and estate, formerly the family residence of Prince Lubomirski, have been converted into a museum and are owned by the state.

Neighbourhood 1979 NW 10:B2

Barbara Danelesko Park

3922–36 Avenue

Barbara L. Danelesko was the victim of one of Edmonton's most notorious murders. A mother of two, the 36-year-old Danelesko was killed in her home during a break-in by two juveniles in April 1994. She was an active member of her community who volunteered with the local hockey league and her children's school. The Barbara Danelesko Park is in the Minchau neighbourhood and has an area of 0.49 ha.

Park 1994 SE 5:B2 *

Barnes Link

East of Barnes Way, west of Blackmud Creek Drive

This road is named in honour of the politician and businessman Samuel Augustus Gordon Barnes (1875–1941). Born in Ontario, Barnes attended the Forest Model School and Toronto Normal School before enrolling at Manitoba University. In 1905 Barnes came to Edmonton to work at Alberta College. He served as a school board trustee from 1911 to 1936 and as a Social Credit MLA from 1935 to 1940. Barnes was, however, perhaps best known for his career in the insurance business as Alberta

manager of the New York-based Mutual Life Insurance Company.

Road 2000 SW 1:A1

Barnes Way

South of Ellerslie Road, west of Calgary Trail

See Barnes Link.

Road 2000 SW 1:A1

Barrie Close

South of Ellerslie Road, west of Calgary Trail

Québec-born Charles E. Barrie (1876–1940) came to Edmonton in the early 1900s and worked for the Banque d'Hochelaga. Some years later he took a position with the Union Bank of Canada and went on to become the secretary of the Franco-Canadian Loan Company. Barrie started working for the Coal Valley Mining Company in 1922, becoming manager of the company in 1924 and president in 1937. He was a member of St. Joachim's parish, the Knights of Columbus and the Edmonton Club. Barrie Close is in the Blackmud Creek neighbourhood.

Road 2000 SW 1:A2 *

Baturyn

Castle Downs Road north to 173A Avenue, 97 Street to 112 Street

Baturyn is named for a famous castle in northeast Ukraine. The town of Baturyn was destroyed by Russian troops in 1708 and rebuilt in 1750. Subdivisions and neighbourhoods in the Castle Downs area are named after castles.

Neighbourhood 1973 NW 10:B1

Baturyn Park

10505–172 Avenue

This Baturyn neighbourhood park has an area of 3.04 ha. *See* Baturyn.

Park 1982 NW 10:B1

Baturyn Road

East of 100 Street between 169 Avenue and 171 Avenue

See Baturyn.

Road 1974 NW 10:C1 *

Beacon Heights

118 Avenue to 122 Avenue, 34 Street to 50 Street

Before 1910, the Beacon Heights neighbourhood was an undeveloped tract of land northeast of the City of Edmonton. In 1913, along with land to the north and south, it was incorporated as part of the Village of Beverly. Beverly amalgamated with Edmonton in 1961. The origin of the Beacon Heights name is not recorded.

Neighbourhood CU NE 6:A1

Beacon Heights Park

4704–121 Avenue

This 0.34-ha. park serves the Beacon Heights neigh-bourhood. *See* Beacon Heights.

Park 2000 NE 6:A1 *

Bearspaw

10 Avenue to 17 Avenue, Calgary Trail west to Blackmud Creek

Chief Masgwaahsid (Bear's Paw) of the Stoney Band was born about 1835. He signed Treaty No. 7 at Blackfoot Crossing on September 22, 1877. It was Bear's Paw's authority that averted an armed confrontation when negotiations leading to the signing of this treaty were being conducted beside the Bow River. Neighbourhood names in the Kaskitayo area honour Aboriginal leaders.

Neighbourhood 1978 SW 1:A1

Bearspaw Drive East

South of 19 Avenue, east of 109 Street

See Bearspaw.

Road 1979 SW 1:A1 *

Bearspaw Drive West

South of 19 Avenue, west of 109 Street

See Bearspaw.

Road 1979 SW 1:A1

Beatrice Carmichael Park

10024–104 Street

Beatrice Carmichael (d. 1964) was Edmonton's Grand Dame of the opera. Born in Indiana, she came to Edmonton in 1919. Around 1923 Carmichael started the University Philharmonic Society and, with the assistance of university staff and students, produced and conducted operas throughout the mid-1920s. In 1935 she founded the Edmonton Civic Opera Company, and directed more than 50 shows in the years that followed. In addition to her light opera and grand opera produc-tions, Carmichael taught voice, violin and piano. She was awarded a citation from the City of Edmonton in 1961. The Beatrice Carmichael Park is in the Downtown neighbourhood and has an area of 0.07 ha.

Park 1986 C 7:C2

Beaver Hills House Park, 1978. (CEA EA–20–5552)

Beaumaris

153 Avenue to 160 Avenue and Beaumaris Road, 97 Street west to Castle Downs Road

The neighbourhood name of Beaumaris is taken from an ancient castle in north Wales. This follows the Castle Downs area theme of naming neighbourhoods and subdivisions after famous castles. Building of the Beaumaris castle began in 1295 on a site chosen by Edward I for what would be his last and largest castle. The site, a water-covered grassland, earned the castle the name Beaumaris, which is French for "beautiful marsh" (*beau mareys*). In the Beaumaris neighbourhood, an illusion of a keep (fortress castle) and moat are created by the houses along Castle Keep road and the Lake Beaumaris stormwater containment area.

Neighbourhood   1973   NW   10:C1

Beaumaris Park

10210–155 Avenue

This park is in the Beaumaris neighbourhood, and has an area of 2.84 ha. *See* Beaumaris.

Park   1982   NW   10:C2

Beaumaris Road

East of Castle Downs Road, north of 153 Avenue

See Beaumaris.

Road   1973   NW   10:B1

Beaver Hills House Park

10404 Jasper Avenue

The Devonian Foundation donated 0.53 ha. of land for this Downtown neighbourhood park and named it Beaver Hills House Park. The name comes from the Cree word *amiskwaskahegan*, which refers to Fort Edmonton's proximity to the Beaver Hills, east of present-day Edmonton.

Park   1977   C   7:C2

Beck Close

South of Ellerslie Road, west of Calgary Trail

Supreme Court judge Nicolas Dominic Beck (1857–1928) was born in Canada West and educated in law at the University of Toronto. Called to the Ontario Bar in 1879, Beck moved west in 1882 and eventually, in the 1890s, came to Edmonton. He was appointed judge of the Supreme Court of Alberta in 1907. Beck Close is in the Blackmud Creek neighbourhood.

Road   2000   SW   1:A1 *

Beechmount Cemetery

12420–104 Street

Opened in 1914 by the City of Edmonton, the Beechmount Cemetery was the first municipal cemetery in Edmonton. It was named for Beechmount subdivision, which dated from around 1910. Possibly a descriptive name as a beech is a long-lived, medium-sized tree with light coloured, smooth bark, while a mount refers to a hill or a mountain. The Beechmount Cemetery is located in the Westwood neighbourhood.

Cemetery   CU   NW   7:C1 *

Belgravia

71 Avenue north to University Avenue, 114 Street and 116 Street west to Saskatchewan Drive

Belgravia is named after a fashionable residential district of nineteenth-century London, England. Robert Tegler (1876–1921), who built the Tegler Building, put this neighbourhood on the real estate market around 1912. In the early 1900s, portions of this neighbourhood were called University Place and University Place Addition.

Neighbourhood   CU   SW   4:B1

Beechmount Cemetery War Memorial, circa 1968. (CEA EA-20-2893)

Belgravia Park

11540–73 Avenue

This Belgravia neighbourhood park has an area of 0.93 ha. *See* Belgravia.

Park   1956   SW   4:B1

Belgravia Road

Joining 122 Street with 71 Avenue at 116 Street

See Belgravia.

Road   1963   SW   4:B1

Bell Court

West of Bowen Wynd and east of 111 Street

James "Jimmy" Bell (d. 1967) was manager of Edmonton's municipal airport from 1930 until his retirement in 1962. Born in Yorkshire, England, and a graduate of Leeds University, Jimmy Bell was a civil engineer who emigrated to Canada in 1911. Two years later, he was hired by the City of Edmonton engineering department. During WWI, Bell enlisted with the 63rd Battalion that was raised in Edmonton. While in London, he considered transferring to the Royal Engineers, but a friend convinced him to join the Royal Flying Corps instead. From 1928, Bell was involved with the Edmonton and Northern Alberta Aero Club, and was one of the first directors of the Edmonton Flying Club when it was formed in 1944. Bell recalled that when he became manager of Edmonton's airfield in 1930, it was nothing more than a strip of grass. During World War II, Bell assisted in ferrying American planes through Edmonton to the Soviet Union. As a result of this "unstinting co-operation rendered American forces landing in Edmonton," Bell was presented with the Medal of Freedom by the United States Air Force in 1947.

Road 2002 SW 1:A2 *

Bellamy Hill

West of Rossdale Road

This road is named in honour of the Bellamy family, who played a prominent role in the city's development. The Bellamys lived at the top of the hill, at 99 Avenue and 102 Street. Thomas (1852–1926) and Lorinda (1855–1937) Bellamy came from Ontario in 1892 and established an agricultural implements business. Thomas was a member of Edmonton town council in 1895 and 1896, and on City Council from 1905 to 1906, 1908, 1912 and 1917. Lorinda organized the first women's missionary society, and was a founder of the YWCA. She was also a charter member of the Women's Christian Temperance Union. The Bellamys' son, Ralph, was the first Rhodes scholar from the North-West Territories (which included present-day Alberta). He was an alderman from 1928 to 1931 and from 1934 to 1935.

Road 1973 C 7:C2

House of George McKay, in Bellevue, 1929.
(CEA EA-160-732)

Belle Rive

153 Avenue to 167 Avenue, 82 Street to 89 Street

This neighbourhood name is taken from the French for "beautiful shore." Neighbourhood names in the Lake District relate to the description of lakes. There is an artificial lake in the southwestern part of the neighbourhood.

Neighbourhood 1979 NE 10:C1

Bellevue

Ada Boulevard north to 118 Avenue, 67 Street west to Wayne Gretzky Drive

Bellevue is likely derived from the French word for "beautiful view." Bellevue sits atop the banks of the North Saskatchewan River and affords a beautiful view of the river valley and Edmonton's downtown skyline. The neighbourhood has existed since at least 1907 and was developed by the Magrath-Holgate real estate company. Bellevue was formerly divided into two subdivisions, Bellevue and Bellevue Addition.

Neighbourhood CU NE 7:D1

Aerial view northeast across Borden Park to Bellevue, 1959. (CEA EA-20-1039)

Belmead

87 Avenue to 95 Avenue, 178 Street to 190 Street

The neighbourhood of Belmead is in the Primrose subdivision. Belmead fits with the pastoral naming pattern adopted for the subdivision, and is an abbreviation of the French term for "beautiful meadows."

Neighbourhood   1971   SW   8:C2

Belmead Park

18131–93 Avenue

This Belmead neighbourhood park has an area of 2.8 ha. *See* Belmead.

Park   1981   SW   8:C2

Belmont

Kennedale Ravine north to 137 Avenue, Victoria Trail west to 40 Street

Belmont is one of the oldest neighbourhoods in the Clareview subdivision. Its name is taken from the French term for "beautiful mountain." Early settlers homesteaded here in the late 1880s. Around 1912, it was subdivided and annexed to Edmonton in 1961. Much of its development, however, did not occur until the 1970s. The origin of the name Belmont is not recorded.

Neighbourhood   1972   NE   11:B2

Belmont Park

3250–132A Avenue

This Belmont neighbourhood park has an area of 3.09 ha. *See* Belmont.

Park   1981   NE   11:B2

Belvedere

LRT tracks north to 137 Avenue, LRT tracks west to 66 Street

This neighbourhood was named after an existing subdivision. Once part of the Village of North Edmonton, Belvedere was annexed to Edmonton in 1910. At that time, industrial and commercial zones began to displace local farms. Residential develop-

Swift Canadian Limited, abattoir in Belvedere, circa 1969. (CEA EA-267-41)

ment did not take place until the 1950s and 1960s. Belvedere may be a descriptive name as a "belvedere" is a raised turret or summerhouse used to view scenery. From the early 1900s, the land between the LRT tracks and Fort Road from 60 Street to 50 Street and 137 Avenue was also known as The Braids.

Neighbourhood   1956   NE   10:D2

Belvedere Park

13223–60 Street

This park in the Belvedere neighbourhood has an area of 1.57 ha. *See* Belvedere.

Park   1983   NE   11:A2

Bergman

122 Avenue north to Yellowhead Trail, 35 Street to 50 Street

Gustave C. Bergman (1872–1962) was the first mayor of the Town of Beverly. He was born in Illinois and came to Edmonton some time after 1901. Beverly was incorporated as a town on August 5, 1914. Bergman was sworn in as mayor a few days later.

Neighbourhood   1964   NE   6:A1

Bergman Park

12310–43 Street

This park is in the Bergman neighbourhood and has an area of 1.71 ha. *See* Bergman.

Park   1987   NE   6:A1

Beringer Crescent

South of Breckenridge Drive, west of Bancroft Close

Music teacher Victor Albert Beringer (1867–1966) was born in England and moved to Edmonton in 1900. He had received musical training at the Royal Academy of Music in London and studied in Germany under Franz Liszt for three years. He taught music in Edmonton from 1902 until his retirement in 1952.

Road   1992   SW   3:B1 *

Beverly

118 Avenue north to Yellowhead Trail, Victoria Trail west to 50 Street

This subdivision incorporates part of the former Town of Beverly. In 1904 the Canadian Pacific Railway named a station in the vicinity after the Beverly township in Wentworth County, Ontario. Most early residents were employed in the coal industry. Beverly was formed as a village in 1913, incorporated as a town in 1914 and annexed to Edmonton in 1961.

Subdivision   1914   NE   6:A1 *

Beverly Bridge

Spanning the North Saskatchewan River at the Yellowhead Trail

Named for its proximity to what was once the Town of Beverly, this bridge was opened in 1972, and handles eastbound traffic on the Yellowhead Trail. Adjacent to it are two other bridges: the railway bridge, which was built in 1907 by the

Beverly Mine trucks and tipple, 1938. (CEA EA-160-482)

Grand Trunk Pacific Railway, and the Clover Bar Bridge, which handles westbound traffic. *See* Beverly.

Bridge   1972   NE   6:B1

Beverly Heights

Ada Boulevard north to 118 Avenue, 34 Street to 50 Street

This neighbourhood was subdivided around 1912 and named after the nearby train station. *See* Beverly.

Neighbourhood   1912   NE   6:A1

Bevington Close

West of Breckenridge Drive

George E. Bevington (1876–1965) was one of the founders of the United Farmers of Alberta (UFA) in 1909. Born in Missouri, Bevington came to Alberta in 1893, homesteading with his family near Bruderheim. Bevington later bought land at Winterburn where he farmed for over 40 years. He was an advocate of monetary reform and testified before Parliament in 1922. In 1955 he was made a life member of the UFA. Bevington Close is in the Breckenridge Greens neighbourhood.

Road   1992   SW   3:B1 *

Bevington Place

South of Breckenridge Drive

See Bevington Close.

Road   1992   SW   3:B1 *

Bhullar Park

8603–38 Avenue

Sohan Singh Bhullar (1882–1968) was an early immigrant from India. He arrived in Canada in 1907, living first in British Columbia before moving to Lethbridge, Alberta. Bhullar worked there on a farm and at the Chisolm Mill, and later farmed his own land. In 1953 he came to Edmonton and, during the late 1950s and early 1960s, housed and helped newly arrived immigrants and students from India. Bhullar Park is in the Richfield neighbourhood and has an area of 0.09 ha.

Park   1985   SE   4:C2

Big Bear Park

1312–109 Street

This 1.74-ha. park in the Bearspaw neighbourhood honours the life of Plains Cree Chief Mistahimaskwa "Big Bear" (c. 1825–1888). By the 1870s, Big Bear, who had been born in what is now Saskatchewan, was a leader of his people. In 1876 he refused to sign Treaty No. 6 because he believed it would destroy his people's way of life. By 1882, however, the threat of starvation finally forced him to submit to the treaty, and with it, to accept the forced relocation of Aboriginal people onto reserves. He was later blamed for the Frog Lake Massacre of 1885. Despite his innocence, Big Bear surrendered at Fort Carleton and faced treason charges. He was found guilty and sentenced to three years at Stony Mountain Penitentiary. Big Bear served two years of his term before being released because of ill health. He returned to the Poundmaker Reserve where he died the following year.

Park 1986 SW 1:A1

Big Bear, no date. (CEA EA-10-1023)

Big Miller Park

11 Tommy Banks Way

See feature story, page 25.

Park 2001 C 7:C2 *

Bingham Crescent

North of Whitemud Drive, east of Winterburn Road

Lloyd Bingham (d. 1968) was the chief constable of the Edmonton Police Department from 1966 to 1968. Bingham joined the Royal Canadian Mounted Police (RCMP) in 1934 and worked in North Battleford until 1943. For the next 20 years he lived and worked across Canada. Bingham had 32 years of service with the RCMP before resigning as acting commissioner in 1966 to become chief of police.

Road 1992 SW 3:B1 *

Bishop Point

North of Whitemud Drive, east of Winterburn Road

Edward S. Bishop was a teacher and civil servant. Born and educated in Ontario, he was ordained a Methodist minister in 1905. After holding various positions in Ontario, Bishop was transferred to Alberta where he worked as a teacher. From 1918 to 1920, he was employed as secretary to the provincial Superintendent of Neglected and Dependent Children, Department of the Attorney General, from 1920 to 1922, as field secretary to the social service board of the Methodist church. He was then appointed commissioner of the province's Liquor Act. Bishop Point is in the Blackmud Creek neighbourhood.

Road 2001 SW 1:B2 *

Big Miller Park

AWARD-WINNING jazz trombonist, blues singer and educator Clarence Horatio "Big" Miller (1922–1992) helped found the Edmonton Jazz City Festival and was considered one of the most acclaimed bluesmen in Canada. Miller, the son of a Sioux father and a mother who was the descendant of a black slave, was born at Sioux City, Iowa. A mix of bad luck and unexpected opportunities led to his becoming a proud Canadian citizen in 1973. It was during a tour of Canada in the late 1960s that Miller became stranded in Vancouver. The show he was performing with ran out of money and he was forced to find work in order to pay his way home.

One of the gigs he took was at Tommy Banks' Embers Club in Edmonton. Embraced by the local music community, Miller made several return engagements, eventually staying and becoming an Edmontonian. He went on to make major contributions to not only the city music scene but provincially, through teaching. Over the course of his 50-year career, Miller performed with some of the world's greatest jazz musicians, including Miles Davis, Wynton Marsalis, Lionel Hampton, Duke Ellington, Count Basie and Woody Herman. He toured internationally and was a regular performer at Switzerland's prestigious Montreux Jazz Festival.

In 1979 Miller won a Juno for *Jazz Canada Montreux 1978*, a live album recorded with the Tommy Banks Orchestra. Among his other albums are *Live From Calgary* (1982), *Big Miller and the Blues Machine: Live at Athabasca University* (1990) and *The Last of the Blues Shouters* (1992), recorded in Southampton, England. The National Film Board of Canada recognized Miller's work with the 1980 biographical film *Big and the Blues*. In 1985 Miller received an honorary doctorate of humanities from Athabasca University in recognition of his teaching of jazz, blues and gospel music. In addition to his busy performing schedule, Miller taught at the Banff School of Fine Arts, Grant MacEwan College and schools throughout Alberta.

The 0.08-ha. Big Miller Park is located in the Strathcona neighbourhood.

Big Miller in concert, 1975. (PAA J.1875)

Bisset

*23 Avenue to 34 Avenue, 34 Street west to
Mill Woods Road East*

Judge Athelstan Bisset (1883–1973) was a WWI
veteran and an alderman from 1934 to 1952. Bisset
was born in Ontario and came to Edmonton in
1893. He served overseas in WWI and upon his
return ran a law practice in Strathcona from 1919
to 1952. He served as an alderman for 15 years and
in 1952 was appointed a judge in family court. In
the late 1910s, the northern portion of the Bisset
neighbourhood was known as Elysian fields.
Ancient Greeks believed that their final destination,
upon death, was the Elysian Fields. More generally,
it can refer to a place of perfect happiness.

Neighbourhood 1976 SE 5:B2

Blackburn Close

North of Ellerslie Road, west of Calgary Trail

John Hiram Blackburn (1896–1972) was an accomplished pilot and businessman. Blackburn was born
in Pennsylvania and in 1911 came with his family to
Alberta. During WWI Blackburn trained as a pilot
but did not see active duty. In 1930 he earned his
private pilot's licence and went on to serve in
WWII. Blackburn won the 1948 Webster Memorial
Trophy as Canada's top amateur pilot. He began
working as an insurance agent in 1930 and was
named president of the Life Insurance
Underwriters Association of Canada in 1962.
Blackburn was the author of two books, *The
Blackburn Story* and *Land of Promise.*

Road 1991 SW 1:A1 *

Blackburn Drive East

North of Ellerslie Road, west of Calgary Trail

See Blackburn Close.

Road 1991 SW 1:A1

Blackburn Drive West

North of Ellerslie Road, west of Calgary Trail

See Blackburn Close.

Road 1991 SW 1:A1

Blackburn Place

North of Ellerslie Road, west of Calgary Trail

See Blackburn Close.

Road 1991 SW 1:A1 *

Blackburne

*Quadrant Avenue south to Ellerslie Road, Calgary
Trail west to 111 Street and Blackmud Creek*

The neighbourhood name Blackburne is derived
from Black Mud Creek, which traverses the property, and "burne," an old English word for stream
or river.

Neighbourhood 1987 SW 1:A1

Blackburne Creek Park

747 Blackwood Crescent

This 1.49-ha. park, in the Blackburne neighbourhood, is located near the Blackmud Creek. *See*
Blackburne.

Park 1995 SW 1:A1

Blackett Wynd

North of Ellerslie Road, west of Calgary Trail

John St. Clair Blackett (1863–1935) was an early
Edmonton entrepreneur. Blackett was born in
Nova Scotia and came to Edmonton in 1904. He
became president of Alberta Agencies (insurance
brokers) and was a director of Acme Brick Co. and
Arctic Ice Co. This road is in the Richford neighbourhood.

Road 1991 SW 1:A1 *

Boy Scouts' Cabin on Blackmud Creek, 1931. (CEA EA-160-668)

Blacklock Way

North of Ellerslie Road, west of Calgary Trail

Thomas M. Blacklock worked as a teacher in
Alberta for 43 years. Blacklock was born in Utah
and came to Edmonton in 1912. He received his BA
degree from the University of Alberta and began
teaching in 1925. After joining the Edmonton
Public School system in 1930, he taught at
Parkdale, Oliver and Queens Avenue schools.
Blacklock was later appointed vice-principal of
King Edward School and principal of Queen
Alexandra, Norwood and Strathearn schools. He
retired in 1968. Blacklock Way is in the Blackburne
neighbourhood.

Road 1991 SW 1:A1

Blackmore Court

*South of Blackmore Way and east of Blackmud
Creek Crescent*

Previously named Bailey Way. *See* Blackmore Way.

Road 2002 SW 1:A2 *

Blackmore Way

*North of Blackmore Court and east of Blackmud
Creek Crescent*

John Horn Blackmore (1890–1962) was a teacher
and Social Credit member of parliament for
Lethbridge. Blackmore was born in the United
States to Mormon parents, and emigrated to the
Cardston area of Alberta with his family in 1892.
Having gained his BA in 1913 from University of
Alberta, and in 1914, his teaching certificate from
the Alberta Normal School, Blackmore embarked
on a 21-year teaching career. In 1935 he left
teaching to run for public office. He served as a
member of parliament for Lethbridge until 1958,
and during this time he was instrumental in
promoting public irrigation of the prairies.

Road 2001 SW 1:A2 *

Blackmud Creek

West of Calgary Trail

The creek flows, within the city limits, into
Whitemud Creek near 130 Street and 23 Avenue.
Whitemud Creek, in turn, flows into the North
Saskatchewan River. The name, noted as early as

1882, is a translation of the creek's original Cree name, *kaskitewâw asiskiy*.

Creek CU SW 2:D2

Blackmud Creek

Ellerslie Road south to 25 Avenue SW, 107 Street to 111 Street

This neighbourhood is named after Blackmud Creek, which borders it along the south and east. It was first named Blackmud Creek neighbourhood in 1994, but later, in 1998, renamed Heritage Valley neighbourhood. After a request by developers, however, the name was changed back to Blackmud Creek. *See* Blackmud Creek *creek*.

Neighbourhood 1999 SW 1:A1

Blackmud Creek Bridge

Spanning the Blackmud Creek at 111 Street

The $5.5 million cost of building the Blackmud Creek Bridge was paid for by both the City and the province. Its construction was spurred by the death of John Shaw, a postal worker, whose postal van was hit by a gravel truck at an unsafe crossing of the creek on 13 August 1992. The bridge was opened in August 1994. *See* Blackmud Creek *creek*.

Bridge 1996 SW 2:D1 *

Blackmud Creek Crescent

Road 1999 SW 1:A2 *
South of Ellerslie Road, west of Calgary Trail

See Blackmud Creek *creek*.

Blackmud Creek Drive

South of Ellerslie Road, west of Calgary Trail

See Blackmud Creek *creek*.

Road 2000 SW 1:A1

Blackmud Creek Ravine

Along the course of Blackmud Creek

See Blackmud Creek *creek*.

Ravine CU SW 2:D1 *

Blackwood Crescent

North of Ellerslie Road, west of Calgary Trail

Matthew Blackwood (1888–1943) was a police chief who served for 31 years with the Edmonton Police Department. The Irish-born Blackwood came to Edmonton with his parents in 1904 and joined the police force in 1912. He was appointed chief of police in 1942. This road is located in the Blackburne neighbourhood.

Road 1991 SW 1:A1

Blue Quill

23 Avenue north to Saddleback Road, 111 Street to 119 Street

In the 1910s, the northeast portion of the Blue Quill neighbourhood was known as Edmonton Place. *See* Blue Quill *subdivision*.

Neighbourhood 1974 SW 4:B2

Blue Quill

23 Avenue to 34 Avenue, 111 Street west to Whitemud Ravine

This subdivision was named in honour of Cree Chief Blue Quill of Saddle Lake Indian Reserve, which was established in 1889. Chief Blue Quill traded in Edmonton in the late 1890s. Blue Quill subdivision was named first, followed by the neighbourhood later in 1974.

Subdivision 1974 SW 4:B2 *

Blue Quill Crescent

East of 123 Street, south of 23 Avenue

See Blue Quill *subdivision*.

Road 1987 SW 4:B2 *

Blue Quill Estates

23 Avenue to 29A Avenue, 119 Street west to Whitemud Park

This neighbourhood is part of the Blue Quill subdivision. *See* Blue Quill *subdivision.*

Neighbourhood   1987   SW   4:B2

Blue Quill Park

11304–25 Avenue

Located in the Blue Quill neighbourhood, this park has an area of 3.07 ha. *See* Blue Quill *subdivision.*

Park   1984   SW   4:B2

Blue Quill Point

North of 29A Avenue, west of 124 Street

See Blue Quill *subdivision.*

Road   1987   SW   4:B2 *

Blyth Crescent

East of Winterburn Road, north of Whitemud Drive

The award-winning photographer Alfred Blyth (1901–1980) was born in Scotland and came to Edmonton in 1913. He later worked for McDermid Studios and in 1928 opened his own firm. Blyth captured scenes of Edmonton life from as early as 1916, taking photographs for the *Edmonton Journal* and the *Edmonton Bulletin*, and serving as the official photographer for visits by the royal family in 1939, 1951 and 1959. He retired in 1970. In 1976 he won an Alberta Achievement Award. His remarkable collection of 25,000 photographs is stored at the Provincial Archives of Alberta.

Road   1992   SW   3:B1 *

Fairway Auto Service, Bonnie Doon, circa 1969.
(CEA EA–88–94)

Bonaventure

CNR railway tracks north to 137 Avenue, St. Albert Trail west to 149 Street

Bonaventure, meaning "good luck" in French, honours the French Canadians who used St. Albert Trail to establish their homesteads, and those who set out on this route during the Klondike Gold Rush. Bonaventure replaced the neighbourhood's earlier names of Radial Park and Brown Estate. At one time the name Klondike was recommended, but it was not adopted.

Neighbourhood   1961   NW   10:A2

Bonnie Doon

Whyte Avenue north to Connors Road, 83 Street west to Mill Creek Ravine Park

The neighbourhood of Bonnie Doon was named around 1912. The name is Scottish for "pleasant, rolling countryside." In the early 1900s, Canadian-born Premier Alexander Cameron Rutherford owned a portion of land east of the Mill Creek which later became part of the Bonnie Doon neighbourhood. Rutherford is believed to have subdivided the land in 1906 and then named it Bonnie Doon in memory of his ancestral homeland, Scotland. He also named a second, nearby, subdivision Scona Brae (the subdivision no longer exists under this name). In keeping with Rutherford's fondness for reminders of Scotland, his second home, located along Saskatchewan Drive, was named Achnacarry, after a castle in the County of Inverness, Scotland.

Neighbourhood   CU   SE   7:C2

Bonnie Doon Park

9263–94 Street

This park, in the Bonnie Doon neighbourhood, has an area of 1.57 ha. *See* Bonnie Doon.

Park   1982   SE   7:C2

Borden Park

11200–74 Street

See feature story, page 31.

Park   CU   NE   7:C1

Borden Park Road

From 73 Street to 79 Street at approximately 114 Avenue

See Borden Park.

Road   1960   NE   7:C1

Bowen Wynd

East of Bell Court and southwest of Blackmud Creek Crescent

John Campbell Bowen (1872–1957) was Alberta's sixth lieutenant-governor. Born in Osgoode, Ontario, Bowen received a degree from McMaster University, and went on to study theology at Brandon College in Manitoba. From 1907 to 1911, he was pastor at the Strathcona Baptist Church. Ill health forced him to resign from his next posting in Winnipeg, and in 1912 he returned to Edmonton. Bowen's new career in the life insurance business was put on hold when, in 1915, he enlisted to serve in WWI with the 63rd Battalion. He was made

chaplain, and assigned the rank of captain. Upon his return to Edmonton in 1918, Bowen resumed his career in life insurance, but two years later changed direction again and entered public life.

In 1920 Bowen was elected to the Edmonton City Council. After only one year as an Alderman, he moved on to the provincial legislature, when he was elected as a Liberal member for Edmonton. Even though he had become Liberal house leader, Bowen's bid for re-election in 1926 did not succeed. Likewise, his campaign to be elected Edmonton's mayor in 1928 was unsuccessful. However, in 1937, Bowen was appointed Alberta's lieutenant-governor, a post he held until 1950. He is perhaps most remembered for the controversy surrounding his refusal, in 1937, to grant Royal Assent to three Bills brought forward by the Social Credit government of Premier William Aberhart. These were the Accurate News and Information Act, the Bank Taxation Act, and the Credit of Alberta Regulation Amendment Act.

Road   2002   SW   1:A2 *

Bowness Wynd

Off Blackmud Creek Crescent, south of Blackmore Way

Ernest W. Bowness (b. 1879) was an engineer who became manager of the Edmonton Electric Light and Power Company in the late 1910s, and was active in Edmonton's business community. Born in PEI, Bowness served in the South African War from 1899 to 1901. He then attended McGill University, receiving a BSc in 1905. After a period teaching in the United States, Bowness came west to make surveys and reports on the Bow River. He was involved in many other projects in western Canada and the US, including a period as an efficiency engineer for the City of Edmonton in 1913. Bowness continued to participate in a variety of engineering projects, including being president of the Edmonton-based Empire Engineering Company, and was identified with the civil and electrical branches of the Professional Engineers of Alberta.

Borden Park

BORDEN PARK, named in honour of Sir Robert Laird Borden (1854–1937), the eighth prime minister of Canada, has been an important Edmonton attraction for almost 100 years. In the early part of the last century, as many as 7,000 people would pour into the park on a Sunday to enjoy picnics, baseball and music. Originally known as East End City Park, it was established in 1906. The 21.99-ha. park was renamed following Prime Minister Borden's visit to Edmonton in 1914. Borden was elected prime minister in 1911 and held office until his retirement in 1920.

One of the city's first three swimming pools was situated in Borden Park. As the *Edmonton Journal* noted in an article published on September 20, 1924: "The whole pool radiates good humor and innocent enjoyment, and is a fitting reply to those prudes who elevate their eyes to high heaven and deplore the 'wickedness' embodied in mixed bathing." The East End swimming pool, the article continued, "will go a long way towards building up a healthy, vigorous, graceful and clean-minded womanhood." In addition to the pool, the park was for many years home to the Edmonton Zoo. Among its first animals was a bear cub named Louise. As well, there were two buffalo, two elk, monkeys, coyotes and peacocks. Other park attractions were a tea room and rides, including a carousel, a giant roller coaster and a tunnel-of-love. The latter, in a bow to decorum, was known as "the Old Mill."

By the mid-1930s, however, the Old Mill had been destroyed by fire and the rides were showing their age. The massive roller coaster, built in 1915 at a cost of $15,000, was dismantled in 1935 and its timbers salvaged by a lumber company. Borden Park has continued to be an important outdoor venue for Edmontonians, though the attractions offered have changed somewhat since its establishment almost a century ago. In the late 1970s, the park's bandshell hosted performances by two of the city's new-wave rock bands, The Silent Movies and Smarties.

Borden Park, circa 1932. (CEA EA-160-1002)

Boyle Street area women's softball game, 1933. (CEA EA-160-746)

He was active in the community as a member of the Edmonton Board of Trade, the Edmonton Club, and the Edmonton Golf and Country Club.

Road   2002   SW   1:A2 *

Boyle Street

101 Avenue north to LRT tracks, 84 Street to 97 Street

Boyle Street, the former street designation for 103A Avenue, is one of the oldest neighbourhoods in Edmonton. The rectangular blocks and straight streets of Boyle Street neighbourhood have existed since 1892 and conform to the original Edmonton Settlement, which was subdivided on the basis of river lots. The Hudson Bay Reserve, located north of Fort Edmonton, forced the emerging town of Edmonton to spread eastward and away from the fort. Consequently, Edmonton's early commercial district was located along Jasper Avenue and 97 Street (Namayo Avenue) near what is now the Boyle Street neighbourhood.

It is likely that Boyle Street was named after an early resident of Edmonton, John R. Boyle (1870–1936). Born in Ontario, Boyle moved west to Regina in 1894 and studied law with McKenzie and Brown. Two years later, Boyle came to Edmonton where he worked at the office of Hedley C. Taylor (later Judge Taylor). After being called to the bar in 1899, Boyle entered into partnership with Taylor. Between 1904 and 1906, Boyle served with K.A. McLeod, Thomas Bellamy, W.H. Clark, J.H. Picard, D.R. Fraser, W.A. Griesbach and, later, Robert Mays and D.G. Latta on the first Municipal Council of Edmonton. Roadways off Boyle Street carried the names of some of these same men—Bellamy, Clark, Picard and Griesbach. Boyle was elected to the provincial legislature in 1905, re-elected in 1909 and remained undefeated until his retirement from provincial politics in 1926. In 1912 he was appointed King's Counsel and minister of education. He was named attorney general in 1918 and, in 1924, a judge.

Neighbourhood   1946   NE   7:C2

Braithwaite Park

8018–112 Street

Dr. Edward A. Braithwaite (1862–1949) was Edmonton's first medical officer. Born in England, Braithwaite came to Canada in 1884. He joined the North West Mounted Police (NWMP) that year and upon his retirement in 1931 had the longest record of service in the history of the force. In 1892 he established a private practice in Edmonton, but retained his connection with the NWMP. During this same period, from 1892 to 1907, he served as medical health officer for Edmonton. Braithwaite was appointed coroner for the North-West Territories in 1896 and became chief coroner and medical inspector for Alberta in 1932, retiring in 1948. Braithwaite Park, in the Garneau neighbourhood, has an area of 1.21 ha.

Park 1956 SW 4:B1

Brander Drive

Northwest of 64 Avenue, west of 148 Street

This road is named for the neighbourhood of Brander Gardens in the Riverbend subdivision. In 1973 the cul-de-sac abutting this road was designated Brander Drive because local residents complained that the previous designation of 62 Avenue was too difficult to locate. The Names Advisory Committee approved the road name clarification on October 10, 1973. *See* Brander Gardens.

Road 1970 SW 4:A1

Brander Gardens

51 Avenue to 66 Avenue, Whitemud Drive west to Whitemud Road

See feature story, page 34.

Neighbourhood 1965 SW 3:D2

Brander Gardens Park

14815–56 Avenue

This park is in the Brander Gardens neighbourhood and has an area of 2.02 ha. *See* Brander Gardens *feature story, page 34.*

Park 1984 SW 4:A1

Breckenridge Bay

East of Winterburn Road, north of Whitemud Drive

See Breckenridge Greens.

Road 1992 SW 3:B1 *

Breckenridge Close

East of Winterburn Road, north of Whitemud Drive

See Breckenridge Greens.

Road 1992 SW 3:B1 *

Breckenridge Court

East of Winterburn Road, north of Whitemud Drive

See Breckenridge Greens.

Road 1992 SW 3:B1 *

Breckenridge Drive

East of Winterburn Road, north of Whitemud Drive

See Breckenridge Greens.

Road 1992 SW 3:B1

Breckenridge Greens

Whitemud Drive north to 87 Avenue, Lewis Farms Boulevard west to Winterburn Road

Gavin Breckenridge Sr. (1870–1946) was a pioneer dairy farmer. News of the Klondike Gold Rush prompted the Ontario-born Breckenridge to travel

Brander Gardens

THIS NEIGHBOURHOOD was named in honour of the gardener George Brander (d. 1933). Brander came to Edmonton from Nova Scotia in 1921 and soon established a peony garden in the Bonnie Doon area. George and his son, prominent Edmontonian Dr. James Frederick Brander (1879–1963), founded the Silver Heights Peony Garden in 1923. The garden, located at 93 Avenue and 85 Street in Bonnie Doon, was a major tourist attraction and the source of most of the peonies in Alberta until the 1940s. In 2002, Fort Edmonton Park completed a recreation of the peony garden, including 26 varieties of peonies.

George Brander and some children in the Silver Heights Peony Garden, 1925. (PAA B.6794)

west to join a group of gold seekers. He arrived in Edmonton in 1898 and found employment in a coal mine. Breckenridge soon discovered, however, that there was an urgent need for milk in the growing community and helped found Edmonton's first dairy farm.

Neighbourhood 1990 SW 3:B1

Breckenridge Lane

East of Winterburn Road, north of Whitemud Drive

See Breckenridge Greens.

Road 1992 SW 3:B1 *

Brennan Court

East of Winterburn Road, north of Whitemud Drive

W. "Daddy" Brennan (b. 1871) worked for more than three decades for Edmonton's street railway. Born and raised in England, Brennan was 40 years old when he emigrated to Edmonton and took a position with the City of Edmonton's street railway. He brought to the job six years of experience working for the Stockport Street railway department in England. Brennan worked for the Edmonton's railway for 35 years, training almost every employee who joined the service.

Road 1999 SW 3:B1 *

Brintnell

153 Avenue to 167 Avenue, Manning Drive west to 50 Street

Following a model of naming neighbourhoods in the Pilot Sound area for pilots, this name was chosen in honour of Wilfred Leigh Brintnell (1895–1971), who was well known for his pioneer flights across unmapped territories. Brintnell was born in Ontario and joined the Royal Flying Corps during WWI. In 1927 he joined Western Canada Airways and flew the first multi-engine flight from

Leigh Brintnell, circa 1937–1939. (GAI NA-463-1)

Winnipeg to Vancouver and return. Brintnell also flew a more than 14,000-kilometre inspection flight and circled Great Bear Lake, the first pilot to do so.

In 1932 he formed Mackenzie Air Service Ltd. in Edmonton. During WWII he was the president of the Edmonton-based Aircraft Repair Ltd., the firm was given a contract for repairing and maintaining Canadian and American military aircraft along the Northwest Staging Route. In 1946 Brintnell received the Order of the British Empire for his outstanding service during the war. Following the war, Brintnell managed Northwest Industries and in 1952 operated Arctic Air Lines. He was inducted into the Canadian Aviation Hall of Fame in 1975.

Neighbourhood 1981 NE 11:A1 *

Britannia Youngstown

Stony Plain Road north to 107 Avenue, 156 Street west to Mayfield Road

Britannia and Youngstown were originally two different subdivisions in the Town of Jasper Place. Britannia appears on early Edmonton maps (1912) and may have been named after the Latin term for Britain, Britannia. The name referred to the three countries of England, Scotland and Wales and was personified in a female figure. The neighbourhood was annexed to Edmonton in 1964. *See* Youngstown Industrial.

Neighbourhood   CU   NW   8:C2

Britannia Youngstown Park

15929–105 Avenue

This park, in the Britannia Youngstown neighbourhood, has an area of 0.58 ha. *See* Britannia Youngstown.

Park   1982   NW   8:D2

Brookside

45 Avenue north to Whitemud Park, Whitemud Park west to Whitemud Drive

The neighbourhood name is derived from its location adjacent to Whitemud Creek.

Neighbourhood   1965   SW   4:A1

Brookside Park

5320–143 Street

This 1.58-ha. park in the Brookside neighbourhood takes its name from a nearby school as well as the neighbourhood. *See* Brookside.

Park   1983   SW   4:A1

Brown Industrial

Yellowhead Trail north to CN railway tracks, St. Albert Trail west to 149 Street

Brown Industrial takes its name from the historic subdivision, Brown's Estate. Brown's Estate was established around 1914 and located at approximately the same site where Brown Industrial exists today. It may have been named after Clifford W. Brown, a real-estate and financial agent who lived in Edmonton in the 1910s. (His name appears in the 1914 local directory.) In 1954 Brown's Estate was replotted and later, in 1960, rezoned for industrial use from Canadian National Railways (CNR) to 137 Avenue and west of 149 Street.

Neighbourhood   1914   NW   7:A1

Buchanan Close

North of Rabbit Hill Road, east of Terwillegar Drive

This road is named in honour of two men, both of whom were named Buchanan but were not related. John Alexander Buchanan was a Canadian senator and a long-time Edmonton resident. James McIntyre Buchanan was a pioneer boat builder. John Alexander Buchanan (1887–1970) was born in Ontario and came to Edmonton in 1910, where he worked for the federal government. He did considerable survey work in the Peace River country and the Northwest Territories. Buchanan was a prominent member of the Conservative Party and was appointed to the Senate in 1959, retiring six years later. James McIntyre Buchanan was born in Scotland in 1884 and came to Edmonton in 1911. He and a partner founded the Alberta Motor Boat Company and manufactured boats used by the Hudson's Bay Company and the RCMP. He died in the late 1930s.

Road   1988   SW   4:A2 *

Buena Vista Park from Mayfair (now William Hawrelak) Park, 1963. (CEA EA-20-989)

Buchanan Place

North of Rabbit Hill Road, east of Terwillegar Drive

See Buchanan Close.

Road   1988   SW   4:A2 *

Buchanan Road

North of Rabbit Hill Road, east of Terwillegar Drive

See Buchanan Close.

Road   1988   SW   4:A2

Buchanan Way

North of Rabbit Hill Road, east of Terwillegar Drive

See Buchanan Close.

Road   1988   SW   4:A2 *

Buena Vista Park

13210 Buena Vista Road

The City of Edmonton began planning a Buena Vista Park in 1957 and purchased the land in 1959. This 80.33-ha. park is located in the Laurier Heights neighbourhood. *See* Buena Vista Road.

Park   1959   SW   4:B1

Buena Vista Road

East of 142 Street on 87 Avenue

This road was named for the former subdivision of Buena Vista. Settled in 1878 and homesteaded in the late 1880s, Buena Vista was subdivided around 1911. Martin Runnalls, developer of Buena Vista, reused the name in 1912 when he built the Buena Vista apartments, which still stand at 102 Avenue and 124 Street. Buena Vista is Spanish for "beautiful view."

Road   1957   SW   4:B1

Bulyea Heights

Rabbit Hill Road north to Whitemud Drive, Whitemud Park west to Terwillegar Drive

George Hedley Vicars Bulyea (1859–1928) was the first lieutenant-governor of Alberta. Born in New Brunswick, he attended the University of New Brunswick and graduated with a Bachelor of Arts in 1878. Between 1878 and 1882, Bulyea was the principal of Sheffield Academy in Sunbury county, New Brunswick. In 1882 he moved west to Winnipeg, Manitoba, and a year later, to Qu'Appelle, Saskatchewan. In 1894, representing South Qu'Appelle, Bulyea won a seat in the North-West Territorial Assembly; he was re-elected in 1898 and again in 1902. Bulyea became the first lieutenant-governor of Alberta in 1905 and served until 1915. While living in Edmonton, he was a member of the Edmonton Club and the Edmonton Golf and Country Club.

Neighbourhood   1972   SW   4:A2

Bulyea Road

East of Terwillegar Drive, north of Rabbit Hill Road

See Bulyea Heights.

Road   1986   SW   4:A2

Lieutenant-Governor G.H.V. Bulyea, seated in carriage on left, with Prime Minister Sir Wilfrid Laurier on the occasion of Laurier's visit to Edmonton, 1910. (CEA EA-10-2051)

Burgess Close

North of Rabbit Hill Road, east of Terwillegar Drive

Cecil Scott Burgess (1870–1971) was born in Bombay and emigrated to Canada in 1903. In 1913 he joined the University of Alberta as professor of architecture, retiring in 1940. As resident architectural consultant to the university from 1913 to 1940, Burgess supervised the construction of the university's Arts and Medical Sciences buildings and designed and supervised the construction of Pembina Hall. He also opened an office for private practice and embarked upon a career as an architect and town planner. From 1929 to 1949, Burgess was a member of the Edmonton Town Planning Commission. The University of Alberta granted him the degree of Doctor of Laws Honoris Causa in 1958.

Road 1988 SW 4:A2 *

Burley Close

North of Rabbit Hill Road, east of Terwillegar Drive

Edward Windham Burley, born in Canada West in 1856, was the first provincial auditor of Alberta. When the provinces of Alberta and Saskatchewan were formed in 1905, he was appointed provincial auditor of Alberta with headquarters at Edmonton.

Road 1986 SW 4:A2 *

Burley Drive

North of Rabbit Hill Road, east of Terwillegar Drive

See Burley Close.

Road 1986 SW 4:A2 *

Burnewood

*Mill Creek Ravine north to Whitemud Drive,
34 Street to 50 Street*

Burnewood originally extended south to 34 Avenue. In 1978 the subdivision was amended to make Mill Creek the southern boundary. The name is descriptive, as Mill Creek traverses the subdivision. "Burne" is a Scots and Old English word for stream or river. Burnewood is compatible with the naming theme for the Mill Woods area, where all subdivisions use "mill" or "wood" in their name.

Subdivision   1975   SE   5:A2 *

Burns Close

*North of Rabbit Hill Road, east of
Terwillegar Drive*

Welsh-born Dr. Patricia Burns (b. 1920) was a recognized expert in the treatment of breast cancer. She received her education and began practising medicine in Scotland before emigrating to Canada. In 1970 she joined the Cross Cancer Institute in Edmonton as a radiotherapist. Dr. Burns retired in 1985 and received an honorary degree from the University of Alberta in 1986.

Road   1992   SW   4:A2 *

Burrows Crescent

*North of Burton Road and west of
Butterworth Way*

Anne Burrows (b. 1922) is an award-winning musician and teacher. She was born in Alberta and studied in Canada before graduating from the Royal College of Music in London, England. Burrows also earned a Master of Music degree in Indiana. She has worked as a music critic, broadcaster, teacher and author. Burrows, who is blind, has been recognized for her excellence in music by the province of Alberta, the YWCA, and the University of Alberta, from which she received an honorary degree. In 1979 she began a foundation to help music students continue their education. She was awarded the Order of Canada in 1992.

Road   1992   SW   4:A2

Burton Close

*North of Rabbit Hill Road, east of
Terwillegar Drive*

Frank Victor Burton (1908–1972) was one of Edmonton's early pilots. Born and raised in Edmonton, Burton joined the Edmonton and Northern Aero Club in 1927. He became a bush pilot, flying into the Yukon, northern Alberta and the Northwest Territories. He helped organize the Edmonton and Northern Alberta Aero Club into what is now known as the Edmonton Flying Club.

Road   1986   SW   4:A2 *

Burton Crescent

*North of Rabbit Hill Road, east of
Terwillegar Drive*

See Burton Close.

Road   1986   SW   4:A2

Burton Loop

*North of Rabbit Hill Road, east of
Terwillegar Drive*

See Burton Close.

Road   1986   SW   4:A2 *

Burton Road

*North of Rabbit Hill Road, east of
Terwillegar Drive*

See Burton Close.

Road   1986   SW   4:A2

Bush pilots at Blatchford Field (now Edmonton City Centre Airport), 1934. (CEA EA-10-2354)

Bush Pilot Road

South of Yellowhead Trail, between 113 Street and 122 Street

Of all cities in Canada, Edmonton was the birthplace of bush pilots. Bush Pilot Road honours the contributions of the many bush pilots who have flown out of the Edmonton City Centre Airport. From this downtown airfield, bush pilots flew on often dangerous missions of mercy, carrying medical supplies to remote communities and ferrying their ill to hospitals in Edmonton, and delivering mail, freight and passengers to far-flung mission outposts and mining camps.

Road   1979   NW   7:B1

Butchart Drive

North of Rabbit Hill Road, east of Terwillegar Drive

At the turn of the twentieth century, the Butchart family established The Great West Land Company. Peter E. Butchart was born in Cananda West in 1859. He later moved to Calgary, where he lived for

several years before relocating to Edmonton in 1902. A year later he helped found Alberta College and started The Great West Land Company, holding the post of secretary when the company was incorporated. He served as the city's finance commissioner from 1908 to 1911 and was a school board trustee from 1910 to 1911.

Road   1986   SW   4:A2

Butchart Wynd

South of Butchart Drive and west of Bulyea Road

See Butchart Drive.

Road   1986   SW   4:A2 *

Butler Memorial Park

15715 Stony Plain Road

Richard D. Butler (1914–1958) was a volunteer firefighter and Jasper Place town councillor. He was killed in a gun battle involving a Jasper Place resident and the town's police and fire departments. Butler was deputy fire chief at the time of his death.

He was first elected to town council in 1950, following the incorporation of Jasper Place. The Butler Memorial Park is located in the West Jasper Place neighbourhood and has an area of 0.40 ha.

Park 1963 NW 8:D2

Butterworth Drive

East of Burton Road, south of Butterworth Way

Mary Butterworth (d. 1973) was a campaigner who fought school district rulings that forced women teachers to stop work upon getting married. Butterworth was born in Scotland and came to Edmonton in 1926. She became an active member of the University Women's Club, serving as president from 1937 to 1939 as well as being a member of the executive of the Local Council of Women prior to WWII. In 1945 she was elected to the Edmonton Public School Board and served for 12 years. She represented Edmonton on the executive of the Provincial School Trustees Association from 1946 to 1957.

Road 1986 SW 4:A2

Butterworth Way

North of Rabbit Hill Road, east of Terwillegar Drive

See Butterworth Drive.

Road 1986 SW 4:A2

Butterworth Wynd

North of Rabbit Hill Road, east of Terwillegar Drive

See Butterworth Drive.

Road 1986 SW 4:A2 *

Byrne Court

South of Ellerslie Road, north of Byrne Crescent

L.D. (Denis) Byrne (d. 1982) came to Edmonton from Birmingham, England, in 1937, upon the request of Premier William Aberhart. Byrne served as minister of economic affairs under the Social Credit government from 1935 until his resignation in 1948. He later joined the British Trade Commission and was high commissioner to Edmonton until he retired in 1971.

Road 1999 SW 1:A2 *

Byrne Crescent

South of Ellerslie Road, east of Blackmud Creek Drive

See Byrne Court.

Road 1999 SW 1:A2

Byrne Place

West of Calgary Trail, south of Ellerslie Road

Byrne Place was originally named Burrows Court but was changed because the name Burrows Crescent already existed in another neighbourhood. *See* Byrne Court.

Road 1999 SW 1:A2 *

Caernarvon

145 Avenue to 153 Avenue, Castle Downs Road west to 124 Street

As with other neighbourhoods in Castle Downs, the name of Caernarvon, located in the Warwick subdivision, is taken from a famous castle. In order to strengthen English influence in Wales, Edward I began building this castle in 1283. Construction was done in two phases and took decades to complete. Architecturally, Caernarvon Castle is considered one of the most impressive of all castles in Wales. Caernarvon was the birthplace of the first English Prince of Wales, Prince Edward (later Edward II) in 1284. After centuries of neglect, repairs to the castle were carried out in the late 19th century.

Neighbourhood 1972 NW 10:B2

Caernarvon Park

14830–118 Street

This park is in the Caernarvon neighbourhood and has an area of 3.04 ha. *See* Caernarvon.

Park 1982 NW 10:B2

Caine Memorial Park

5420–106 Street

This 0.33-ha. park, located in the Pleasantview neighbourhood, was named in honour of the WWII flying ace John Todd Caine (1920–1995). The Edmonton-born Caine grew up working on his father's 6-ha. fox and mink ranch west of Mount Pleasant Cemetery, on the outskirts of the city. In 1929 this land became the site of the Harry L. Caine Market Garden. In 1939 John Caine attempted to enlist in the Royal Canadian Air Force (RCAF), but was rejected because of his lack of education. He then enrolled in Royal Canadian Legion correspondence courses and, in a little over a year, upgraded his education from grade eight to grade 11. He was then accepted into air crew training and became a Mosquito Bomber pilot.

Caine went on to be awarded the Distinguished Flying Cross medal with two bars, one of only six such honours to be bestowed. Following the war he became a partner in his father's fur farm and later opened his own farm. By 1966 the Caine mink ranch was one of the largest in Canada. He closed the business in 1973.

Park 1998 SW 4:B1 *

Cairns Bay

North of 155 Avenue, west of 133 Street

James Mitchell Cairns emigrated from Scotland with his family in 1910 and settled on a farm in Nelson, British Columbia. Since there was no law school in British Columbia at the time, Cairns enrolled at the University of Alberta. After graduation he moved to Calgary where he worked at a law firm headed by the father of future Alberta premier Peter Lougheed. In 1952, Cairns was appointed a justice of the Alberta Supreme Court, and in 1965 became a judge of the Appellate Division of the Supreme Court.

Road 1999 NW 10:B2 *

Cairns Place

South of 155 Avenue, west of 133 Street

See Cairns Bay.

Road 1999 NW 10:B2

Calder

127 Avenue to 132 Avenue, 113A Street to 127 Street

See feature story, page 45.

Neighbourhood 1910 NW 10:B2

Calder Community Park

12721–120 Street

This Calder neighbourhood park has an area of 1.73 ha. *See* Calder *feature story, page 45.*

Park 1978 NW 10:B2

Calder

THE EARLY DEVELOPMENT of Calder is linked to the construction of the Grand Trunk Pacific Railway (GT&P), which arrived in Edmonton in 1909. After connecting the railway to Edmonton, the GT&P located its roundhouse and railway yards in the area.

In July 1910, the village of West Edmonton was established. Many GT&P employees settled there and the village became known as a railway colony. In 1913 the City of Edmonton annexed the land surrounding the village of West Edmonton and a few years later, in 1917, annexed West Edmonton itself.

The Calder Land Company, a real-estate firm owned by Hugh Alfred Calder and J. R. McIntosh, began to subdivide the area around 1910. The land was originally settled by the McRoberts family. Hugh Alfred Calder (1872–1964) arrived in Strathcona in 1902 and became a partner in the Calder Land Company in 1907. He went on to serve as a city alderman, first for Strathcona and then Edmonton after amalgamation, from 1908 to 1916. After serving in WWI, Major Calder returned to the Edmonton area and took up farming.

Although some of Calder's houses were pre-1910, most were built after WWII. Generally, newer structures are located in the northern portion of the neighbourhood while older structures are located in the vicinity of the Calder Railway Yards. The present-day Calder neighbourhood includes the former village of West Edmonton (west of 120 Street) and Elm Park (east of 120 Street). The Elm Park subdivision was established around 1907 and became part of the city of Edmonton in 1913.

Calder Yards, circa 1935. (CEA EA-495-131)

Calgary Trail

South from Saskatchewan Drive to city limits, west of Gateway Boulevard

The road has a rich and storied history beginning in 1873. That was the year that the Rev. John McDougall and his brother, David, cleared a trail from Fort Edmonton to the mission at Morley, about 80 kilometres west of Calgary. The trail followed, in part, older trails blazed by Aboriginal people and early traders of European descent. When Fort Calgary was established in 1875, the NWMP completed the southern leg of this trail from the Lone Pine Stopping House, near Bowden, to Calgary. After the 1883 arrival of the Canadian Pacific Railway in Calgary, the Calgary-Edmonton Trail became a busy supply route with regular mail and stagecoach services.

   The use of the Trail declined after the completion of the Calgary and Edmonton Railway in 1891. Since the advent of the automobile, however, the "Trail" has become the most heavily travelled highway in Alberta. Calgary Trail Southbound, connecting Edmonton to Calgary via Highway 2, was renamed Calgary Trail in 2000 because a southbound identifier was considered no longer necessary after Calgary Trail Northbound was renamed, also in 2000, Gateway Boulevard.

Road 2000 SW 1:A2

Calgary Trail North

Whitemud Drive north to 63 Avenue, CP railway tracks west to Calgary Trail

This neighbourhood has no residential development and is used for industrial and commercial purposes. *See* Calgary Trail.

Neighbourhood 1984 SW 4:C1

Calgary Trail South

23 Avenue north to Whitemud Drive, CP railway tracks west to Calgary Trail

This neighbourhood has no residential development and is used for industrial and commercial purposes. *See* Calgary Trail.

Neighbourhood 1984 SW 4:C2

Callingwood North

69 Avenue north to Whitemud Drive, 170 Street to 178 Street

Annexed to Edmonton in 1969, the Names Advisory Committee named the neighbourhood Callingwood. In 1979 the neighbourhood of Callingwood was divided into two sections and renamed Callingwood North and Callingwood South. The origin of the Callingwood name is not recorded.

Neighbourhood 1979 SW 3:C1

Callingwood Park

17740–69 Avenue

This 6.4-ha. park, in the Callingwood North neighbourhood, was originally named West Jasper Place Park. *See* Callingwood North.

Park 1989 SW 3:C1

Callingwood Road

North of 61 Avenue, 170 Street to 199 Street

This curvilinear avenue forms the southern boundary of Callingwood South at approximately 62 Avenue, west of 170 Street. *See* Callingwood North.

Road 1971 SW 3:C1

Callingwood South

Callingwood Road north to 69 Avenue, 170 Street to 178 Street

See Callingwood North.

Neighbourhood 1979 SW 3:C1

Riverdale, near Cameron Avenue, October 1977. (CEA EA-263-91)

Cameron Avenue

East of 95 Street, south of 100A Avenue

John Cameron was a pioneer citizen and businessman who lived at the north end of the road that now bears his name. He arrived in Edmonton from Winnipeg in 1881, bringing with him merchandise to start a business. Cameron was president of the city's first Board of Trade, a member of the first town council in 1892 and 1895, and served as chairman of the Edmonton School Board. Cameron died in 1919 at the age of 74. Originally named Cameron Street, it was renamed Cameron Avenue around 1953.

Road   CU   SE   7:C2

Cameron Heights

South of 45 Avenue, west of 184 Street

The Cameron Heights neighbourhood was rezoned for residential use in 2001. It is under development. *See* Cameron Avenue.

Neighbourhood   2001   SW   3:B1 *

Campbell Bridge

Spanning the Whitemud Creek at Fox Drive

The current Campbell Bridge, which opened in 1969, takes its name from a bridge built by Duncan L. Campbell across Whitemud Creek in 1904. Campbell was born in Canada West in 1847, and brought his family to Strathcona in 1898. In 1902 he bought a farm and later built the bridge on his own land. He sold the farm in 1912, but the bridge was still standing in 1920. He was a member of the Old Timers' Association and helped found the Knox Presbyterian Church (now known as Knox-Metropolitan United Church) in 1907.

Bridge   1969   SW   4:A1

Campbell Road

North of St. Albert Trail and 156 Street

After the turn of the 20th century, a station siding along the Edmonton, Dunvegan and British Columbia Railway line (ED & BC, now Canadian National Railway) between Edmonton and

St. Albert was named after Alex Campbell. At the time, he was a traffic manager for the ED & BC. His name has been perpetuated in the City of St. Albert, and within Edmonton by this road.

Road 1988 NW 9:D1

Canon Ridge

Hyndman Road north to Kennedale Ravine, Hermitage Park west to Victoria Trail

See Newton.

Neighbourhood 1972 NE 6:B1

Canora

Stony Plain Road north to 107 Avenue, 149 Street to 156 Street

In 1948 the West Jasper Place School District held a contest to name a new elementary school built at 154 Street and 105 Avenue. The winner of the contest was a grade-eight student who noted that the site of the school was near the old Canadian Northern Railway line. By combining the first two letters of each word—Ca-no-ra—the new name was created. The Canora School was officially opened February 4, 1949. The neighbourhood became known by its school's name.

Neighbourhood CU NW 8:D2

Canora Park

10425–152 Street

This Canora neighbourhood park has an area of 2.48 ha. *See* Canora.

Park 1968 NW 8:D2

Canossa

167 Avenue north to the proposed outer ring road, 112 Street west to Rapperswil

The name is consistent with the famous castles theme of the Castle Downs area. The Canossa castle

was built around 940 AD near Bologna in northern Italy. Over the next three centuries, Canossa sheltered many notable guests, including Pope Gregory VII. The castle later fell into the hands of imperial troops and was destroyed in 1255. Though it was restored numerous times over the centuries, Canossa today lies in ruins.

Neighbourhood 1982 NW 10:B1

Capilano

106 Avenue north to Capilano Park, 43 Street west to Hardisty Drive

The Capilano neighbourhood in the Hardisty subdivision was likely named after the Capilano River, Capilano River Canyon and the Capilano Suspension Bridge in North Vancouver, BC. *Capilano* is an adaptation of a Salish word that means "the people of Kiap." It was also the hereditary name of the Chief of the Squamish, Central Coast Salish who traditionally lived in what is today North Vancouver. Edmonton's Capilano was an existing subdivision name dating back to the early part of the twentieth century. It was subdivided in 1910, but remained mostly farmland until the 1950s. Capilano was annexed to Edmonton in 1954.

Neighbourhood 1956 NE 6:A1

Capilano Bridge

Spanning the North Saskatchewan River at Wayne Gretzky Drive

This bridge was built in 1969. *See* Capilano.

Bridge 1967 NE 6:A1

Capilano Community Park

10810–54 Street

This park in the Capilano neighbourhood has an area of 3.18 ha. *See* Capilano.

Park 1987 NE 7:D1

Capilano Bridge under construction, 1969. (CEA ET–2–12)

Capilano Crescent

Connects with 109 Avenue; northwest of 56 Street

See Capilano.

Road   1956   NE   7:D2

Capilano Park

10988–50 Street

This park in the Capilano neighbourhood has an area of 13.76 ha. *See* Capilano.

Park   1964   NE   7:D1

Capilano Ravine

Separating the Capilano and Forest Heights neighbourhoods; 106 Avenue at 74 Street

See Capilano.

Ravine   CU   NE   7:D2

Capilano Street

106 Avenue northwest to 65 Street

See Capilano.

Road   1956   NE   7:D2

Capital City Recreation Park

River Valley, east from the Provincial Legislature

This park in the river valley is actually a 16-kilometre network, officially opened on July 9, 1978, which stretches from below the Provincial Legislature to Hermitage Park. Capital City Recreation Park has 55 kilometres of hiking and biking trails and includes four wooden bridges and a number of steel bridges and overpasses. The total area of the park, including both land and water, is approximately 1,215 hectares.

Park   1974   C   7:B2 *

Carleton Square Industrial

118 Avenue north to CN railway tracks, 163 Street to 170 Street

Carleton Square Industrial was annexed to the City of Edmonton in 1962. The name Carleton (sometimes Carlton) Square has been in use since 1912. According to a 1911 township map, James Tough owned what is now Carleton Square Industrial. By 1920 the property belonged to K.A. McLeod, a pioneer and businessman. Maps produced in the 1950s refer to it as Carleton Estate.

The name may honour a local individual named Carleton. Another theory is that the neighbourhood was named for Guy Carleton, 1st Baron Dorchester (1724–1808), governor of Québec in the late 1700s, or for Thomas Carleton, a brother of Guy Carleton and the first lieutenant-governor of New Brunswick, from 1784 to 1817. However, the name may also be a variation of Carlton. A nearby street, now 142 Street, for example, was once called Carlton. In this case, the name may refer to Fort Carlton. *See* Carlton *neighbourhood.*

Neighbourhood   CU   NW   8:C1

Carlisle

137 Avenue to 145 Avenue, Castle Downs Road west to 123 Street

The Carlisle neighbourhood in the Warwick subdivision is named after a famous castle in England, in accordance with the naming theme of the Castle Downs area in which it is located. In the early 1900s, a portion of the Carlisle neighbourhood was named GTP Addition. The original Carlisle Castle is located south of England's border with Scotland; construction of the castle was begun in 1093 by King William II. Carlisle was the backdrop for several historical events. In the 1800s Carlisle Castle went through extensive renovations and is today one of the best preserved castles in England.

Neighbourhood   1972   NW   10:B2

Carlisle Park

14240–117 Street

This park is located in the Carlisle neighbourhood and has an area of 3.13 ha. *See* Carlisle.

Park   1981   NW   10:B2

Carlson Close

South of Rabbit Hill Road, west of Carter Crest Road

Nellie Mildred Carlson (b. 1927) was the first president of the Alberta group Indian Rights for Indian Women. She was born on the Saddle Lake Indian Reserve. After moving to Edmonton, Carlson lobbied the federal government to revise the Indian Act so that Aboriginal women who married non-Aboriginal or Métis men could retain their First Nation status. With the successful passage of Bill C-31, enacted in 1985, Aboriginal women regained band membership. Carlson was the recipient of the 1988 Persons Award.

Road   1990   SW   4:A2 *

Carlton

153 Avenue to 167 Avenue, 133 Street to 142 Street

This neighbourhood is named after Fort Carlton. Throughout The Palisades area, neighbourhoods are named after fur trade forts, posts or houses. Fort Carlton, located near the junction of the North and South Saskatchewan Rivers, was established as a Hudson Bay Company fur trade and provision post in 1798. Its strategic location made it a focal point for western trade and commerce. In the 1870s, the Métis, displaced from their lands around Winnipeg and Red River, Manitoba, followed the buffalo west and settled near the fort. A North West Mounted Police detachment was later dispatched to the fort to keep it secure. In 1885 the detachment was ordered to leave Fort Carlton and help quell the North-West Rebellion (the Métis and Aboriginal uprising). The fort was later destroyed in a series of fires: the first fire was started by accident; two others were set by the rebels.

Neighbourhood   1998   NW   10:A1

Carmichael Close

South of Rabbit Hill Road, east of Terwillegar Drive

Scottish-born Anne Carmichael (1904–1999) was a pioneer Edmonton teacher who taught for more than four decades and supported programs to improve the education system. She emigrated from Scotland to Edmonton in 1911 and began teaching in 1928. Carmichael served as assistant to the director of elementary education in 1953 and earned a Master of Education degree from the University of Alberta in 1954. She was appointed to the senate of the University of Alberta Teachers' Association; served twice as president of the Edmonton Education Local; was president of the Edmonton Education Society and a school board director until her retirement in 1969.

Road   1993   SW   4:A2 *

Carmichael Wynd

South of Rabbit Hill Road, east of Terwillegar Drive

See Carmichael Close.

Road 1993 SW 4:A2 *

Carse Lane

South of Rabbit Hill Road, east of Terwillegar Drive

Ruth Carse (1916–1999) was the founder and artistic director of the Alberta Ballet Company. The Edmonton-born dancer performed in Canada and abroad and began teaching dance in 1954. She formed Dance Interlude, a small amateur troupe that performed throughout Alberta, which later became the Alberta Ballet Company. Carse was the company's artistic director until her retirement in 1975. She also founded the Alberta Ballet School in 1971 and was principal of the school until 1983. Carse received the Queen's Silver Jubilee Medal (1977), the Canada Dance Award (1990), an honorary degree from the University of Alberta (1991) and was appointed a member of the Order of Canada (1992).

Road 1993 SW 4:A2 *

Carter Crest

Approximately 29 Avenue north to Rabbit Hill Road, east of Terwillegar Drive

Robert I. Carter (1858–1931) was an agent for the Canadian government who advised Americans on their prospects as immigrants in Canada. In 1906, after numerous visits to Edmonton from his home in Ohio, he purchased a farm in what is now Terwillegar Park, naming it Riverside Farm. While Carter moved to Strathcona in 1910, his sons continued to work on the farm until 1946. Carter was active in the affairs of Strathcona, serving on the council for rural districts, as president of the

Conservative Association of Strathcona and as a member of the Masonic Order. In 1923 Carter and his wife returned to the United States and lived in Long Beach, California, for the rest of their lives.

Neighbourhood 1981 SW 4:A2

Carter Crest Road

South of Rabbit Hill Road, east of Terwillegar Drive

See Carter Crest.

Road 1990 SW 4:A2

Carter Crest Way

South of Rabbit Hill Road, east of Terwillegar Drive

See Carter Crest.

Road 1990 SW 4:A2 *

Casselman

144 Avenue to 153 Avenue, 50 Street to 58 Street

Politician and veteran Frederick C. Casselman (1885–1941) served two terms on city council, in 1937 and 1939, and was elected as a member of parliament in 1940. He was awarded the Military Cross for his service during WWI. Prior to entering civil and federal politics, Casselman served for many years, beginning in 1928, on the public school board. Casselman was born in Montana and moved with his family to Ontario when still a child. In 1913, after completing an arts degree at Queen's University and an education degree at the University of Toronto, he came to Edmonton. He later graduated from the University of Alberta with a law degree.

Neighbourhood 1969 NE 10:D2

Lake Beaumaris in Castle Downs, 1983. (CEA A90–90, File 40)

Castle Downs

137 Avenue north to the proposed outer ring road, 97 Street to 127 Street (excluding 137 Avenue to 153 Avenue, 97 Street west to Castle Downs Road)

Castle Downs was the developer's second choice of name for this area. The original choice, Athabasca Downs, was rejected by the City. Subdivisions and neighbourhoods, as well as many parks and roads in the Castle Downs area are named for famous castles. The original northern limit of Castle Downs was 174 Avenue. In 1977 the Castle Downs Extension area was created, extending the northern boundary to the proposed outer ring road. In 1982, the Extension area became part of Castle Downs.

Area   1971   NW   10:B1 *

Castle Downs Road

113A Street at 153 Avenue, northeast to 97 Street and 167 Avenue

See Castle Downs.

Road   1973   NW   10:C1

Castle Keep

158 Avenue and 109 Street

See Castle Downs.

Road   1977   NW   10:B2

Centennial Plaza

101A Avenue to the Stanley A. Milner Library, 99 Street to 100 Street

This 0.36-ha. plaza is located in the Downtown neighbourhood. It was named after the adjacent library, known as the Centennial Public Library from its construction in 1967 until 1996, when it was renamed the Stanley A. Milner Library. Funds towards the cost of this project were donated by Molson Breweries, which marked its 200th anniversary in 1986.

Park   1986   C   7:C2

Central McDougall

105 Avenue to 111 Avenue, 101 Street to 109 Street

John Alexander McDougall (1879–1928) was an early Edmonton businessman who was twice elected mayor (town mayor in 1897; city mayor in 1908). He also served as an MLA, on the senate of the University of Alberta, the school board and city council. McDougall was born in Ontario and came to Edmonton in 1879, opening the first general store on Jasper Avenue. In 1897 McDougall went into partnership with Richard Secord (1860–1935). Together, they ran a fur trading business and, later, a finance company. During the real estate boom of 1912, the Hudson's Bay Company (then the owner of this neighbourhood) paved 3.2 km of Portage Avenue (present-day Kingsway) and offered lots for sale. In 1913 McDougall School was built at 10930–107 Street.

Neighbourhood CU C 7:C2

Chalmers Park

12310–131 Avenue

This park is named after Chalmers Church, the well-known Calder community landmark. The name was chosen through a public contest organized by the Calder Action Committee. This church was named in honour of Thomas Chalmers (1780–1847), a leading Scottish theologian, philosopher, mathematician and moderator of the Free Church of Scotland. Many churches around the world bear his name. Chalmers Church in Edmonton dates back to 1911, when the first service was held in an Oddfellows Hall. Chalmers Park is in the Calder neighbourhood and has an area of 0.45 ha.

Park 1978 NW 10:B2

Chambery

174 Avenue north to the proposed outer ring road, 105 Street to 112 Street

As with other neighbourhoods in the Castle Downs area, the name Chambery is taken from a famous castle. The original Chambery castle was founded in 1232 and served as the capital of the mountain

Charles Anderson. (CEA EA-600-3908)

Duchy of Savoy until the sixteenth century. In 1860 Savoy became part of France. The ancient ducal castle, restored many times, still stands today.

Neighbourhood 1983 NW 10:B1

Charles Anderson Park

3803–105 Street

Scottish-born Charles Anderson (b. 1901) was a pioneer railroad man who came to Edmonton in 1911. He delivered newspapers for the *Edmonton Journal* before being hired as a chainman for the Grand Trunk Pacific Railway Company (GTP) in 1918. In 1923 the GTP was amalgamated with the Canadian National Railways and Anderson went to work in the accounting department of the Alberta and Great Waterways Railway (A & GW). He later became chief clerk with the Alberta government-owned Edmonton, Dunvegan and British Columbia

(ED & BC) Railway. In 1928 this railway merged with the A & GW, the Canada Central Railway and the Pembina Valley Railway to form the Northern Alberta Railways (NAR). By 1950 Anderson was the NAR's chief accounting and finance officer. He retired in 1967 but returned to work four years later as director and then managing director of the Alberta Resources Railway. He continued working until 1995 when, at the age of 94, he retired for the second and last time. In 1996 he was appointed a member of the Order of Canada for his contributions to industry, commerce and business. Anderson celebrated his 100th birthday in 2001. The Charles Anderson Park is in the Duggan neighbourhood and has an area of 2.05 ha.

Park 1984 SW 4:C2

Charles B. Hill Park

3450 Hillview Crescent

Charles B. Hill (1891–1972) was a child welfare worker for more than 40 years. Over this period, "Uncle Charlie" supervised the adoption of more than 20,000 babies. Hill was born in England and began his career in the English Poor Law service. He came to Canada in 1910 and began working for the provincial government in 1915, first as a welfare inspector, then as chief clerk for the department. He was named child placement officer in 1923, deputy of child welfare in 1940, and became superintendent in 1944, retiring from this post in 1956. The Charles B. Hill Park is in the Hillview neighbourhood and has an area of 0.41 ha.

Park 1983 SE 5:A2

Charles Simmonds Park

7830–115 Street

English-born Charles Simmonds (1893–1962) was an alderman and long-serving president of the Edmonton Federation of Community Leagues. Before emigrating to Canada in 1921, Simmonds served as a major in the British Army during WWI

and was awarded the Military Cross. After moving to Edmonton in 1934, he became an active member of the community, serving on city council as an alderman from 1954 to 1955 and filling the post of president of the Edmonton Federation of Community Leagues 13 times. The Charles Simmonds Park is in the Belgravia neighbourhood and has an area of 1.53 ha.

Park 1965 SW 4:B1

Cheriton Crescent

South of Rabbit Hill Road, east of Terwillegar Drive

Edith Muriel Cheriton was one of the first women to graduate from the University of Alberta Faculty of Engineering. Cheriton, born and raised in Edmonton, graduated with a Bachelor of Science degree in Electrical Engineering in 1946. She went on to work for Calgary Power and later accepted a post with Canadian General Electric in Toronto. In 1963, Cheriton and her husband established an engineering consulting firm in Edmonton.

Road 1990 SW 4:A2 *

Cherry Grove Place

North side of 160 Avenue, east of 82 Street

This crescent, located in the Mayliewan neighbourhood, takes its name from the Cherry Grove subdivision, which existed here in the early 1900s. The original owners of the land were George and Elizabeth Cresswell, who settled it in 1905. They originally planned to subdivide their property. The crash of Edmonton's real estate market in 1913, however, bankrupted many land speculators and brought the city's remarkable pre-WWI growth to a halt. The city would not see a boom in the land market again until after WWII. Because of this, many of the neighbourhoods that had been subdivided and named in the first decade of the twentieth century remained farmland and were not developed until well after the 1950s. The Cresswell family continued to farm here until the 1970s, when the land was finally developed for residential use. It is possible that chokecherries, which are native to this region, are the source of this name.

Road   1993   NE   10:C1 *

Cherrydale Park

13824–74 Street

At the turn of the 20th century, the district where this park is located was known as Cherrydale. The name Cherrydale Park was chosen for this 2.81-ha. park, in the Kildare neighbourhood, through a naming contest sponsored by the *Londonderry Colloquium*, a northeast Edmonton community newspaper. Mary Ostapiw won a $25 prize for her winning entry.

Park   1976   NE   10:C2

Churchill Crescent

North of 102 Avenue, east of 132 Street

Sir Winston Churchill (1874–1965) was one of the most important figures of the 20th century. As prime minister of Great Britain during WWII, he led the allied campaign against Nazi Germany and the Axis powers. Churchill Crescent, in the Glenora neighbourhood, was originally two numbered streets. It was in 1941, during WWII, that residents petitioned the City to join the two streets and name the new street after the British prime minister.

Road   1941   NW   7:B2 *

Clareview

Kennedale Ravine north to 153 Avenue, North Saskatchewan River west to Manning Drive

Francis C. Clare (d. 1941), an important spokesperson for agriculture, farmed in this vicinity from 1906 to 1959. In 1914 he sued the City and obtained a court judgement restraining the City of Edmonton from increasing its deposits of sewage in the North Saskatchewan River. The City was at that time dumping unfiltered waste water into the river, making it impossible for Clare to water his dairy cows. The judgement also ordered the City to construct a sewage treatment plant. Clare was a member of the United Grain Growers Board, Edmonton Exhibition Board, United Farmers of Alberta and the local school board. Many of the neighbourhoods in this subdivision are named after Edmonton pioneers, including Bannerman, Fraser, Kernohan and Kirkness.

Subdivision   1969   NE   11:B2 *

Clareview Business Park

137 Avenue to 144 Avenue, CN railway tracks west to Manning Drive

This neighbourhood is a component of a development plan formulated in 1979, but never implemented. Known as Clareview Town Centre, it had two parts. This portion would provide space for business ventures, while the adjacent Clareview Campus neighbourhood would be devoted to school and recreational facilities. The Clareview Town Centre name has largely been replaced in popular usage by Clareview Business Park and Clareview Campus, despite the lack of development.

Neighbourhood   CU   NE   11:A2

Clareview Campus

137 Avenue to 144 Avenue, 36 Street west to CN railway tracks

See Clareview Business Park.

Neighbourhood   CU   NE   11:B2

Clareview Road

East of Victoria Trail, south of 135 Avenue

This winding road was named for the Clareview subdivision in which it is located. *See* Clareview.

Road   1976   NE   11:B2

Clover Bar, circa 1904. (CEA EA–264–112)

Clifton Place

South of 102 Avenue at 126 Street

This road, overlooking the Groat Ravine, has been in existence since around 1935. The name may refer to the road's cliff-top location.

Road   CU   SW   7:B2 *

Clover Bar

Yellowhead Trail north, and 33 Street NE west to the North Saskatchewan River

Thomas H. Clover (b. 1829) was a California "forty-niner," a veteran of the California gold rush of 1849, who mined gold from sandbars along the North Saskatchewan River. He was born in Missouri and is believed to have arrived in the area around 1859. It would be many years, however, before Clover Bar was settled by European home-steaders. Beginning in 1881, the rich farming land and the discovery of coal drew settlers to the area.

The Clover Bar name was in use before 1900, evidenced by the establishment of the Clover Bar Post Office in 1884 and the Clover Bar School District in 1891.

Area   CU   NE   11:C2

Clover Bar Bridge

Spanning the North Saskatchewan River at the Yellowhead Trail

Work on the Clover Bar Bridge started in 1951 but was halted a year later because of a shortage of steel. Construction resumed months later and the superstructure was completed in March 1953. This bridge was informally known as the Beverly Bridge, a name later officially given to its twin. The Clover Bar Bridge carries westbound traffic on the Yellowhead Trail. *See* Clover Bar *area.*

Bridge   1966   NE   6:B1

Clover Bar Cemetery

2025 Yellowhead Trail NE

Clover Bar Cemetery was established in 1901 behind the Clover Bar Church, which had been built in 1899. Homesteader W. F. Wilkinson donated his land for the cemetery, and he and nine other local residents formed a cemetery company. Originally surrounded by countryside, the cemetery has an area of 1.21 ha. The City took over management of the facility in 1995. *See* Clover Bar *area.*

Cemetery 1995 NE 6:C1 *

Clover Bar Industrial

118 Avenue to 130 Avenue, 17 Street NE west to Meridian Street

Prior to annexation, this name was established through common usage. *See* Clover Bar *area.*

Neighbourhood 1982 NE 6:C1 *

Cloverdale

Connors Road and Strathearn Drive north to the North Saskatchewan River

Cloverdale was named for the Clover Bar Road, which ran from this neighbourhood to Clover Bar. Clover Bar and Cloverdale are named after Thomas H. Clover, a pioneer who mined the North Saskatchewan for gold. The neighbourhood was originally called Gallagher Flats, after the landowner Cornelius Gallagher, who owned a meat store and was later a mayor of Edmonton. The name Cloverdale seems to have emerged in the 1930s. For instance, the local Bennett School Community League was renamed the Cloverdale Community League in 1934. Both Cloverdale and Gallagher Flats were used to refer to the district until the 1950s, when the name Cloverdale was used on maps and in the *Henderson's Greater Edmonton Directory. See* Clover Bar *area.*

Neighbourhood CU SE 7:C2

Cloverdale and the Low Level Bridge, 1914.
(CEA EA-184-24)

Cloverdale Hill

92 Street and 97 Avenue

This road was commonly referred to by several names, including Cloverdale Road, Cloverdale Hill Road and Cloverdale Hill. In 1973 Cloverdale Hill was recognized as the official name. *See* Cloverdale.

Road 1973 SE 7:C2

Colonel F.C. Jamieson Park

5403–190 Street

The Colonel F.C. Jamieson Park is in the Jamieson Place neighbourhood and has an area of 3.08 ha. *See* Jamieson Place.

Park 1992 SW 3:C1

Confederation Park

11204–43 Avenue

This 10.72-ha. park, in the Royal Gardens neighbourhood, commemorates the 1967 centenary of Canada's confederation. It was established with the cooperation of the Public School Board, the Separate School Board and the City of Edmonton Parks and Recreation Department.

Park 1965 SW 4:B2

Coal Fields

AS EARLY AS THE 1840s, the Hudson's Bay Company was mining coal from the banks of the North Saskatchewan River. By the late 1800s, the area was becoming known for its abundance of hard coal and prospectors staked their claims along the riverbank.

One of the first mines, located just below the present-day MacDonald Hotel, was worked from 1881 by Donald Ross and George Moore. The largest mine was the Clover Bar, which produced most of the 13 million tonnes of coal mined in Edmonton up to 1970. The first customers used the coal to heat their homes. Later, after the arrival of the railways, Edmonton coal was shipped to British Columbia and Manitoba.

Among the 100 mines worked in the city and river valley, most were seasonal, small-scale operations. Some of the more important early mines included the Humberstone and Bush coal mines in Beverly, now part of northeast Edmonton; the Dawson coal mine, southeast of the present-day Dawson Bridge; the Strathcona coal mine, on the south bank of the North Saskatchewan River just east of the High Level Bridge; the Twin City mine, in Mill Creek Ravine; and the Chinook coal mine, in Riverdale. The Coal Fields subdivision, now part of the Beverly Heights neighbourhood, was located in north-east Edmonton, near the coalfields of the Beverly area.

Seventeen of the biggest mines continued operation into the twentieth century and, for a time, provided employment for a large number of Edmontonians. By the 1950s, however, Edmonton's coal mines were pretty much history. This was the direct result of the "dieselization" of locomotive engines, as well as an increasing dependence on oil for home heating. Over the years, subsidence of coal tunnels has caused problems for homeowners located above abandoned workings.

Coal industry, Samis Collieries, domestic coal mine, 1947.
(CEA EA–600–600E)

Connaught Drive

West of Groat Road, south of Stony Plain Road to 102 Avenue

This road, which has existed since around 1912, was probably named after His Royal Highness Arthur William Patrick Albert, 1st Duke of Connaught and Strathcarn (1850–1942). The third son of Queen Victoria and Prince Albert, he was governor general of Canada from 1911 to 1916 and was the first member of the royal family to be appointed to the position. He was considered to have taken the post seriously, sometimes disagreeing with the government and causing tension between himself and Minister of Militia Sam Hughes and Prime Minister Robert Borden. He visited Edmonton in 1912, when he officially opened the Legislature Building.

Road   CU   NW   7:B2

Connors Road

Off the Low Level Bridge southeast from 98 Avenue to the traffic circle at 86 Street and 90 Avenue

William H. Connors was a land investor and the proprietor and part owner of the Imperial Hotel at 99 Street and 101A Avenue. In the late 1800s and early 1900s, he owned River Lot 21, where Connors Road is located. He was also involved in the fur trade. Connors Road has been a feature in Edmonton since the early 1900s.

Road   1965   SE   7:C2

Constable Ezio Faraone Park

11004–97 Avenue

See feature story, page 61.

Park   1991   C   7:B2

Lieutenant-Governor G.H.V. Bulyea, centre, greeting Governor General, HRH the Duke of Connaught, left, 1911. (CEA EA-10-786)

Conway Farrell Park

11704–114 Avenue

Conway McAllister Grey Farrell (1898–1988) was an early bush pilot and a veteran who served with both the Royal Flying Corps and Royal Canadian Air Force (RCAF), receiving the Distinguished Flying Cross. After the WWI, "Con" Farrell attended the University of Manitoba. In 1928 Farrell joined Western Canada Airways and was in charge of instruction at Winnipeg. Between 1929 and 1931 he flew airmail out of Edmonton to Regina and Lethbridge. As a bush pilot, he was considered one of the "birdmen of the north."

In WWII, Farrell served as the first commanding officer of the Northwest Staging Route of the RCAF between Edmonton and Calgary. After the war he joined Canadian Pacific Airlines and worked at Dawson City, in Japan as superintendent of the Oriental service, and later as superintendent of the British Columbia district. The 0.30-ha. Conway Farrell Park is located within the Edmonton City Centre Airport, on the site where the RCAF's administration building was located during WWII.

Park   2000   NW   7:B1 *

W. Connors, 1904. (CEA EA-10-669.19)

Cormack Crescent

North of Leger Boulevard, west of Rabbit Hill Road

See feature story, page 62.

Road 1989 SW 4:A2

Coronation Park

11425–142 Street

The City bought this land in 1906, but it lay undeveloped for many years. Initially called Westmount Park, or West End City Park, the name was changed in 1953 to mark the coronation of Queen Elizabeth II. An elm tree was planted in the 35.41-ha. Woodcroft neighbourhood park to mark its official naming and dedication.

Park 1953 NW 7:A1

Coronet Addition Industrial

CN railway tracks north to Argyll Road, 75 Street to 91 Street

In 1957 the land adjoining the residential developments of Argyll, Avonmore and Hazeldean, south from Argyll Road and 63 Avenue to the then city limits, and from present-day Gateway Boulevard to 75 Street, was renamed Coronet. This included Coronet Addition Industrial and Coronet Industrial. The origin of the name Coronet is not recorded.

Neighbourhood 1957 SE 4:C1

Coronet Industrial

51 Avenue north to CN railway tracks, 91 Street west to CP railway tracks

Before this neighbourhood was named Coronet, part of it was called Speedway. In 1956 city council approved the replotting of Avonmore Addition, Belleville Gardens and Broadview for industrial land use, and named it Coronet Industrial. A decade later, the boundaries were extended south of the Canadian National Railway tracks to the neighbourhood's present limits. The origin of the name Coronet is not recorded.

Neighbourhood 1957 SE 4:C1

Coronet Road

77 Street to 88 Street, south of Argyll Road

See Coronet Addition Industrial.

Road 1957 SE 4:D1

Cote Crescent

North of Cumberland Road, south of 149 Avenue, west of 131 Street

Jean Léon Côté (1867–1924) was a pioneer land surveyor and politician. Born and educated in Québec, Côté passed the Dominion Land Surveyor's examination in 1890. He worked for the Department of Interior for about five years before forming a partnership with the Cautley brothers of

Constable Ezio Faraone Park

Const. Ezio Joseph Faraone (1957–1990) was a dedicated city police officer who was killed in the line of duty. A ten-year veteran of the force, Faraone was the third Edmonton police officer since 1918 to be killed while on duty.

The 33-year-old officer, a member of the elite task force unit, was gunned down on June 25, 1990, as he approached a car believed to have been used in a bank robbery. Two men were later convicted of his murder. In the wake of Faraone's killing, new police policy was adopted requiring all task force members to wear bullet-proof vests.

The Ezio Faraone Park includes a larger-than-life bronze sculpture of the late police officer by Edmonton artist Danek Mozdzenski. The sculpture depicts a uniformed Faraone kneeling beside a young boy. The park commemorates not only Faraone but also Edmonton's two other slain officers, Const. Frank Beevers (d. 1918) and Const. William Leslie Nixon (d. 1919); both men were shot by assailants. The 4.25-ha. park, at the north end of the High Level Bridge, was officially opened on 21 June 1992. Edmonton also has a park dedicated to the memory of firefighters who gave their lives in the line of duty. Fire-Fighters' Memorial Plaza is located in Strathcona.

Memorial sculpture, Constable Ezio Faraone Park, circa 1990s. (CEA.2000/169)

61

Cormack Crescent

BARBARA VILLY CORMACK (1903–1991) and her husband, Col. Eric Wyld Cormack (1899–1987), helped establish the Edmonton, Strathcona County, Alberta and Canadian Associations for the Mentally Retarded, now known as the Alberta and Canadian Associations for Community Living, as well as the Winnifred Stewart and Robin Hood Schools for the Mentally Retarded. The couple began their lengthy involvement with mentally handicapped children after their youngest son was born with Down's syndrome. Barbara Cormack was born in England and came to Canada in 1914. She authored several books, including *Seed Time and Harvest,* and *Beyond the Classroom: The first 60 years of the University of Alberta's Department of Extension.* She was also involved with the Girl Guides in Alberta, and received an Alberta Achievement Award, an honorary degree from the University of Alberta, and was a member of the Order of Canada.

Eric Cormack was born in Scotland and came to Canada after serving in WWI. He had 50 years of decorated service with the British and Canadian armies. The Eric Cormack Centre, which specializes in educating people with developmental disabilities, was named in his honour. He was also awarded the Alberta Achievement Award in 1978, the Order of Canada in 1980 and in 1983 was made an Honorary Doctor of Laws by his alma mater, the University of Alberta.

Barbara Cormack, no date. (CEA.87/130)

Dawson City. The company relocated between 1903 and 1904 before being dissolved in 1907. Côté then formed Côté & Smith with F. B. Smith. In 1909 Côté became a member of parliament for the Athabasca riding. In 1918 he was named to the Alberta cabinet as provincial secretary, and was also minister of Mines and Railways. In 1919 Côté helped form the Scientific and Industrial Research Council of Alberta. He was named to the Senate in 1923.

Road 1984 NW 10:B2

Country Club Place

West of Edmonton Country Club and Golf Course, south of Wanyandi Road

This road is adjacent to the Edmonton Golf and Country Club. Golf was first played in Edmonton around 1896. The Edmonton Golf and Country Club was formed in 1911 and shortly after acquired its present location.

Road 1989 SW 3:D1 *

Country Club Point

West of Edmonton Country Club and Golf Course, south of Wanyandi Road

See Country Club Place.

Road 1989 SW 3:D1 *

Country Club Road

West of Edmonton Country Club and Golf Course, south of Wanyandi Road

See Country Club Place.

Road 1989 SW 3:D1

Country Club Wynd

East of Wilkin Road, south of Wilson Lane

See Country Club Place.

Road 1989 SW 3:D1

Hon. Jean Léon Côté, circa 1923. (CEA EA-272-01)

CPR Irvine

63 Avenue north to Whyte Avenue, 99 Street west to CP railway tracks

At the beginning of the 1900s this land was owned by Nancy Irvine and called the Irvine Estate. In 1906 she sold part of her land to Canadian Pacific Railway (CPR) and a station was built there in 1908. It was also here that the terminus of the Edmonton, Yukon and Pacific Railway was located. In 1912 the neighbourhood was still known as Irvine Estate. In 1997 the south side Canadian Pacific and Canadian National railway yards east of Gateway Boulevard were amalgamated into one neighbourhood, CPR Irvine.

Neighbourhood 1997 SE 4:C1

CPR West

63 Avenue north to Whyte Avenue, CP railway tracks west to Calgary Trail

This neighbourhood belongs to the Canadian Pacific Railway (CPR) Company and is used for railway purposes. It is located to the west of another CPR holding. The first train to come to Strathcona (now Edmonton) was the CPR-operated Calgary and Edmonton Railway line in 1891. The CPR soon established an infrastructure in Edmonton. In 1902 a wooden freight shed measuring 67 metres by 7.4 metres was built at 103 Street and 80 Avenue. It was dismantled in the 1960s. The 1908 Strathcona CPR Station still exists and is now a bar and restaurant.

Neighbourhood   CU   SW   4:C1

Crawford Plains

10 Avenue north to Mill Woods Road South and 16A Avenue, 34 Street to 50 Street

Neil Crawford (1931–1992) was an alderman, an MLA for Edmonton Parkallen, a Progressive Conservative cabinet minister, government house leader and attorney general. He was one of the first to be elected in 1971 in the defeat of the Social Credit Party by the Peter Lougheed-led Progressive Conservatives. Crawford held portfolios in both the Lougheed and, later, the Don Getty governments. He died in 1992 after a long battle with ALS.

Neighbourhood   1976   SE   1:C1

Crawford Plains Park

4012–12 Avenue

This park is in the Crawford Plains neighbourhood and has an area of 2.19 ha. *See* Crawford Plains.

Park   1985   SE   1:C1

Creek's Crossing Park

South of 41 Avenue, west of 38 Street

Located near Mill Creek, this park is in the Kiniski Gardens neighbourhood and has an area of 2.45 ha.

Park   1997   SE   5:B2 *

Crestwood

McKenzie Ravine north to MacKinnon Ravine, Riverside Drive west to 149 Street

Crestwood neighbourhood was developed around 1952. It had formerly been known as the Jasper Place and Capital Hill subdivisions. City council allowed the local community league to help choose and vote on the new name.

Neighbourhood   1952   SW   7:A2

Crestwood Park

14325–96 Avenue

This park is in the Crestwood neighbourhood and has an area of 2.06 ha. *See* Crestwood.

Park   1982   SW   8:D2

Cromdale

Jasper Avenue north to 114 Avenue, 76 Street west to 84 Street and LRT tracks

Cromdale is one of Edmonton's oldest inner-city neighbourhoods. Its development began soon after a streetcar line was extended from the city's central business district east along Jasper Avenue, north on Kinnaird Street (82 Street) and then east again on Pine Avenue (112 Avenue). Cromdale, meaning "crooked valley," is also a place in Scotland. Over the past century, parts of Cromdale have had different names. The area north of Jasper Avenue and east of Kinnaird (now 82) Street was once known as Cromdale Place. The area north of Jasper Avenue and east of 78 Street was originally called View Point. Among the historical residences are the oldest house on Jasper Avenue, the house of the

Royalite Service Station at 8120–106 Avenue in Cromdale, June 9, 1966. (CEA EA–88–23)

first woman professional photographer in western Canada, and the homes of two former Edmonton mayors and of Edmonton's first sheriff.

Neighbourhood   CU   C   7:C1

Crystallina Nera

South of the proposed outer ring road, east of 82 Street

The name of this Lake District area neighbourhood is derived from the Greek *krystallos nero*, meaning "crystal water."

Neighbourhood   1979   NE   10:C1 *

Cumberland

Cumberland Road north to 153 Avenue, 127 Street to 142 Street

The name is based on the theme of adopting names of early forts and posts for neighbourhoods in The Palisades area. Cumberland House was the first Hudson's Bay Company inland trading post. It was built by Samuel Hearne in 1774, on the Saskatchewan River, near the present-day Manitoba-Saskatchewan boundary. The post was named in honour of the first governor of the Hudson's Bay Company, Prince Rupert, Duke of Cumberland.

Neighbourhood   1984   NW   10:A2

Cumberland Park

14816–129 Street

See Cumberland.

Park 2002 NW 10:B2 *

Cumberland Road

West of 127 Street to 135 Street and 145 Avenue

See Cumberland.

Road 1984 NW 10:B2

Cutts Court

South of 155 Avenue, west of Cairns Place

War veteran and postmaster Edward Cutts was
born in St. Johnsbury and educated in Sherbrooke,
Québec. During WWI, Cutts served with the 117th
Eastern Battalion Canadian Expeditionary Force.
After the war he worked at the Sherbrooke post
office until 1922, when he was transferred to
Edmonton. In 1928 he was appointed to the investigations branch and in 1947 was promoted to post
office inspector. In 1955 he became Edmonton's
ninth postmaster. Cutts retired in 1963 after 46
years of service.

Road 2000 NW 10:A2

Cy Becker

167 Avenue north to the proposed outer ring road,
Manning Drive west to 50 Street

Charles "Cy" Becker (1908–1965) was one of the
pioneers of the transportation industry in Canada's
North. Becker started his flying career as a pilot
with the Royal Naval Air Service in WWI. He
completed a law degree at the University of Alberta
in 1923, and in 1929 formed the firm of
Commercial Airways Limited with partner "Wop"
May. From 1927 to 1932, Becker was associated
with the Edmonton Flying Club. Around 1932 he
established the Northern Waterways Company
which provided transport on the Mackenzie River.
Becker was appointed Queen's Council in 1946 and
was police court crown prosecutor in Edmonton
from 1931 to 1937.

Neighbourhood 1981 NE 11:A1 *

Dalhousie Crescent

South of Lessard Road, east of 183A Street

James Andrew Broun Ramsay (1812–1860), first Marquess of Dalhousie, was Governor General of India from 1847 to 1856. He helped to centralize the Indian state and, through his conquests and annexations, to create the map of modern India. Dalhousie's changes were so radical that he was often held responsible for the Indian Mutiny, which occurred in 1857. The names of roads in the Donsdale neighbourhood were chosen to celebrate Canada's historical connections to England.

Road   2000   SW   3:C2 *

Dalhousie Way

South of Lessard Road, east of 184 Street

See Dalhousie Crescent.

Road   2000   SW   3:C2

Daly Grove

16A Avenue north to 23 Avenue, 34 Street west to Mill Woods Road East

Thomas Daly (1861–1908) was an early pioneer who started homesteading in the Clover Bar area in 1883. He received worldwide attention after showing the superiority of Alberta-grown oats by winning first prize at the Chicago World's Fair in 1893. He was involved with the Clover Bar school and the Clover Bar municipality and was a member of the Edmonton Exhibition Association. Daly also served on city council in 1907.

Neighbourhood   1976   SE   1:C1

Daly Grove Park

1880–37 Street

This Daly Grove neighbourhood park has an area of 3.05 ha. *See* Daly Grove.

Park   1987   SE   1:C1

Danbury Boulevard

Southeast of Lessard Road, northwest of Donsdale Drive

Danbury Boulevard is named after the small town of Danbury in the County of Essex in southeastern England. Names in the Donsdale neighbourhood conform to the theme of celebrating Edmonton's connection with Britain.

Road   1997   SW   3:C1 *

Darlington Crescent

South of Lessard Road, east of 183A Street

Darlington Crescent is named after a district in the southern extreme of the county of Durham, England. Names in the Donsdale neighbourhood conform to the theme of celebrating Edmonton's connection with Britain.

Road   1997   SW   3:C1 *

Darlington Gate

Southeast of Lessard Road, northwest of Donsdale Drive

See Darlington Crescent.

Road   1997   SW   3:C2 *

Dartmoor Crescent

East of Lessard Road, south of 53 Avenue

Dartmoor Crescent is named after the moorland of Dartmoor in the south of England. Names in the Donsdale neighbourhood conform to the theme of celebrating Edmonton's connection with Britain.

Road   1997   SW   3:C2 *

Dartmouth Cove

South of Lessard Road, east of 183A Street

The name Dartmouth Cove originates from either the city of Dartmouth, named for Sir William Legge, the Earl of Dartmouth, in Nova Scotia or from its English namesake. Names in the Donsdale neighbourhood conform to the theme of celebrating Edmonton's connection with Britain.

Road 1997 **SW** 3:C1 *

Dartmouth Point

Southeast of Lessard Road, northwest of Donsdale Drive

See Dartmouth Cove.

Road 1997 **SW** 3:C2 *

David Ure Park

14211–57 Street

David Alton Ure (1910–1953) was a teacher, farmer and minister of agriculture. Ure was born and raised at Delburne, Alberta. In the 1930s he taught at Clarendon and later Innisfail, where he also operated a small farm on the outskirts of town. He retired from teaching a few years later and worked for farm equipment and auctioneering businesses. In 1943 he was elected to the legislature as part of Ernest Manning's Social Credit government. Ure retained his seat and advanced to the position of minister of agriculture, a portfolio he held until his death in 1953. In addition to his numerous interests and activities, Ure was a member of the Lions Club and the Knights of Pythias. The David Ure Park is in the York neighbourhood and has an area of 0.95 ha.

Park 1987 **NE** 10:D2

Davies Industrial East

From CN railway tracks north to CP railway tracks and Sherwood Park Freeway, 50 Street to 75 Street

Arthur Davies (1862–1927) arrived from Wales in 1895; he was mayor of Strathcona in 1905 and served on city council for three years. Re-elected as Strathcona's mayor in 1910, he oversaw the amalga-

Aerial view of Davies Industrial West, 1959. (CEA Vol. 4, YC 270 A-15)

mation of Strathcona with Edmonton in 1912. He served as the first chairman of the Strathcona Library Board, was president and co-founder of the Commercial Life Assurance Company, and served as a director on the Edmonton Exhibitions Board and Robertson Theological College.

Neighbourhood 1965 **SE** 4:D1

Davies Industrial West

CN railway tracks north to CP railway tracks, 75 Street to 91 Street

This neighbourhood is an extension of the original Davies Industrial subdivision. *See* Davies Industrial East.

Neighbourhood 1965 **SE** 4:D1

Davies Road

South of Argyll Road, connecting 86 Street to Wagner Road

On January 26, 1965, the Names Advisory Committee (NAC) approved Davies Road as the roadway connecting 86 Street and 75 Street at 62

The Dawson Bridge and Dawson Coal Mine, 1931. (CEA EA–160–819)

Avenue. A year later, however, City Council rejected the name. NAC resubmitted it on June 15, 1966 and this time City Council approved the committee's recommendation. But the matter was still not entirely resolved, and later that same year the NAC recommended that Davies Road be renamed Wagner Road, and that the road connecting 86 Street to Wagner Road at approximately 77 Street be named Davies Road. *See* Davies Industrial East.

Road   1966   SE   4:D1

Dawson Bridge

Spanning the North Saskatchewan River connecting Rowland Road to 106 Avenue

This bridge was originally called the East End Bridge. It was later named to honour H. S. Dawson, who came to Edmonton in 1892. Dawson established the Dawson Coal Mine in this area in 1907. Construction of this bridge began in 1911 and was completed the following year.

Bridge   CU   NE   7:C2

Dawson Park

10298–89 Street

Dawson Park is named for John Forsyth Dawson (1892–1962). He was a WWI veteran and one of the province's pioneer geologists. Dawson was born in Ontario and came to Edmonton with his parents as a child. Dawson studied engineering at the University of Alberta and Upper Canada College in Toronto and worked in northern Alberta as a geologist. In 1913 he travelled to Australia. While there, he joined the Australian Imperial Force and was posted to Europe, where he was wounded at Vimy Ridge. Dawson returned to Canada in the early 1920s and worked in the Turner Valley oil fields. He later accepted a position with the Dominion Oil Fields Supply Company in Edmonton and remained with this firm until his retirement in 1954. The Dawson Bridge was named after his father, H. S. Dawson, who established the Dawson Coal Mine. Dawson Park is located in Capital City Recreation Park and has an area of 10.75 ha.

Park   1990   NE   7:C2

Dechene

*Lessard Road north to Callingwood Road,
178 Street to 184 Street*

Joseph Miville Déchêne (1879–1962) was born in
Quebec and moved with his family to Alberta in
1892. They were among the first homesteaders in
the Morinville district. In 1903 Déchêne moved to
Edmonton and, in 1912, opened a tobacco and
news store. He later entered the political arena, and
from 1921 to 1935 was a member of the Alberta
Legislature. In 1940 he was elected as a member of
parliament for Athabasca. Déchêne retained this
seat until his retirement in 1958.

Neighbourhood   1979   SW   3:C1

Dechene Lane

North of Lessard Road, east of 184 Street

See Dechene.

Road   1979   SW   3:C2 *

Dechene Park

18209–57 Avenue

This park is in the Dechene neighbourhood and has
an area of 2.02 ha. *See* Dechene.

Park   1990   SW   3:C1

Dechene Road

North of Lessard Road, east of 184 Street

See Dechene.

Road   1980   SW   3:C1

Dechene Way

North of Lessard Road, east of 184 Street

See Dechene.

Road   1986   SW   3:C1 *

Decker Way

South of Drysdale Run, east of Dalhousie Way

Dr. George Edward Decker (1909–1984) was born
in Saskatchewan and received his Doctorate of
Dental Surgery from the University of Alberta in
1932. After completing his two-year internship at
the University Hospital, he went on to practise
dentistry for the next 43 years in Lacombe,
Lloydminster and Edmonton. During WWII, Dr.
Decker served in the Canadian Dental Corps. He
continued to serve in the reserve unit of the corps
until 1957, reaching the rank of lieutenant-colonel.
Dr. Decker was also chairman of the Canadian
Dental Association's Council and executive director
and registrar of the association from 1961 to 1976.
As well, Dr. Decker lectured at the University of
Alberta, was editor of the *ADA News Information*
from 1976 to 1982, was a fellow of the International
College of Dentists, and served as president of the
Edmonton and District Dental Society, the
University of Alberta Dental Alumni Association,
the Kinsmen Club and the Rotary Club.

Road   2001   SW   3:C2 *

Decoteau Trail

From 80 Avenue to 87 Avenue east of 184 Street

See feature story, page 72.

Walkway   1971   SW   3:C1 *

Delton

*122 Avenue north to Yellowhead Trail, 86 Street
to 97 Street*

This neighbourhood is named after Edward
Delegare "Del" Grierson, who came to Edmonton
in the 1890s while working on the CPR and went
on to own property along Jasper Avenue. In the
early 1900s Grierson served a number of terms on
City Council. The name of Delton has been in use
since around 1907 and has been part of the city
since 1908. Grierson was active in real estate

Decoteau Trail

SGT. ALEX WUTTUNEE DECOTEAU (1887–1917) was an Olympic athlete and Canada's first Aboriginal police officer. Born on the Red Pheasant Reserve, near Battleford, in present-day Saskatchewan, Decoteau was the only Albertan on the Canadian team that competed in the 1912 Olympic Games in Stockholm, Sweden. Between 1909 and 1916 Decoteau won nearly every track event in Alberta.

In 1911 Decoteau was hired as a police officer by the City of Edmonton. As well as being the first Aboriginal person to hold such a post in Canada, Decoteau is said to have been the country's first motor-cycle policeman. By 1916, when he took leave from the police force to enlist in the Canadian Army, he had reached the rank of sergeant. He continued to run, even while stationed in England. After winning a one-mile race in Salisbury, England, Decoteau was presented with a gold pocket watch by King George V. The watch, taken from the King's own waistcoat, was a last-minute replacement for a misplaced trophy.

Decoteau would never see Canada again. He was hit by a sniper's bullet and tragically died at the Battle of Passchendaele on October 30, 1917. The German who shot Decoteau then stole the gold pocket watch. Days later, the sniper was killed by Decoteau's fellow soldiers and the watch returned to Decoteau's mother in Canada. Decoteau was buried at Ypres, northern France.

In 1985 friends and relatives of the famed runner held a belated Cree burial service for Decoteau in his birthplace of Red Pheasant Reserve. Band council members, Aboriginal veterans and family members walked to a sacred burial ground where singers chanted a burial song to guide the spirit of the long-dead Decoteau home. With them was a ten-member honour guard from the Edmonton Police Service and Canadian Army personnel. Decoteau was inducted into the City of Edmonton Sports Hall of Fame in 1967, and the Alberta Sports Hall of Fame in 2001. Decoteau Trail, in the Aldergrove neighbourhood, is one of a number of trail names approved between 1969 and 1971.

Alexander Decoteau, 1912. (CEA EA-10-2072)

speculation, and there have been a number of developments incorporating his nickname, including Delwood, New Delton, East Delton, New Delton Addition, North Delton, West Delton, Delton Gardens, Delton Addition and Delton Industrial. Today only Delton and Delwood remain. *See* Grierson Hill.

Neighbourhood CU NE 7:C1

Delton Park

12325–88 Street

The park has an area of 1.49 ha. in the Delton neighbourhood. *See* Delton.

Park 1984 NE 7:C1

Delwood

132 Avenue to 137 Avenue, 66 Street to 82 Street

This neighbourhood name has existed since the early 1900s and is likely named after Edward Delegare "Del" Grierson, the prominent landowner and politician. Delwood replaced the old subdivision names of Industrial Centre, Queen's Park and East Delton. *See* Delton *and* Grierson Hill.

Neighbourhood 1956 NE 10:C2

Delwood Park

7505 Delwood Road

This park is in the Delwood neighbourhood and has an area of 4.71 ha. *See* Delwood.

Park 1983 NE 10:C2

Delwood Road

North of 132 Avenue, east of 80 Street, west of 68 Street

This is the main loop collector road that extends north of 132 Avenue. *See* Delwood.

Road 1963 NE 10:C2

Delton in flood, 1940. (CEA EA–160–849)

Diamond Park

9813–101 Street

The 2.1-ha. Diamond Park in the Rossdale neighbourhood was most likely named for the baseball diamond that was built on this site in 1907. In 1906, Frank Gray, a local businessman who owned the Edmonton baseball franchise, leased a parcel of land in the Ross Flats area of the river valley from landowner Donald Ross. He then constructed a sports field that became known as Diamond Park. For many years the park was the site of Edmonton sporting events, including baseball, soccer and football.

Park CU C 7:C2

Dickens Loop

South of Lessard Road, north of Donsdale Drive, surrounded by Darlington Crescent

Reflecting the area's naming theme, Dickens Loop is named for Charles Dickens (1812–1870), the

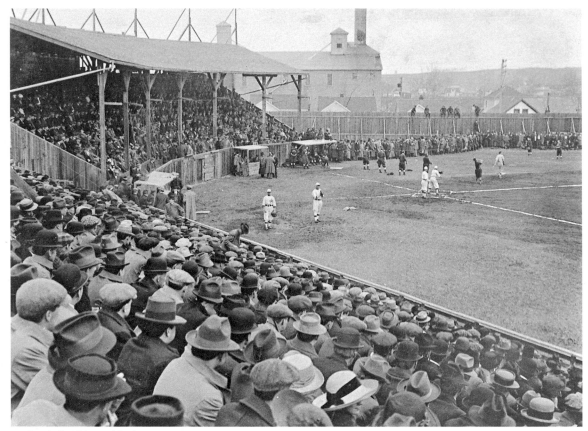

Baseball at Diamond Park, 1920. (CEA EB–23–2)

famous English author. Among his many novels are *Oliver Twist*, *Great Expectations* and *A Christmas Carol*.

Road   1997   SW   3:C1 *

Dickinsfield

137 Avenue to 153 Avenue, 82 Street to 97 Street

Clennell H. "Punch" Dickins (1899–1995) was one of the original officers of the Royal Flying Corps and the first pilot to transport airmail across the prairies. Dickins was born in Manitoba and came to Edmonton in 1907. He went on to serve in WWI and was awarded the Distinguished Flying Cross. After the war, Dickins was part of the official opening of Edmonton's Blatchford Field, the first municipal airport in Canada. In 1928 he piloted the first airmail flights across the prairies and earned

the McKee Trophy, also known as the Trans-Canada Trophy, for outstanding achievement in the field of aerospace operations. The McKee Trophy is Canada's oldest aviation honour and was first awarded in 1927. As a bush pilot, Dickins flew across the unmapped expanses of Canada's north and helped open up the Arctic territory. Dickins received the Order of the British Empire in 1936 and the Order of Canada in 1968. He was inducted into Canada's Aviation Hall of Fame in 1973.

Subdivision   1966   NE   10:C2 *

Dr. Anne Anderson Park

10515–162 Street

See feature story, page 75.

Park   1985   NW   8:D2

Dr. Anne Anderson Park

ANNE ANDERSON (1906–1997) pioneered the teaching of the Cree language in western Canada. A Métis elder once described Anderson as "the heart of the [Métis] Nation." In her long and active life, Anderson was a nurse, a teacher and the author of more than 90 books on Métis history and culture and the Cree language. Apart from her language tapes, Anderson was probably best known for her *Cree Dictionary*. She also researched and documented traditional herbal remedies.

Anderson was one of ten children born to Elizabeth "Betsy" Callihou and William Joseph Gairdner on the river lot they farmed east of St. Albert. Her parents were of Cree, French and Scottish descent. Anderson attended school to Grade 10 and then worked on the family farm. After marrying and having two children, she moved to Edmonton in the mid-1940s and became a nurses' aide.

After 15 years of nursing, Anderson began what was to be her most important work—the preservation of the Cree language. Recalling the dying words of her convent-raised mother, Anderson set out to record and teach the Cree language. She founded Cree Productions, which published Cree dictionaries and instructional materials. She also served on the Alberta Cultural Heritage Council. She initiated Cree classes at schools and centres across Canada and lectured at the University of Alberta, Grant MacEwan Community College, Fairview College, the Charles Camsell Hospital and Fort Saskatchewan Correctional Facility.

Anderson received the Native Council of Canada Award, an honorary Doctorate of Laws from the University of Alberta and the Order of Canada. Among her many books were *The First Métis…A New Nation*, which documented the history of the Métis in Alberta. Anderson died at the age of 91. The Dr. Anne Anderson Park is in the Britannia neighbourhood and has an area of 0.07 ha. The park features a bronze sculpture of a buffalo.

Dr. Anne Anderson, circa 1978. (CEA EA–742–1)

Dr. Francis Crang Park

10503–48 Avenue

Dr. Francis William Crang (1869–1947) was a pioneer Edmonton doctor. Dr. Crang was born in Ontario and, after completing public school, went to work for his father as a bricklayer and stone mason. At the age of 25 he completed high school and entered McGill University, graduating in 1901. Following his marriage in 1903, he moved to Strathcona where he practised medicine for nearly 40 years. He served on the Canadian Medical Council for four years and the Edmonton Public School Board from 1911 to 1937. Dr. Crang was also chairman of the Edmonton Boxing and Wrestling Commission, serving as its doctor for 25 years, and was medical examiner and advisor for the world-famous Commercial Graduates Basketball Club, better known as the Edmonton Grads. Dr. Francis Crang Park is in the Empire Park neighbourhood and has an area of 1.41 ha.

Park 1984 SW 4:C2

Dr. Wilbert McIntyre Park

8303–104 Street

Dr. Wilbert McIntyre (1867–1909) was the first member of parliament for Strathcona. When McIntyre died in 1909, his constituents collected donations and built a commemorative fountain in the middle of 104 Street at 83 Avenue. This fountain was destroyed when a car crashed into it in 1952. A replica fountain, paid for by donations to the Old Strathcona Foundation, was erected in this park in 1991. The Dr. Wilbert McIntyre Park, in the Strathcona neighbourhood, has an area of 0.21 ha. *See* McIntyre Industrial.

Park 1989 C 7:C2 *

Dr. William Rowan Park

8830–152B Avenue

William Rowan, PhD (1891–1957) was an internationally recognized ornithologist and the first

Dr. Wilbert McIntyre, circa 1909. (CEA EA-10-2549)

chairman of the University of Alberta's Department of Zoology. In the 1920s Rowan discovered a connection between changes in seasonal light intensity and the hormones that trigger the migratory instincts of birds. In addition to his scientific research, he contributed to the founding of Edmonton's Storyland Valley Zoo and was an accomplished artist. One of his drawings of whooping cranes was selected by the Canadian Post Office Department, in 1955, for use in its wildlife stamp series.

William Rowan was a member of the British Ornithological Union, a fellow of the Zoological Society of London and a fellow of the Royal Society of Canada. In 1946 he was awarded the Flavelle Medal of the Royal Society. Rowan headed the University of Alberta's Department of Zoology for nearly four decades. The Dr. William Rowan Park is in the Evansdale neighbourhood and has an area of 0.74 ha.

Park 1983 NE 10:C2

Dominion Industrial

118 Avenue north to Yellowhead Trail, 142 Street to 149 Street

In the early 1900s, this area was developed for residential use and called Dominion Park. Decades later, it was renamed Dominion and rezoned for industrial use. It is now known as Dominion Industrial. A dominion is a territory that is subject to a governmental authority. The British North America Act created the Dominion of Canada in 1867.

Neighbourhood   1957   NW   7:A1

Donnan Park

9105–80 Avenue

Belfast-born John Donnan (1870–1933) came to Strathcona in 1901, establishing a lumber yard and dairy and serving as alderman for the area. The 5.34-ha. Donnan Park is in the King Edward Park neighbourhood on the east side of Mill Creek. The land was part of the Donnan estate and was given to the city for use as a park.

Park   1967   SE   4:C1

Donnell Road

North of 95 Avenue, west of 92 Street

This road is named for George Donnell, an early landowner who homesteaded River Lot 21, in what is now Strathearn, around 1882.

Road   1948   SE   7:C2 *

Donsdale

45 Avenue north to Lessard Road, Donsdale Drive west to 184 Street

Donsdale, located in the Lessard subdivision, is named for Frank Doncaster (d. 1955), who owned a large tract of land in the area around 1946 to 1947. After the area's annexation, the use of the name

Donsdale continued. The approved naming theme of the Donsdale neighbourhood honours the British aspect of Edmonton's heritage.

Neighbourhood   1972   SW   3:C2

Donsdale Crescent

South of 45 Avenue, east of 183A Street

See Donsdale.

Road   1997   SW   3:C2 *

Donsdale Drive

Southeast of Lessard Road, north of 45 Avenue, east of 183A Street

See Donsdale.

Road   1997   SW   3:C2

Douglas

Lansdowne Drive north to Grandview Drive, 122 Street west to Whitemud Park; excluding University of Alberta Farm

The name honours three brothers—James, Robert and Henry Douglas—who came to Edmonton from Ontario at the turn of the 20th century and went on to become prominent members of the business and political communities. The brothers were the sons of Rev. James Douglas, a Scottish Presbyterian minister, and Margaret (nee Blyth). The first to arrive, in 1894, was James McCrie Douglas (1867–1950). He was a member of Strathcona's city council and served as the member of parliament for Strathcona from 1909 to 1921. From 1922 to 1926 he was an alderman and was elected Edmonton's mayor in 1930 and 1931. He was re-elected and afterwards served as an alderman.

Five years after James arrived in Edmonton, he was joined by his younger brother, Robert Blyth Douglas (1869–1953). Together, they opened a mercantile store, Douglas Brothers Ltd., in Strathcona. Robert served several terms on

Strathcona and Edmonton city councils and was chosen to head the Alberta Liquor Control Board. In 1902 the third brother, Henry W. B. Douglas (1873–1944), made the journey west, first opening a stationery store and later a printing business. Henry was a member of Edmonton's first city council and an alderman from 1912 to 1913. He also served on the Edmonton Public School Board. The subdivision name Douglas replaced the existing name of Grandview Heights, the latter then becoming a neighbourhood within the Douglas subdivision.

Subdivision   1956   SW   4:B1 *

Dovercourt

118 Avenue to 124 Avenue, St. Albert Trail west to 142 Street

This area had its name by 1910, and may have been named for Dovercourt village in Essex, England. The Edmonton neighbourhood of Dovercourt was annexed to Edmonton in 1913 but remained undeveloped until it was replotted in the 1950s.

Neighbourhood   CU   NW   7:A1

Dovercourt Avenue

139 Street to 122 Avenue

See Dovercourt.

Road   1954   NW   7:A1

Dovercourt Crescent

137 Street to 122 Avenue

See Dovercourt.

Road   1955   NW   7:A1

Dovercourt Park

13510 Dovercourt Avenue

This park is in the Dovercourt neighbourhood and has an area of 2.09 ha. *See* Dovercourt.

Park   1982   NW   7:A1

Downtown Edmonton, 1980. (CEA EA-340-384)

Downey Way

Adjoining and south of Drysdale Run

Melvin McKenzie Downey (1874–1959) was a civil servant and politician. Born in Ontario, Downey joined the Canadian Pacific Railway in 1891 and worked as a sectionman and a brakeman. He then became a mail clerk and, in 1904, moved to Medicine Hat. Relocating to Calgary, he left the mail service and took work with the Attorney General's Department. In 1922 he moved with his family to Edmonton and until 1924 served with the prohibition staff of the Provincial Government. Between 1924 and 1939 he worked as a supervisor of the Alberta Liquor Control Board and from 1940 to 1955 as magistrate of the Small Debts Court. As well, Downey served on the Edmonton Public School Board from 1939 to 1943, as a city alderman from 1943 to 1945, and on the Exhibition Board from 1945 to 1947.

Road   2001   SW   3:C2 *

Downtown

97 Avenue to 104 Avenue, 97 Street to 109 Street

In the late 1800s, as the town of Edmonton began to develop outside Fort Edmonton, Edmonton's downtown was established to the east of the Hudson's Bay Company Reserve. At the turn of the 20h century, Jasper Avenue and 97 Street were the hub of downtown activity. Much of the Downtown neighbourhood is now located to the west, within the southern portion of the original Reserve. By the 1980s, Edmonton's downtown was being challenged for its position as the city's centre of business and commerce by suburban shopping malls and commercial strips. Nevertheless, the Downtown neighbourhood continues to be an important cultural, historic, governmental and business area.

Neighbourhood CU C 7:C2

Drysdale Run

East of Dalhousie Way, south of Lessard Road

James Roy Drysdale (1888–1954) was a WWI veteran and lawyer. Born in Nova Scotia, Drysdale spent a year at Dalhousie University in Halifax before attending the University of Alberta, where he completed a Bachelor of Arts and a Bachelor of Laws. He enlisted with the 196th Battalion of the Canadian Expeditionary Force in 1917 and served overseas, participating in the Battle of Lens (September 1917) and the Battle of Passchendaele (October 1917), where he was wounded. Drysdale returned to Edmonton in 1919 and established a private law practice. In 1920, he formed a partnership with S.S. Cormack.

Road 2001 SW 3:C2 *

Dudley B. Menzies Bridge

Spanning the North Saskatchewan River at LRT line

Dudley Blair Menzies (1906–1995) was Edmonton's longest-serving commissioner. He was born in England and came to Edmonton when his family moved here in 1908. After graduating from the University of Alberta in 1931 he worked as an

J.J. Duggan, 1899. (CEA EA-10-709)

engineer for the city and the province. Menzies was the public works commissioner from 1945 to 1970, and an alderman from 1971 to 1974.

Bridge 1989 C 7:B2 *

Duggan

34 Avenue to 40 Avenue, Calgary Trail west to 111 Street

Two-time mayor John Joseph Duggan (1868–1952) was born in Ontario and came to Strathcona in 1891. He went on to run a successful lumber yard. In 1899, the year that Strathcona was incorporated as a town, Duggan was elected as an alderman. He served as mayor in 1902 and 1903, and again from 1908 to 1910. Duggan neighbourhood is located on land once owned by John Duggan.

Neighbourhood 1961 SW 4:B2

Duggan Bridge under construction, 1957. (CEA EA-75-784)

Duggan

*34 Avenue to 51 Avenue, Calgary Trail west to
111 Street*

See Duggan *neighbourhood*.

Subdivision 1961 SW 4:B2 *

Duggan Bridge

Spanning Fort Hill road at Saskatchewan Drive

This bridge was built in 1957 and opened in 1958.
See Duggan *neighbourhood*.

Bridge 1958 C 7:C2 *

Duggan Park

3728–106 Street

This park is in the Duggan neighbourhood and has
an area of 3.23 ha. *See* Duggan *neighbourhood*.

Park 1986 SW 4:B2

Duncan Innes Park

8102–80 Avenue

Nova Scotia-born Duncan R. Innes (1900–1969)
was politician, radio broadcaster and teacher. After
graduating from the University of Alberta, Innes
began teaching at Garneau High School in 1928. In
1948 he was appointed principal of Strathcona
Composite High School, retiring from that position in 1965. In the 1940s Innes broadcast a weekly
radio program, *The Word Man*, that instructed

Dunvegan Road

THIS ROAD IS LOCATED in an area that has been part of the city since the early 1900s, when it was known as Dunvegan Yards. The railway yard and depot of the Edmonton, Dunvegan and British Columbia (ED & BC) Railway were built here, making Edmonton the southern terminus of the railway. Dunvegan, in the Peace Country, was a major point along the line to British Columbia. Between 1915 and 1926 Dunvegan Yards even had a school—Dunvegan Yards School—for the children of the employees of the ED & BC Railway.

Dunvegan Yards played an important part as a staging point in the settlement of the Peace River District and Northern Alberta. It was also the focal point for supplies and men coming from all over North America during the construction of the Alaska Highway during WWII. In 1981 the Canadian National Railway (CNR) bought the land from the Northern Alberta Railway Company (NAR). Three years later, Dunvegan became the area's official name. Subsequently, Dunvegan became part of the Athlone neighbourhood, and today Dunvegan Road is a reminder of the community's long association with the railway.

The name of Dunvegan was taken from a castle in northern Scotland. Located on the Isle of Skye, the castle is the ancestral home of the McLeod family and the oldest inhabited castle in the region. Archibald Norman McLeod of the fur-trading North West Company is believed to have brought the name with him when he established Fort Dunvegan on the Peace River in 1805.

Dunvegan Yards, 1917. (CEA EA-494-1)

Duncan Innes, 1952. (CEA EA-10-2611.4)

listeners on the correct usage of the English language. He served as alderman in 1951 and 1952. He also served as an officer commanding the 92nd Field Battery, Royal Canadian Artillery (Militia); was a member of the Geographic Board of Alberta; was active in both the provincial and federal wings of the Liberal Party; was president of the Garneau Community League and the South Side Kiwanis Club; and was associated with the Federation of Community Leagues and the Edmonton Historical Board. The Duncan Innes Park is in the King Edward Park neighbourhood and has an area of 0.66 ha.

Park 1986 SE 4:D1

Dunluce

153 Avenue to 167 Avenue, Castle Downs Road west to 127 Street

The Dunluce neighbourhood is in the Warwick subdivision of the Castle Downs area. Consistent with the area's naming theme, the name is taken from a historical castle. Dunluce Castle, on the northern coast of Ireland, occupied a position of great strategic importance that was fought over for centuries. The castle remained the property of the McDonnells, "Lords of the Isles," from the 16th century until 1928 when it was transferred to the state for preservation.

Neighbourhood 1973 NW 10:B1

Dunluce Park

11620–162 Avenue

This park is in the Dunluce neighbourhood and has an area of 2.95 ha. *See* Dunluce.

Park 1987 NW 10:B1

Dunluce Road

161 Avenue to 115 Street

The original Dunluce Road, in 1974, was west of 121 Street and 162 Avenue. This road was later given the numerical designation of 161 Avenue, and Dunluce Road was reassigned to its present route. *See* Dunluce.

Road 1978 NW 10:B1

Dunvegan Road

West of 135 Street, north of 127 Avenue

See feature story, page 81.

Road 1994 NW 10:A2

E.L. Hill Park

10518–86 Avenue

Ethelbert Lincoln Hill (1863–1960) was Edmonton's first librarian. Hill, born in Canada West, came to Edmonton in 1909, taking up the position of inspector of schools for Strathcona District. Finding no library, Hill campaigned until both Strathcona and Edmonton built libraries in 1913. He was chosen as the first librarian and remained in the post for 24 years. The E.L. Hill Park is in the Strathcona neighbourhood and has an area of 0.2 ha.

Park 1988 C 7:C2

E.L. Smith Road

East of 184 Street at 35 Avenue

This roadway accesses the E.L. Smith Water Treatment Plant. The plant and the road were named after Eugene Lloyd Smith (1902–1960), the first water treatment chemical engineer in Edmonton. He was a pioneer in several treatment processes and was considered the leading authority on water treatment methods in western Canada. Smith was born in Nova Scotia and moved with his family to the Edmonton area in 1919. He graduated from the University of Alberta in 1930 and, beginning in 1935, Smith was employed in a city water treatment plant. Under his supervision, the facility was upgraded and its capacity tripled.

Road 1976 SW 3:C2

Earl Samis Park

5680 Hardisty Drive

Earl L. Samis (1895–1970) supported the development of Edmonton's sports programs for more than 40 years. Samis was born near Edmonton and was a school teacher before joining the civil service. His contribution to sports began in 1918 when he became involved with the Edmonton Eskimos, the Canadian Football League team. For his outstanding contributions to hockey, soccer, baseball and foot-

ball, Samis was inducted into the City of Edmonton Sports Hall of Fame in 1963. He was also honoured by the Edmonton Sportswriters and Sportscasters Association as Edmonton Sportsman of the Year in 1967, and received awards from the National Recreation Association and the Canadian Amateur Hockey Association. The Earl Samis Park is in the Capilano neighbourhood and has an area of 1.23 ha.

Park 1982 NE 7:D1

Eastgate Business Park

92 Avenue to 101 Avenue, 34 Street to 50 Street

Eastgate Industrial was the original name given to this area. The name is likely descriptive.

Neighbourhood 1982 SE 6:A2

Easton Road

East of 91 Street, south of Edwards Drive

Dr. Donald R. Easton was a prominent Edmonton physician. During WWII he served with the Royal Canadian Air Force. In 1945 he became a senior medical officer and returned to Canada with the rank of wing commander. From 1945 to 1947 Easton was district medical officer for the Department of Veteran's Affairs. From 1948 until his resignation in 1961 he was the superintendent of the Royal Alexandra Hospital. Easton was a fellow of the American College of Hospital Administrators, served on the board of the American Hospital Association and was an advisor to Blue Cross.

Road 2001 SE 1:B1 *

Eastwood

118 Avenue to 125 Avenue, 75 Street east to 89 Street

Likely a descriptive name, Eastwood was part of the Village of North Edmonton until amalgamation with the City of Edmonton in 1912. Parts of

Edgar Millen Park dedication, 1968. (CEA EA-20-35)

Eastwood were subdivided as early as 1906; eastern sections were divided in 1910 and 1913. A streetcar line began servicing 118 Avenue in 1910. A portion of Eastwood (approximately 75 Street to 82 Street and 118 Avenue to about 120 Avenue) was once called Wedgewood.

Neighbourhood CU NE 7:C1

Eastwood Park

8508–118 Avenue

This park is in the Eastwood neighbourhood and has an area of 1.58 ha. *See* Eastwood.

Park 1984 NE 7:C1 *

Eaux Claires

153 Avenue to 167 Avenue, 91 Street to 97 Street

This neighbourhood is in the Lake District. Its name is French for "clear waters."

Neighbourhood 1979 NE 10:C1

Ebbers Industrial

144 Avenue to 151 Avenue, CN railway tracks west to Manning Drive

John Rudolph Ebbers was a well-known area dairy farmer. Ebbers was born in 1895 in the Netherlands and came to Edmonton in 1912. He worked for the city's electrical department, and then ventured into the farming business. In 1937 the City decided to expand the nearby airport, Blatchford Field (now the City Centre Airport), which had begun operation more than a decade earlier, in 1926. Ebbers' dairy farm was on the land slated for expropriation. He was offered $2,200 in compensation for the loss of his business, land and buildings. Ebbers then purchased a quarter section of land in northeast Edmonton and established Ebbers Dairy, later known as Ebberdale Farm. Today, only 2.43 ha. of the Ebberdale farm remains.

Neighbourhood 1981 NE 11:B2

Eddy Mark Shaske Jr. Park

8751–153 Street

Edmonton-born Eddy Mark Shaske Jr. (1957–1982) was an internationally known trap shooter. From 1969 to 1974, Shaske was Alberta's trap champion. In 1977 he was a member of the Canadian National Team and represented Canada at an international competition in Mexico. He also competed at world championships in France, Korea, Italy and Argentina, and Grand Prix events in Wales and Brazil. In 1980 he qualified for Canada's Olympic team but did not participate following Canada's boycott of the Moscow-hosted games in protest of the Soviet invasion of Afghanistan. He was posthumously inducted into Edmonton's Sports Hall of Fame in 1983, and into the Alberta Sports Hall of Fame in 1990. The Eddy Mark Shaske Jr. Park is in the Jasper Park neighbourhood and has an area of 1.86 ha.

Park 1988 SW 8:D2

Edgar Millen Park

11424 Fort Road

Edgar Millen (1901–1932) was an RCMP officer who died in the line of duty in the Northwest Territories. He was shot by Albert Johnson, "the mad trapper of Rat River," during the famous manhunt. Johnson fired upon officers after he was accused of trapping on established Aboriginal traplines. The Edgar Millen Park in the Parkdale neighbourhood has an area of 0.08 ha.

Park 1967 NE 7:C1

Edinboro Park

9304–118 Street

This name was in common usage before it was formally recognized. Edinboro Park is in the Windsor Park neighbourhood and has an area of 0.2 ha. *See* Edinboro Road.

Park 1956 C 7:B2

Edinboro Road

West of 116 Street, north of 92 Avenue

This name appeared on the original registered plan of Windsor Park (c. 1912). At some point, however, the name fell into disuse. In 1932 residents of Windsor Park petitioned to have 93 Avenue formally changed to Edinboro Road because they had seen the name on early maps. The name's origin is not recorded but may be a derivation of Edinburgh, the capital of Scotland.

Road CU C 7:B2 *

Edmiston Industrial

111 Avenue north to Yellowhead Trail, 178 Street to 184 Street

William S. Edmiston (d. 1903) was the mayor of Edmonton in 1898 and 1899. Born in Scotland, Edmiston settled in the Clover Bar area in 1882. He was an architect by profession and in 1893 designed the first post office. Edmiston moved to Edmonton around 1895 and served as a town councillor from 1895 to 1896. During the 1910s, this area was called Edmonton Heights.

Neighbourhood 1975 NW 8:C1

Edmonton

41 Avenue SW to 195 Avenue NW, 31 Street NE to 231 Street NW

See feature story, page 87.

City 1795 C 7:C2 *

Edmonton Cemetery

11820–107 Avenue

Many of Edmonton's first settlers are buried here. In 1886, Edmonton pioneers formed the Edmonton Cemetery Company to oversee a cemetery established on land donated by the Hudson's Bay Company. In 1964 the City of Edmonton

Edmonton

EDMONTON IS ONE OF THE OLDEST AREAS of "European" settlement in what is now the province of Alberta. Fort Edmonton was established in 1795 as a fur trade post of the Hudson's Bay Company (HBC). It was built as part of the HBC's western expansion during its competition for trade and influence with the rival firm, the North West Company (NWC). Fort Edmonton was named for the English birthplace of Sir James Winter Lake. He was present at the meeting of the governors of the HBC when it was decided to establish a fort on the North Saskatchewan River.

The first Fort Edmonton was built some 32 kilometres further down the North Saskatchewan from the current city, across the river from present-day Fort Saskatchewan. For mutual protection, it was built in close proximity to the NWC's post, Fort Augustus, constucted earlier that same year. For a number of reasons, including the lack of readily available firewood and threats by local Aboriginal groups, both companies abandoned this site in 1801, and moved to what is now Rossdale, in downtown Edmonton. They stayed at this site for nine years and then, in 1810, moved to a spot at the confluence of the North Saskatchewan River and White Earth Creek, about 15 kilometres east of the town of Smoky Lake, northeast of present-day Edmonton. A number of forts, including NWC's Fort Augustus, and the HBC's Fort Edmonton were relocated to this site. The forts shared the same stockade and were known as the Lower Terre Blanche Houses.

Another move occurred in the winter of 1813–1814, when this location was abandoned in favour of the site where the Rossdale Power House now is situated. The third Forts Edmonton and Augustus became Fort Edmonton after 1821, when the two companies merged under the HBC banner. Following a flood in 1825, Chief Factor John Rowand decided to rebuild further above the flats. In 1830, the fortified trading post was located just below the present-day Province of Alberta's Legislature Buildings in Edmonton. The last buildings of this fort were demolished in 1915.

With the influx of settlers in the late 1800s, and its historical significance as a "gateway to the north," Edmonton prospered. In 1892 it was officially made a town and in October 1904 it was given the status of a city. Because of its geographically central location and its political influence and connections, in 1906 Edmonton became the capital of the newly created province of Alberta.

The name "Edmonton" is derived from the Anglo-Saxon Christian name Eadhelm and "tun" or "ton," which means a "field" or "enclosure."

The old fort being demolished; new Legislature buildings in the background, 1915. (CEA EA-10-79)

Hangar and airplane at Blatchford Field, now Edmonton City Centre Airport, 1937. (CEA EA-160-1332)

assumed management of this 11.00 ha. cemetery in the Queen Mary Park neighbourhood and renamed it Edmonton Cemetery.

Cemetery   1964   C   7:B2 *

Edmonton Grads Park

12103–109 Avenue

See feature story, page 89.

Park   1989   C   7:B1

Edmonton Municipal Airport

Kingsway and Princess Elizabeth Avenue north to Yellowhead Trail, 106 Street to 121 Street

In 1926 the area now home to the Edmonton City Centre Airport was called Blatchford Field, in honour of Mayor Ken Blatchford. At that time the Edmonton airport was the first licensed municipal airport in Canada. It was later renamed the Edmonton Industrial Airport and, in 1975, the Edmonton Municipal Airport. In 1996, after all scheduled passenger services were consolidated at the Edmonton International Airport, 54 kilometres south of the city, the centrally located airport facility was renamed Edmonton City Centre Airport. It is today a general aviation airport used by private planes and charter traffic. The area in which the airport is located is still known as Edmonton Municipal Airport.

Area   1996   NW   7:B1

Edmonton Northlands

Borden Park Road north to 118 Avenue, 73 Street west to LRT tracks

Until 1979 this area was known as the Edmonton Exhibition Grounds. Edmonton's first agricultural fair was held at Rossdale in 1879, but moved here in 1909. The Skyreach Centre [historically known as Northlands Coliseum and Skyreach Centre, and now as Rexall Place], home of the Edmonton Oilers National Hockey League (NHL) team is located here.

Neighbourhood   1979   NE   7:C1

Edmonton Grads Park

DR. JAMES NAISMITH (1861–1939), the Canadian-born inventor of basketball, said of the Edmonton Commercial Graduates Basketball Club: "The Grads have the greatest team that ever stepped out on a basketball floor." The players of the legendary Grads were all alumnae of McDougall Commercial High School. In the 25-year career of the Grads, the team won an unparalleled 502 of 522 games. These wins included 21 Western Canadian championships, and every Canadian championship from 1922 to 1940. The Edmonton Grads disbanded in 1940, in part because the team's gymnasium had been taken over by the British Commonwealth Air Training Plan as part of the war effort.

On the international level, the team won so regularly that the international Underwood Trophy was given to them for permanent possession in 1940. The Grads participated in four Olympic exhibition tournaments from 1924 to 1936, in Paris, Amsterdam, Los Angeles and Berlin. The team won all 27 of its Olympic matches. Remarkably, only 38 women played with the Grads throughout the team's illustrious 25-year history. In addition to bringing Edmonton great fame and honour, the Grads helped dispel the common belief that involvement in competitive sports was somehow dangerous or unhealthy for young women.

The team's coach was J. Percy Page (1887–1973), who came to McDougall Commercial High School as a teacher in 1912. Page and his assistant, Bill Tate, developed a farm system to hone the skills of promising basketball players. After the Grads disbanded, Page ran successfully for the Alberta Legislative Assembly first as an Independent (1940, 1944), then as a Conservative (1952, 1955). After being defeated in the 1959 election, Page was appointed lieutenant-governor of the Province of Alberta, a post he held until 1966.

The 1987 film *Shooting Stars: The Amazing Story of the Edmonton Grads* was directed by the local filmmaker and broadcaster Allan Stein. The Edmonton Grads Park is located in the Inglewood neighbourhood.

Edmonton Grads basketball team, 1923. (CEA EA-160-192)

Klondike Days midway at Edmonton Northlands, July 1963. (CEA EA-10-2112)

Edmonton Research and Development Park

9 Avenue to 23 Avenue, 91 Street west to Parsons Road

This area was previously named Poundmaker. The industrial neighbourhood, opened on October 4, 1979, was designed to attract high tech enterprises. Although the Names Advisory Committee gave its support for the name in 1980, the neighbourhood was named by the province. Originally developed as the Edmonton Industrial Research Park, the Edmonton Research and Development Park Authority Act was passed on May 22, 1980.

Neighbourhood   1980   SE   1:B1

Edwards Drive

East of 91 Street and south of 2 Avenue

Frank J. Edwards (1907–1967) was an alderman on the Edmonton City Council from 1965 until he died, while driving home from City Hall. Edwards was born in Edmonton and educated at local schools and the University of Alberta. During World War II he served in the Royal Canadian Air Force, attaining the rank of squadron leader. In civilian life, Edwards worked variously for the Canadian Pacific Railway, as a salesman for Robin Hood flour, and later as a teacher and principal at Grovenor School. Edwards was also active in

community life. He served as president of the Alberta Teachers' Association, was a member of the Alberta Curling Association, the Belgravia Community League, the United Church, and the Air Cadet League.

Road   2001   SE   1:B1 *

Ekota

Mill Woods Road South north to 23 Avenue, 66 Street west to Mill Woods Road

This neighbourhood is in the Knottwood subdivision of the Mill Woods area. *Ekota* is a Cree word meaning "special place."

Neighbourhood   1972   SE   1:B1

Ekota Crescent

West of 66 Street, north of Mill Woods Road, south of 17 Avenue

See Ekota.

Road   1973   SE   1:B1

Ekota Park

1415 Knottwood Road North

Ekota Park is located in the Ekota neighbourhood and has an area of 2.02 ha. *See* Ekota.

Park   1983   SE   1:B1

Eleniak Road

Connecting 50 Street to 43 Street

Wasyl Eleniak (1859–1956) was one of the first Ukrainian settlers in Canada. Eleniak came to Canada in 1891 and, after first working in Winnipeg, settled in Alberta. In 1941, Eleniak was an honoured guest at the celebrations of the 50th anniversary of Ukrainian immigration to Canada. In 1947, shortly after the Canadian Citizenship Act came into effect, Eleniak received his citizenship at a special ceremony in Ottawa.

Road   1974   SE   5:A1

Ellerslie

*City limits north to 10 Avenue, 66 Street to
111 Street*

The name Ellerslie has been used to designate this
area since before the turn of the twentieth century.
Some sources say the name is taken from Ellerslie
House, believed to be the birthplace of William
Wallace, an insurgent against Edward I of England.
Ellerslie village is located on the Clyde River in
Renfrewshire, Scotland. Other sources claim this
Edmonton area was named by the brothers John
and James McLaggan, who owned the first store
and post office, after a favourite character in a novel
by Sir Walter Scott. The Ellerslie School District
was established in 1895; the Ellerslie Post Office
began operation in 1896.

Area 1982 SE 1:B2 *

Ellerslie

*Quadrant Avenue south to Ellerslie Road,
66 Street to 91 Street*

That part of the Ellerslie neighbourhood from
2 Avenue SW south to Ellerslie Road and from
66 Street to 78 Street was formerly known as
Wernerville. Christian and Emilie Werner owned
the land that later became the neighbourhood of
Wernerville. They had come to Canada from
Volhynia, now part of Ukraine, along with Karl and
Amanda Werner, who owned nearby land.
Wernerville, a former locality, was annexed to
Edmonton in 1982. *See* Ellerslie *area.*

Neighbourhood 2001 SE 1:B1

Ellerslie Road

*South of Quadrant Avenue, from east of 17 Street
to 215 Street*

See Ellerslie *area.*

Road 1982 SW 2:B1

*Ellingson Park with paddling pool and Parkallen
Elementary School, circa 1968. (CEA EA-20-4898)*

Ellerslie Rugby Park

10950 Ellerslie Road

The Edmonton Rugby Union, a private enterprise,
sought and received official park status for the
Ellerslie Rugby Park in order to ensure that the
facility would be identified on city maps. The
Ellerslie Rugby Park is in the Richford neighbourhood near the southern edge of the city and has an
area of 12.14 ha. *See* Ellerslie *area.*

Park 1984 SW 1:A1 *

Ellingson Park

11104–65 Avenue

Joseph L. Ellingson (1902–1979) was the principal
of Parkallen School from 1952 to 1967. When he
retired, members of the Parkallen community
requested the park in tribute of his "years of
faithful service given so patiently, so untiringly and
with so deep an understanding to our children and
community." Ellingson Park, in the Parkallen
neighbourhood, has an area of 2.76 ha.

Park 1967 SW 4:B1

Emily Murphy, 1919. (CEA EA-10-1970)

Elmwood

Whitemud Drive north to 87 Avenue, 159 Street to 170 Street

Elmwood was originally part of the Town of Jasper Place. Development of Elmwood was begun around 1963 and it was annexed by Edmonton in 1964. A section of Elmwood, approximately 79 Avenue to 87 Avenue and 156 Street to 159 Street, was once called West Lynnwood and was first developed around 1959. In the 1910s, the western portion of Elmwood was named Eureka.

Neighbourhood 1963 SW 3:C1

Elmwood Park

122 Avenue north to Yellowhead Trail, Fort Road west to 82 Street

Formerly Grierson Estate (named after Edward Delgare "Del" Grierson), it was renamed around 1945. Since the area was developed to accommo-date returning veterans, most of the residences were built in the late 1940s and 1950s. Veterans were given elm trees to plant along the boulevards.

Neighbourhood 1945 NE 7:C1

Elsinore

174 Avenue to 180A Avenue, 97 Street to 105 Street

As with other names in the Castle Downs area, the name Elsinore is taken from a European castle. The original Elsinore Castle, in Elsinore, Denmark, was made famous by Shakespeare's *Hamlet*. The Dutch Renaissance-style castle was built between 1574 and 1584 by Frederick II and replaced an earlier fortress. It boasted a 61-metre-long banquet hall and a commercial and maritime museum. It was used as a barracks from 1785 to 1922 and completely restored in the late 1920s.

Neighbourhood 1982 NW 10:C1

Elsinore Close

West of 97 Street, south of 174 Avenue, north of 173A Avenue

See Elsinore.

Road   1989   NW   10:C1 *

Elsinore Place

West of 97 Street, south of 174 Avenue, north of 173A Avenue

See Elsinore.

Road   1989   NW   10:C1 *

Emily Murphy Park

11904 Emily Murphy Park Road

Emily Murphy (1868–1933) was the first female police magistrate in the British Empire (1916). The City's Names Advisory Committee originally decided to name the park "Jancy Canuck," Murphy's pen name, but Murphy's daughter convinced the committee to change the name before it went to City Council. Murphy was born in Ontario and came to Edmonton in 1907. Already a popular author, she lobbied for provisions in the Dower Act that entitled a woman to part of her husband's estate. She campaigned for female suffrage, and became a judge in 1916. Her efforts in the Persons Case, as part of the Famous Five, saw women legally declared to be "persons," giving women the right to become members of the Senate. The Emily Murphy Park is located in the river valley and has an area of 11 ha.

Park   1958   C   7:B2

Emily Murphy Park Road

Joins Saskatchewan Drive and Groat Road, bordering Emily Murphy Park

See Emily Murphy Park.

Road   1958   C   7:B2 *

Empire Park

Whitemud Drive north to 51 Avenue, Calgary Trail west to 111 Street

Although not developed until the 1960s and 1970s, the 1.05-ha. Empire Park has existed since the early 1910s. The name is probably a reference to the British Empire; many early Edmontonians were of British origin. Its original boundaries were west of 107 Street to 110A Street and south of 51 Avenue to 45 Avenue.

Neighbourhood   1910   SW   4:B2

Empire Park

4804–107 Street

Empire Park is in the Empire Park neighbourhood and has an area of 1.05 ha. *See* Empire Park *neighbourhood.*

Park   1983   SW   4:B2

End of Steel Park

30 Tommy Banks Way

In 1891, the Calgary and Edmonton Railway came to South Edmonton (as the Town of Strathcona was known until 1899). The development of the railway network was crucial to the growth and prosperity of Strathcona. "End of steel" refers to the terminus of the railway line. End of Steel Park is located in the Strathcona neighbourhood and has an area of 0.93 ha.

Park   1991   C   7:C2

Ermineskin

23 Avenue to 30 Avenue, Calgary Trail west to 111 Street

Chief Ermineskin of Hobbema was the Cree chief who headed the group located in the Ermineskin Indian Reserve No. 138, established in the 1880s, just south of Wetaskiwin at Bear Hills. The members of the group were among those who signed Treaty No. 6. This neighbourhood follows

Chief Ermineskin, first left of cairn, commemorating treaty between Cree and Blackfoot, 1927. (CEA EA–10–2503)

the Aboriginal naming theme of the Kaskitayo area in which it is located.

Neighbourhood 1975 SW 4:B2

Ermineskin

23 Avenue to 34 Avenue, Calgary Trail west to 111 Avenue

See Ermineskin *neighbourhood.*

Subdivision 1975 SW 4:B2 *

Ermineskin Park

10704–25 Avenue

Ermineskin Park is in the Ermineskin neighbourhood and has an area of 8.91 ha. *See* Ermineskin *neighbourhood.*

Park 1990 SW 4:B2

Ermineskin Trail

From 178 Street to 184 Street north of 89 Avenue

The name of this trail, a major walkway in the Belmead neighbourhood, reflects the theme of most of Edmonton's walkways, which are named for prominent Aboriginal people or bear a relationship with Aboriginal heritage. Ermineskin Trail is one of a number of trail names approved between 1969 and 1971. *See* Ermineskin *neighbourhood.*

Walkway 1971 SW 8:C2 *

Eusebio Garcia Park

9225–179 Avenue

Dr. Eusebio Garcia (b. 1930) has made important contributions to the Hispanic community. He was born in Spain in 1930 and emigrated to Edmonton in 1956. Dr. Garcia was instrumental in bringing the first Spanish-speaking church service to Edmonton in 1975. He served as president of the Ibero American Cultural Society and was the founding president of the Spanish Cultural Society in Edmonton. The Eusebio Garcia Park is in the Lago Lindo neighbourhood and has an area of 0.73 ha.

Park 1985 NE 10:C1 *

Evansdale

144 Avenue to 153 Avenue, 82 Street to 97 Street

Harry Marshall Erskine Evans (1876–1973) was the mayor of Edmonton in 1918. Evans was born in Ontario and moved to Edmonton in 1907, where he established a finance company. He was president of Edmonton Board of Trade in 1916, chairman of the Alberta Coal Commission in 1925, and served as a financial advisor to the provincial government. He received the Order of the British Empire in 1946. In 1961, the Evansdale neighbourhood, along with much of the land extending from the Dickinsfield subdivision to Beverly, was annexed to Edmonton. Most of Evansdale's development took place in the 1970s.

Neighbourhood 1967 NE 10:C2

Evansdale Park

9123–150 Avenue

The Evansdale Park is in the Evansdale neighbourhood and has an area of 4.16 ha. *See* Evansdale.

Park 1984 NE 10:C2

F.W. Barclay Park

14613–90 Avenue

F.W. "Slip" Barclay (1900–1984) was an Edmonton magistrate from 1954 to 1970. Barclay was born in Ontario and moved to Edmonton in 1912. After serving in WWI, he studied law, graduating in 1925. In 1949 Barclay was appointed sheriff, clerk of the court and magistrate for Wetaskiwin. In 1953 he was transferred to Edmonton as RCMP court magistrate, and in 1954 appointed the magistrate of Edmonton's municipal courts. He retired in 1970. Barclay died soon after this park was named in his honour. The F.W. Barclay Park is in the Parkview neighbourhood and has an area of 0.34 ha.

Park 1984 SW 8:D2

Fairway Drive

Joining Westbrook Drive and 119 Street

This name is descriptive; Fairway Drive runs alongside the Derrick Golf and Country Club.

Road 1963 SW 4:B2

Faith Clifton / Alan Macdonald Memorial Park

13725–101 Avenue

Edmonton actress Marguerite "Mickey" Macdonald requested that a park in the Glenora neighbourhood be named in honour of her mother and husband. Faith Clifton (1901–1959) was born in Saskatchewan and came to Edmonton around 1932. Clifton was involved in Edmonton's early theatre groups and was instrumental in opening Edmonton's original Canadian National Institute for the Blind building in 1949. In recognition of her 23 years of service, Clifton was made the organization's first life member. Macdonald's husband was the Edmonton-born lawyer Alan F. Macdonald (1913–1981). They were married before Macdonald went overseas to serve in WWII. He was awarded the Order of the British Empire. After the war he resumed his position with the City, retiring in 1973. Macdonald was also active with the Kiwanis Club and Edmonton's community theatres. The Faith Clifton/Alan MacDonald Memorial Park in the Glenora neighbourhood has an area of 0.43 ha.

Park 1997 NW 7:A2

Falconer Court

South of Rabbit Hill Road, west of Terwillegar Drive, east of Riverbend Road

See Falconer Heights.

Road 1989 SW 4:A2*

Falconer End

South of Rabbit Hill Road, west of Terwillegar Drive, east of Riverbend Road

See Falconer Heights.

Road 1989 SW 4:A2*

Falconer Gate

South of Rabbit Hill Road, west of Terwillegar Drive, east of Riverbend Road

See Falconer Heights.

Road 1989 SW 4:A2*

Falconer Heights

Falconer Road north to Rabbit Hill Road, Terwillegar Drive west to Riverbend Road

James F. Falconer (b. 1916) was involved in the formation of the Names Advisory Committee in 1956 and served on the committee until 1979. He was a school board trustee for 15 years, beginning in 1953, and was elected to city council in 1955 and 1957. For 27 years he served continuously on civic boards and committees.

Neighbourhood 1980 SW 3:D2

James F. Falconer, 1957. (CEA EA-267-509)

Falconer Link

South of Rabbit Hill Road, west of Terwillegar Drive, east of Riverbend Road

See Falconer Heights.

Road   1989   SW   4:A2 *

Falconer Place

South of Falconer Road

See Falconer Heights.

Road   1989   SW   4:A2 *

Falconer Road

South of Rabbit Hill Road, west of Terwillegar Drive, east of Riverbend Road

See Falconer Heights.

Road   1989   SW   4:A2

Farnell Close

East of Falconer Road, north of Ferguson Place

See feature story, page 100.

Road   1989   SW   4:A2 *

Father Ivor Daniel Park

7415–18 Avenue

Father Ivor J.E. Daniel was a Roman Catholic priest who ministered overseas during WWI, in Edmonton and as a missionary in British Columbia. Born in England in 1883, he moved to Edmonton sometime after 1906. Father Daniel was ordained in 1913 and assigned as an assistant priest at St. Joachim's Church. With the outbreak of WWI, he was sent overseas to serve as a chaplain. When he returned he ministered at St. Joseph's Church before accepting missionary duties in British Columbia. Father Daniel also served as a justice of the peace, acted as a juvenile court judge, translated the "Appendix to the Roman Ritual," and was the author of *Travelling for Christ* and a series of missionary sketches that appeared in the *Catholic Register* in 1922. The Father Ivor Daniel Park is in the Ekota neighbourhood and has an area of 1.33 ha.

Park   1986   SE   1:B1

Ferguson Place

East of Falconer Road, between Ferris Way and Farnell Close

Kathleen "Kay" Ferguson was an Edmonton Public School Board teacher for 35 years. Aside from her teaching duties, she acted as a consultant for five Edmonton schools and helped develop a unique science course for inclusion in the public school curriculum. Ferguson retired from Kildare Elementary School in 1976.

Road   1989   SW   4:A2 *

Farnell Close

EDMONTON-BORN Margaret "Peggy" O'Connor Farnell (1916–2004) was an agent for the British Secret Intelligence Service (SIS) during WWII; from 1942 to 1945 she worked in Central America, South America and the Caribbean for the SIS. Farnell attended the University of Alberta, where she majored in French and German, and Simmons College in Boston, where she studied library science. In 1937 Farnell returned to Edmonton and began working as a reference librarian at the Rutherford Library at the University of Alberta. The outbreak of war in Europe, however, soon brought dramatic changes to her life.

With the help of a friend in Toronto, Farnell made contact with the British Secret Service in New York, and was soon hired as a secret agent. She later said she had no idea she had applied for a job as a spy. Farnell was stationed at the British Security Coordination headquarters in New York for one year, working for the head of western hemisphere operations, Sir William Stephenson—the man called Intrepid. After a year in New York, she held one-year postings in Port-au-Prince, Haiti, and Montevideo, Uruguay, where she worked for the SIS station chief. In Haiti, among her many responsibilities, Farnell reported on German submarine activity and decoded cables.

After the war Farnell returned to Edmonton. She married WWII veteran Gordon Farnell and raised three sons. She also resumed her position at Rutherford Library, where she worked from 1963 to 1981, when she retired as head of the Humanities and Social Sciences Library. In 1982, with the expiry of a 35-year secrecy limit under Britain's Official Secrets Act, Farnell granted several interviews about her wartime work to local media. Farnell is the author of *Old Glenora*, a history of the neighbourhood where she was born and lived for most of her life. Her parents were George Bligh O'Connor, an Alberta Supreme Court Chief, and Margaret Farlie O'Connor, a journalist and theatre critic.

Peggy Farnell, 1995. (Photo courtesy Farnell family.)

Firefighters, circa 1913. (CEA EA-10-2704)

Ferris Way

East of Falconer Road, south of Ferguson Place

W.D. "Grace" Ferris (d. 1962) was one of the first
Canadian women to work in England's military
canteens during WWI. Ferris was born in Toronto
and came to Edmonton in 1904. When her husband
went overseas during WWI, she joined him, and
became one of the first Canadian women to work
for the British army. Ferris was active in social and
community work in Edmonton and served as a
school trustee from 1930 to 1936. She helped
organize the Local Council of Women in 1908, a
children's home and the YWCA. Ferris was also
active in the Imperial Order Daughters of the
Empire and the Women's Canadian Club.

Road 1989 SW 4:A2 *

Fire-Fighters' Memorial Plaza

10318–83 Avenue

Located west of the Walterdale Playhouse
(formerly Fire Hall #6) in the Strathcona neighbourhood, this plaza honours the nine Edmonton
firefighters who have lost their lives in the perform-
ance of their duties. The centerpiece of the plaza is
a life-size bronze sculpture by Edmonton artist
Danek Mozdzenski depicting a firefighter on a
ladder rescuing a little girl. The Fire-Fighters'
Memorial Plaza has an area of 0.15 ha.

Park 1999 C 7:C2 *

Flight Line Road

East of 121 Street, north of Kingsway

This road is in the Edmonton City Centre Airport.
A "flight line" is a parking and servicing area for
airplanes.

Road 1987 NW 7:B1

Jasper Avenue and 91 Street looking south across the river to Forest Heights, circa 1915. (CEA EA-302-6)

Floden Park

10906–40 Street

Charles Floden (1879–1960) was a mayor of the Town of Beverly. He came to Beverly around 1910, and over the next fifty years served on the school board and the town council. He was mayor of Beverly from 1951 to 1957. In September 1959, after residents petitioned city council, a park was named in his honour. Floden Park is in the Beverly Heights neighbourhood and has an area of 4.21 ha.

Park 1967 NE 6:A1

Forbes Close

South of Rabbit Hill Road, north of Falconer Gate

M.M. "Jerry" Forbes (1923–1981) was the manager of CHED radio station and a dynamic force behind Santas Anonymous, a charity event in support of underprivileged children. Forbes was born in Innisfail, Alberta, but lived most of his life in Edmonton. After returning from WWII, he worked at CFRN radio. In 1954 he joined the fledgling CHED radio. In 1955 he organized the first Santas Anonymous toy drive.

Road 1989 SW 4:A2 *

Forbes Way

East of Riverbend Road, south of Rabbit Hill Road

See Forbes Close.

Road 1989 SW 4:A2

Forest Capital Trail

River valley trail between John Walter Museum and the north end of the Whitemud Nature Reserve

The City of Edmonton was designated the National Forestry Capital of Canada for 1994. Forest Capital Trail marks this honour.

Walkway 1994 C 7:B2

Forest Heights

98 Avenue north to Rowland Road, Wayne Gretzky Drive west to Forest Heights Park

Windsor Realty first developed Forest Heights in 1911. It is assumed that the owner of Windsor Realty, James H. McKinley, an Edmonton alderman from 1909 to 1911, chose the name. Although this area became part of Edmonton in 1913, it remained agricultural land until the late 1940s, development beginning only after the end of WWII. The area between 72 Street and 79 Street and 106 Avenue and the river valley was once called West Capilano.

Neighbourhood CU NE 7:D2

Forest Heights Park

10104–84 Street

Forest Heights Park is in the Forest Heights neighbourhood and has an area of 25.5 ha. *See* Forest Heights.

Park 1960 NE 7:C2

Forest Lane

East of Falconer Road, south of Falconer Gate

Jean Forest (b. 1926) is a member of the Senate and was the first woman chairperson of the Edmonton Catholic School Board. Forest was born in rural

Reconstructed fort at Fort Edmonton Park, 1973. (CEA EA-20-640)

Manitoba and came to Edmonton in 1947. In addition to the school board, she also served on the Alberta Human Rights Commission and the University of Alberta Board of Governors and Senate. She was the University of Alberta's first woman chancellor and in 1983 was awarded an honorary Doctor of Laws degree. Forest was named to the Order of Canada in 1987 and appointed to the Canadian Senate in 1996.

Road   1989   SW   4:A2 *

Forsland Park

8003–99 Avenue

Staff Sgt. Erling F. Forsland (1905–1985) was a member of the Edmonton police force from 1935 to 1970. Forsland was born in Ontario and came to Edmonton in 1912. Forsland Park is in the Forest Heights neighbourhood and has an area of 2.34 ha.

Park   1983   SE   7:D2

Fort Edmonton Park

7000–143 Street

The reproduction of Fort Edmonton at Fort Edmonton Park most closely resembles the final structure as it appeared about 1846. Fort Augustus was established in 1795 by the North West Company (NWC) across the North Saskatchewan River from what is now Fort Saskatchewan. Later that same year the Hudson's Bay Company (HBC) built Edmonton House, also called Fort Edmonton, beside Fort Augustus. In 1802 both forts were rebuilt on the north bank of the North Saskatchewan River, near the present-day Rossdale Water Treatment Plant. After being moved 80 kilometres downstream, the two forts were returned to the city area in the winter of 1812–1813. The HBC and the NWC merged in 1821. In 1830 Fort Edmonton was rebuilt on the bank of the North Saskatchewan River, just below the present-day site of the Alberta Legislature Building. Fort Edmonton Park is located just north of the Brander Gardens neighbourhood and has an area of 62.73 ha.

Park   1966   SW   4:A1 *

Fort Edmonton Park Road

Fort Edmonton Park

This road is the entrance to Fort Edmonton Park. *See* Fort Edmonton Park.

Road 1987 SW 4:A1 *

Fort Hill

106A Street north of 87 Avenue

This road was previously known as Old Fort Hill Road and may have originated at the turn of the nineteenth century, when Aboriginal people travelled down the south bank of the North Saskatchewan River to cross the river and trade at Fort Edmonton. In 1875, John Walter built a house directly across the river from where Fort Edmonton then stood. This road ran through his property and led to the ferry he operated, transporting passengers and cargo across the river.

Road 1973 C 7:B2 *

Fort Road

115 Avenue and 86 Street northeast to 227 Avenue NE and 17 Street NE

See feature story, page 105.

Road 1962 NE 10:D2

Fortway Drive

Connects River Valley Road to 107 Street

This road was called Fortway because it provided access from the North Saskatchewan River to Fort Edmonton (on the bank of the North Saskatchewan River, just below the present-day site of the Alberta Legislature). Before being officially named, it was sometimes referred to as Parliament Hill Road.

Road 1964 C 7:C2 *

Fox Drive

Connects Whitemud Drive to Belgravia Road

Thomas Fox (1909–1995) was a WWII pilot, a champion horseman, race-car driver and airline operator. Born in British Columbia, Fox moved to Edmonton in 1941. He was involved in numerous organizations and projects, including the Edmonton Community Chest and the YMCA. Fox was inducted into Canada's Aviation Hall of Fame in 1983. Thomas and his wife, Clara, donated land in the Whitemud area to the City. The Names Advisory Committee (NAC) originally approved Foxdale Drive as the name of this road. City Council did not, however, approve this recommendation, and the name was revised by the NAC.

Road 1968 SW 4:B1

Frank and Etta Wild Park

9503–178 Street

North Dakota-born Frank (1881–1944) and Etta (1892–1971) Wild were early settlers in the area now known as Winterburn Industrial. The Wilds, married in 1914, came to Alberta and settled their land in 1915. The Frank and Etta Wild Park is in the Terra Losa neighbourhood and has an area of 5.4 ha.

Park 1996 SW 8:C2 *

Frank Oliver Memorial Park

9955 Jasper Avenue

The unveiling ceremony for the 0.27-ha. Frank Oliver Memorial Park in the Downtown neighbourhood took place on August 17, 1964. *See* Oliver.

Park 1963 C 7:C2 *

Fort Road

THE ORIGINAL FORT ROAD was little more than a dirt track. It was part of the fur trade trail system stretching east to Lower Fort Garry (Winnipeg). Known as the Carleton Trail after Fort Carlton, located midway along the route, it was established in the mid-1800s. By the 1880s, Fort Road had gained importance as the trail connecting the booming communities of Fort Saskatchewan and Fort Edmonton. The journey was considered a difficult one, with lengthy diversions to avoid swamps and other hazards. In 1883, a resting place for weary travellers, known as the Halfway House, was built northeast of Fort Edmonton.

Fort Road was a crucial link between the two forts and traffic was heavy: on just one morning in 1905, 175 teams were said to be on the trail. The route was gravelled in 1926 and oiled in 1930.

It has also been known as Fort Saskatchewan Road, Fort Saskatchewan Trail and Fort Trail. Fort Road, as it is now known, originally wound its way from Jasper Avenue through northeast Edmonton to Fort Saskatchewan. One of the earliest published references to its existence is an 1884 report in the *Edmonton Bulletin* newspaper in which the roadway was referred to as the "old" Fort Saskatchewan Trail.

Fort Saskatchewan is located about 35 kilometres northeast of Edmonton. The North West Mounted Police established Fort Saskatchewan in 1875, making it the force's second post (the first was Fort Macleod) and the first in the region. When the national transcontinental railway was first surveyed in the 1870s, a more northerly route was being considered. For a time it was thought that Fort Saskatchewan would become the major centre in the vicinity, much to the displeasure of Fort Edmonton. In an attempt to ensure Canadian sovereignty north of the 49th Parallel, another path was chosen, and in 1883 the Canadian Pacific Railway's route took it through Calgary to the south. Fort Saskatchewan became a town in 1904 and a city in 1985.

Fort Trail (now Fort Road), circa 1909. (CEA EA–500–17)

TRANSIT HOTEL

Frank Oliver Park, September 1964. (CEA EA-97-805)

Fraser

144 Avenue to 153 Avenue, proposed outer ring road west to Victoria Trail

Like other neighbourhoods in the Clareview subdivision, Fraser is named for an Edmonton pioneer. John Fraser (1840–1919) was the son of Hudson's Bay officer Colin Fraser. Born at Jasper House, Fraser apprenticed to the Hudson's Bay Company as a boat builder and dog driver. In 1871, Fraser moved to the "lower settlement" (now known as Highlands neighbourhood) and homesteaded there.

Neighbourhood 1979 NE 11:B2

Fraser Park

14720–21 Street

Fraser Park is in the Fraser neighbourhood and has an area of 3.04 ha. *See* Fraser.

Park 1986 NE 11:B2

Fraser Ravine

East from 147 Avenue and 15 Street

See Fraser.

Ravine CU NE 11:B2

Fred A. Morie Park

9004–100 Street

Fred A. Morie (d. 1981) transformed land that was being used as a garbage dump into a park. Beginning in 1944, Morie beautified this open space that local residents had turned into a waste site. City Council originally approved "Morie Park," however, Morie wished to have his full name associated with the park. The Fred A. Morie Park in the Strathcona neighbourhood has an area of 0.29 ha.

Park 1965 C 7:C2

Fulton Creek

Flowing northwest from the eastern city limits south of Whitemud Drive to the North Saskatchewan River at the Capilano Bridge

The Fulton family homesteaded land near the creek in the Clover Bar area. Leander Fulton (b. 1839) came west from Nova Scotia in 1883 and a year later was joined by his wife and their children. Their eldest son, Daniel, farmed an area near his father's and, in 1889, Daniel and his wife built their first home there. They named it Burnside, after the Scottish word for creek, because of its proximity to Fulton Creek. As the name Fulton Creek was noted on a federal government map of 1903, it is likely that it had been in use for some time before. The course of Fulton Creek has been interrupted by city development between approximately 72 Avenue at 46 Street, and Terrace Road at 67 Street.

Creek CU SE 5:A1 *

Fulton Drive

Connecting to and south of 106 Avenue, northwest of 63 Street

See Fulton Creek.

Road 1956 NE 7:D2

The road crossing Fulton Ravine from Burnside, the Fulton's Farm, 1931. (CEA EA-160-1728)

Fulton Place

101 Avenue to 106 Avenue, 50 Street west to Fulton Drive

See Fulton Creek.

Neighbourhood 1956 NE 7:D2

Fulton Place Park

10340–56 Street

This park is in the Fulton Place neighbourhood and has an area of 1.93 ha. *See* Fulton Creek.

Park 1982 NE 7:D2

Fulton Ravine

Along the course of Fulton Creek; north of 101 Avenue at 67 Street

See Fulton Creek.

Ravine CU NE 7:D2

Fulton Road

West of 50 Street, connecting 103 Avenue with 63 Street

See Fulton Creek.

Road 1956 NE 7:D2

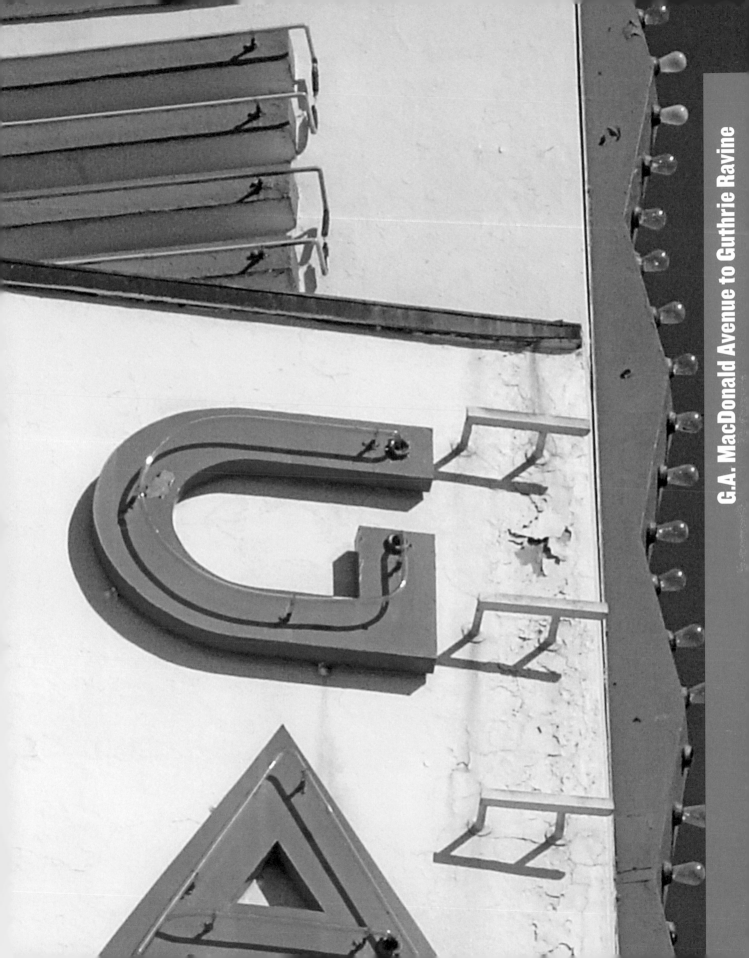

G.A. MacDonald Avenue

Between Calgary Trail and Gateway Boulevard at 39A Avenue

George A. MacDonald (b. 1929) was born and raised in Wainwright and worked with Dun and Bradstreet before moving to the Alberta Motor Association (AMA) as an assistant accountant in 1951. In 1964 MacDonald became the president and chief executive officer of the AMA, the position he held until his retirement in 1991. Active in the community, he has also served on many boards including the Edmonton Junior Chamber of Commerce, the Yellowhead Interprovincial Highways Association, and the Mayfair Golf and Country Club. The AMA's administration centre is located on this road.

Road   1992   SW   4:C2 *

G. Edmund Kelly Park

14909–79 Street

George Edmund Kelly (1886–1972) was one of the province's first electrical engineers and played an important role in the provision of electricity to rural Alberta. Kelly was born in Edmonton and established Alberta's pioneer electrical utility industry before joining Canadian Utilities in 1927. In the decades that followed, he compiled a preliminary report on rural electrification and arranged for the supply of power to Canada's first electrically driven oil well pumping unit. During WWII he introduced the use of electricity on farms. Kelly retired from Canadian Utilities in 1951 and was made an honorary director of the company. The G. Edmund Kelly Park is in the Kilkenny neighbourhood and has an area of 2.11 ha.

Park   1984   NE   10:C2

G.M.V. Bulyea Park

East of Terwillegar Drive, west of Bulyea Road

An error occurred in the official naming of this park, leaving the initials for George Hedley Vicars

George Gagnon, 1904. (CEA EA-10-669.22)

Bulyea incorrect. The G.M.V. Bulyea Park is in the Bulyea Heights neighbourhood and has an area of 2.2 ha. *See* Bulyea Heights.

Park   1984   SW   4:A2

Gagnon Estate Industrial

123 Avenue north to CN railway tracks, 149 Street to 163 Street

This neighbourhood was most likely named for George Gagnon, who once owned the land on which Gagnon Estate Industrial is now located. Gagnon came to the region in 1873 and settled along the St. Albert Trail. He was a resident of Edmonton and the St. Albert area until his death in 1912 at the age of 79.

Neighbourhood   CU   NW   8:D1

Gainer Industrial

Sherwood Park Freeway north to Whyte Avenue, 50 Street to 71 Street

John Gainer (1858–1938) was an Edmonton pioneer businessman whose name remains synonymous with the meat-packing industry. Born in Canada West, Gainer moved to Strathcona and in 1891 opened a butcher shop on Whyte Avenue. Gainer's was incorporated in 1911 and a new plant established near the Mill Creek Ravine, south of Whyte Avenue.

Neighbourhood 1968 SE 5:A1

Galbraith Close

South of 69 Avenue, east of Glastonbury Boulevard

Scottish-born Alexander Galbraith (1853–1928) was an early educator at agricultural schools. Galbraith emigrated from Scotland to the United States in 1883. There, he formed a partnership with his three brothers and became an importer and breeder of Clydesdale, Suffolk and Shire horses. After the firm's collapse in 1893, Galbraith went to work as a lecturer at the Farmers' Institute at the University of Wisconsin. In 1901 he moved to Manitoba and in 1915 to Edmonton. In Edmonton, he became the provincial superintendent of fairs and institutes and was a lecturer at agricultural schools in the province.

Road 1998 SW 3:B1 *

Galbraith Gate

Connecting Galbraith Close to Glastonbury Boulevard

See Galbraith Close.

Road 1998 SW 3:B1 *

Gallagher Park

Cloverdale Road north to 97 Avenue, Cloverdale Road west to 95 Street

This area was originally known as Grassy Hill but was renamed in honour of Cornelius Gallagher (1854–1932), an Edmonton pioneer who had owned the land, the riverside portion of which had been known as Gallagher Flats. Born in New Brunswick, Gallagher came to Edmonton in 1891 and went on to serve as alderman and mayor. Gallagher Park is located in the Cloverdale neighbourhood and has an area of 6.52 ha.

Park 1958 SE 7:C2 *

Galland Close

West of Glastonbury Boulevard, south of 69 Avenue

Arthur Galland (b. 1872) left Ontario at the age of 19 and moved west, first to Saskatchewan, then Winnipeg, Manitoba, and later, in 1913, to Edmonton. In Edmonton, he was employed by the Arctic Ice Company. After two years, Galland purchased an interest in the company and eventually became the owner and manager.

Road 2000 SW 3:B1 *

Galland Crescent

East of Glastonbury Boulevard, south of 69 Avenue

Originally called Garnett Crescent, Galland Crescent was renamed in April 2000 and the name Garnett reassigned to another road. *See* Galland Close.

Road 2000 SW 3:B1

Gariepy

River valley north to Callingwood Road, 170 Street to 178 Street

Joseph Hormidas Gariépy (1852–1927) was a pioneer businessman, real estate investor and

Looking northeast over Garneau, 1930. (CEA EA-10-159)

politician. Gariépy was born in Canada East, now Quebec, and came to Edmonton in 1893. That same year he bought a lot on Jasper Avenue at the corner of McDougall Avenue (now 100 Street) and opened a general store. Gariépy was also a town alderman for Edmonton from 1897 to 1898.

Neighbourhood   1972   SW   3:C1

Gariepy Crescent

East of 172 Street, south of Callingwood Road

See Gariepy.

Road   1976   SW   3:C2

Gariepy Park

17404-57 Avenue

This park is in the Gariepy neighbourhood and has an area of 2.45 ha. *See* Gariepy.

Park   1982   SW   3:C1

Garneau

Whyte Avenue and University Avenue north to Saskatchewan Drive, 107 Street to 112 Street

Laurent Garneau (1840–1921) was of Métis descent and is believed to have been born in Michigan. He later moved to the Red River Colony in Manitoba, and in 1869 took part in the Red River uprising under Louis Riel, which led to the formation of Manitoba in 1870. By 1874 he had moved west to Fort Edmonton and by 1883 had been granted River Lot 7 in the Edmonton Settlement, on the south side of the North Saskatchewan River. He was active in local affairs and politics. After 1901, Garneau moved to St. Paul. His property, known as "The Garneau," became part of the Town of Strathcona, and later, in 1912, part of Edmonton. That part of Garneau south of Whyte Avenue was part of a subdivision formerly known as Strathcona Place.

Neighbourhood   CU   C   7:B2

Garneau Park

10943–84 Avenue

Garneau Park is in the Garneau neighbourhood and has an area of 0.63 ha. *See* Garneau.

Park 1984 C 7:B2

Garnett Close

Encircled by Garnett Way

Lt. Col. Charles E. Garnett (1887–1970) was a WWI veteran and prominent businessman. He was born in England and emigrated to Canada in 1910, arriving in Edmonton after the war. Garnett worked as a sales engineer for Gorman's Ltd. until 1928, at which time he bought the company. He then started the Edmonton Elevator Service. During WWII Garnett served in the Canadian Army Reserve. He was active in many business associations and served as chairman of the board of the Great Northern Gas Utilities for 15 years, and president of the Edmonton Chamber of Commerce and the Edmonton Chamber of Mines and Resources.

Road 1999 SW 3:B1 *

Garnett Court

West of Garnett Way, north of Guardian Road

See Garnett Close.

Road 1999 SW 3:B1 *

Garnett Way

West of 199 Street, north of Guardian Road

See Garnett Close.

Road 1999 SW 3:B1 *

Garside Industrial

114 Avenue to 118 Avenue, 149 Street to 156 Street

Thomas Emsley Garside (1890–1958) was a King's Counsel who spent 36 years working for the City.

Laurent Garneau, with Eleanor, and the fiddle that made nights merry. (CEA EA-58-3)

Garside emigrated from England to Edmonton and attended the University of Alberta. After serving overseas in WWI, he returned to Edmonton and beginning in 1920 was employed by the City as a legal clerk. He became a City solicitor in 1934 and retired in 1956.

Neighbourhood 1967 NW 8:D1

Gateway Boulevard

North from city limits to Saskatchewan Drive, east of 104 Street

Calgary Trail Northbound and 103 Street were renamed Gateway Boulevard as part of a business-sponsored beautification project. The area along the roadway was landscaped and trees were planted in order to improve the roadway's appearance. The name was chosen because Edmonton is often called

*Calgary Trail north, now Gateway Boulevard,
circa1960s. (CEA EA–275–1270)*

the "Gateway to the North" and because the
roadway is a major corridor into the city.

Road   2000   SE   4:C2

Gateway Park

2404 Calgary Trail Southwest

The site represents a gateway to the city because of
its location and function. Gateway Park offers
tourist information services, an oil industry inter-
pretive centre and park area. The original derrick
from Imperial Leduc No. 1, the starting point of
Alberta's oil boom in 1947, has been reassembled
on this site. Gateway Park has an area of 9.58 ha.

Park   1986   SW   1:A2 *

George Close

North of Glastonbury Boulevard

John "Jack" George (b. circa 1918) had a distinguished military record, receiving the
Distinguished Service Order in 1953 for his
"strength of action in early December (1952) when
the Canadian Forces carried out several midnight
raids and captured Communist positions" in Korea.
George's first experience with the military came
when he enlisted with the Loyal Lancashire
Regiment before WWII. After the war, he held
civilian jobs, including a stint from 1949 to 1951 as

Edmonton's Assistant Building Inspector. He re-
enlisted in May 1952, and was wounded in action in
Korea later that year. After receiving training at
Kingston in 1953, George was appointed company
commander in the Second Battalion of the Royal
Canadian Regiment, First Canadian Light Infantry
Brigade, and was posted to Germany. George
retired from the military in 1961.

Road   2001   SW   3:B1 *

George F. Hustler Memorial Plaza

98 Avenue and 96 Street

George Francis Hustler (1882–1958), an ordained
minister and WWI veteran, was the principal of
Bennett School from 1924 to 1945. Hustler was
born in England and came to Edmonton in 1909.
He founded the Cloverdale Community League
and in 1961 was inducted into Edmonton's Sports
Hall of Fame in recognition of his coaching of local
sports teams. The Bennett School Alumni spoke
affectionately of him on the 75th anniversary
reunion of Bennett School in 1988. At that time
they committed themselves to creating a suitable
monument in his memory. The Bennett School,
located at 9703–94 Street, was closed in 1973. In
1981 the Edmonton Public School Board reopened
the facility as the Bennett Environmental
Education Centre. The George F. Hustler Memorial
Plaza has an area of 0.76 ha.

Park   1989   SE   7:C2 *

Germaine Dalton Park

West of 57 Street, north of 123 Avenue

Germaine Dalton (1913–1984) was a veteran
community newspaperwoman. She was born in
Quebec and came to Edmonton in 1942. In 1953
Dalton started the *Beverly Page*, a community newspaper, and worked as its editor and publisher until
1977. The Germaine Dalton Park is located in the
Newton neighbourhood and has an area of 0.9 ha.

Park   1990   NE   6:A1 *

Giovanni Caboto Park was once known as Patricia Park, 1946. (CEA EA-20-6252)

Gillespie Crescent

South of Glastonbury Road

Dr. Alexander Gillespie (b. 1854) was a prominent member of Edmonton's medical community, arriving here in 1906. He was born in Canada West and graduated from the Trinity Medical College at the University of Toronto in 1884. Gillespie then took postgraduate work in Scotland, earning his Licentiate of the Royal College of Physicians. After practising medicine in Manilla, Ontario, for 11 years, he moved, in 1895, to Lindsay and practised for another 11 years. He then relocated to Edmonton where he spent the remainder of his career.

Road   1999   SW   3:B1 *

Giovanni Caboto Park

9403–109A Avenue

Formerly named Patricia Square (Patricia Park), this park lies in the centre of the Italian District on 95 Street north of the downtown. The Italian community petitioned to have this park renamed in honour of Giovanni Caboto (John Cabot), the Italian navigator and explorer. Caboto landed on the North American coast, most likely Newfoundland or Cape Breton Island, in 1497. The Giovanni Caboto Park is located in the McCauley neighbourhood and has an area of 1.78 ha.

Park   1981   NE   7:C1

Girard Industrial

CN railway tracks north to Argyll Road, Sherwood Park Freeway west to 75 Street

Girard Industrial, or Girard Place as it was originally called, may have been named after Napoleon Girard, who farmed in the area in the early part of the 20th century. A 1914 source listed him as owning land around 98 Street and 83 Avenue. The Girard Place subdivision, dating from 1913, was replotted in 1965 and 1966 and became known as Girard Industrial. During the 1910s, a portion of this area was known as the Eden subdivision.

Neighbourhood   1965   SE   4:D1

Girard Road

South of 76 Avenue, east of Argyll Road

See Girard Industrial.

Road   1965   SE   5:A1

Glastonbury

South of Whitemud Drive, west of 199 Street

The developers wanted the names of The Grange area to evoke a period in England's past when estates were known as granges. Glastonbury, the name of a monastery in England, reflects this theme. One legend associated with Glastonbury is that of King Arthur. According to the ancient story, Glastonbury was the place where the Holy Grail was kept and where King Arthur and Queen Guinevere were buried.

Neighbourhood   1990   SW   3:B1

Glastonbury Boulevard

West of 199 Street at 69 Avenue

See Glastonbury.

Road   1998   SW   3:B1

Glastonbury Court

North of Glastonbury Boulevard

See Glastonbury.

Road   1998   SW   3:B1 *

Glengarry

132 Avenue to 137 Avenue, 82 Street to 97 Street

Glengarry replaced the older subdivisions of Sunalta and Namayo Park, which had existed from as early as 1912. Glengarry, meaning "a rough water glen," was named after a glen in Invernesshire, Scotland.

Neighbourhood   1956   NE   10:C2

Glengarry Park

8520–132 Avenue

This park is in the Glengarry neighbourhood and has an area of 8.77 ha. The name was in common usage before the Names Advisory Committee approved it. *See* Glengarry.

Park   1967   NE   10:C2

Glenora

River valley north to 107 Avenue, Groat Road west to 142 Street

The development of the Glenora neighbourhood began in 1906. Land originally owned by Malcolm Groat was bought by Montreal businessman and developer James Carruthers. Carruthers named the area and persuaded the city to bridge Groat Ravine at 102 Avenue. Carruthers placed a caveat on the development, dictating housing standards in the area. The regulations were implemented in order to ensure that Glenora would be an upscale development. In 1909 the Alberta Government built Government House in Glenora as the official residence of the lieutenant-governor.

Neighbourhood   CU   NW   7:A2

Glenora Crescent

Connecting 103 Avenue to Stony Plain Road

See Glenora.

Road 1958 NW 7:B2 *

Glenora Park

10410–136 Street

This park is in the Glenora neighbourhood and has an area of 0.74 ha. *See* Glenora.

Park 1982 NW 7:A2

Glenora Pointe

South of Stony Plain Road at 128 Street

Local residents of the Westmount neighbourhood cul-de-sac petitioned for the road's naming, arguing that the cul-de-sac had a longstanding association with the Glenora neighbourhood. At the north end of road is the Old Glenora School, which operated between 1918 and 1940, and the south end points across the Groat Ravine to the Glenora neighbourhood. *See* Glenora.

Road 2001 NW 7:B2 *

Glenwood

95 Avenue north to Stony Plain Road, 156 Street to 170 Street

This neighbourhood was once part of the Town of Jasper Place, which amalgamated with Edmonton in 1964. It incorporates the former neighbourhood of Westlawn, which was established in about 1912. Glenwood is likely a descriptive name as "glen" means a valley. It has been named since approximately 1907.

Neighbourhood CU SW 8:C2

Glenwood Park

16430–97 Avenue

This park is in the Glenwood neighbourhood and has an area of 1.32 ha. *See* Glenwood.

Park 1982 SW 8:C2

Glenwright Court

West of Glenwright Crescent, north of Glenwright Gate

Nova Scotia-born John W. Glenwright (1875–1951) migrated west with his mother in 1882. After living in Winnipeg for some time, he moved to Calgary in 1908 and then to Edmonton in 1918. In Edmonton, he founded the Alberta Saskatchewan Life Insurance Company, which later became the Commercial Life Assurance Company of Canada. In 1939, the company's head offices were relocated to Toronto and he was transferred there. Glenwright continued to work as the company's managing director until he retired in 1949. While living in Edmonton, he was president of the Edmonton Chamber of Commerce, the Kiwanis Club, and the northern division of the Alberta Motor Association.

Road 1998 SW 3:B1 *

Glenwright Crescent

North of 69 Avenue, west of 199 Street

See Glenwright Court.

Road 1998 SW 3:B1

Glenwright Gate

Connecting Glastonbury Boulevard to Glenwright Crescent

See Glenwright Court.

Road 1998 SW 3:B1 *

Gold Bar

101 Avenue to 106B Avenue, Goldstick Park west to 50 Street

This area was originally known as Gold Bar Farm. The name Gold Bar was in common usage when the neighbourhood was officially named in 1956. The name might be a reference to early prospectors who panned for gold along the North Saskatchewan River.

Neighbourhood   1956   NE   6:A2

Gold Bar Community Park

4620–105 Avenue

This park is in the Gold Bar neighbourhood and has an area of 1.01 ha. *See* Gold Bar.

Park   1987   NE   6:A2

Gold Bar Park

109A Avenue, east of 50 Street

The Gold Bar Park is north and east of the Gold Bar neighbourhood, and has an area of 3.63 ha. *See* Gold Bar.

Park   1973   NE   6:A1

Gold Bar Ravine

East of Gold Bar neighbourhood; south of the North Saskatchewan River to 101 Avenue, east of 40 Street

This ravine is located to the east of the Gold Bar neighbourhood. *See* Gold Bar.

Ravine   1973   NE   6:B2 *

Goldstick Park

101 Avenue and 44 Street

See feature story, page 119.

Park   1984   NE   6:A2

Goodspeed Lane

North of Glastonbury Boulevard, west of George Close

Frederick G. Goodspeed (b. 1881) was the district engineer for the Dominion Public Works for northern Alberta. Originally from eastern Canada, Goodspeed worked on the Georgian Bay ship canal survey from 1904 to 1907. Between 1907 and 1910, he was employed by the Dominion Public Works in St. John, New Brunswick, where he was also an assistant engineer and part-time engineer in charge. In 1910, Goodspeed came to Edmonton to take up his post as district engineer for northern Alberta.

Road   2001   SW   3:B1 *

Gordon Drynan Park

10320–166 Street

Gordon Drynan (1901–1982) was a dedicated volunteer who worked in support of physically handicapped children. Born in Ontario, Drynan moved to Alberta and began working with Canadian National Railways in 1919. He joined the Shriners in 1949, becoming the charity organization's transportation coordinator. Drynan provided transport to train stations, bus depots and airports for thousands of children from Alberta and British Columbia en route to and from treatment at the Shriners' Hospital for Crippled Children in Winnipeg. In 1974 the Edmonton Junior Chamber of Commerce recognized his contributions by naming him the Citizen of the Year. The Gordon Drynan Park is in the Britannia Youngstown neighbourhood and has an area of 1.21 ha.

Park   1985   NW   8:C2

Gorman Industrial East

North of 153 Avenue, 18 Street west to CN railway tracks

George W. Gorman (d. 1942) piloted the first commercial flight in western Canada. He was born

Goldstick Park

Rabbi Hyman Goldstick (1882–1978), Edmonton's first rabbi, and his Edmonton-born son, Cecil "Tiger" Goldstick (1915–), were prominent members of the religious and sporting communities. Latvian-born Rabbi Goldstick came to Edmonton in 1906 to assume teaching and religious leadership of the city's small Jewish community. In 1912 he moved to Edson and served as mayor, town councillor and school board member.

One of four children born to Hyman and Bessie Goldstick, "Tiger" served with the Royal Canadian Navy in WWII and held the navy lightweight wrestling championships for three consecutive years. The diminutive athlete acquired his nickname for his tenacity and volatility in the ring. In 1946, after returning from the war, Tiger was named Outstanding Sportsman of the Year by Edmonton sportswriters and sportscasters.

He went on to have a successful career as a trainer for the Edmonton Eskimos, the Eskimos Baseball Club and the Edmonton Flyers hockey team, and as a radio and television broadcaster for CFRN. He became a household name through his work as host of "Tiger's Den," a featured segment on CFRN-TV's popular children's program *Popcorn Playhouse* that aired in the 1960s and 1970s.

Tiger's contributions to local sports and his generosity to children's causes earned him recognition from local and provincial organizations. He was honorary captain of Edmonton's school patrol for more than four decades. In 1975 he received the Max Bell award for outstanding reporting of amateur sport, and in 1982 he was inducted into the Edmonton Boxing and Wrestling Hall of Fame. He received the Order of Canada in 1990. Goldstick Park is located in the Gold Bar Ravine and has an area of 12.63 ha.

Cecil "Tiger" Goldstick, 1947. (CEA EA–524–78)

in Oregon and came to Edmonton in 1906. Gorman served in WWI and afterwards established an aircraft company. In 1919 he flew a plane to Wetaskiwin, carrying *Edmonton Journal* newspapers. Gorman "delivered" the newspapers by tossing them out of the airplane as he flew. Neighbourhoods in this area of this city are named after pilots.

Neighbourhood 1981 NE 11:B1

Gorman Industrial West

153 Avenue to 167 Avenue, CN railway tracks west to Manning Drive

See Gorman Industrial East.

Neighbourhood 1981 NE 11:B1

Government House Park

128 Street and 102 Avenue

Government House, officially opened in 1913, was home to Alberta's first six lieutenant-governors. In 1951 the federal government purchased Government House and for some years used it as a convalescent home for disabled WWII veterans. In 1964 the provincial and federal governments decided to use the land surrounding Government House for the Provincial Museum and Provincial Archives of Alberta. These opened in 1967 and the control of Government House reverted to the provincial government. Government House was reopened to the public in 1976. There are just under 10 ha. of lawns and gardens surrounding the Glenora neighbourhood mansion. The park-like grounds of the estate overlook the North Saskatchewan River.

Park CU NW 7:B2 *

Gowan Park

South of 78 Avenue, east of 114 Street

Elsie Park Gowan (1905–1999) was an award-winning Alberta playwright and actor. Gowan was

Elsie Park Gowan, 1954. (PAA OS.1809)

born in Scotland and came to Edmonton in 1911. After graduating from the University of Alberta, she began to write plays for the stage and radio. A number of Gowan's plays are based on historical events. In 1954, she wrote a pageant for Edmonton's golden jubilee, "Who Builds a City," that traced the city's growth through the story of one family. She received an honorary degree from the University of Alberta in 1982. Gowan Park is located in the McKernan neighbourhood and has an area of 0.64 ha.

Park 1991 SW 4:B1 *

Graham Court

Intersecting with Graham Gate and Graham Wynd, south of Guardian Road

Thorton Andrews Graham (1886–1982) was a businessman and active in several volunteer organizations. Graham, who moved to Edmonton from Ontario in 1910, started out as a bookkeeper for Western Supplies Ltd., a wholesale plumbing firm. Within 15 years, he held controlling interest in the company and served as its chairman until his retirement in 1975. Graham was a member of the Masonic Order, the Shriners and the Kiwanis Club; from the latter membership, he held the world record for attendance, having not missed a meeting in 54 years.

Road   1999   SW   3:B1

Graham Gate

Connecting Guardian Road to Graham Court

See Graham Court.

Road   1999   SW   3:B1 *

Graham Wynd

South of Guardian Road, west of 199 Street

See Graham Court.

Road   1999   SW   3:B1 *

Grand Meadow Crescent

North of 38 Avenue, east of 66 Street

Located Greenview, Grand Meadow Crescent follows the pattern of similar-sounding names in the neighbourhood, including Granlea Crescent and Greenoch Crescent.

Road   1974   SE   5:A2

Grand Trunk Park

13025–112 Street

This park is named after the Grand Trunk Pacific Railway. Grand Trunk Park is dedicated to the railway pioneers who helped develop Edmonton. It was informally known as Onion Park, apparently because the original property owner grew onions there in a large market garden. Grand Trunk Park is

located in the Lauderdale neighbourhood and has an area of 16.27 ha.

Park   1962   NW   10:B2

Grand View Drive

West of 123 Street, north of 62 Avenue

See Grandview Heights *neighbourhood.*

Road   1973   SW   4:B1

Grand View Park

6223–124 Street

This park is in the Grandview Heights neighbourhood and has an area of 0.74 ha. *See* Grandview Heights *neighbourhood.*

Park   1984   SW   4:B1

Grandisle Point

East of 199 Street, north of 9 Avenue SW

The name of this road refers to the nearby location of the Big Island; Grandisle is French for "big island." In the early 1900s, the island, 25.7 km upstream from Edmonton and 28.3 ha. in size, was a popular recreation and picnic spot. For one dollar, Edmontonians could take *The City of Edmonton*, a sternwheeler owned by John Walter, to the tree-covered island. Picnicking on the island stopped in 1914 and by 1918 the island was abandoned. It was eventually logged. Grandisle Point was previously known as Riverview Crescent.

Road   1982   SW   2:A1

Grandisle Road

East of 199 Street, north of 9 Avenue SW

Grandisle Road was originally named River Valley Street. *See* Grandisle Point.

Road   1982   SW   2:A1 *

Grandisle Way

East of 199 Street, north of 9 Avenue SW

Grandisle Way was formerly known as Valleyview Crescent. Its name was changed to avoid confusion with the already-existing road by the same name in Parkview. *See* Grandisle Point.

Road   1982   SW   2:A1 *

Grandview Heights

62 Avenue north to Grand View Drive, 122 Street west to Whitemud Park

Strathcona was incorporated as a city in the spring of 1907. A month later, Premier A.C. Rutherford announced that a provincial university would be built there. Although this area was outside the Strathcona boundaries, it was subdivided in anticipation of the new city's rapid development and named Grand View Heights. The name probably refers to the view of the river valley and the ravine that border the area. In 1913 this area, as part of Strathcona, was annexed to Edmonton. Grandview Heights was officially adopted as the neighbourhood name in 1956.

Neighbourhood   1956   SW   4:B1

Grange, The

45 Avenue north to Whitemud Drive, 199 Street west to Winterburn Road

A grange is a country house with farm buildings or the dwelling of a gentleman farmer. The names of the neighbourhoods in this area are taken from English history.

Neighbourhood   1984   SW   3:B1 *

Granlea Crescent

North of 40 Avenue at 60 Street

Granlea was the name of an early (1913) Alberta district. A combination of "grain" and "lea" (a meadow or pasture), the name reflected the agricul-

tural nature of the area. Located in Greenview, Granlea Crescent follows the pattern of similar-sounding names in the neighbourhood, including Grand Meadow Crescent and Greenoch Crescent.

Road   1974   SE   5:A2

Grant Court

Encircled by Grant Way

Charles H. Grant (1884–1973) was a prominent lawyer and active member of the community. Born in Ontario, Grant first worked as a school teacher and as an assistant postmaster before moving west in 1905 to study law with A.C. Rutherford (the first premier of Alberta) and F.C. Jamieson. In 1910 he was called to the Alberta Bar. Between 1910 and 1922, Grant practised law with Rutherford and Jamieson and, from 1917 to 1919, he was a city alderman. In 1936, Grant defended a client who refused to accept scrip money issued by the provincial Social Credit government. His client won and the court found that the scrip was not legal tender. In 1923 Grant was one of the first men to drive an automobile from Edmonton to Jasper. The trip took 14 hours and 40 minutes. He was the first president of the Alberta Motor Association and a member of the Council of Edmonton Chamber of Commerce and the National Parks Highways Association. In 1968 he was appointed King's Counsel and received an honorary law degree from the University of Alberta.

Road   1999   SW   3:B1 *

Grant Gate

Connecting Grant Way and Grantham Drive

See Grant Court.

Road   1999   SW   3:B1 *

Grant Moellmann Bridge

Spanning the LRT tracks at Wayne Gretzky Drive

Grant Moellmann (1935–1994) was a construction foreman who lost his life building this bridge. For 44 years, Moellmann was a respected ironworker in Edmonton. He was involved in the construction of a number of building projects in Edmonton, including the Jubilee Auditorium, the Kinsmen Fieldhouse and the Rossdale Power Plant, and was recognized as a leader in the structural steel and construction industry.

Bridge 1995 NE 7:D1

Grant Notley Park

11603–100 Avenue

Walter Grant Notley (1939–1984) was a leader of the New Democratic Party (NDP) of Alberta. Born in Didsbury, Alberta, Notley graduated from the University of Alberta and soon became involved in politics. In 1962 he was named the first provincial secretary of the Alberta NDP and in 1968 became provincial leader of the party. From 1971 until his death in an airplane crash, he represented the riding of Spirit River/Fairview in the Legislative Assembly. Following the election of 1982, he became leader of the opposition. The Grant Notley Park is in the Oliver neighbourhood and has an area of 1.69 ha.

Park 1985 C 7:B2

Grant Way

South of Guardian Road, east of Whitemud Drive

See Grant Court.

Road 1999 SW 3:B1

Grantham Drive

West of Grant Way, south of Guardian Road

Manitoba-born Madge Grantham (d. 1961) was a hospital worker, editor and volunteer. A graduate of Brandon College, Madge Grantham moved to Edmonton in 1946 and worked at the Charles Camsell Hospital as a member of the education staff. Grantham was responsible for providing support to nonresident Aboriginal and Inuit patients, many of whom travelled long distances to receive health care and were without relatives or family in Edmonton. Grantham later founded and served as editor of the *Camsell Arrow*, a hospital publication. She was a member of the Imperial Order Daughters of the Empire (IODE), the University Women's Club and the Business and Professional Women's Club. Before being named, Grantham Drive was known as 205 Street.

Road 1999 SW 3:B1

Graunke Park

South of 34 Avenue, east of 50 Street

William (d. 1983) and Mary (d. 1985) Graunke were homesteaders in south Edmonton. Born in what is now Mill Woods, William continued the family tradition, farming land that had belonged to his father. The Graunkes were active church members, and Bill was a member of the Old Timers' Association. Graunke Park is in the Weinlos neighbourhood and has an area of 2.33 ha.

Park 1994 SE 5:A2

Graydon Court

Encircled by Glenwright Crescent

George Hughes Graydon (1858–1940) was a member of the North West Mounted Police and a prominent pharmacist. Born in Canada West, Graydon graduated from the Ontario College of Pharmacy in 1876 and came west with the NWMP in 1886. In 1891, he left the police and joined the drug firm of Martin, Bole, Wynne and Co. in Winnipeg. In 1894, he opened his own drugstore in Edmonton. Graydon was an honorary president of the Canadian Pharmaceutical Association, president

Grierson Hill, [date]. (CEA EA-275-331)

of the Alberta Retail Druggists' Association and a lifetime member of the Alberta Pharmaceutical Association.

Road 1998 SW 3:B1 *

Greenfield

34 Avenue to 40 Avenue, 111 Street to 119 Street

Herbert Greenfield (1867–1949), leader of the United Farmers of Alberta Party, was Premier of Alberta from 1921 to 1925. He was born in England and came to Alberta to homestead in 1906. After his retirement from politics, Greenfield became a successful businessman working in the oil industry. Greenfield neighbourhood is located in the Petrolia subdivision, the naming theme of which is the petroleum industry.

Neighbourhood 1962 SW 4:B2

Greenfield Park

3755–114 Street

This park is in the Greenfield neighbourhood and has an area of 3.13 ha. *See* Greenfield.

Park 1983 SW 4:B2

Greenoch Crescent

North of 40 Avenue, west of 50 Street

Located in Greenview, Greenoch Crescent follows the pattern of similar-sounding names in the neighbourhood, including Grand Meadow Crescent and Granlea Crescent. Greenoch is a port on the Firth of Clyde in Scotland.

Road 1974 SE 5:A2

Greenview

38 Avenue north to the Mill Woods Golf Course, 50 Street to 66 Street

This neighbourhood overlooks the Mill Woods Golf Course, hence the name Greenview. Some roads in this neighbourhood are named, and incorporate the word green or refer to open green spaces: Grand Meadow Crescent, Granlea Crescent, Greenoch.

Neighbourhood 1974 SW 5:A2

Greenview Park

5804–38 Avenue

This park is in the Greenview neighbourhood and has an area of 0.79 ha. *See* Greenview.

Park 1983 SW 5:A2

Grierson Hill

South of 101 Avenue at 95 Street

The prominent landowner and politician Edward Delgare "Del" Grierson (1861–1922) owned the Queen's Hotel on Jasper Avenue and 98 Street, and in 1903 rebuilt the Alberta Hotel across the street. Both buildings overlooked the hill. In the early part of the 1900s this road, which did not then run all the way down the hill, was called Grierson Street. In 1933 City Council renamed it Grierson Avenue. The road later became known as Grierson Hill. *See* Delton.

Road 1973 C 7:C2

Griesbach Road

97 Street and 146 Avenue

Maj. Gen. William Antrobus Griesbach (1878–1945) was a veteran, lawyer and the city's youngest ever mayor. W.A. Griesbach had a law firm in Edmonton in the early 1900s and served as an alderman from 1903 to 1905. He was mayor in 1907 at the age of 29. From 1917 to 1921 he served as member of parliament. In 1921 he was named to the Senate and commissioned as a major general for his service to the armed forces. Griesbach had a long military career, serving in the Boer War (1899–1902), WWI (1914–1918) and, as Inspector General of Western Canada, WWII (1939–1945).

William A. Griesbach, circa early 1900s.
(CEA EA-10-1545)

During WWI, Griesbach helped organize Edmonton's 49th Battalion. Griesbach's name was chosen for the roadway after a naming contest was held at the school located on CFB Griesbach. William Griesbach was the son of Arthur Henry Griesbach, one of the first members of the North West Mounted Police.

Road 1992 NW 10:B2

Groat Bridge

Spanning the North Saskatchewan River at Groat Road

Malcolm Groat, a Scottish-born carriage maker and farmer, and one-time employee of the Hudson's Bay Company from 1861, was granted River Lot 2

Groat Road, 1966. (CEA EA-20-5360)

in the original Edmonton Settlement in the early 1880s. In 1903, Malcolm Groat sold portions of his land to William Tretheway, and he, in turn sold it to James Carruthers in 1905. Carruthers subdivided the land, forming Glenora and large estates, known as Groat Estates, on the east bank of the ravine. In 1911, Carruthers placed a caveat on Groat Estates, ensuring that no house under $5000 was built in the area and that no building would be closer than 25 feet to the street. The first residents were prominent Edmontonians, who built grand country homes, as the area was still largely undeveloped. Less affluent Edmontonians christened the area "Robber's Row" or "Robber's Roost."

The northern end of the Groat Bridge runs through part of River Lot 2 below Malcolm Groat's 1907 home at 10131 Clifton Place. In 1953 the City of Edmonton Archives and Landmarks Committee recommended that this bridge be named Malcolm Groat Bridge. City Council compromised and named it Groat Bridge. After delays in construction, the bridge was completed in 1955.

Bridge 1954 C 7:B2

Groat Ravine

Separating the Westmount and Glenora neighbourhoods; south of 107 Avenue at Groat Road to the North Saskatchewan River

Malcolm Groat was the original owner of the land this ravine runs through. The name Groat Ravine was in use by 1912. In 1954 Groat Road was constructed in the Ravine. *See* Groat Bridge.

Ravine CU NW 7:B1

Groat Ravine Bridge

Spanning the Groat Ravine at 102 Avenue

Work began on this bridge, originally known as the Iron Bridge, in 1910. *See* Groat Bridge *and* Groat Ravine.

Bridge   CU   NW   7:B2 *

Groat Road

South of 118 Avenue at 132 Street, across the North Saskatchewan River to 87 Avenue

This road was built in 1954 as an approach to the Groat Bridge, via Groat Ravine on the north side and William Hawrelak Park (formerly Mayfair Park) on the south side. *See* Groat Bridge.

Road   1954   NW   7:B1

Grovenor

MacKinnon Ravine north to 107 Avenue, 142 Street to 149 Street

The name Grovenor began to be used after WWII: the Grovenor School (named after the district) was named in 1949 and the Grovenor Community League in 1952. Part of Grovenor neighbourhood, was formerly known as Westgrove, which was developed around 1907. The origin of the name Grovenor is not recorded.

Neighbourhood   CU   NW   7:A2

Grovenor Park

14325–104 Avenue

This park is in the Grovenor neighbourhood and has an area of 1 ha. *See* Grovenor.

Park   1982   NW   7:A2

Guardian Road

West of 199 Street, south of Whitemud Drive

The road's name reflects the area naming theme of monastic images and the Glastonbury neighbour-

Groat Ravine—Taking a walk in the park, circa 1912. (CEA EA 267–185)

hood theme of roads beginning with the letter "G." "Guardian" is defined not only as being one that guards, but also as a superior of a Franciscan monastery.

Road   1990   SW   3:B1

Guinevere Park

1704 Glastonbury Boulevard

This ornamental park was named after Queen Guinevere, the wife of King Arthur, of England's Arthurian legends. The name was requested by area developers because it fit with their proposed Arthurian marketing theme. Guinevere Park is located in the Glastonbury neighbourhood and has an area of 0.61 ha.

Park   1991   SW   3:B1 *

Gurdwara Road

Portion of Mill Woods Road East and Mill Woods Road South

A *gurdwara*, which translates into "house of God," is the Sikh place of worship. There are four gurdwaras in Edmonton, two of which are located in

Grovenor Elementary School, 1968.
(CEA EA-20-4253)

the Mill Woods area. To celebrate the tercentennial of the founding of the Sikh order of Khalsa, a portion of Mill Woods Road East and Mill Woods Road South that connects the two gurdwaras was named Gurdwara Road.

Road   1999   SE   1:C1 *

Guthrie Point

South of 5 Avenue Southwest, east of 207 Street Southwest

This road was formerly known as Ravine Drive. *See* Guthrie Ravine.

Road   1982   SW   2:A1

Guthrie Ravine

West of the North Saskatchewan River at 9 Avenue SW

Paul Guthrie (1904–1993) was a pioneer oilman, rancher and horse breeder. Guthrie was born in Michigan and came to Canada with his parents in 1910, settling near Edgerton. In 1922 he helped build Lloydminster's first gas well and, 25 years later, after oil was discovered in Leduc, set up Leduc's first independent oil well. Later, Guthrie's company discovered oil near Valleyview. After his retirement from the oil field, Guthrie established a ranch and bred Polish Arabian horses. The Guthrie Ravine is located on property he once owned.

Ravine   1982   SW   2:A1 *

H.W. Heathcote Park

West of 119 Street, south of Westbrook Drive

Henry W. Heathcote (1853–1936) emigrated from England to the Edmonton area in 1894. While his family settled near present-day New Sarepta, Heathcote took up work in Edmonton. He was employed at the Imperial Bank of Canada for more than thirty years. The H.W. Heathcote Park is located in the Westbrook Estates neighbourhood and has an area of 0.92 ha.

Park   1983   SW   4:B2 *

Habitat Crescent

North of Hermitage Road at 46 Street to 48 Street

Located in the Homesteader neighbourhood, the name of this road is consistent with the neighbourhood naming theme. A habitat is a locality in which a plant or animal grows or lives.

Road   1973   NE   11:A2

Haddow

Proposed outer ring road north to Heath Road, Terwillegar Drive west to Hector Road

Albert Walker "Bert" Haddow (1884–1958) was Edmonton's city engineer for 40 years. Born in Ontario, Haddow came to Edmonton in 1910 to work for the city engineering department, becoming the city engineer in 1919. Aside from the bridges, underpasses and roads constructed during his tenure as engineer, he can be credited with laying out and supervising construction of the City Centre Airport. Before his retirement in 1950, Haddow was also instrumental in developing the Riverside Golf Course and promoting and implementing the concept of using former landfill sites as recreational areas.

Neighbourhood   1987   SW   3:D2

Albert W. Haddow, left, and A. Latournell, circa 1910. (CEA EA–10–1601)

Haddow Close

North of Riverbend Road, west of 156 Street

This road is a portion of Haddow Drive, renamed Haddow Close in 1996 to enable proper addressing procedures. *See* Haddow.

Road   1996   SW   3:D2

Haddow Drive

West of Terwillegar Drive, south of Riverbend Road

See Haddow.

Road   1996   SW   3:D2

Hagen Way

South of Hunters Green and west of 156 Street

Raymond George Hagen (1895–1983) served in Europe during WWI, and had a long and distinguished career as a public servant with the Alberta Department of Welfare. Hagen was born in Ontario in about 1895. Already a member of the reserves, having enlisted with the 97th Regiment Algonquin Rifles in 1910, Hagen joined the active army in 1915, after the outbreak of WWI. He saw action in the battles of the Somme, Vimy Ridge and Amiens, was decorated with the Military Medal and received a field commission.

Upon returning to Canada in 1919, Hagen married his childhood sweetheart, Margaret, and found work in the insurance business. In 1924 they moved west to the Rabbit Hill district near Edmonton, where Hagen operated his own farm and worked for a nearby farmer. He began a new career in 1935, when he joined the Alberta public service as an accountant. In 1936 he became chief accountant of the Alberta Department of Welfare, and in 1957 was made the deputy minister of that department. During his tenure with the government of Alberta, Hagen was instrumental in organizing early seniors' housing and establishing social welfare courses at the University of Alberta. In 1959, he was the first Albertan ever elected to the National Welfare Council. Hagen retired in 1960, and died in 1983 at age 89.

Road   2002   SW   3:D2 *

Hagmann Estate Industrial

Yellowhead Trail north to CN railway line, 121 Street west to St. Albert Trail

This neighbourhood is part of the land that was farmed by John Hagmann at the turn of the 20th century. In 1898, John Hagmann, a real estate businessman, bought 145 acres (58.7 ha.) from the Hudson's Bay Company for $10 an acre. In 1912, he sold his property for the remarkable sum of $850,000. With the collapse of the speculative land boom in 1913, however, it is unlikely that Hagmann ever received the total amount. The west corner of the Hagmann estate was leased by the Edmonton Airplane Company; the Edmonton City Centre Airport is now situated on this tract of land.

Neighbourhood   CU   NW   7:B1

Hairsine

137 Avenue to 144 Avenue, Victoria Trail west to 36 Street

Albert Hairsine (1906–1979) was mayor of the Town of Beverly from 1948 to 1951. His administration is credited with introducing modern ideas of planning and carrying out badly needed sanitation reforms. Hairsine also established the first industrial subdivision in Beverly after the closing of some area coal mines in the 1930s.

Neighbourhood   1978   NE   11:B2

Hairsine Park

3120–139 Avenue

This park is in the Hairsine neighbourhood and has an area of 2.46 ha. *See* Hairsine.

Park   1987   NE   11:B2

Haliburton Close

South of Haliburton Road, west of Haliburton Court

Edmonton Eskimo Leroy Lawrence Haliburton (1890–1976) was inducted into the Edmonton, Alberta and Canadian Sports Halls of Fame. The champion track and field athlete and football player also coached, refereed and organized amateur sports teams.

Road   1999   SW   3:D2 *

Haliburton Court

South of Haliburton Road, west of Haddow Drive

See Haliburton Close.

Road   1999   SW   3:D2 *

Haliburton Crescent

North of Haliburton Road, west of Haddow Drive

See Haliburton Close.

Road   1999   SW   3:D2 *

Haliburton Road

Connecting Hector Road to Haddow Drive

See Haliburton Close.

Road   1999   SW   3:D2 *

Hamilton Crescent

Off Harvest Road, west of 40 Street

Robert Winslow Hamilton (b. 1911) served as an alderman from 1943 to 1945. Born in England, Hamilton became a chartered accountant after graduating from the University of Alberta.

Road   1973   NE   11:A2 *

Hampton Court

South of Heath Road, west of Holgate Place

Polish-born Stanley John Hampton (1923–1985) held several senior positions during his 28-year career working for the City of Edmonton. Hampton and his family immigrated to Canada, arriving in Edmonton when Hampton was only five years old. After receiving a BSc degree in Engineering at the University of Alberta, Hampton went to work for the City of Edmonton as an electrical engineer in 1946. Five years later he was promoted to chief electrical engineer. In 1965 he was named superintendent of Edmonton Telephones. He became commissioner of utilities and engineering in 1967, and in 1972 was appointed chief commissioner. Heart attacks and a stroke led to his early retirement in 1974. In 1977 Hampton received a Canadian Silver Jubilee Medal in recognition of his almost three decades of public service. Hampton was also active in the community, volunteering for cultural organizations and the Edmonton Exhibition Association.

Road   1997   SW   3:D2 *

Hamptons, The

45 Avenue to approximately 54 Avenue, 199 Street west to Winterburn Road

This neighbourhood is under development. "The Hamptons" is best known as the fashionable residential area on Long Island, New York, but the name originates in the United Kingdom. Early connections include London's Hampton Court, the favourite residence of King Henry VIII (reigned 1509–1547).

Neighbourhood   1998   SW   3:B1

Harbin Road

102 Avenue between 95 Street and 99 Street

See feature story, page 133.

Road   1986   C   7:C2

Hardisty

101 Avenue north to the river valley, 50 Street west to Wayne Gretzky Drive

See feature story, page 134.

Subdivision   1956   NE   6:A2 *

Hardisty Drive

South of the North Saskatchewan River, connecting to and north of 106 Avenue, running to 65 Street

See Hardisty *feature story, page 134.*

Road   1956   NE   6:A1

Harbin Road

EDMONTON WAS TWINNED with the northern Chinese city of Harbin in 1985, following an official visit to Harbin by Edmonton Mayor Laurence Decore. The following year, in May 1986, the mayor of Harbin, Gong Benyan, brought a delegation to Edmonton. During his visit, 102 Avenue from 95 Street to 97 Street was renamed Harbin Road. Harbin Road was later extended to 99 Street and now intersects with Hull Street, which was named for Edmonton's Canadian twin city in Quebec. In honour of the twinning of Edmonton and Harbin, a 4.7-kilometre segment of Xinyang Road, along the route to Harbin's airport, was renamed Edmonton Boulevard.

The city of Harbin is in the northern Chinese province of Heilongjiang; Alberta was twinned with Heilongjiang in the early 1980s. By 2002, the estimated population of Harbin had reached 2.54 million. The twinning of Harbin and Edmonton was promoted as a way to increase trade. The city of Harbin produces leather goods, textiles, metal and mineral products, household appliances and farming equipment.

In the late 1980s, the City flew in construction workers from Harbin to construct the Chinatown Gate, the decorative archway at the entrance of Edmonton's first Chinatown at 102 Avenue and 97 Street. There were also visits to Harbin, on the invitation of the mayor, by Edmonton high school students. A decade later, there was criticism that the twinning of Edmonton and Harbin was merely symbolic and had failed to create business opportunities.

Edmonton Boulevard in Harbin, China, 1985. (CEA EA-353-15)

133

Hardisty

RICHARD HARDISTY (1831–1889) was the chief factor of Fort Edmonton from 1872 to 1882. He was born at Fort Mistassini near James Bay, in present-day Québec, and began working for the Hudson's Bay Company (HBC) in 1849. Hardisty's role as chief factor made him one of Edmonton's pioneer leaders. In 1874 he built the first house outside the walls of the fort, and in 1888 was appointed Alberta's first senator.

Hardisty came from a family of fur traders. His father and his grandfather had also worked for the HBC. He was educated at the Red River Academy at Fort Garry, later known as St. John's College, Winnipeg. Hardisty worked at Fort Garry, Cumberland House, Fort Carlton, Fort Victoria (now known as Pakan), Rocky Mountain House and Fort Edmonton. In 1867 Hardisty married Eliza Victoria McDougall, eldest daughter of Rev. George McDougall, the first Protestant missionary to live in the district.

By the late 1870s, the massive herds of buffalo that had once ranged across the prairies were dwindling rapidly. As chief factor of Fort Edmonton, Hardisty dealt with the imminent disappearance of the buffalo and the very real threat of hunger by establishing HBC cattle ranches. This decision was to bring great change to the region as settlers soon arrived to take part in the increasingly land-based, rather than fur trading, opportunities. Hardisty was also responsible for the building of lumber and flour mills.

In 1888, the same year he became a senator, the HBC promoted Hardisty to inspecting chief factor. He died the next year in Winnipeg after breaking his neck in a road accident. The two-storey Hardisty home, known as the "Big House," was located at the present-day site of the Alberta Legislature.

Richard Hardisty, no date. (CEA EA-10-2095)

Harker Close

North of Hunter's Green

Yorkshire-born Fredrick F. Harker (b. 1879) immigrated to Canada with his family at the age of eight. At the age of 10, then living in Toronto, he began working and in 1893 entered the service of F. Wilson & Co. Eight years later, Harker took work with the Robert Simpson Company. In 1908, he moved to Portland, Oregon, where he commenced employment with the Olds, Wortman and King Department Store. In 1919 Harker accepted the position of general manager with the Edmonton store of the Hudson's Bay Company. He left the company's employ in 1922.

Road   1999   SW   3:D2 *

Harrison Drive

North of Hermitage Road at 45 Street

Arthur Gregory Harrison (1870–1954) was a city commissioner from 1912 to 1918. New Brunswick-born Harrison came to Edmonton in 1896. In addition to his work as a civil servant, he was involved with the Edmonton Board of Trade and the Edmonton Exhibition.

Road   1973   NE   11:A2

Harrow Circle

East of 40 Street at 130 Avenue

The harrow is a farming tool used to till the soil. A set of iron teeth or discs attached to a heavy frame, the harrow is pulled across fallow cropland to break it up and to root up weeds. Harrow Circle follows the naming theme of the Homesteader neighbourhood, in which it is located.

Road   1973   NE   11:B2

Harry Farmer Park

9824–170 Avenue

Harry Farmer (1911–1986) was for many years the organist of the Edmonton Symphony Orchestra and St. Paul's United Church. Farmer was born in England and came to Edmonton in 1958. He was musical director at CFRN-TV for 15 years, and choirmaster and organist at St. Paul's United Church for 21 years. He was also the music director of the Alberta Opera Society and organist for the Edmonton Symphony Orchestra. As well, Farmer launched a recreation centre for seniors. Harry Farmer Park is in the Baturyn neighbourhood and has an area of 0.73 ha.

Park   1984   NW   10:C1

Harry Hardin Park

5620–101A Avenue

Harry F. Hardin (1899–1979) was a pharmacist and the owner of several drugstores. Born in Ukraine, Hardin came to Edmonton in 1912. He graduated from the University of Alberta in 1927. He operated a drugstore in Forestburg until 1938, then became the proprietor of a number of drugstores in Edmonton, retiring from business in 1972. The Harry Hardin Park is in the Fulton Place neighbourhood and has an area of 0.27 ha.

Park   1986   SE   6:A2

Harvest Road

North of Hermitage Road at 40 Street

This road is in the Homesteader neighbourhood; its name follows the agrarian theme.

Road   1973   NE   11:A2 *

Haswell Close

Southwest of Haswell Way

English-born George Frederick Haswell (1891–1961) served in both the Boer War and WWI. In 1910, he immigrated to Edmonton and then enlisted in the 10th Battalion in 1915. He returned to Edmonton in 1919 and established a plumbing business. Haswell was president of the

Boer War Veterans group, an honorary life member of the Army and Navy War Veterans' Association and active in the Royal Canadian Legion.

Road 1999 SW 2C1 *

Haswell Court

West of Haswell Way

See Haswell Close.

Road 1999 SW 2:C1 *

Haswell Cove

North of Haswell Way, west of Haddow Drive

See Haswell Close.

Road 1999 SW 2:C1 *

Haswell Gate

Connecting Haswell Road to Haddow Drive

See Haswell Close.

Road 1999 SW 2:C1 *

Haswell Place

Intersecting Haswell Way and Haswell Gate

See Haswell Close.

Road 1999 SW 2:C1 *˙

Haswell Way

South of Hector Road, west of Haddow Drive

See Haswell Close.

Road 1999 SW 2:C1

Hawin Park Estate Industrial

118 Avenue to 123 Avenue, 156 Street to 163 Street

William Hawrysh was the manager of a real-estate company, Hawrysh Agency, that was active in the

1950s. Luke Winterburn was a real estate agent, buying and selling Edmonton property as early as 1913. The name of this neighbourhood is a combination of their names. An industrial area, it was annexed by the City of Edmonton in 1964, along with the adjacent Town of Jasper Place. The name of Hawin Park Estate did not appear on maps until the late 1950s.

Neighbourhood CU NW 8:D1

Hawkins Park

North of 25 Avenue, east of 46 Street

William Forbes McLeod Hawkins (1872–1960) was an area pioneer whose original purchase of land in southeast Edmonton has remained in the Hawkins family for five generations. He was also a member of the East Edmonton District School Board for 22 years. Hawkins Park is in the Weinlos neighbourhood and has an area of 0.41 ha.

Park 1983 SE 5:A2 *

Haynes Close

North of Heath Road

Elizabeth Sterling Haynes (1898–1957) was an arts pioneer who contributed to Alberta theatre for more than 30 years. Haynes not only acted but served as a producer and director of live theatre. She was the founder of the Alberta Drama League, the Dominion Drama Festival, the Edmonton Little Theatre, the Women's Theatre Guild and the Studio Theatre.

Road 1997 SW 3:B2 *

Hayter Road

North of Yellowhead Trail, west of Meridian Street

Henry "Harry" W. Hayter (1900–1974) was born in Prince Edward Island and served in WWI. He earned his pilot's licence in 1927 and in 1932 established his own air operation at Fort McMurray.

During WWII he managed an aircraft maintenance plant in Edmonton. Hayter retired from professional flying in 1950, and was named to Canada's Aviation Hall of Fame in 1973.

Road 1982 NE 6:B1

Hayward Crescent

North of Hodgson Boulevard, east of Rabbit Hill Road

George E. Hayward (b. 1882), founder of Hayward Lumber Company, began his career in Manitoba at the age of 18 with the Hanbury Manufacturing Company. He was later transferred to British Columbia, and, in 1905 moved to Vermilion, Alberta where he founded the Hayward Lumber Co. Initially selling lumber from a tent, he soon gained enough capital to build a frame structure. With the influx of settlers, his business swelled and he purchased the Northern Lumber Company of Edmonton in 1915. The following year, he transferred his head office from Vermilion to Edmonton. Hayward's business grew, and in 1919 he purchased an entire block adjoining his property. Branches were soon opened throughout Alberta and the Pacific coast.

Road 2001 SW 4:A2 *

Hazeldean

63 Avenue to 72 Avenue, Mill Creek Ravine Park west to 99 Street

In 1907, this area was annexed to the City of Strathcona. By 1910, it had been subdivided and named Hazeldean. Although its origin is not recorded, the name may have been descriptive. Two species of hazelnuts, the American hazelnut and beaked hazelnut, are native to the area. Hazels are small bushes or trees that have nuts as their fruit. A dean is a vale or a valley.

Neighbourhood CU SE 4:C1

Hazeldean Park

9630–66 Avenue

This park is in the Hazeldean neighbourhood and has an area of 0.87 ha. *See* Hazeldean.

Park 1981 SE 4:C1

Heacock Road

South of Rabbit Hill Road, southeast of Heffernan Drive, northwest of Riverbend Road

Ontario-born Kenneth E. Heacock (1887–1964) was a long-time RCMP officer. He joined the Alberta Provincial Police in 1917 and was posted to Athabasca and Vegreville. He became an RCMP sergeant in the 1930s and was transferred to Edmonton in 1941. He retired in 1945.

Road 1988 SW 3:D2

Heagle Crescent

Off Healy Road, west of Riverbend Road

H. A. Heagle was the manager of Edmonton's National System of Baking. Born in Ontario, Heagle worked as a salesman, ran a general store and established three bakeries before opening his Edmonton bakery in 1920.

Road 1981 SW 3:D2

Healy Road

West of Riverbend Road, south of Heath Road

Frank J. Healy (1890–1976) was the founder of Healy Motors. Born in Ontario, Healy came to Edmonton in the early 1920s. In 1927 he became a car salesman and in 1932 established Healy Motors. He retired in 1963.

Road 1981 SW 3:D2

Heath Road

West of Riverbend Road at 32 Avenue

William G. Heath (b. 1890) was a long-time employee at Alberta College. He was born in Ontario but moved west and joined the college in 1913. Heath was the registrar at the college for 50 years, retiring in 1963.

Road 1981 SW 3:D2

Heavener Bay

South of Heacock Road, east of Heffernan Drive

Edythe Heavener (1918–1990) was the founder of Alberta's oldest established dance school. A native Edmontonian, she co-founded the Heavener School of Dance and Physical Culture in 1936. Heavener was the first Alberta teacher to receive a scholarship to the National Ballet School of Toronto and was instrumental in bringing examinations for the Royal Academy of Dance and the Imperial Ballet to Alberta. She was also a founding member of the Alberta Professional Dance Teachers' Association. In 1978 she was the recipient of an Excellence Award for Dance from the Alberta government.

Road 1990 SW 3:D2 *

Hector Place

East of Hector Road

Sir James Hector (1834–1907) was a surgeon and geologist with the famed Palliser Expedition, the scientific exploration of the Rocky Mountains and prairies that set out in 1857. On the expedition, Hector's horse kicked him and rendered him unconscious for several hours; Kicking Horse Pass, 60 km northwest of Banff, is named for this incident. During the expedition, Hector stopped several times at Fort Edmonton. After completing his expedition service in 1860, Hector was appointed geologist to the New Zealand government in 1865. He retired in 1903.

Road 1974 SW 3:D2 *

Hector Road

North of 23 Avenue, west of Holgate Place

See Hector Place.

Road 1974 SW 3:D2

Hedley Way

West of Heath Road at 30B Avenue

Robert W. Hedley (1871–1965) was a pioneer in Alberta art education. Born in Ontario, Hedley came to Edmonton in 1912. He was the art supervisor in Edmonton public schools from 1914 to 1929, and a lecturer at Edmonton Normal School for the next several years. After retirement, Hedley became the director of the Edmonton Museum of Arts and an art critic. In 1953 he was awarded an honorary doctorate of law degree by the University of Alberta.

Road 1981 SW 3:D2 *

Heffernan Close

North of Heffernan Drive

Jeremiah W. Heffernan (b. 1884) was a pioneer lawyer. Born in Ontario, he came to Edmonton in 1912. Heffernan was a prosecuting attorney in 1914, a Crown prosecutor from 1914 to 1919, and made King's Counsel in 1921. From 1921 to 1926 he was an MLA.

Road 1981 SW 3:D2 *

Heffernan Drive

West of Heath Road at 31 Avenue

See Heffernan Close.

Road 1981 SW 3:D2

Hegler Crescent

West of Heath Road, east of Heffernan Drive

Michigan-born Herbert S. Hegler (b. 1873) was an early Edmonton businessman, arriving in the city in

The Henderson family and its famous round barn, 1898. (CEA EA-80-4)

1910. He was involved in a number of local businesses, including real estate, construction and insurance. He was stationed in Edmonton during WWI.

Road 1981 SW 3:D2

Hemingway Road

West of 199 Street, south of 53 Avenue

Peter G. Hemingway (1929–1995) emigrated from England to Canada in the 1950s, responding to the government of Alberta's demand for more architects. Initially, he worked with the Alberta Department of Public Works, but later left to pursue a career in the private sector, first in partnership with Charles Laubenthal and later as sole proprietor. Hemingway was a notable Edmonton modernist architect. He was the first Alberta architect to be awarded the Massey Medal for

Architecture, an honour he received twice. Among his most outstanding projects were the Coronation Swimming Pool, the Stanley Building, the Muttart Conservatory, and the Central Pentecostal Tabernacle Building.

Road 2002 SW 3:B2 *

Henderson Estate

Heagle Crescent north to Rabbit Hill Road, Riverbend Road west to river valley

Thomas Henderson (1837 or 1838–1926) was a pioneer who homesteaded in the Riverbend area in the 1800s. After living in Ontario and British Columbia, Henderson and his family came to the Edmonton area in 1880. The family farmed on several homesteads before finally settling near Rabbit Hill. In 1888, while travelling in eastern Canada, Henderson shipped Italian bees to his farm.

W. J. Hendra, no date. (CEA EA-10-2071)

These bees are said to have been the first swarm of honeybees in Edmonton. After seeing similar structures in Ontario and Florida, Henderson built a round barn in 1898. This barn is one of the few remaining round barns and can be seen at Fort Edmonton Park. This neighbourhood bears Henderson's name because his homestead was located nearby, 1.6 km west of Whitemud Creek on 23 Avenue in the Rabbit Hill area.

Neighbourhood 1979 SW 3:D2

Henderson Park

East of Henderson Street, north of Hendra Crescent

This park is in the Henderson Estate neighbourhood and has an area of 3.51 ha. *See* Henderson Estate.

Park 1990 SW 3:D2 *

Henderson Street

North of Heath Road

See Henderson Estate.

Road 1981 SW 3:D2

Hendra Crescent

North of Heath Road, west of Riverbend Road

William J. Hendra (1878–1966) was a choral leader and founder of the Edmonton Male Chorus. Born in Wales, Hendra came to Edmonton in 1906 as a stonemason. His interest and training in music motivated him in 1908 to found the Alberta Music Festival. In 1911 he organized the Edmonton Male Chorus. Hendra was for decades a church choir conductor and a teacher at Alberta College.

Road 1981 SW 3:D2

Henri Legay Park

West of 50A Street, south of 141 Avenue

Henri Legay owned land around 137 Avenue and Manning Drive that he donated to the Roman Catholic church. A school was built on the site in 1955. The Henri Legay Park is in the York neighbourhood and has an area of 1.13 ha.

Park 1995 NE 11:A2 *

Henrietta Louise Edwards Park

Between 98 Avenue and the North Saskatchewan River, east of the Low Level Bridge to 89 Street

See feature story, page 141.

Park 1989 SE 7:C2

Henry Avenue

North of Hermitage Road, west of Homestead Crescent

William T. Henry (1870–1952) was the mayor of Edmonton between 1914 and 1917. Henry was born in Prince Edward Island and came to

Henrietta Louise Edwards Park

HENRIETTA LOUISE (MUIR) EDWARDS (1849–1931) was one of Canada's most important feminists and the legal adviser for the "Famous Five." In 1927, at the age of 78, Edwards joined Nellie McClung, Emily Murphy, Irene Parlby and Louise McKinney in a petition demanding that Canadian women be granted the status of "persons" under the British North America Act, therefore making them eligible to hold a seat in the Senate.

On March 14, 1928, the Supreme Court of Canada met to consider the question put to it by the five Alberta women: "Does the word 'person' in Section 24 of The British North American Act include female persons?" Five weeks later, the Court gave its ruling: "No, it does not." With the support of then Prime Minister Mackenzie King, the Famous Five appealed the ruling to the Judicial Committee of the Privy Council in London, then the highest court of appeal. On October 18, 1929, the five-member Privy Council ruled unanimously in favour of the petition, declaring women to be "persons" and clearing the way for women to hold all public offices.

Edwards was responsible for much of the backroom work required for the "Persons Case," preparing legal opinions, carrying out research and writing letters. She was already a recognized authority on the law, having written two handbooks on legal matters affecting women, *Legal Status of Women in Canada* (1917) and *Legal Status of Women in Alberta* (1925).

Edwards was born and raised in Montreal. As a young woman, she established the Working Girls' Association in downtown Montreal, a forerunner to the Young Women's Christian Association. She also published Canada's first women's magazine, *Women's Work in Canada*. In addition, Edwards helped found the National Council of Women in 1893 and the Victorian Order of Nurses in 1897. She served as provincial president of the Council of Women and later was the chair of the National Council of Laws.

Edwards and her husband, Dr. Oliver Cromwell Edwards, moved to Fort Macleod, in southern Alberta, in 1903. Dr. Edwards was posted there as medical officer to the Blood Indian Reserve, west of Lethbridge. Together, they had three children.

The Henrietta Louise Edwards Park is in the river valley, to the north of the Muttart Conservatory, and has an area of 14 ha.

Henrietta Louise Muir Edwards, no date. (PAA PA.3665)

Edmonton in 1893. At the beginning of the 1900s, he was an Edmonton alderman, and from 1924 to 1926 was a member of the provincial legislature.

Road   1973   NE   11:B2

Henry Singer Park

14940–142 Street

Henry Singer (1911–1980) was one of Edmonton's leading personalities. Singer, the son of a clothing merchant, was born in Saskatchewan. After a number of years in the music business and a short stint at his father's store, Singer opened a men's clothing store in Edmonton. He served with the Royal Canadian Air Force in WWII (he was the first man in the Force's entertainment unit), returning to his clothing business after the war.

Singer was involved in the revival of the Edmonton Eskimos football team, served on its board of directors, and was a colour commentator on radio broadcasts. For his efforts, Singer was inducted into Edmonton's Sports Hall of Fame in 1981. He served as president of the B'nai B'rith and the Better Business Bureau; headed the United Way campaign; was instrumental in establishing a games competition for the handicapped in Edmonton; was one of the originators of the Klondike Days theme; and wrote the children's book *Little Johnnie Greenhorn*. The Henry Singer Park is within Rampart Industrial and has an area of 56.8 ha.

Park   1989   NW   9:D2

Henson Close

North of Herring-Cooper Way, east of Heffernan Drive

Percy H. Henson (1891–1975) was a talented artist who also served as Director of the Edmonton Art Gallery. He was born in England, and came to Canada in 1910. In 1950, after decades working for the YMCA, he took up the senior post at the Edmonton Art Gallery. Henson was also an instructor in the Extension Department of the University of Alberta. As well, he painted the *Now No More* series, which earned him the Performing and Creative Arts Award from the City of Edmonton in 1971, and the Performing and Creative Arts Award of Distinction from the Alberta Historical Society in 1974. Henson was also president of the Edmonton Art Club, a member of the Alberta Society of Canadian Painters and Engravers, and an original member of the Visual Arts Board of Alberta.

Road   1990   SW   3:D2 *

Hepburn Avenue

Connecting Heffernan Drive and Henderson Street

Charles Hepburn (1879–1961) was a pioneer businessman and an alderman. Born in Ontario, Hepburn came to Edmonton in 1907. In 1909 he opened a confectionery, which he ran until 1924. Hepburn later managed a second candy store and manufactured a brand of potato chips under his name. He was elected as an alderman in 1918.

Road   1981   SW   3:D2 *

Herb Link Park

South of Dunluce Road, west of Warwick Road

Dr. Herb Link (1953–1994) was a well-known dentist and soccer enthusiast who lived in the Dunluce neighbourhood. He graduated from the University of Alberta in 1978. In 1988 Link was given an Ambassador of the City award after he chaired the Canadian Dental Association's annual convention. He was also involved in organizing, playing and coaching soccer. Link suffered a head injury and died at the age 40 after colliding with another player while playing soccer at the Kinsmen Sports Centre. The Herb Link Park is in the Dunluce neighbourhood and has an area of 5.66 ha.

Park   1994   NW   10:B1

Herbert Hart Park

16103–88 Avenue

Herbert "Bert" Hart (1883–1960) was an early city employee. Hart was born in England and came to Edmonton in 1910. In 1913 he joined the Edmonton Telephone Department. He served in WWI and in 1919 rejoined the telephone department, retiring in 1948. The Herbert Hart Park is in the Meadowlark Park neighbourhood and has an area of 0.46 ha.

Park   1982   SW   8:D2

Heritage Trail

*Connecting downtown to the High Level and
Low Level Bridges*

The Heritage Trail walkway is part of a circuit that begins in the downtown core and extends westward along the upper portion of the river valley, crossing the North Saskatchewan River on the High Level Bridge and the Low Level Bridge. This promenade traces the path that once connected the Hudson's Bay Company's Fort Edmonton to Edmonton's original downtown. The walkway was constructed by the City's Program to Improve Downtown Edmonton (PRIDE).

Walkway   1989   C   7:C2 *

Hermitage

*CN tracks north to Kennedale Ravine, river valley
west to 50 Street*

The first district headquarters of the Church of England was established in this area in the late 1800s by the Rev. Canon William Newton (1828–1912). Newton called the settlement The Hermitage (the home of a hermit or a secluded dwelling). The Canon Ridge, Homesteader and Overlanders neighbourhoods are within the Hermitage subdivision. *See* Newton.

Subdivision   1967   NE   6:B1 *

Hermitage Park

1496 Hermitage Road

Between 1969 and 1979, the City of Edmonton acquired parcels of land in the Hermitage area. By 1979 the area had been turned into a park and included in the Capital City Recreation Park system. Hermitage Park is in the Hermitage subdivision and has an area of 36.81 ha. *See* Hermitage.

Park   1979   NE   6:B1

Hermitage Road

*East from 50 Street to Victoria Trail, north of
Yellowhead Trail*

See Hermitage.

Road   1973   NE   11:B2

Herring-Cooper Way

Connecting Heacock Road with Heffernan Drive

Irish-born William Herring-Cooper (1860–1930) was an early pioneer who immigrated to Canada in 1880 and joined the North West Mounted Police. Later, he moved to Edmonton and from 1893 to 1910 was the territorial/provincial licence inspector. In 1897, at a special ceremony given in his honour by Cree bands from Stony Plain, Hobbema and Onion Lake, Herring-Cooper was made honorary chief of the Cree and given the title of Mekupuckiwan. In 1912 he moved to St. Albert.

Road   1990   SW   3:D2 *

Hetu Lane

South of Herring-Cooper Way

Bertha Hétu (1864–1943) was a pioneer woman entrepreneur. After immigrating to Canada from England, Hétu settled first in Lethbridge, where she lived for a decade before moving to Edmonton in 1898. She bought the Queen's Hotel at 9733 Jasper Avenue in 1902 and ran it until 1936.

Road   1990   SW   3:D2 *

High Level Bridge under construction, 1911. (CEA EA-134-1)

Hewes Way

53 Street and 23 Avenue

See feature story, page 145.

Road 1984 SE 1:C1

Hewgill Place

East of Heffernan Drive, north of Herring-Cooper Way

Col. William H. Hewgill (b. 1874) was a businessman with a distinguished military career. Hewgill was born in Ontario and enlisted in 1902. In 1910 he came to Edmonton and entered the insurance business before going overseas with the Alberta Battalion. When WWI ended, Hewgill returned to Edmonton and in 1923 became the manager of a pharmaceutical company. He was a recipient of the Order of the British Empire (Military Division).

Road 1990 SW 3:D2 *

High Level Bridge

Spanning the North Saskatchewan River at 109 Street

The High Level Bridge was designed by P.M. Motley, a bridge engineer for the Canadian Pacific Railway, and constructed between 1910 and 1913 at a cost of $2 million. The 8,000-ton steel bridge, held together by 1.4 million rivets, was the first in Canada to carry four different modes of traffic— rail, streetcar, automobile and pedestrian. The first passenger train, seven cars long with 200 passengers, crossed the bridge from Strathcona to Edmonton on June 2, 1913.

The High Level Bridge is approximately 0.8 km long and stands 46.3 metres above the mean river level. The construction of the High Level Bridge was a significant engineering achievement for the time and remains a distinctive city landmark. For Alberta's 75th anniversary in 1980, local artist Peter Lewis created the Great Divide Waterfall, which

Hewes Way

ELIZABETH "BETTIE" JANE HEWES (1924–2001) was a long-serving politician and community volunteer. Born in Ontario, Hewes came to Edmonton in 1949. For ten years, beginning in 1974, she served as an alderman. In 1984, Hewes became the first woman chair of CN Rail.

From 1986 to 1997, Hewes was a Liberal member of the Alberta Legislature; from 1988 to 1994 she was deputy leader of the Liberal Party; in 1994 she served as interim Liberal leader. During Hewes' brief leadership, the Liberals, as the *Edmonton Journal* described it, "hammered" the ruling Conservatives. At the time of her election in 1986, Hewes became the first Liberal woman to sit in the legislature since Nellie McClung in 1921.

Throughout her career in provincial politics, Hewes considered herself an advocate for women and seniors. The public also strongly identified her with health and social services. In the 1993 election, Hewes led all candidates in Alberta, receiving more votes than Premier Ralph Klein.

Hewes received an occupational therapy degree from the University of Toronto in 1944. She was active with the Canadian Mental Health Association, serving as the Edmonton branch's executive director from 1964 to 1967; in 1967 she became the planner and acting director of the Edmonton Social Planning Council and established the Women's Emergency Shelter and the Edmonton Society for the Retired and Semi-Retired; and sat on many public and community service boards. She was also one of the founders of Urban Reform Group Edmonton (URGE), a civic party, and the Urban Design Group, a nonprofit organization that sought to improve public architecture and preserve historic buildings in Edmonton.

Bettie Hewes, circa 1985. (CEA EA-340-1457)

Highlands streetcar, 1942. (CEA EA-201-3)

cascades off the bridge's upper deck on special occasions during the summer months, including Canada Day on July 1.

Bridge CU C 7:B2

High Park

107 Avenue to 111 Avenue, 149 Street to 156 Street

This neighbourhood was formerly part of the Town of Jasper Place, which was annexed to the City of Edmonton in 1964. High Park has existed as an area name since around 1912. It may have been named after one of the two High Parks in northeast England.

Neighbourhood CU NW 8:D1

High Park

11032–154 Street

This park in the High Park neighbourhood and has an area of 0.71 ha. *See High Park neighbourhood.*

Park 1982 NW 8:D1

High Park Industrial

111 Avenue to 114 Avenue, 149 Street to 156 Street

The Town of Jasper Place began to develop its industrial areas in the 1950s. Among them was High Park Industrial, which has existed since at least 1953 and is adjacent to the neighbourhood of High Park. *See High Park neighbourhood.*

Neighbourhood 1953 NW 8:D1

Highlands

Ada Boulevard north to 118 Avenue, 50 Street to 67 Street

Now, in the early 21st century, the Highlands neighbourhood can boast some of Edmonton's best preserved historic homes and streetscapes, dating from 1912. In the 1880s, this area was known as the "lower settlement" and was originally owned by three Hudson's Bay Company employees who were bought out by J.A. McDougall in 1888. By 1910 the real estate developers Magrath, Holgate and Company, acting as brokers for McDougall, sponsored a contest to select a name for the district. The judges awarded the prize of $50 in gold to a 19-year-old law clerk, S. Loughlin, who suggested the name "The Highlands," which is descriptive of its position on the banks above the North Saskatchewan River.

In 1910 William J. Magrath and Bidwell Holgate advertised the area as Edmonton's newest "high class" neighbourhood. Its selling features included the healthful, beautiful setting, large lots, and a $2500 minimum cost per house to ensure the standard of building would be high. So enthused were they about the area, they bought out J.A.

McDougall's interest in the land in 1913. Messrs Holgate and Magrath also built houses next to each other on Ada Boulevard in 1912–1913. Their houses were worth $49,000 and $76,000 respectively.

Neighbourhood   CU   NE   7:D1

Highlands Park

11333–62 Street

This park is in the Highlands neighbourhood and has an area of 1.21 ha. *See* Highlands.

Park   1984   NE   6:A1

Hill View Crescent

South of 38 Avenue, west of 50 Street

See Hillview.

Road   1974   SE   4:D2

Hilldale Park

17415–106A Avenue

The origin of the name Hilldale Park is not recorded. This park is in the McNamara Industrial neighbourhood and has an area of 2.23 ha.

Park   1995   NW   8:C2

Hilliard Close

East of Rabbit Hill Road, north of Hodgson Boulevard

Frederick A. Hilliard (1878–1961) was instrumental in the formation of the Alberta Horticultural Association. Hilliard came to Edmonton from Ontario in 1906, and opened a branch of the Dominion Life Insurance Company, a company which had been founded by his father, Thomas Hilliard. An avid horticulturist, Hilliard was noted for his gladiolus, for which he won prizes. Hilliard wrote a weekly gardening column in the *Edmonton Journal* newspaper, and helped to found the Alberta Horticultural Association and the Edmonton

Hillside Crescent area, 1947. (CEA EA-160-323)

Horticultural Society (EHS). For 40 years he was on the board of the EHS, serving as president from 1948 to 1956.

Road   2001   SW   4:A2 *

Hilliard Green

East of Rabbit Hill Road, north of Hodgson Boulevard

See Hilliard Close.

Road   2001   SW   4:A2 *

Hillside Crescent

South of Ada Boulevard at 48 Street

Likely named for its location, Hillside Crescent was renamed from Hillcrest Crescent between 1964 and 1965. Hillcrest Crescent appears in sources dating from 1955.

Road   1965   NE   6:A1 *

Hillview

34 Avenue to 38 Avenue, 50 Street to 66 Street

This neighbourhood is situated on the only hill in the Mill Woods area.

Neighbourhood   1974   SE   5:A2

Hillview Park

East of 58 Street on Woodvale Road East

This park is in the Hillview neighbourhood and has an area of 4.59 ha. *See* Hillview.

Park   1982   SE   5:A2

Hodgson

23 Avenue to approximately 29 Avenue, Whitemud Park west to Rabbit Hill Road

John Hodgson (1888–1969) was the City of Edmonton's comptroller and financial commissioner for almost 40 years. Born in England, he gained his early accounting experience there in a shipping office, and with a firm of chartered accountants. In 1913, he came to Edmonton and joined the civil service. Hodgson became chief audit clerk in 1920, was named city comptroller in 1924, and was the City's finance commissioner for 16 years. He was employed by the City of Edmonton until his retirement in 1953. In 1973 a planned road in the Homesteader neighbourhood was named after John Hodgson, but the road was never constructed.

Neighbourhood   1990   SW   4:A2

Hodgson Boulevard

South of Hilliard Green, east of Rabbit Hill Road

See Hodgson.

Road   2001   SW   4:A2 *

Hodgson Road

Southeast of Hodgson Boulevard

See Hodgson.

Road   2001   SW   4:A2 *

Hodgson Way

North of 23 Avenue, east of Rabbit Hill Road

See Hodgson.

Road   2001   SW   4:A2 *

Holgate Place

South of Heath Road, west of Hunter's Run

Bidwell A. Holgate (1877–1928) was a prominent lawyer and businessman. Originally from Ontario, Holgate moved to Edmonton in 1908 and became involved in the booming real estate and financial investment market. In 1909 he purchased John H. Hart's interest in the Magrath-Hart real estate company and, in 1911, the company was renamed the Magrath-Holgate Company.

Road   1997   SW   3:D2

Hollands Landing

Connects Hodgson Road to Hollingsworth Bend

Fred V. Hollands (1884–1952) was a prominent manager with Edmonton's Johnstone Walker deptment store. Hollands was born in England, but immigrated to Canada, arriving in Saskatoon in 1906. There he studied window trimming and advertising for three years with the J. F. Cairns department store. After a short time in Portage La Prairie, he came to Edmonton and entered into the employ of Johnstone Walker. In 1918 he became manager of advertising and sales, a position he retained until his death. Hollands had an interest in horticulture and had an elaborate garden. An avid sportsman, he enjoyed duck hunting and fishing.

Road   2001   SW   4:A2 *

Hollick-Kenyon

153 Avenue to 163 Avenue, 50 Street to 59A Street

Herbert "Bertie" Hollick-Kenyon (1897–1975) piloted flights over the Antarctic that enabled the first mapping of the then uncharted territory. He was born in England and, after serving in WWI, joined the Royal Flying Corps and earned his pilot's licence. Hollick-Kenyon flew airmail across the Prairies and piloted numerous search and rescue flights, including a lengthy search in the western Arctic for a lost mining exploration party. As a tribute to his northern explorations, a major land area on the Antarctic continent was named for him. In 1942 Hollick-Kenyon joined Canadian Pacific Airlines, retiring in 1962. He was named to Canada's Aviation Hall of Fame in 1973. Neighbourhoods in Pilot Sound are named after famous aviators.

Neighbourhood   1981   NE   11:A1

Hollick-Kenyon Road

156A Avenue to 162B Avenue, connecting to Hollick-Kenyon Way

See Hollick-Kenyon.

Road   1991   NE   11:A1

Hollick-Kenyon Way

Connecting to 54 Street, abutting Hooke Road

See Hollick-Kenyon.

Road   1991   NE   11:A1

Hollinger Close

South of Hooke Road, west of Victoria Trail

Following his discharge from the Royal Canadian Air Force, Ontario-born Bruce B. Hollinger moved to Edmonton and entered the roofing business. Hollinger was a master of Masonic Lodge Temple No. 167. He also raised, showed and ran Chesapeake Bay retrievers.

Road   1998   NE   6:B1 *

Hollingsworth Bend

South of Hilliard Green, east of Hodgson Boulevard

Clare Millar Hollingsworth (1908–2002) was an educational leader whose career spanned over 40 years. Born and raised in Edmonton, he received his education at the University of Alberta and the University of Toronto. Hollingsworth's teaching career began in rural Alberta schools, but he soon moved into the Edmonton Public School system. Over the years he taught University of Alberta summer school courses, served with the Department of Education Curriculum Committee on Business Education and was a member of the Advisory Committee on Secretarial Science at the Northern Alberta Institute of Technology. At the end of his teaching career, he received several honours in recognition of his outstanding contributions to business education. Hollingsworth was also prominent in the field of sport. From 1936 to 1940 he coached the famous Edmonton Commercial Graduates basketball team. He served as Secretary Treasurer for the Canadian Wheelchair Games, was an original member of the Commonwealth Organizing Committee and served as official timekeeper for the Canadian Football League and Junior Football. For his efforts, he was inducted into the Edmonton and the Alberta Sports Halls of Fame and the Canadian Basketball Hall of Fame.

Road   2001   SW   4:A2 *

Hollingsworth Green

North of Hodgson Road, west of Hollingsworth Bend

See Hollingsworth Bend.

Road   2001   SW   4:A2 *

Holyrood

90 Avenue to 98 Avenue, 75 Street to 85 Street

This area has had four names since it was first developed in the early 1900s. In 1912 it was called Mount Pleasant and East Edmonton Gardens.

Decades later, after the area was resubdivided, it was named Balmoral. In 1953, because of a duplication in subdivision names, the area was renamed Holyrood. Holyrood may take its name from the Holyrood Abbey, which was built by James V in Edinburgh, Scotland. The origin of "Holyrood" is from medieval English, meaning a holy rood or the cross of crucifixion.

Neighbourhood 1953 SE 7:D2

Holyrood Park
8035–95 Avenue

This park is in Holyrood neighbourhood and has an area of 3.43 ha. *See* Holyrood.

Park 1982 SE 7:D2

Holyrood Road
80 Street and 95 Avenue

See Holyrood.

Road 1953 SE 7:D2 *

Homestead Crescent
North of Hermitage Road at 38 Street

See Homesteader.

Road 1973 NE 6:B1

Homesteader
Yellowhead Trail north to the Kennedale Ravine, 37 Street to 50 Street

This neighbourhood was named in honour of the men and women who first settled the Edmonton area. Most homesteading in western Canada occurred in the late 1800s and early 1900s, as European immigrants, as well as people from the United States and eastern Canada, arrived to farm the undeveloped land of western Canada. Under the Dominion Lands Policy, settlers or homesteaders

could claim 160 acres (64.75 ha.) of land for a filing fee of $10; and could gain title to the land after prescribed improvements had been made.

Neighbourhood 1973 NE 11:A2

Homesteader Park
575 Hermitage Road

This park is in the Homesteader neighbourhood and has an area of 3.1 ha. *See* Homesteader.

Park 1981 NE 6:A1

Hooke Court
North of Hooke Road, east of Victoria Trail

See Hooke Road.

Road 2002 NE 6:B1 *

Hooke Place
North of Hooke Road, east of Victoria Trail

See Hooke Road.

Road 2002 NE 6:B1 *

Hooke Road
North of Hermitage Road

Alfred J. Hooke (1905–1992) was a long-serving politician and author. Born in England, Hooke came to Alberta in 1913. He worked as a school teacher until he was elected to the provincial legislature in 1935. For the next 36 years Hooke held a number of cabinet posts. After his retirement in 1971, he authored several books on Alberta politics, including *30/5, I know, I was There.*

Road 1975 NE 6:B1

Hooper Crescent

North of Hooke Road, west of Victoria Trail

Staff Insp. Stanley G. Hooper served as an Edmonton police officer for 45 years. Born in England, Hooper came to Edmonton in 1924. Two years later he enlisted with the Royal Canadian Mounted Police and was stationed in the Northwest Territories. In 1928 he joined the city police. After serving in WWII, he returned to the force. Hooper retired in 1971.

Road   1975   NE   6:B1

Horner Road

North of Hooke Road, west of Victoria Trail

William "Reg" Horner (1898–1980) was born in Medicine Hat and came to Edmonton in 1905. After serving in WWI, Horner was employed at the Northern Alberta Dairy Pool, where he remained for many years. Horner served on the Edmonton Historical Board and was president of the Old Timers' Association.

Road   1975   NE   6:B1

Horsehills Creek

Flowing southeast into the North Saskatchewan River from 50 Street and 240 Avenue

Horsehills Creek was named after the nearby Horse Hills, the area that the Hudson's Bay Company at Edmonton House had once used as a wintering place for their horses. The Horse Hills post office operated between 1896 and 1919.

Creek   CU   NE   11:C1

Horsehills Road

Parallel to Manning Drive at 195 Avenue NW and 18 Street NW, to 211 Avenue NW and Meridian Street

This road crosses over Horsehills Creek. *See* Horsehills Creek.

Road   1982   NE   12:B2

Horseshoe Lake

5 km southwest of St. Albert, west of 199 Street

This name has been in use since 1963 and describes the lake's horseshoe shape.

Lake   1963   NW   8:B1

Howson Crescent

North of Hermitage Road, east of Victoria Trail

William Robinson Howson (1883–1952) was chief justice of the Alberta supreme court. Howson was born in Ontario and came to Edmonton in 1910. After graduating from the University of Alberta, Howson served in WWI. He was elected to the Alberta Legislature in 1930, appointed justice of Alberta's Supreme Court in 1936, and in 1944 became chief justice.

Road   1975   NE   11:A2 *

Hudson

Hudson Way north to Cumberland Road, west to 137 Street

Hudson House was a Hudson's Bay Company (HBC) post built in 1779, 40 km west of present-day Prince Albert, Saskatchewan. It was built by William Tomison, an Inland Chief of the HBC. The company was named after the explorer Henry Hudson, whose ship was the first to enter the Hudson Strait and Hudson Bay in 1610. Named after a historical fort, Hudson follows the Palisades' area naming theme.

Neighbourhood   1997   NW   10:B2

Hudson Bend

127 Street and 142 Avenue

See Hudson.

Road   1998   NW   10:B2 *

Hudson's Bay Reserve

IN 1870 the Hudson's Bay Company (HBC) sold
Rupert's Land to the Dominion of Canada. For 200
years the company had been absolute lords and propri-
etors of the vast territory. A deed of surrender, under
which the HBC agreed to relinquish its claim to
Rupert's Land, was negotiated between the government of Canada and the HBC in 1869. The terms of
this agreement allowed the HBC to retain parcels of
land around each of its posts. These lands became
known as Hudson's Bay Reserves. The HBC claimed
3000 acres (1,214 ha.) surrounding Fort Edmonton.
The property was bounded by present-day 101 Street
on the east, 121 Street on the west, 118 Avenue on the
north and the North Saskatchewan River to the south.
In addition to land, the HBC received £300,000, and
title to one-twentieth of all farmland within the territory, some 2.8 million ha. of land in all.

The Hudson's Bay Reserve was eventually sold to
settlers, the first lots being put up for sale by the HBC
as early as 1883. On May 13, 1912, the company sold
the remainder of its substantial Edmonton properties
by public lottery. Despite attempts to keep the location
secret, more than 2,000 people lined up for the sale; the
HBC received $4.3 million from the sale of some 1,500
lots. The excitement surrounding the release of the
Hudson's Bay Reserve lots marked the peak of the land
boom. A year later the overheated land market crashed;
the recession that followed lasted until the mid-1920s.

*Map: Municipality of the Town of Edmonton, Alberta, N.W.T.,
1903. (CEA EM52)*
*Photograph: Hudson's Bay Company sale of land, 1912.
(CEA EA-10-785)*

Hudson Way

127 Street and 142 Avenue

See Hudson.

Road   1998   NW   10:B2

Hudson's Bay Reserve

North Saskatchewan River north to 118 Avenue, 97 Street to 121 Street

See feature story, page 152.

Subdivision   CU   C   7:B1 *

Huff Bremner Estate Industrial

111 Avenue to 118 Avenue, 142 Street to 149 Street

This area was once a portion of the Huff Estate and the Bremner Estate. Warren Huff founded W.P. Huff's Dairy (located at 127 Street and 112 Avenue) in 1907. He changed the name to Huff's Jasper Dairy in 1914 and the next year moved the business to the Jasper Place area (now Crestwood and West Jasper Place neighbourhoods). Thomas Logan owned section 11-53-25-W4 in the 1880s, having acquired it under the Western Lands Grant program. This section included the land which was named Bremner Estate in about 1912. The origin of the name Bremner is not recorded, although a James C.C. Bremner was an early landowner in the immediate vicinity.

Neighbourhood   CU   NW   7:A1

Huffman Crescent

West of Humberstone Road, south of Hermitage Road

Bertram "Bert" M. Huffman (b. 1921) worked in the City of Edmonton engineer's department for 28 years. He was born in High River and graduated from the University of Alberta in 1949. Huffman began working for the city after serving in WWII. He retired at the end of 1975.

Road   1975   NE   6:B1

Hughes Road

Joins with and is confined by Huffman Crescent

Katherine Hughes (1877–1925) was Alberta's first provincial archivist. Hughes was born in Prince Edward Island and came to Edmonton in the early 1900s. Starting in 1906, she worked as a journalist at the *Edmonton Bulletin*. She was appointed provincial archivist in 1908. Hughes was the author of several books, including *Father Lacombe: The Black-Robe Voyageur.*

Road   1975   NE   6:B1 *

Humberstone Road

East of Huffman Crescent, south of Hermitage Road

William Humberstone (1836–1922), born in Canada West, was an early Edmonton businessman. He arrived in Edmonton in 1880 and went on to establish a coal mine in Beverly and a brickyard in Riverdale. Humberstone was also a partner in John Walter's sawmill.

Road   1975   NE   6:B1 *

Hunt Road

Joins Hermitage Road to Humberstone Road

Reginald Hunt (1884–1978) was the inventor and pilot of Alberta's first airplane. His pioneer flight took place on September 8, 1909, when he and his aircraft rose 15.2 metres and stayed aloft for a remarkable 35 minutes. After a crash in 1910 (he was uninjured), Hunt left Edmonton.

Road   1975   NE   6:B1

Hunter's Close

West of Haddow Drive, south of Hunter's Gate

Vernon Harper Hunter (1906–1985) was part of the crew that drilled the famous Leduc No. 1 well on February 13, 1947, heralding the start of Alberta's oil boom. Born in Nanton, Alberta, and educated in

Billboard for Humberstone Coal, no date. (CEA EA–160-334)

Blairmore and Calgary, Hunter began a career in the oil patch after graduating from high school in 1923. Working for Imperial Oil, he was promoted to field superintendent in 1947, the year of the Leduc discovery. Hunter was manager of the drilling department at the time of his departure from Imperial Oil in 1967. He then established the company, V.H. Hunter & Associates, Drilling Consultants, from which he retired in 1977. Hunter was inducted into the Canadian Petroleum Hall of Fame in 1997.

Road   1996   SW   3:D2 *

Hunter's Gate

Connecting Hunter's Run with Haddow Drive

See Hunter's Close.

Road   1996   SW   3:D2 *

Hunter's Green

South of Riverbend Road, southeast of Haddow Drive, west of Terwillegar Drive

See Hunter's Close.

Road   1996   SW   3:D2 *

Hunter's Run

West of Riverbend Road, north of Haddow Drive

See Hunter's Close.

Road   1996   SW   3:D2

Hunter's Way

Northeast of Hunter's Green

See Hunter's Close.

Road   1996   SW   3:D2 *

Hyndman Crescent

East of Victoria Trail, south of Hermitage Road

James Duncan Hyndman (1874–1971) was an alderman and a judge on Alberta's Supreme Court. Born in Prince Edward Island, Hyndman came to Edmonton in 1903. He was an alderman from 1910 to 1911. In 1914 Hyndman was appointed to the Supreme Court of Alberta. From 1921 to 1931 he served as justice of the appellate division.

Road   1975   NE   6:B1

Hyndman Road

East of Victoria Trail, south of Hyndman Crescent

See Hyndman Crescent.

Road   1975   NE   6:B1

Looking east at Industrial Heights, 1963.
(CEA EA-267-48)

Idylwylde

Whyte Avenue north to 90 Avenue, 75 Street to 83 Street

This area was subdivided and named sometime around 1914. An "idyll" is a short poem that describes a simple, country life.

Neighbourhood CU SE 7:D2

Idylwylde Park

8631–81 Street

This park is in the Idylwylde neighbourhood and has an area of 0.5 ha. *See* Idylwylde.

Park 1982 SE 7:D2

Industrial Heights

Yellowhead Trail north to CN railway tracks, 50 Street west to LRT tracks

This area was named as early as 1912, when it was first proposed as an industrial area. The Swift Canadian Co. packing plant, which opened in 1908, was located here, conveniently close to the railroad tracks. In 1983, the boundaries of this area were expanded to include the portion west of 62 Street.

Neighbourhood 1983 NE 7:D1

Inglewood

111 Avenue to 118 Avenue, 122 Street west to Groat Road

In the 1870s this land was owned by John A. Norris (c. 1829–1916), a Scottish immigrant and Hudson's Bay Company employee. Norris came to Fort Edmonton in 1849 and later became a successful store owner. The land was annexed to the City of Edmonton in 1904 and development of the Inglewood neighbourhood began a year later. A section of this area, 114 Avenue to 118 Avenue and Groat Road to 127 Street, was once called Hempriggs. Hempriggs is located in the Scottish county of Caithness. John Norris was born in John O'Groat, which is also in the county of Caithness. In Gaelic, an ingle is a hearth or fireplace. In the early 1880s, Inglewood was used as the name for one of the first communities in Calgary.

Neighbourhood CU NW 7:B1

Inglewood Park

12815–116 Avenue

This park is in the Inglewood neighbourhood and has an area of 0.65 ha. *See* Inglewood.

Park 1967 NW 7:B1

Irene Parlby Park

9545–100 Street

Mary Irene Marryat Parlby (1868–1965) was the first woman in Alberta and second woman in the British Empire to serve as a cabinet minister. Parlby was born in England and came to Alberta in 1897. After helping to establish the women's auxiliary of the United Farmers' of Alberta (UFA), she became the provincial president of the United Farm Women of Alberta in 1916. From 1921 to 1935 Parlby was a member of the provincial legislature in the UFA government. She served on the Board of Governors of the University of Alberta from 1919 to 1921 and

Inglewood Park, circa 1968. (CEA EA-20-5235)

was the first woman to receive an honorary doctorate of laws degree from the University of Alberta. Parlby was a member of the "Famous Five" who, in 1929, won the "Person's Case" before the Privy Council of England, granting women the right to hold a seat in the Canadian Senate. She was named to the Canadian delegation that attended the League of Nations at Geneva in 1930. The Irene Parlby Park has an area of 3.7 ha.

Park   1991   C   7:C2

Isabelle Connelly Park

9835–148 Street

Isabelle Connelly (1880–1963) was the first woman in Alberta to work as a licensed embalmer. Born in Ontario, Connelly came to Edmonton in 1901. Six years later she married J. William Connelly, and the following year they founded the province's first funeral home. The firm still exists as Connelly-

McKinley. Connelly was active in the Catholic Women's League and helped establish a retreat for Roman Catholic women. She was also a member of the Third Order of St. Francis and the League of the Sacred Heart. Connelly was awarded the Lateran Cross in 1952. The Isabelle Connelly Park is in the Crestwood neighbourhood and has an area of 0.57 ha.

Park   1987   SW   8:D2

Izena Ross Park

12166 Fort Road

Izena Ross (d. 1945) was elected to City Council in 1922, becoming Edmonton's first woman councillor. Ross was also a school board member and president of the Local Council of Women. The Izena Ross Park is in the Eastwood neighbourhood and has an area of 0.08 ha.

Park   1995   NE   7:C1 *

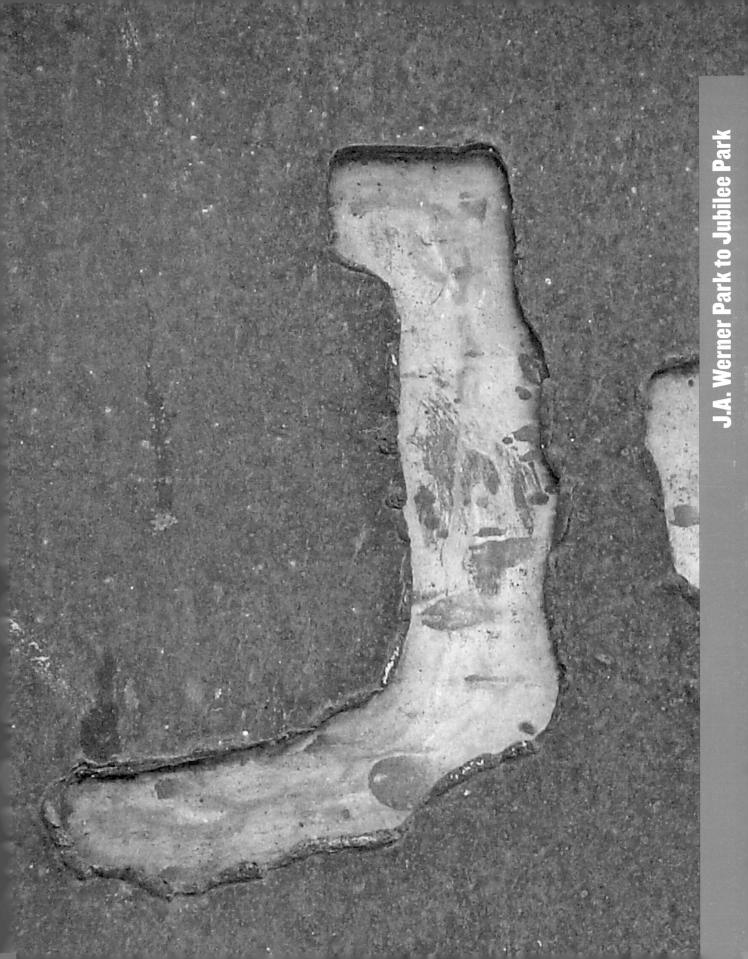

Jackie Parker, right, and Don Getty, circa 1955. (CEA A2003-42 File 12)

J.A. Werner Park

11420-35 Avenue

Ontario-born Jacob A. Werner (1873–1963) was a
pioneer merchant who came to Edmonton in 1906.
He established a hardware store on the north side,
retiring in 1945. Werner was a member of the
Highlands Baptist Church, the Edmonton Shriners,
and Al Azhar Temple. He was also a life member of
the Masonic Lodge. The J. A. Werner Park is directly
west of the W. E. Werner Park in the Greenfield
neighbourhood and has an area of 0.7 ha.

Park 1984 SW 4:B2

J. Dean Whittaker Park

13415-105 Street

J. Dean Whittaker (1912–1981) was a WWII veteran
and a prominent Edmonton engineer. Whittaker
was born in British Columbia and graduated from
the Faculty of Engineering at the University of
British Columbia in 1934. He enlisted in the Royal
Canadian Engineers in 1940, serving in England,
Gibraltar and northern Europe during WWII, and
becoming chief structural engineer for the
Department of National Defence. Major Whittaker
left the Canadian Army in 1953 with the rank of
major and moved to Edmonton. He then became a
partner in the engineering firm of Whittaker,
Laviolette and Leckie, which specialized in struc-

tural and civil engineering. The J. Dean Whittaker Park is in the Rosslyn neighbourhood and has an area of 0.85 ha.

Park 1982 NW 10:C2

Jack Horan Park

16919–99 Avenue

John W. "Jack" Horan (1908 or 1909–1971) was instrumental in improving recreational facilities in Jasper Place. He was born in England and came to Edmonton in 1929. Horan was a Jasper Place MLA from 1963 until his death. The Jack Horan Park is in the Glenwood neighbourhood and has an area of 0.99 ha.

Park 1982 NW 10:C2

Jackie Parker Recreation Area

4204–50 Street

Jackie Parker (b. 1932) was a legendary football player with the Edmonton Eskimos. He was born in Tennessee and signed as a player with the Eskimos in 1954. At that year's Grey Cup game Parker recovered a fumble during the last minutes of play, ran for a touchdown that tied the game, and the Eskimos won 26–25. Parker led the team to three Grey Cups in the mid-1950s; collected three Schenley awards as the league's most outstanding player in 1957, 1958 and 1960; was voted all-star for nine consecutive years from 1954 to 1962; and won most valuable player in the west for seven of the nine years he played for the Eskimos. Parker was traded in 1962 but later returned to Edmonton as a radio colour commentator. In 1978 he was selected the Canadian Football League's most outstanding player of the past quarter century. Parker rejoined the Edmonton Eskimos in 1983 as head coach. He retired in 1987 and that same year was inducted into the Canadian Sports Hall of Fame. The Jackie Parker Recreation Area is located in the Mill Woods area and covers an area of 24.69 ha.

Park 1989 SE 5:A1

Jackson Heights

40 Avenue north to Whitemud Drive, Johns Road west to 50 Street

Annie B. Jackson (1879–1959) was Edmonton's first woman police officer and the first woman constable in Canada. Born in Ontario, she came west in 1909 to visit her sister who lived in Lacombe. In 1910, she came to Edmonton and worked for the Children's Aid Society and the Ruthenian Home for Girls, which helped immigrant women find employment and learn English. In 1912, Jackson was hired by the Edmonton Police Department; her primary responsibility was to protect the morals of young women and girls. She later became the first woman constable in Canada, receiving worldwide acclaim when her photograph appeared in London's *Daily Mirror*. Jackson was a probation officer until 1918.

Neighbourhood 1976 SE 5:A2

Jackson Road

East of 50 Street, south of Whitemud Drive

See Jackson Heights.

Road 1980 SE 5:A2

Jacob Prins Park

12037–53 Street

Dutch-born Jacob Prins (1886–1963) was an area farmer who provided support for his fellow émigrés from Holland. In 1927 Prins and his wife, along with their eight children, emigrated to Edmonton, settling on the former Humberstone Mine property. He soon became involved in aiding newly arrived Dutch immigrants, helping them to settle and find work. The Jacob Prins Park is in the Newton neighbourhood and has an area of 0.33 ha.

Park 1983 NE 6:A1 *

James MacDonald Bridge and Edmonton skyline at night, circa 1970. (CEA EA–340–387)

James A. Christiansen Park

400 Kirkness Road

James A. Christiansen (1889–1953) was a prominent Edmonton businessman who sponsored the Mercurys and Oil Kings hockey clubs and the Meteors basketball club. His Mercurys hockey club brought Edmonton worldwide recognition by winning the world's amateur championship in 1950 and the Olympic hockey championship in 1952. Born in Denmark, Christiansen arrived in Edmonton in 1935 and went on to become president of Waterloo Industries.

Among his volunteer activities, he was president of the Edmonton Kiwanis Club in 1942; chairman of the Citizens' Committee and the Chamber of Commerce Highways Committee; and president, in 1951, of the Alberta Automotive Dealers' Association. Christiansen received the Junior Chamber of Commerce Citizenship Award in 1952, and was named honorary president of the Edmonton Chamber of Commerce in 1953. The

James A. Christiansen Park is in the Kirkness neighbourhood and has an area of 0.55 ha.

Park 1985 NE 11:B2 *

James Crescent

East of 50 Street, north of 44 Avenue

Ontario-born Harry James (1895–1967) came to Alberta in 1907 and moved to Edmonton in 1918, where he worked as a fruit wholesaler. He managed the Brown Fruit Company, a subsidiary of the Dominion Fruit and Wholesale Company, and later, in 1959, was promoted to supervisor of the parent company's provincial operations.

Road 1980 SE 5:A2

James Kidney Park

11845A–77 Street

James Kidney (b. 1909) was a dedicated community volunteer. He was born in Edmonton and served in WWII. In 1954 he moved to the Eastwood neigh-

bourhood and became active in the community
league, organizing hockey games and ice shows.
Kidney served as president of the Eastwood
Community League for 10 years and oversaw
construction of the community hall. The James
Kidney Park is in the Eastwood neighbourhood
and has an area of 0.33 ha.

Park   1995   NE   7:C1 *

James MacDonald Bridge

*Spanning the North Saskatchewan River
connecting 97 Avenue and 98 Avenue*

James D. MacDonald (1901–1966) was a city engineer who took part in the design and construction
of five of the bridges that span the North
Saskatchewan River. He graduated from the
University of Alberta and joined the City in 1923.
MacDonald was appointed field engineer in 1925,
later becoming the resident engineer, assistant city
engineer in 1939 and city engineer in 1949. The
James MacDonald Bridge was opened in 1971.

Bridge   1967   C   7:C2

James Ramsay Park

15016–43 Avenue

James Ramsay (1864–1939) was an early Edmonton
businessman and politician. He was born in
Michigan and in 1868, while still a small child,
moved with his family to Ontario. Ramsey came to
Edmonton in 1911 and established a department
store. He served as an alderman in 1915 and 1916,
and as a MLA from 1917 to 1921. Ramsey sold his
store to the T. Eaton Company in 1928 and retired.
The James Ramsay Park (the misspelling of
Ramsey's name in the park name has been noted by
the City but has not been corrected) is in the
Ramsay Heights neighbourhood and has an area of
3.19 ha.

Park   1991   SW   4:A2

Sam and Vera Jamha, circa 1960.
(Photo courtesy of Miriam Shawley nee Jamha.)

Jamha Road

East of 50 Street, south of Whitemud Drive

Sam Jamha (1890–1974) was one of Alberta's first
immigrants from Lebanon, arriving in Canada when
he was 15. A year later, he came to Edmonton and
took up fur trading. In 1938, by then well established, Jamha helped build the Al Rashid mosque in
Edmonton—the first mosque in Canada. After 50
years as a fur trader, Jamha retired in 1969. His
descendants continue to have a prominent role in
Edmonton's business and Muslim communities.
This road was originally named Jamha Crescent.

Road   1980   SE   5:A2 *

Jamieson Place

*51 Avenue north to Callingwood Road, 184 Street
to 191 Street*

Frederick Charles Jamieson (1875–1966) was a
prominent lawyer and politician who came to the
Edmonton/Lacombe district in 1895. Born and
educated in Ontario, he was admitted to the bar of
the North-West Territories in 1899 and went on to
practise law with A.C. Rutherford, the first premier
of Alberta. Jamieson served in both the Boer War

Col. Fred Jamieson, centre, and the 260th Battalion Officers, circa 1915. (CEA EA-227-3)

and WWI. From 1931 to 1935 he held a seat in the Alberta legislature. Jamieson was presented with a life membership in the Edmonton Bar Association in 1953. He retired in 1962.

Neighbourhood 1972 SW 3:C1

Jane Salisbury Park

11125–77 Street

Jane Thompson Salisbury was a Grand Matron of the Order of the Eastern Star. Salisbury was born in Quebec and came to Edmonton as a child. She joined the Order of the Eastern Star in 1953 and was grand matron from 1976 to 1982. Salisbury spent almost 30 years doing volunteer work for elderly people living in the Cromdale neighbourhood. From 1949 to 1987, as part of a project run by the Order of the Eastern Star, senior citizens were housed in cottages on this site. The Jane Salisbury Park is in the Cromdale neighbourhood and has an area of 0.59 ha.

Park 1990 NE 7:C1 *

Jarvis Crescent

East of 50 Street, south of Whitemud Drive; both ends joining with Jamha Crescent

William Drummer Jarvis (1834–1914) was one of the first members of the North West Mounted Police (NWMP). He was born in Upper Canada and served with the East Suffolk Regiment in the militia of Upper Canada. When the NWMP was first organized in 1873, Jarvis was appointed as a superintendent. He came to Edmonton the following year to establish a military post on the south side of the North Saskatchewan River, across from Edmonton House (Fort Edmonton). Instead, Jarvis chose a site 32 km downstream. Under his command, the Fort Saskatchewan NWMP post was built in 1875.

Road 1980 SE 5:A2

Jasper Avenue

101 Avenue, from 77 Street to 125 Street

See feature story, page 165.

Road CU C 7:C2

Jasper Park

87 Avenue to 92 Avenue, 149 Street to 156 Street

This neighbourhood has existed since 1912. It was within the Town of Jasper Place and was annexed to the City of Edmonton in 1964. *See* Jasper Avenue *feature story, page 165.*

Neighbourhood CU SW 8:D2

Jasper Place Jubilee Park

9200–160 Street

This park is located in the Meadowlark Park neighbourhood and has an area of 3.93 ha. It was named in 1955 by the Town of Jasper Place in honour of the 50th anniversary of Alberta's creation as a province. *See* West Jasper Place.

Park 1967 SW 8:D2

Jasper Avenue

JASPER HAWES was a trapper from Missouri who, in 1817, was put in charge of the North West Company's trading post at Brûlé Lake, which at first was known as Rocky Mountain House and later became known as Jasper's House. This post may have existed as early as 1801, and was rebuilt on the shores of Jasper Lake around 1828. It remained in operation until 1884, when it was abandoned. Jasper Avenue (first surveyed in 1882), the town of Jasper, Jasper Lake and Jasper National Park were all named after Jasper Hawes.

Most of Edmonton's early businesses were located along Jasper Avenue, east of 97 Street. Among these, in 1899, were Lauder's Bakery, the Alberta Hotel, Ross Brothers' Hardware store, the CPR Land Office, the Sheriff's Office and the Bulletin Block. By 1907, Jasper Avenue was so congested with traffic that the City enforced a bylaw requiring all vehicles, including those that were horse-drawn, to keep to the right. A portion of Jasper Avenue was paved in 1910. In 1933, at the corner of 101 Street and Jasper Avenue, the street became the first in Edmonton to have a traffic light, replacing a uniformed traffic-control officer who had directed traffic at this intersection.

Jasper Avenue, looking west from 100 Street, circa 1930s.
(CEA EA–275–1039)

Jasper Place welcome sign, circa 1960.
(CEA EA-275-323)

Jefferson Road

North of and joining to Jackson Road, west of
34 Street, south of Whitemud Drive

Brig. James C. Jefferson (1906–1973) was a decorated soldier who served in WWII. He was born in
England and came to Canada in 1914, moving to
Edmonton after 1918. Jefferson joined the
Edmonton Regiment, was commissioned in 1927
and went overseas in 1939. He assumed command
of the Edmonton Regiment in 1942. Jefferson was
decorated with the Distinguished Service Order
and Bar, and the Croix de Guerre (France). He was
made a Companion of the British Empire. In 1949
he was appointed as the Director of Civil Defence
for Edmonton. Jefferson worked for Northwestern
Utilities from 1953 to 1967.

Road   1980   SE   5:B2

Jefferys Crescent

East of 50 Street, south of Whitemud Drive;
both ends joining Jamha Crescent

Charles W. Jefferys (1869–1951) was a talented
painter, lithographer and illustrator. Born in
England, he moved to Ontario with his parents in

1879. Before beginning his career as an illustrator,
Jefferys apprenticed with a lithographer and
worked for the *New York Herald*. He painted and
drew illustrations depicting Canadian history,
including early explorers and pioneers. In addition
to lecturing, teaching and writing, Jefferys received
commissions to paint murals and to design a medal
and a stamp.

Road   1980   SE   5:A2

Jellett Way

North of Jackson Road, west of Jefferson Road

Born in Canada West in 1859, St. George Jellett
came west with a survey party in 1859. After a few
years of farming at Clover Bar, Jellett moved to
Edmonton where he worked as an insurance agent.
He was the secretary-treasurer of the Edmonton
District Telephone Company and the Edmonton
Electric Light Company. This road was originally
named Jellett Crescent.

Road   1980   SE   5:A2 *

Jenner Cove

East of Jones Crescent, south of Whitemud Drive

Manitoba-born Frederick Thomas Jenner
(1909–1976) was a WWII veteran and a successful
businessman. In 1929 he began working for
General Motors in Alberta. In 1951, after serving in
WWII, Jenner opened his own dealership, Jenner
Motors, in Edmonton. He retired from the
Canadian Army as a brigadier in 1954. He
continued to run Jenner Motors until its sale in
1970. Jenner was a senator and chairman of the
Board of Governors of the University of Alberta. In
1976 he was awarded an honorary doctorate of laws
degree from University of Alberta. This road was
originally named Jenner Road.

Road   1980   SE   5:B2 *

Joe Clarke Athletic Grounds

JOSEPH A. CLARKE (1869–1941), one of early Edmonton's most indefatigable politicians, was responsible for the building of Edmonton's first stadium. He was a three-time alderman (1912, 1914–1915, 1925) and twice served as mayor (1919–1920, 1935–1937). The 3,000-seat Clarke Stadium was built in 1938 on federal land in the McCauley neighbourhood. Clarke was born in Ontario, and after an ignominious stint in the North West Mounted Police—he was charged with desertion—he studied law before heading to the Yukon during the gold rush. Clarke was elected to the Yukon Territorial Council for 1903–1904. In 1908 he came to Edmonton to practise law. He was instrumental in the purchase of the land on which Clarke Park sits.

As early as 1929, at the onset of the Great Depression, Clarke urged the city to construct a stadium complex as a relief work program that would benefit "a substantial number of married unemployed." While the athletic park, including a baseball diamond, running track and soccer field, was approved, the stadium proposal was not. In 1930 Clarke, a friend of Prime Minister W.L. Mackenzie King, persuaded the federal government to lease the land to the City of Edmonton. The lease was for 99 years at a cost to the city of one dollar a year. In honour of "Fighting" Joe's efforts, the original stadium was named Clarke Stadium.

Over the decades, Clarke Stadium was expanded from its original 3,000 seats to some 25,000. The Edmonton Eskimos of the Canadian Football League made their home at Clarke Stadium from 1938 until 1978, when the 60,000-capacity Commonwealth Stadium, adjacent to Clarke Stadium, was completed. The original Clarke Stadium was torn down and completely rebuilt for the eighth International Amateur Athletics Federation (IAAF) 2001 World Championships. The new Clarke Stadium, with seating for 2,500, was used as a warm-up facility for athletes participating at the IAAF at Commonwealth Stadium. Clarke Stadium continues to be used for amateur sports events, including soccer and football. Clarke Park, a triangular-shaped area, encompasses Clarke Stadium and Commonwealth Stadium.

Joseph Clarke, 1919. (CEA EA–160–205)

167

Joe Morris, circa 1900. (CEA EA–231–5)

Jennings Bay

North of Jefferson Road, east of Jillings Crescent

Reginald Jennings (1893–1968) was a WWI veteran and the chief of Edmonton's police force. He was born in England and came to Edmonton in 1911, joining the police force two years later. In 1915, however, he enlisted and went overseas. After WWI he rejoined the force and in 1923 was appointed acting detective. He was appointed sergeant in 1931, and chief constable in 1943. Jennings retired in 1954. This road was originally named Jennings Crescent.

Road   1980   SE   5:B2 *

Jillings Crescent

North of Jefferson Road, east of Jennings Bay

David Jillings (1919–1977) was chairman of the Edmonton Civic Employees' Charitable Assistance Fund. He was born in England and joined the Royal Air Force in 1939. In 1941 Jillings was posted to Canada as air crew instructor. Following WWII he returned to Edmonton and for the next 29 years was employed by Edmonton Power and the International Brotherhood of Electrical Workers. Jillings was an active volunteer, board member and sports enthusiast.

Road   1980   SE   5:B2 *

Joe Clarke Athletic Grounds

11100 Stadium Road

See feature story, page 167.

Park   2001   NE   7:C1 *

Joe Morris Park

10824–78 Avenue

In 1904, Joseph Henry Morris (1868–1939) became the proud owner of Edmonton's first automobile. Morris was born in Ontario and came to Edmonton in 1896, where he became a retail merchant and politician. He owned the J.H. Morris & Company store and wholesale grocery. Morris was also a town councillor in 1901 and 1902. The Joe Morris Park is in the Queen Alexandra neighbourhood and has an area of 0.38 ha.

Park   1982   SW   4:B1

John A. Norris Park

12808–112 Avenue

Scottish-born John A. Norris (1829–1916) came to Fort Edmonton in 1849 as a Hudson's Bay Company employee. He was a trader for the company before opening his own business in the

1880s. The Norris & Carey Store sold groceries and hardware. The John A. Norris Park is in the Inglewood neighbourhood and has an area of 0.19 ha.

Park 1988 NW 7:B1

John Devoldere Memorial Park

16415–83 Avenue

John Devoldere (d. 1993) was a firefighter for 35 years and a resident of the Elmwood neighbourhood for 33. He was an active volunteer, involved in the Boy Scouts and little league baseball. Before its renaming, this park was known as Elmwood Park. The John Devoldere Memorial Park is in the Elmwood neighbourhood and has an area of 3.4 ha.

Park 1996 SW 3:C1

John Ducey Way

96 Avenue, east of 103 Street

John Ducey (1908–1983), known as "Mr. Baseball," is an Edmonton sports legend. Born in New York, he moved with his family to Edmonton in 1909. Ducey started his 60-year involvement in Edmonton's baseball scene as a batboy. He went on to become an umpire, a player and, finally, a promoter. Ducey was inducted into the Edmonton Sports Hall of Fame in 1972, the Alberta Sports Hall of Fame in 1980, and the Canadian Baseball Hall of Fame in 1983. On March 13, 1984, City Council renamed Renfrew Park to John Ducey Park, again renamed in 1995 to Telus Field.

Road 1997 C 7:C2 *

John Fry Park

9700–28 Avenue

John Wesley Fry (1876–1946) served as an alderman from 1932 to 1936 and mayor from 1937 to 1945. Fry was born in Woodstock, Ontario. In 1897 he moved west to Regina, where he attended Normal

John "Lefty" Ducey at Edmonton's Boyle Street Park, shortly after beginning his umpiring career in the summer of 1931. (CEA EA-524-20)

School (teachers' college). Having received his teaching certificate, he moved to Gainsborough, Lloydminster and finally, in 1911, to Edmonton, where he went into business as a contractor and realtor. Fry was an alderman for four years, and mayor for eight consecutive years. During this time he played a significant role in devising a plan to re-finance Edmonton's debt during the final bleak years of the Great Depression and guiding Edmonton through WWII. Fry lobbied Ottawa to remedy Edmonton's housing crisis. Eventually his efforts paid off with greater involvement in the Wartime Housing Scheme. Though he did not live to see the oil boom, it was largely through the efforts of John Fry that Edmonton was well-positioned to take advantage of it when it came. The John Fry Park is in the Parsons Industrial neighbourhood and has an area of 5.5 ha.

Park 1979 SE 4:C2

Mayor Fry welcoming King George VI and Queen Elizabeth to Edmonton, 1939. (CEA EA–174–4)

John G. Niddrie Park

12707–111 Avenue

John G. Niddrie (1887–1972) was a teacher and principal for more than 50 years. He was born in Manitoba and moved to Alberta as a child in 1889. His family helped to build the first school in Eagle Valley, Alberta: Niddrie would later teach at this very school. In 1917 he began teaching in Edmonton and in 1921 graduated from the University of Alberta. The John G. Niddrie Park is in the Westmount neighbourhood and has an area of 0.06 ha.

Park 1988 NW 7:B1

John Patrick Gillese Park

671 Glenwright Crescent

John Patrick Gillese (1926–1999) was an award-winning writer who published more than 5,000 articles and books. Born in Ireland, he and his family immigrated to Rochfort Bridge, Alberta, in the mid-1920s. His first story was published in 1939, but his career only began to take off after he wrote the short story "Ashamed to Go Home." In 1944, Gillese moved to Edmonton where he worked as a freelance writer. In 1971, the Alberta Department of Culture, Youth and Recreation hired him as the provincial supervisor of creative writing. Gillese won several awards for his writing, including the Catholic Press Association Award for fiction and nonfiction, the Vicky Metcalf Award and the Rothman's Award. Among his many books were *People and Progress: Hospital District 24's World of Extended Care, 1961–1986* and *Murder Will Out*. The John Patrick Gillese Park is in the Glastonbury neighbourhood and has an area of 0.39 ha.

Park 1999 SW 3:B1 *

Johnny Bright Sports Park

9217–165 Street

Indiana-born John Bright (1930–1983) was an award-winning football player, coach and teacher. His Canadian Football League (CFL) career began in 1952, when he joined the Calgary Stampeders. Two years later, he came north to play fullback with the Edmonton Eskimos. Bright remained with the team for 11 years, during which he helped the Eskimos win three straight Grey Cup victories in the mid-1950s. In 1959 Bright became the first black player to win the Schenley award as the CFL's most outstanding player. He retired in 1964 and was later inducted into the Edmonton Sports Hall of Fame and the Canadian Football League Hall of Fame. In 1969 he graduated from the University of Alberta and went on to work as a school teacher, administrator and football coach. The Johnny Bright Sports Park is in the West Meadowlark Park neighbourhood and has an area of 6.73 ha.

Park 1984 SW 8:C2

Johns Close

Intersecting with Johns Road near the east end of Jackson Road

Walter Hugh Johns (1908–1985) was president of the University of Alberta from 1959 to 1969. He was born in Ontario and began teaching in the Classics Department at the University of Alberta in 1938. In 1945 he was made assistant to the dean of arts and science; in 1947, academic assistant to the president; in 1952, dean of arts and science; in 1957, vice-president of the university. After the end of his presidency, Johns returned to teaching, retiring in 1973. He was named to the Order of Canada in 1978 and received an Alberta Order of Excellence. He wrote *A History of the University of Alberta, 1908–1969*, which was published by the University of Alberta Press in 1981.

Road   1990   SE   5:B2 *

Johns Road

Intersecting with Jackson Road at 38 Street

See Johns Close.

Road   1990   SE   5:B2

Johnsonwood

23 Avenue to 34 Avenue, 50 Street to 66 Street

R. Vernon Johnson (d. 1980) was a member of the Edmonton public school board for 20 years. Johnson was born in Edmonton and graduated from the University of Alberta in 1950. In 1957 he was elected to the public school board and served as chairman in 1961 and 1970. From 1963 to 1964, Johnson was president of the Canadian School Trustees' Association. Johnsonwood is compatible with the naming theme for the Mill Woods area, all subdivisions using "mill" or "wood" in their name.

Subdivision   1978   SE   4:D2 *

Jones Crescent

East of Jefferys Crescent, west of Jenner Cove, south of Whitemud Drive

This road may have been named after either Maria Anne Jones, who came to Edmonton in 1910, or Douglas Bonnell Jones, who arrived here a decade later. English-born Maria Anne Jones (d. 1960) lived in Edmonton for 50 years and, with her husband, ran the James and Jones' Fish Market. She continued to work at the market after her husband's death in 1925 and did not retire until 1956.

Douglas Bonnell Jones was born in Nova Scotia in 1898 and came to Edmonton in 1920, where he attended the University of Alberta. Upon graduating, Jones went to work for the Hayward Lumber Company, where he soon became superintendent. Jones left the company in 1931 and established the Western Canada Subscription Agencies and Western Canada News (also known as the Palace of Sweets).

Road   CU   SE   5:A2

Jordan Crescent

South of Johns Road, east of 44 Street

Most Rev. Anthony Jordan (1901–1982) was the Roman Catholic Archbishop of Edmonton. Born in Scotland, he came to Alberta with his family in 1913. After his ordination, he served in Saskatchewan, Ontario and British Columbia before coming to Edmonton in 1955. He was named archbishop in 1964. Jordan founded *The Western Catholic Reporter* and the Newman Theological College. He received an honorary doctorate of laws degree from the University of Alberta in 1971. Jordan retired in 1973.

Road   1980   SE   5:A2

Josef Chelen Park

6820–135 Avenue

Josef Chelen (1896–1956) was a pioneer market gardener in the Beverly area. Chelen was born in Poland and immigrated to Edmonton in 1929. In 1932 Chelen moved to Beverly and in 1940 purchased 143 ha. of land in the area now known as Rundle Park. The Josef Chelen Park is in the Delwood neighbourhood and has an area of 0.62 ha.

Park   1983   NE   10:D2

Joviz

South of the proposed outer ring road, west of 66 Street

Neighbourhood names in the Lake District area describe water. *Joviz* is Hungarian for "good water."

Neighbourhood   1979   NE   10:D1 *

Joyce Crescent

South of Jones Crescent, east of Jefferys Crescent

Annie C. Joyce (1891–1970) worked at the Edmonton Public Library for 41 years. She was born in Scotland and came to Edmonton in 1913. Joyce joined the library soon after arriving in the city. In 1916 she was appointed cataloguer and in 1953 became assistant librarian. Among her many accomplishments, Joyce helped establish the city's bookmobile service. She retired in 1954. Joyce Crescent was originally named Joyce Street.

Road   1980   SE   5:A2

Joyce Road

North of Jackson Road, intersecting with Jones Crescent

See Joyce Crescent.

Road   1980   SE   5:A2

Jubilee Park

4203–120 Avenue

This park was originally known as Beverly Jubilee Park and was named as part of Alberta's Golden Jubilee in 1955, before the Town of Beverly amalgamated with Edmonton. In 1989 the park's name was revised at the request of the Beacon Heights Community League. The Names Advisory Committee approved dropping the word "Beverly" since the current neighbourhood name is Beacon Heights. Beverly Heights is the neighbourhood to the south. Jubilee Park has an area of 1.12 ha.

Park   1989   NE   6:A1

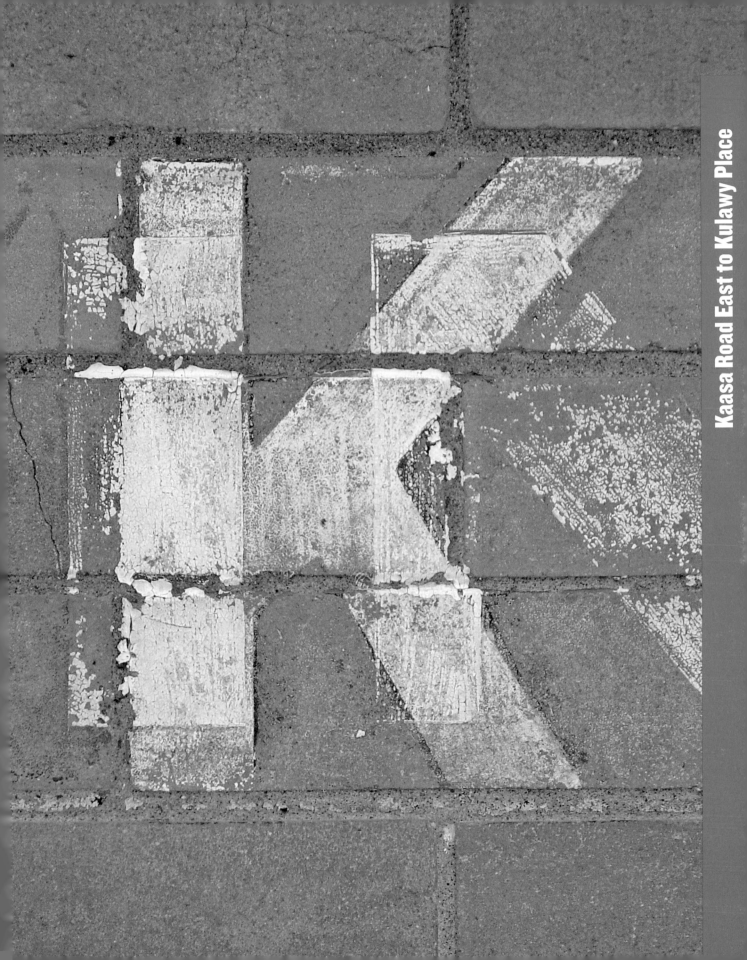

John Kaasa, circa 1961–1962. (GAI NA-4204–1)

Kaasa Road East

West of 34 Street, south of 38 Avenue

Minnesota-born John Kaasa (1894–1978) was an explorer and photographer who settled on a farm in Saskatchewan in 1913. Later, in 1932, he settled at Fort St. John, BC. He documented his explorations in the Arctic, Alaska and Canada's northwest in photographs, films and the collection of artifacts. Kaasa moved to Millet in 1938 and to Edmonton a decade later. He established a museum in British Columbia and for many years gave public lectures and showed his films.

Road   1991   SE   5:B2

Kaasa Road West

West of 34 Street, south of 35 Avenue; connecting to Kramer Way and Kaasa Road East

See Kaasa Road East.

Road   1991   SE   5:B2 *

Kainai Park

11714–32A Avenue

Names in the Kaskitayo area are in honour of Aboriginal culture. Kainai is a Blackfoot word meaning "many chiefs." The Kainai Chieftainship is bestowed by the Blood (of the Blackfoot Nation) upon distinguished persons in recognition of their work with Aboriginal people. This honour may be held by only 40 living persons at a time. Edward, the Prince of Wales, was the first to receive the Kainai Chieftainship in 1919, and Charles, the present Prince of Wales, has also been honoured and bears the name of Chief Red Crow. The Kainai Park is in the Sweet Grass neighbourhood and has an area of 0.39 ha.

Park   1982   SW   4:B2

Kameyosek

28 Avenue to 34 Avenue, 66 Street west to Mill Woods Road

Kameyosek is said to be the Cree word for "the beautiful."

Neighbourhood   1972   SE   4:D2

Kameyosek Park

260 Lakewood Road North

This park is in the Kameyosek neighbourhood and has an area of 3.03 ha. *See* Kameyosek.

Park   1987   SE   4:D2

Kane Wynd

South of 38 Avenue, west of 34 Street

Edward William Scott Kane (b. 1899) was a justice of the Alberta Supreme Court. Kane was born in Ireland and came to Canada with his parents in 1900. He moved to Edmonton in 1916 and graduated from the University of Alberta in 1920. Kane received his law degree in 1922, was called to the bar in 1922 and practised law for four decades. In 1961 he was appointed justice of the Alberta Supreme Court, appellate division.

Road 1991 SE 5:B2

Karl Clark Road

Off Parsons Road, south of 23 Avenue, west of 91 Street

Ontario-born Karl A. Clark (1888–1966) developed the hot-water method of extracting oil from the Athabasca tar sands. He obtained a PhD in chemistry from the University of Illinois in 1916 and came to Edmonton in 1920 to work for the forerunner of the Alberta Research Council. In 1938 he was appointed professor of metallurgy at the University of Alberta. He retired from the University in 1954 but continued working for the Research Council until his retirement in 1964. This semicircular roadway, located within the Edmonton Research and Development Park, was originally named Research Centre Loop. Later, however, it was felt that the names used in the park should honour prominent scientists and researchers. As a result, the road was renamed in honour of Karl Clark.

Road 1981 SE 1:B1

Kaskitayo

10 Avenue and Blackmud Creek north to 34 Avenue, Calgary Trail west to Whitemud Creek

Originally spelled "Kaskiteeo," this name is derived from the Cree word, noted by J.B. Tyrrell in the 1870s as *kas-ki-tee-oo-asiki*, meaning "blackmud creek." Subdivisions and neighbourhoods in this area have an Aboriginal naming theme.

Area 1970 SW 4:B2 *

Kaskitayo Park

1921–111 Street

This 11.79-ha. park is in the Keheewin neighbourhood. It is named for the Kaskitayo area in which it is located. *See* Kaskitayo.

Park 1980 SW 1:A1

Kathleen McAllister Park

10517–50A Street

Kathleen McAllister (1886–1981) was an early activist for women's rights and marched with Nellie McClung in the fight for women's suffrage. Born in Ballacola, Ireland, she immigrated to Canada with her family at the age of three. She and her husband, Robert McAllister, farmed in Retlaw, Alberta, from 1910 to 1916. They then moved to a farm along the North Saskatchewan River and remained there until Robert's death in 1946. Later in life, McAllister worked at the Manyberries Research Station, the Hobbema Reserve Agent's Office, a law office in Vegreville and at St. Paul's United Church. She retired in 1974 but continued to be involved in a variety of causes. McAllister volunteered for several women's groups and organizations concerned with the welfare of minorities. The Kathleen McAllister Park is located in the Fulton Place neighbourhood and has an area of 0.39 ha.

Park 1982 NE 6:A2

Kaufman Way

North of 34 Avenue, west of 34 Street

This road is named in honour of Dr. Stanley and Carolyn (Reesor) Kaufman. Born in Ontario, Dr.

Kaufman graduated from the University of Toronto in 1908. He then worked at London Hospital and graduated as a member of the Royal College of Surgeons of England. He married Carolyn Reesor in 1912, and they moved to Edmonton where Dr. Kaufman practised medicine for 51 years. Dr. Kaufman was one of the original members of the Alberta St. John Ambulance medical advisory board and was an instructor with the organization for 30 years. Carolyn Kaufman, also born in Ontario, was a painter and author who wrote and illustrated *Historic Churches of Alberta and the Canadian Northwest*. She was a member of the Alberta Society of Artists and served as president of the Federation of Canadian Artists. Both of the Kaufmans died in 1968.

Road   1991   SE   5:B2 *

Keheewin

17 Avenue to 23 Avenue, Calgary Trail west to 111 Street

Some of the neighbourhoods names in the Kaskitayo area honour Aboriginal leaders. Keheewin was a Cree chief. His name means "Eagle." Chief Keheewin signed the Treaty No. 6 in 1876. He died in 1887 at Onion Lake, Saskatchewan; the Kehewin First Nation, located south of Bonnyville, bears his name.

Neighbourhood   1978   SW   1:A1

Keheewin Park

10710–19 Avenue

This park is in the Keheewin neighbourhood and has an area of 5.99 ha. *See* Keheewin.

Park   2001   SW   1:A1 *

Keillor Farm, 1962. (CEA ET-2-30)

Keillor Road Trail

North of Fox Drive

Dr. Frederick A. Keillor (1883–1971) was the city's coroner and served as alderman for two terms. Born in Ontario, Keillor moved to Edmonton in 1912 and established a medical practice. After serving in WWI, he returned to Edmonton and in 1919 bought the land this trail runs through. Keillor donated part of his river valley property in 1928 and requested that a road be built to provide better access to his farm and Whitemud Park. He was a coroner for the city, and an alderman from 1926 to 1927 and 1929 to 1932. Keillor Road closed to vehicular traffic in 1995 and is now used as a bicycle and walking trail.

Walkway   1974   SW   4:A1 *

Ken Newman Park

10802–150 Street

Alberta-born Ken Newman (b. 1917) was a WWII veteran and the last mayor of the Town of Jasper Place. After serving overseas, he began farming in Jasper Place. Newman was elected to the Jasper Place town council in 1952 and served for five years. In 1957 he was elected mayor and served until the town amalgamated with Edmonton in 1964. That same year Newman was elected as an Edmonton alderman and served (except for 1966 to 1968) until his retirement in 1983. The Ken Newman Park is in the High Park neighbourhood and has an area of 1.3 ha.

Park   1987   NW   8:D2

Kenilworth

Whyte Avenue north to 90 Avenue, 58 Street to 75 Street

This neighbourhood was named in the early 1900s and appears on early Edmonton maps. Kenilworth may be named after the town and castle of Kenilworth in Warwickshire, England. The name has existed in England since at least 1086. The word may mean "Kenulph (or Kenelm's) Place" as "Kenil" likely refers to the name of an early land owner, Kenulph or Kenelm, and "worth" is a Saxon term for a mansion or dwelling-place. The castle of Kenilworth was built in 1122.

Neighbourhood   CU   SE   7:D2

Kenilworth Field

8302–64 Street

This park is in the Kenilworth neighbourhood and has an area of 2.63 ha. *See* Kenilworth.

Park   1967   SE   7:D2

Kenilworth Park

7104–87 Avenue

This park is in the Kenilworth neighbourhood and has an area of 2.37 ha. *See* Kenilworth.

Park   1982   SE   7:D2

Kennedale Industrial

CN Railway tracks north to 137 Avenue, 50 Street west to CN Railway tracks

H.P. Kennedy came to Edmonton from Ontario in 1911 and bought this property and other sites in north Edmonton. He was a real estate developer and named the area after himself. Prior to being named as a neighbourhood, the area was known as the Kennedale subdivision. The name is a long-standing one, having been in common usage since 1913. The area was replotted in 1961.

Neighbourhood   CU   NE   11:A2

Kennedale Industrial, looking northeast from Kenward Drive and 50 Street, 1976. (CEA EA-264-38)

Kennedale Ravine

Separating the Hermitage and Clareview subdivisions, east of 50 Street at 131 Avenue

Around 1912, H.P. Kennedy named this area Kennedale Park. Before the ravine's formal naming in 1972, the name Kennedale Ravine was in common usage. *See* Kennedale Industrial.

Ravine   1972   NE   11:B2

Kennedale Ravine Bridge

Spanning the Kennedale Ravine at Victoria Trail

Construction on this bridge over the Kennedale Ravine began in 1980. It connects the Hermitage neighbourhood with Clareview along Victoria Trail. *See* Kennedale Industrial.

Bridge   1980   NE   6:B1

Kennedy Drive

East of 56 Street, north of 129 Avenue

This road was most likely named for H.P. Kennedy. Local maps indicate that this road has existed since at least 1914. *See* Kennedale Industrial.

Road   CU   NE   11:A2 *

Kensington

132 Avenue to 137 Avenue, 113A Street to 127 Street

This name replaces the subdivisions of Grand Trunk Annex and Queen Mary Park (not to be confused with the current Queen Mary Park neighbourhood). Kensington was the name of a subdivision located to the east of the present-day neighbourhood and appears as early as 1907. The name may have been taken from the Kensington area of London, England, which has been part of the British capital since 1899.

Neighbourhood 1957   NW   10:B2

Kensington Park

12130–134B Avenue

This park is in the Kensington neighbourhood and has an area of 5.88 ha. *See* Kensington.

Park   1982   NW   10:B2

Kensit Place

East of Kaasa Road East, north of Kramer Place

William Kensit (1902–1984) was a self-taught photographer who worked for the *Edmonton Bulletin* and the *Edmonton Journal*. Kensit was born in England and moved to Edmonton with his parents. From 1945 to 1965, he ran his own photography studio. Photographs from the Kensit Studios are now at the Provincial Archives of Alberta.

Road   1993   SE   5:B2 *

Kernohan

Kennedale Ravine north to 137 Avenue, 22 Street west to Victoria Trail

Like other neighbourhoods in the Clareview subdivision, Kernohan is named for an Edmonton pioneer. James Kernohan came west to the Edmonton area from Ontario in the early 1880s. In

Frank and Lulu Kernohan, children of James Kernohan, circa 1910. (CEA EA-745-222)

1883, the shanty that Kernohan lived in the Belmont area burned down. Two years later, his wife, Mary Elizabeth, and their children joined him. He then moved to property owned by J. Rowland, and later owned some land on the Hudson's Bay Reserve. Kernohan, a farmer and a member of the Belmont School Board, also tried his hand at shopkeeping. Between July and September 1892, he owned part of W.A. Ibbotson & Kernohan, a store that sold fruits and vegetables, as well as ice cream. Mary Elizabeth Kernohan owned one of the first millinery shops in Edmonton. Her store was in operation between 1889 and 1891. Mary Elizabeth died in 1894. Their eldest son was an Edmonton postal worker in 1887; another son successfully reached the Klondike. In 1899, Kernohan moved to Leduc.

Neighbourhood   1978   NE   11:B2

Kernohan Park

551 Clareview Road

This park is in the Kernohan neighbourhood and has an area of 3.03 ha. *See* Kernohan.

Park 1987 NE 11:B2 *

Keyano Park

12963–119 Street

The Calder neighbourhood held a contest to name this park, choosing Keyano, which means "sharing" in Cree; proponents of the name gave the meaning as "unity." The community believed the name was appropriate for commemorating the Commonwealth Games being held in Edmonton in 1978. Keyano was also the name given to the games' mascot, the Commonwealth Bear. The Keyano Park is in the Calder neighbourhood and has an area of 1.01 ha.

Park 1978 NW 10:B2

Kikino Trail

From 77 Avenue to 87 Avenue at 177 Street

The name of this trail, a major walkway in the Thorncliff neighbourhood, reflects the theme of most of Edmonton's walkways, which are named for prominent Aboriginal people or bear a relationship with Aboriginal heritage. *Kikino* is said to be the Cree word for "our home." Kikino Trail is one of a number of trail names approved between 1969 and 1971.

Walkway 1969 SW 3:C1 *

Kildare

137 Avenue to 144 Avenue, 66 Street to 82 Street

The name of this neighbourhood is taken from the county and town of Kildare in Ireland. St. Bridget (453–523) founded a nunnery there and changed the name from the Celtic words *Druim Criaidh* to

Cill-dara, which means church of the oak. Kildare is the anglicized form of *Cill-dara*. The name reflects other Irish names in the area, including Kilkenny, Killarney and Londonderry.

Neighbourhood 1964 NE 10:D2

Kildare Park

14224 74 Street

This park is in the Kildare neighbourhood and has an area of 1.72 ha. *See* Kildare.

Park 1983 NE 10:C2

Kilkenny

144 Avenue to 153 Avenue, 66 Street to 82 Street

The name of this neighbourhood is taken from the inland county and town of Kilkenny in Ireland. Its name is derived from the Celtic phrase *Cill Chainnigh*, meaning the church of St. Canice (also Cainneach) or Kenny (also Kenneth), in its anglicized form. St. Canice was a sixth-century Irish monk who founded a monastery in Kilkenny. The church dates back to 1052 and is the second largest place of worship in Ireland, after St. Patrick's Church in Dublin. The name reflects other Irish names in the area, including Kildare, Killarney and Londonderry.

Neighbourhood 1964 NE 10:C2

Kilkenny Park

7245–149A Avenue

This park is in the Kilkenny neighbourhood and has an area of 1.78 ha. *See* Kilkenny.

Park 1983 NE 10:C2

Wright's Grocery in King Edward Park, no date. (CEA EA-275-1132)

Killarney

127 Avenue to 132 Avenue, 82 Street to 97 Street

This name is taken from the town of Killarney in Ireland, the origin of its name being the Gaelic *Cill Airne*, meaning church of the sloes. A sloe is the small black or purplish fruit of the blackthorn, a thorny bush. Killarney is the anglicized version of *Cill Airne*. The name reflects other Irish names in the area, including Kildare, Kilkenny and Londonderry.

Neighbourhood 1956 NE 10:C2

Killarney Park

8720–130A Avenue

This park is in the Killarney neighbourhood and has an area of 0.78 ha. *See* Killarney.

Park 1983 NE 10:C2

King Edward Industrial

Argyll Road and Whyte Avenue west to 71 Street

This area is east of the King Edward Park neighbourhood and was named for King Edward VII. *See* King Edward Park *neighbourhood.*

Subdivision 1968 SE 4:D1 *

King Edward Park

76 Avenue north to Whyte Avenue, 71 Street west to Mill Creek Ravine Park

James Inkster (1854–1938) farmed this land before the turn of the 20th century. He was born in Manitoba and came to Edmonton in 1880, settling on this land the following year. In about 1909, he sold much of his property. The neighbourhood was named before it was annexed to the City of Edmonton in 1913. The name commemorates Edward VII (1841–1910), the eldest son of Queen Victoria, who became king in 1901.

Neighbourhood CU SE 4:C1

King Edward Park

7708–85 Street

This park is in the King Edward Park neighbourhood and has an area of 0.82 ha. *See* King Edward Park *neighbourhood.*

Park 1983 SE 4:C1

Kingsway

118 Avenue southeast to 101 Street at 108A Avenue

Kingsway Avenue and Portage Avenue were renamed Portage Avenue (later Princess Elizabeth Avenue) and Kingsway, respectively, in 1939. Bylaw 928 switched the names of the two intersecting streets just days before the June 2, 1939 visit of King George VI and Queen Elizabeth. The change was made so that the royal procession could travel along Kingsway, instead of Portage Avenue.

Road 1939 NW 7:B1

Kiniski Crescent

44 Avenue and 38 Street

See Kiniski Gardens *feature story, page 182.*

Road 1980 SE 5:B2

Kiniski Gardens

Mill Creek Ravine north, and 34 Street northwest to Kiniski Crescent, Kirkwood Avenue and Kline Crescent

See feature story, page 182.

Neighbourhood 1976 SE 5:A2

Kiniski Gardens Park

4120–41 Street

This park is in the Kiniski Gardens neighbourhood and has an area of 1.88 ha. *See* Kiniski Gardens *feature story, page 182.*

Park 1987 SE 5:B2

George J. Kinnaird, 1904. (CEA EA-10-669-102)

Kinnaird Bridge

Spanning the Kinnaird Ravine at 82 Street

The Kinnaird Bridge passes over the Kinnaird Ravine between 111 and 112 Avenues. *See* Kinnaird Park.

Bridge 1951 NE 7:C1

Kinnaird Park

78 Street and 111 Avenue

George Johnston Kinnaird (1857–1922) was a pioneer Edmonton civil servant. He came from Scotland to apprentice with the Hudson's Bay Company (HBC) at Fort Qu'appelle (near present-day Regina) in 1875. Ten years later, Kinnaird arrived in Edmonton. He left the HBC in 1900 to become Edmonton's town clerk, and later became a city commissioner. In 1910 he established an accounting firm and in 1915 was appointed auditor for the City.

Kiniski Gardens

POLISH-BORN Julia Kiniski (1899–1969) was a colourful and determined Edmonton politician who was credited with breathing new life into Edmonton civic politics. After ten failed attempts, Kiniski was elected as an alderwoman in October 1963. She was only the third woman to win a seat on City Council. As president of the Civic Rights Protective Association, Kiniski campaigned against wasteful city spending during the two-decade-long domination of municipal affairs by politicians connected to the Civil Government Association.

Kiniski emigrated from Poland to Chipman, Alberta, with her family in 1912 and married at the age of 16. She left school after completing Grade 7; as an adult, she attended extension courses in psychology and philosophy at the University of Alberta. She and her husband moved to Edmonton in 1936.

Between 1945 and 1962, in the course of her ten unsuccessful runs for office, "Big Julie," as she was known, became an accomplished, albeit unconventional, speaker. Her 1963 victory was said to have reinvigorated public interest in City Council. While Kiniski's outspoken criticism of city spending did not make her popular with civic administrators, her defence of the "little people" captured the public's imagination. A local radio personality, Jerry Forbes, recorded a song about her set to the tune of "Hello Dolly." By 1968, in her last election, Kiniski had so greatly increased her share of the votes that she led all other candidates by a clear margin.

After her election in 1963 she was re-elected three times (1964, 1966, 1968) and served until her death from a heart attack in 1969 at the age of 70. Kiniski was the mother of six children, including the professional wrestler Gene Kiniski. During the late 1910s, the southern portion of Kiniski Gardens was known as Edmonton Market Gardens.

Julia Kiniski, circa 1960. (CEA EA–117–19)

Kinsmen Park, looking northeast toward Rossdale and Downtown, circa 1960. (CEA EA-20-1033)

The land on which the Kinnaird Park and Kinnaird Ravine are located was once owned by James McDonald (River Lot 24) and James Kirkness (River Lot 26). The City acquired the property in the early 1900s and named the park in 1916. Kinnaird Park lies between the Virginia Park and Cromdale neighbourhoods and has an area of 1.05 ha.

Park CU NE 7:C1 *

Kinnaird Ravine

East of 82 Street, south of 112 Avenue in Cromdale

This ravine was originally called Rat Creek Ravine, after the creek of the same name that ran through the ravine. It eventually became known as Kinnaird Ravine, most likely after nearby Kinnaird Street, now 82 Street. The name was in common usage before it was adopted by the Names Advisory Committee in 1967. *See* Kinnaird Park.

Ravine CU NE 7:D1

Kinokamau Lake

North of Yellowhead Trail, west of 170 Street, east of 184 Street

This name has been in use since 1895. While its origin is not recorded, the name is taken from the Cree word *kinokamâw*, which means "a long lake."

Lake 1958 NW 8:C1

Kinsmen Park

9100 Walterdale Hill Road

From 1953 to 1963 the Kinsmen Club leased this land from the City of Edmonton. The club carried out a ten-year project to develop the site as a sports and recreational area. Several facilities have since been built in the park, including the Kinsmen fieldhouse in 1967 (a Centennial project) and an aquatic centre in 1977 (for the Commonwealth Games). These comprise the Kinsmen Sport Centre, and include five swimming pools and an indoor running track. The Kinsmen Park has an area of 21.45 ha. and is located in the river valley.

Park 1969 C 7:B2

Kirk Lake

North of Highway 16, between 199 Street and 184 Street

The name was approved by the province in 1963 and likely honours Horace Kirk, who homesteaded the land to the east of the lake.

Lake 1963 NW 8:B1

Kirkness

144 Avenue to 153 Avenue, Victoria Trail west to CN railway tracks

Like other neighbourhoods in the Clareview subdivision, Kirkness is named for an Edmonton pioneer. James Kirkness (d. 1911) was an early Edmonton settler who came to Canada from Scotland in 1864 with the Hudson's Bay Company. By the 1870s, Kirkness was living in Edmonton and had purchased and settled on River Lot 26 (the present-day site of Edmonton Northlands).

Neighbourhood 1979 NE 11:B2

Kirkness Park

630 Kirkness Road

This park is located in the Kirkness neighbourhood and has an area of 3.04 ha. *See* Kirkness.

Park 1986 NE 11:B2

Kirkness Road

144 Avenue northeast to Victoria Trail

See Kirkness.

Road 1979 NE 11:B2

The Ebbers dairy farm at 153 Avenue east of 34 Street, later Kirkness neighbourhood, 1976. (CEA EA-264-27)

Kirkpatrick Crescent

Joining Kiniski Crescent east of 38 Street

George R. F. Kirkpatrick (1868–1943) was the manager of Edmonton's first bank. He was born in Ontario and in 1891 came to Edmonton to open a branch of the Imperial Bank of Canada. He remained bank manager until his retirement in 1936. From 1892 to 1898, Kirkpatrick was also Edmonton's first town treasurer.

Road 1980 SE 5:B2 *

Kirkwood Avenue

North of 43 Avenue, east of 38 Street

Harry Kirkwood (d. 1977) was born in Ireland and came to Edmonton with his parents in 1912. He worked with his father, the founder of Kirkwood Dairy, until 1951. Kirkwood spent the next 23 years as a custodian at Bonnie Doon High School, retiring in 1973.

Road 1990 SE 5:B2

Kirkwood Way

Joining Kirkwood Avenue and 43 Avenue, west of 34 Street

See Kirkwood Avenue.

Road 1990 SE 5:B2

Kitchener Park

11411–103 Avenue

Horatio Herbert Kitchener (1850–1916) was a British field marshal and statesman, and one of the most celebrated personalities to represent the British Empire at the height of its power. Kitchener took part in the Battle of Omdurman and the defeat of Mahdist forces in Sudan in 1898, and served in South Africa in the Boer War until 1902. He was then sent to India as commander in chief of British forces there, remaining in the position until 1909; served as consul general to Egypt from 1911 to 1914; and was recalled to England at the outbreak of WWI and made secretary of state for war. He died in 1916 en route to a mission in Russia when his ship struck a German mine and sank. In 1925, the Kitchener Park was known as Kitchener Square. Prior to that, *Henderson's Directory* listed it as Old School Grounds. Kitchener Park is in the Oliver neighbourhood and has an area of 0.65 ha.

Park   1967   C   7:B2

Kittlitz Park

2850–36A Avenue

Karl (1865–1943) and Anna (1869–1904) Kittlitz came to Edmonton from Poland in 1897. Upon arrival in south Edmonton, they purchased land in the Colchester district, just east of the present-day Silver Berry neighbourhood. Later, the Kittlitz family owned and farmed the land that is now known as Kittlitz Park. This park is in the Wild Rose neighbourhood and has an area of 1.0 ha.

Park   1995   SE   5:B2 *

Klarvatten

167 Avenue to 180 Avenue, 82 Street to 91 Street

Klarvatten is Swedish for "clear water." This neighbourhood is part of the Lake District area.

Neighbourhood   1979   NE   10:C1

Klarvatten Bay

Joining Klarvatten Road, north of 167 Avenue, east of 90 Street

See Klarvatten.

Road   1990   NE   10:C1 *

Klarvatten Close

Joining Klarvatten Lake Wynd, north of 167 Avenue, west of 84 Street

See Klarvatten.

Road   1990   NE   10:C1 *

Klarvatten Court

Joining Klarvatten Road, northeast of 170A Avenue, west of Klarvatten Lake Wynd

See Klarvatten.

Road   1990   NE   10:C1 *

Klarvatten Cove

Joining Klarvatten Road, south of Klarvatten Court, west of Klarvatten Lake Wynd

See Klarvatten.

Road   1990   NE   10:C1 *

Klarvatten Lake Wynd

Joining Klarvatten Road, north of 167 Avenue, west of 84 Street

See Klarvatten.

Road   1990   NE   10:C1 *

Klarvatten Road

North of 167 Avenue, east of 91 Street

See Klarvatten.

Road   1990   NE   10:C1

H.B. Kline and Sons Jewellers, 1918. (GAI NC-6-4022)

Kline Crescent

North of Kirkwood Avenue, west of 34 Street

Irving Kline (1893–1971) was an early Edmonton optometrist and jeweller. He was born in Montreal and came to Edmonton with his family in 1904. His father opened a jewellery store and Irving studied optometry. In 1917 Irving opened an optical dispensary and, soon after, began selling jewellery as well as eyeglasses.

Road   1980   SE   5:B2 *

Knottwood

9 Avenue to 23 Avenue, 66 Street to 91 Street

Daniel K. Knott (1879–1959) was a linotype operator, alderman and mayor. Knott was born in Ontario and, after apprenticing as a printer in the

United States, came to Edmonton in 1905 to work at the *Edmonton Bulletin*. He later joined the *Edmonton Journal* and remained there for 35 years. Knott was first elected to city council in 1923. He served as an alderman for many years and as mayor from 1932 to 1934. The Knottwood subdivision name is compatible with the Mill Woods area naming theme, which requires use of "mill" or "wood."

Subdivision   1972   SE   1:B1 *

Knottwood Road East

Intersecting Mill Woods Road South, west of 69 Street

See Knottwood.

Road   1974   SE   1:B1

Mayor Daniel K. Knott mailing first air mail, Edmonton, 1931. (GAI ND-3-5935)

Knottwood Road North

Intersecting Mill Woods Road, south of 23 Avenue, west of 74 Street

See Knottwood.

Road 1974 SE 1:B1

Knottwood Road South

Between Knottwood Road East and West, north of 11 Avenue

See Knottwood.

Road 1974 SE 1:B1

Knottwood Road West

Between Knottwood Road North and South, east of 89 Street

See Knottwood.

Road 1974 SE 1:B1

Kramer Place

East of Kaasa Road East, north of Kaufman Way

Edward Kramer (1888–1976) was press foreman at the *Edmonton Journal* for 35 years. Kramer was born in Quebec and worked in Winnipeg, Chicago and Boston before coming to Edmonton in 1914. After installing presses at the *Edmonton Journal*, he took the position of press foreman and remained there until his retirement in 1950. During the 1920s and 1930s, Kramer and his wife also ran a lake resort at Alberta Beach.

Road   1991   SE   5:B2 *

Kramer Way

West of Kaasa Road East, north of Kaufman Way

See Kramer Place.

Road   1991   SE   5:B2 *

Kulawy Drive North

North of 38A Avenue, west of 44 Street

This road in the Kiniski Gardens neighbourhood is named after three brothers, two of whom were murdered in the Auschwitz concentration camp in German occupied Poland during WWII. Polish-born brothers Albert, John and Paul Kulawy were all Oblate priests. Albert Kulawy (1871–1942) moved to Ottawa in 1894 and was ordained as a priest in 1898. For the next five years, he was based in Winnipeg. Albert later left the Oblate Order and from 1905 to 1921 served in the Diocese of Philadelphia. He returned to Poland in 1923 and ministered there until 1939. When the Germans invaded Poland in 1939, Albert fled and sought sanctuary at the Oblate Hospital in Swiety Krzyz. He died of natural causes at the hospital in 1942.

Jan "John" Kulawy (1872–1941) came to Canada with his elder brother, Albert. He worked in Ottawa and published a Polish-language Roman Catholic newspaper. He was the first of the three brothers to return to Europe, leaving Canada in 1905. In 1919 John was appointed superior-general of the Oblates of Mary Immaculate in Poland. The third brother, Paul Kulawy (1877–1941), arrived in Canada in 1903. He was attached to various parishes in Alberta for 18 years. During this period, in 1915, he founded the Holy Rosary Parish in Edmonton. Paul returned to Poland in 1921 and

continued his religious service there. In 1941, John and Paul were both arrested, on the same day, by the German Gestapo. The two brothers were interned at the Auschwitz concentration camp and died a short time later.

Road   1991   SE   5:B2 *

Kulawy Drive Point

West of Kulawy Drive North, north of 39 Avenue

See Kulawy Drive North.

Road   1991   SE   5:B2 *

Kulawy Gate

North of Kulawy Place, between Kulawy Drive North and 44 Street

See Kulawy Drive North.

Road   1991   SE   5:B2 *

Kulawy Place

North of 38A Avenue, east of Kulawy Drive North

See Kulawy Drive North.

Road   1991   SE   5:B2 *

La Perle

95 Avenue to 100 Avenue, 178 Street to 191 Street

In 1898, Eléodore Joseph "Leo" LaPerle (1895–1980) and his family travelled west from Ontario to Winterburn. There, in 1906, Leo's father opened a general store. Leo LaPerle enlisted in the army in 1917 and was stationed in England. He was discharged in 1919 as a sergeant. In 1929, LaPerle began running the family store and the Winterburn Post Office. The store remained in operation until 1969, when the building was torn down.

Neighbourhood 1978 SW 8:C2

La Perle Park

18527–97A Avenue

This park is in the La Perle neighbourhood and has an area of 2.09 ha. *See* La Perle.

Park 1985 SW 8:C2

Lago Lindo

167 Avenue to 180A Avenue, 91 Street to 97 Street

Lago Lindo is Spanish for "beautiful lake." This neighbourhood is in the Lake District area.

Neighbourhood 1979 NE 10:C1

Lago Lindo Crescent

168 Avenue and 95 Street

See Lago Lindo.

Road 1980 NE 10:C1

Lago Lindo Park

17123–95 Street

This park is in the Lago Lindo neighbourhood and has an area of 3.07 ha. *See* Lago Lindo.

Park 2000 NE 10:C1 *

Lake District

153 Avenue to 181 Avenue, 66 Street to 97 Street

This area was named for the abundance of lakes (stormwater management facilities) built here. Neighbourhood names in this area relate to water and lakes.

Area 1979 NE 10:C1 *

Lakewood

23 Avenue to 34 Avenue, 66 Street to 91 Street

The name is compatible with the naming theme for the Mill Woods area, all subdivision names using "mill" or "wood."

Subdivision 1972 SE 4:D2 *

Lakewood Road East

Joining Lakewood Road North at 71 Street, north of 28 Avenue

See Lakewood.

Road 1974 SE 4:D2 *

Lakewood Road North

Between Lakewood Road East and West, north of 32 Avenue

See Lakewood.

Road 1974 SE 4:D2

Lakewood Road South

Between Lakewood Road West and Mill Woods Road, north of 24 Avenue

See Lakewood.

Road 1974 SE 4:D2

Marcel Lambert, front right, with other scholastic award winners prior to leaving for the coronation of King George VI, 1937.
(CEA EA–10–2600)

Lakewood Road West

Between Lakewood Road North and South, west of 83 Street

See Lakewood.

Road 1974 SE 4:C2

Lamb Crescent

North of Leger Way, west of Rabbit Hill Road

Jack Lamb (b. 1935) was an Edmonton-born football player who played for both the Edmonton Eskimos and the Calgary Stampeders between 1955 and 1965. He also owned a real estate company, Lamb Realty.

Road 1999 SW 4:A2 *

Lambert Court

North of 23 Avenue, west of Leger Way

Federal politician Marcel Lambert (1919–2000) served in WWII and was taken prisoner by German forces at Dieppe. After Lambert's tank broke down during the assault on the beaches of Dieppe, he and his crew were captured by German troops and spent the next three years as prisoners of war. After the war, Lambert, a Rhodes scholar, went on to have a successful political career. He served as member of parliament for Edmonton-West from 1957 to 1984, as Speaker of the House from 1962 to 1963, as minister for veterans affairs in 1963 and was named to the National Transportation Agency in 1985.

Road 1999 SW 4:A2 *

Lambton Industrial

CP railway tracks north to 92 Avenue and west to 50 Street

This industrial area has existed since about 1911 and was formerly known as Lambton Park. It may have been named after John George Lambton, the first Earl of Durham. Lord Durham (1792–1840) was governor general of British North America for five months in 1838. Lord Durham resigned after the British government rejected his plans to exile political prisoners. He was famous for the Durham Report that recommended responsible government and the union of Upper and Lower Canada.

Neighbourhood 1975 SE 6:A2

Lansdowne

53 Avenue south to Whitemud Drive, 122 Street west to Whitemud Park

This neighbourhood in the Douglas subdivision honours Sir Henry Charles Keith Petty-Fitzmaurice (1845–1927), fifth Marquess of Lansdowne, sixth Earl of Kerry and Governor General of Canada from 1883 to 1888.

Neighbourhood 1962 SW 4:B1

Lansdowne Drive

East of Whitemud Park, west of 122A Street, north of Whitemud Drive

See Lansdowne.

Road 1964 SW 4:B1

Lansdowne Park

4915–124 Street

This park is in the Lansdowne neighbourhood and has an area of 1.77 ha. *See* Lansdowne.

Park 1983 SW 4:B1

David G. Latta, circa 1906. (CEA EA-302-39)

Larkspur

38 Avenue north to Whitemud Drive, 17 Street to 34 Street

This neighbourhood, in The Meadows area, was named for the larkspur, a wildflower or ornamental plant that blooms in many colours. The showy stalks of the larkspur tend toward blue flowers but vary to red, white, pink, yellow and violet.

Neighbourhood 1982 SE 5:B2

Larkspur Park

2928–41 Avenue

This park is in the Larkspur neighbourhood and has an area of 12.23 ha. *See* Larkspur.

Park 1992 SE 5:B2

Latta Bridge

Spanning the Latta Ravine at Jasper Avenue

By 1911, a trestle bridge had been built across the Latta Ravine, and in 1936 a steel bridge replaced it. While the bridge was called Latta Bridge from the time of its construction, the name was not formally recognized until 1951, when a plaque honouring David G. Latta was placed on the bridge. *See* Latta Ravine.

Bridge 1951 NE 7:C2

Latta house from Latta Ravine, circa 1940.
(CEA EA–302–99)

Latta Ravine

Jasper Avenue and 90 Street

David G. Latta (1869–1948) was a pioneer Edmonton businessman. He was born in Ireland and came to Canada in 1889. Before arriving in Edmonton in 1897, Latta was a member of the North West Mounted Police. In 1902 he opened a blacksmith shop and in 1906 was elected as an alderman. In 1907 David Latta built a house next to what is now known as Latta Ravine. *See* Latta Bridge.

Ravine CU NE 7:C2 *

Lauder Avenue

South of 132 Avenue at 105 Street

See Lauderdale.

Road 1960 NW 10:C2

Lauderdale

127 Avenue to 132 Avenue, 97 Street to 113A Street

James Lauder (1843–1924) and his son Tom (1863–1949) owned and farmed this land before the turn of the 20th century. Both were born in Scotland and came to Canada in 1874. In 1881 the Lauders travelled west to Edmonton and acquired a homestead. James opened a bakery in 1885 and Tom soon joined the business. In 1900, after James became ill, the bakery was sold. Tom later became the chief of the fire brigade.

Neighbourhood CU NW 10:B2

Lauderdale Park

12935–107 Street

This park is in the Lauderdale neighbourhood and has an area of 1.81 ha. *See* Lauderdale.

Park 1982 NW 10:C2

Lauderdale Road

North of 129 Avenue at 104 Street

See Lauderdale.

Road 1959 NW 10:C2 *

Laurier Drive

South of 80 Avenue, from 149 Street east to 142 Street

See Laurier Heights.

Road 1968 SW 4:A1

Edmonton Mayor Robert Lee, no date. (CEA EA-10-1610)

Laurier Heights

*Laurier Drive north to 87 Avenue,
Buena Vista Park west to 149 Street*

Sir Wilfrid Laurier (1841–1919), a Liberal, was Canada's prime minister from 1896 to 1911. He was in power when Alberta became a province in 1905. Sir Wilfrid Laurier Park (originally Laurier Park) pre-dates Laurier Heights. The Laurier Heights neighbourhood incorporates most of the former subdivision of Buena Vista. Development in this neighbourhood occurred during the 1950s and 1960s. *See* Sir Wilfrid Laurier Park.

Neighbourhood   1956   SW   4:A1

Laurier Heights Park

14405–85 Avenue

This park is in the Laurier Heights neighbourhood and has an area of 2.51 ha. Although the name was officially adopted in 1987, it has been in use since 1912. *See* Laurier Heights.

Park   1987   SW   4:A1 *

Laurier Place

East of 139 Street, south of 79 Avenue

See Laurier Heights.

Road   1968   SW   4:A1

Lavigne Road

North of Saskatchewan Drive between 90 Avenue and 91 Avenue

This road takes its name from an informal river valley subdivision that existed as far back as the late 1890s. Lavigne, or Skunk Hollow, lies to the north of Saskatchewan Drive and covers an area 91.4 metres by 91.4 metres. The origin of the name Lavigne is not recorded.

Road   CU   C   7:C2 *

Layton Court

North of Leger Boulevard, west of Rabbit Hill Road

Roberta Layton (1916–1987) was an Edmonton humanitarian who helped to improve the lives of others. Layton was an active participant in many organizations, including the Junior League of Edmonton, the University Women's Club and the United Way. Between 1985 and 1987, she was on the Board of Directors of the Big Sisters of Edmonton. In 1987, shortly after Layton's death, the Big Sisters of Edmonton named a trust fund in her honour; it is today known as the Children's Scholarship Plan.

Road   1998   SW   4:A2 *

Lee Ridge

34 Avenue to 38 Avenue, 66 Street west to Mill Woods Road

Robert Lee (1862–1925) was the mayor of Edmonton from 1909 to 1910. He was born in Canada West and came to Edmonton in 1898. Before serving as an alderman in 1908, Lee was a

Looking west, Lavigne "Skunk Hollow" neighbourhood in foreground, circa 1920. (CEA EA-10-1066)

town alderman and school board member. Lee was also a businessman involved in real estate.

Neighbourhood 1972 SE 4:D2

Lee Ridge Park

460 Millbourne Road East

This park is in the Lee Ridge neighbourhood and has an area of 2.79 ha. *See* Lee Ridge.

Park 1984 SE 4:D2

Lee Ridge Road

Joining 36 Avenue and Millbourne Road East

See Lee Ridge.

Road 1972 SE 4:D2

Leger

23 Avenue to approximately 29 Avenue, Rabbit Hill Road west to Terwillegar Drive

Long-serving politician Edmund Hugh Leger (1927–1990) was first elected as a city councillor in 1959, and went on to serve for 25 years. In 1961 he made a failed bid for mayor, but returned to City Council in 1963 as an alderman. Although his political career was often controversial, Leger was considered to be the city's "watchdog." He entered politics accusing city officials of acting improperly and of accepting bribes. In particular, he charged Mayor Hawrelak with "gross misconduct." The mayor later resigned over the provincial inquiry into a number of questionable land sales in which he was involved. Leger's last term ended in 1986, when he lost his seat in the election.

Neighbourhood 1990 SW 4:A2

Leger Boulevard

West of Rabbit Hill road, north of Lindsay Crescent

See Leger.

Road 1998 SW 4:A2

Leger Way

West of Rabbit Hill Road, north of 23 Avenue

See Leger.

Road   1999   SW   4:A2

Leigh Crescent

*North of Leger Boulevard, west of
Rabbit Hill Road*

Zebulon Lewis "Lewie" Leigh (b. 1906) had a
distinguished civilian and military aviation career.
Inducted into the Canadian Aviation Hall of Fame
in 1974, he was also a member of the Order of the
British Empire. Born in England, Leigh served with
Air Transport Command during WWII. After D-
Day, large numbers of casualties were evacuated
from the war zone by aircraft under his command.
He was also an aviation instructor and flew
numerous rescue missions within Canada.

Road   1998   SW   4:A2 *

Lendrum Place

51 Avenue to 61 Avenue, 111 Street to 115 Street

Irish-born Robert Watt Lendrum (1834–1912)
immigrated to Canada West in 1850 and went on to
become a surveyor. Lendrum came to south
Edmonton in 1892 as a Dominion land surveyor
and later settled on a homestead in the Rabbit Hill
area. The property that he once owned now makes
up the Lendrum Place neighbourhood while the
lake on this site was known as Lendrum Lake.

Neighbourhood   1959   SW   4:B1

Lendrum Place Park

11325–57 Avenue

This park is in the Lendrum Place neighbourhood
and has an area of 3.55 ha. *See* Lendrum Place.

Park   1981   SW   4:B1

Leo LeClerc Bridge

Spanning the Yellowhead Trail at 50 Street

Leo LeClerc (1923–1994) was a founding director
of the Yellowhead Highway Association and a key
figure in the designation of the Yellowhead
Highway as a Trans-Canada Highway Route. Born
in Alberta, he was active in many Edmonton organizations, including the Edmonton Exhibition
Association and the United Community Fund.
LeClerc helped to develop and organize
Edmonton's first Klondike Days in 1962. He was
also involved in the formation of the Edmonton
Oil Kings hockey club in 1950, and managed the
team until 1965.

Bridge   1994   NE   6:A1

Lessard

*40 Avenue north to Callingwood Road, 170 Street
to 191 Street*

P. Edmond Lessard (1873–1931) was an Edmonton
businessman and politician. Born in Quebec,
Lessard was a bookkeeper before coming to
Edmonton in 1898. He began working for a retail
business and by 1901 was a partner in the store.
Lessard was also president of a financial company
and the director of a weekly newspaper. He was
active in the French-Canadian community and
promoted settlement by francophone Canadians. In
1909 he was elected as an MLA and appointed as a
cabinet minister. Lessard continued to serve in the
Alberta Legislature until 1921. In 1925, Lessard was
appointed to the Canadian Senate.

Subdivision   1972   SW   3:C1 *

Lessard Drive

North of 53 Avenue, east of 174 Street

See Lessard.

Road   1980   SW   3:C1

Lessard Road

*Northeast of 45 Avenue, south of
Callingwood Road*

See Lessard.

Road 1980 SW 3:C1

Lewis Estates Boulevard

North of Whitemud Drive, west of Picard Drive

See Lewis Farms.

Road 1991 SW 3:B1

Lewis Farms

*Whitemud Drive north to Stony Plain Road,
Anthony Henday Drive west to 231 Street*

Ernie Lewis (1903–1987) was an award-winning
farmer and active school board member. Born in
Calgary, Lewis graduated from the University of
Alberta in 1929. In 1932, he bought a farm in the
Winterburn area. His farm went on to receive the
Master Farm Family Award in 1956. Lewis joined
with other potato growers and formed the
Edmonton Potato Growers. Lewis also served on
the Winterburn District School Board, the Stony
Plain School Board and the Parkland County
School Board. From 1966 to 1969, he was on the
Board of Governors of the University of Alberta.
The naming theme in the Lewis Farms area uses the
names of early pioneers, settlers and farmers, along
with the word "Greens" to reinforce the identity of
the neighbourhood as a golf course community.

Area 1982 SW 8:B2 *

Liliput Park

9637–74 Avenue

The name of this park was chosen by local residents
through a contest sponsored by the Ritchie
Neighbourhood Improvement Committee. It may
have been named for the fictional country of
Lilliput in Jonathan Swift's satirical work, *Gulliver's*

*Laura Lindsay on the CFRN Stage at the Edmonton
Exhibition, no date. (CEA A.2001–17)*

Travels. Liliput Park is located in the Ritchie neighbourhood and has an area of 0.21 ha.

Park 1980 SE 4:C1

Lincoln Crescent

South of Leger Way, west of Rabbit Hill Road

Manitoba-born George Edward Lincoln
(1921–1988) was an award-winning musician and
decorated WWII veteran. During WWII, Lincoln
joined the Royal Canadian Air Force and received
the Distinguished Service Order Award. Following
the war, he returned to Canada and resumed his
music studies at the University of Manitoba,
receiving his Licentiate in Music, Manitoba (LMM).
In 1946, he won the Gold Medal of Music. After
several years teaching and performing, Lincoln
became a professor of music at the University of
Alberta. He was also the director of the Western
Board of Music and co-founded Lincolnberg
Homes Ltd., which was the genesis of the Man Cap
Group of Companies.

Road 1999 SW 4:A2 *

Lindsay Crescent

South of Leger Boulevard, west of Rabbit Hill Road

Laura Lindsay (1914–1988) was a local television personality who hosted a homemakers' show, from 1955 to 1968, on CFRN-TV called Laura. Lindsay went on the air live five days a week. "Lindsay," however, was her stage name; her real name was Laura Banks (her son is the renowned Edmonton musician Senator Tommy Banks). Her television show was done live, with no rehearsals and no taping. Lindsay interviewed celebrities, cooked and sewed. When the daily show was finished, she cleaned up the set and prepared for the next day's broadcast. *Laura's Recipes*, a cookbook published in 1964, sold 30,000 copies.

Road 1998 SW 4:A2 *

Little Mountain Cemetery

16025–50 Street

The district of Little Mountain has existed since at least the early 1880s. In 1895 a site was scouted in Little Mountain for a cemetery to serve the northeast districts of what is now Edmonton. The *Edmonton Bulletin* reported, on 11 February 1895, that the cemetery would be located on the highest point in the area of Little Mountain. By the early 1900s, Little Mountain Cemetery had become a public burial ground. In 1985 the City of Edmonton assumed responsibility for the cemetery. This cemetery is located in the Brintnell neighbourhood and has an area of 2.00 ha.

Cemetery CU NE 11:A1 *

Livingstone Court

South of Leger Boulevard, west of Rabbit Hill Road

Irish-born Sam Livingstone emigrated to the United States in 1847, remaining there until the 1860s when he moved to the Canadian west. Livingstone, along with James Gibbons, was considered one of the first to pan for gold along the North Saskatchewan River in the Edmonton area.

Little Mountain Cemetery, 1976. (CEA EA-264-49)

Livingstone and his wife, Jane Howse, eventually settled on a farm in southern Alberta, in the area that later became part of the city of Calgary. Their farm was flooded in 1929 for the construction of the Glenbow Dam and Reservoir in what is now southwest Calgary. A respected member of the Calgary community, Livingstone was also honoured in Calgary by having a school and a federal building named for him.

Road 1998 SW 4:A2 *

Loewen Court

North of Leger Way, west of Lamb Court

Joel I. Loewen (b. 1907) was born in Saskatchewan and began to study the piano at an early age. Later, his interest turned to the tuning and repair of pianos. In 1944 he moved west to work at the Edmonton division of Heintzman & Co., where he was put in charge of piano servicing. In 1955 Loewen became an independent tuner, servicing pianos at the University of Alberta's Department of Music and at radio and, later, television stations. Loewen was the first honorary member of the Alberta Piano Tuner Technicians' Association.

Road 1999 SW 4:A2 *

Londonderry

137 Avenue to 153 Avenue, 66 Street to 82 Street

The name of this subdivision is taken from the town of the same name in Ireland. *Derry* or *doire* is Gaelic for "oak grove." As many places in Ireland were called Derry, it was necessary to add a second name to differentiate between the various towns. In 1609, "London" was added to "Derry" after King James I granted the merchants of London a charter to settle in the town. The name reflects other Irish names in Edmonton, including Kildare, Kilkenny and Killarney.

Subdivision   1964   NE   10:C2 *

Londonderry Athletic Grounds

14627–72 Street

This park is located in the Kilkenny neighbourhood and has an area of 10.89 ha. *See* Londonderry.

Park   1972   NE   10:D2

Lorelei

From Beaumaris Road, Stirling Road and 160 Avenue north to Castle Downs Road, 97 Street west to Castle Downs Road

This neighbourhood is in Castle Downs and is named after a historical castle located on the Rhine River in Germany. It is said that a large rock on the bank of the Rhine emits an echo. Legend has it that this is the site where a lovelorn maiden named Lorelei threw herself into the river. According to the story, Lorelei was transformed into a siren who lured fishermen to their deaths.

Neighbourhood   1973   NW   10:C1

Lorelei Park

16220–103 Street

This park is in the Lorelei neighbourhood and has an area of 3.06 ha. *See* Lorelei.

Park   1984   NW   10:B1

Lorne Street Park

9120–113 Avenue

Lorne Street, now 92 Street, was named in about 1908. It may have been named after John Douglas Sutherland Campbell (1845–1914), the Marquess of Lorne, fifth governor general of Canada (1878–1883), who was later the ninth Duke of Argyll. Lorne Street Park is located in the Alberta Avenue neighbourhood and has an area of 0.1 ha. *See* Argyll.

Park   2000   NE   7:C1 *

Lougheed Court

South of Lindsay Crescent, west of Livingstone Court

Peter Lougheed was the premier of Alberta from 1971 to 1985, leading the province during a period of tremendous economic growth fuelled by the oil and gas industries. It was also a time of political conflict between the province and the federal government, as Alberta sought to protect its resource-based wealth from federal government control. Born in Calgary in 1928, Lougheed, the grandson of Sir James Lougheed, came to Edmonton to attend the University of Alberta and graduated with a degree in law in 1952. He then went to Harvard University and in 1954 earned an MBA. Lougheed was called to the Alberta Bar the following year.

In 1956 he joined the Mannix Company Ltd., later becoming the company's vice-president. He returned to private law practice in 1962, and in 1965 was elected leader of the Alberta Progressive Conservative Party. In 1967 he was elected to the Legislative Assembly, where he served as leader of the official opposition. Lougheed became the premier of Alberta in 1971, when his party defeated the Social Credit Party, gaining 45 of the 75 seats. In 1987 he became a Companion of the Order of Canada.

Road   1998   SW   4:A2

*Depression era housing and Grierson Dump, now the site
of Louise McKinney Riverfront Park, 1938.*
(CEA EA-160-325)

Louise McKinney Riverfront Park

9529 Grierson Hill

Louise Crummy McKinney (1868–1931) was the
first woman to be elected to a legislature in Canada
and the British Empire. She was born in Ontario
and settled in southern Alberta in the early 1900s.
In 1917 she was elected to the Alberta Legislature
as an independent representative for the
Claresholm constituency, a position she held until
1921. McKinney was also an organizer of the
Women's Christian Temperance Union (WCTU)
and president of its Alberta branch, acting president of the national organization and
vice-president of the international WCTU.
McKinney was one of Alberta's "Famous Five," the
group of women who campaigned for women's
political rights in the Persons Case of 1929. This
landmark case won women the right to sit in the
Canadian Senate. The Louise McKinney Riverfront
Park is located south of the Boyle Street neighbourhood and has an area of 2.17 ha.

Park   2000   C   7:C2

Low Level Bridge

*Spanning the North Saskatchewan River
connecting Rossdale Road and Scona Road*

The Low Level Bridge was the first bridge to be
built in Edmonton. Construction on the bridge
began in 1898 and was completed on April 4, 1900.
Donald Ross, Edmonton's first hotelier and a well-
regarded pioneer, had the honour of driving in the
last rivet. In 1902, railway track was laid across the
bridge so that the Edmonton, Yukon and Pacific
Railway could use it, thus making it a bridge for
pedestrians, wagons, trains and, later, automobiles.
The first streetcar was driven across the bridge in
1908. The bridge was actually named somewhat
later for its proximity to the High Level Bridge,
constructed between 1910 and 1913. By the 1940s,
it was apparent that the city's growing volume of
traffic was too much for the single-laned bridge.
City engineer A.W. Haddow suggested the bridge
be twinned, and a new bridge, based on the original
plans but with a wider bridge deck, was built next
to the existing Low Level Bridge in 1949. More
than a half a century later, southbound traffic
continues to use the "new" bridge while northbound traffic travels over the original structure.

Bridge   CU   C   7:B2

Lymburn

*69 Avenue north to Whitemud Drive, 178 Street to
191 Street*

John F. Lymburn (1880–1969) was born in Ayr,
Scotland. He graduated as a law agent from
Glasgow University in 1906 and arrived in
Edmonton in 1911, where he worked with the firm
of Short & Cross for more than a year before
opening his own office. In 1926 Lymburn was

Low Level bridge, south entrance, circa 1960. (CEA EA-275-332)

elected to the Legislative Assembly as a member of the United Farmers of Alberta (UFA). He served as the attorney general from 1926 to 1935, when the UFA was defeated by the Social Credit Party.

Neighbourhood 1971 SW 3:C1

Lynnwood

Whitemud Drive north to 87 Avenue, 149 Street to 159 Street

This area was formerly part of the Town of Jasper Place and was named prior to the annexation of Jasper Place by Edmonton in 1964. A "lynn" or "linn" refers to a linden or lime tree; the term may also be used to describe the wood of this tree.

Neighbourhood 1957 SW 3:D1

Lynnwood Athletic Field

15625–80 Avenue

This park is in the Lynnwood neighbourhood and has an area of 2.02 ha. *See* Lynnwood.

Park 1969 SW 3:D1

Lynnwood Park

15525–84 Avenue

This park is in the Lynnwood neighbourhood and has an area of 1.89 ha. *See* Lynnwood.

Park 1983 SW 3:D1

Lynnwood Way

North of Whitemud Drive, west of 149 Street

See Lynnwood.

Road 1989 SW 1:D1

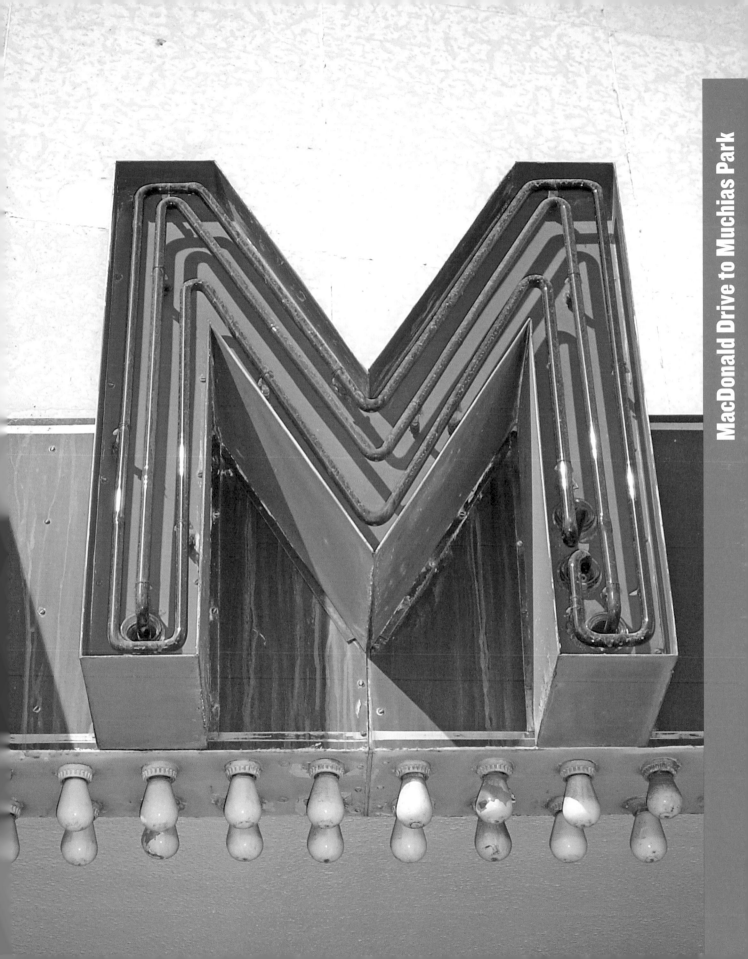

MacDonald Drive

100 Avenue from 100 Street to 102 Street

In the 1890s and early 1900s this road was called College Avenue. It was renamed McDonald Drive in 1914 and in 1921 the spelling was changed to MacDonald Drive. There are at least two possible origins for the name. MacDonald Drive (or McDonald Drive, as it was originally spelled) may have been named after James McDonald (d. 1908), a contractor and real estate agent who came to Edmonton in 1879. McDonald became wealthy from subdividing the Cromdale district. In 1890 he built a large home at 102 Street and 100 Avenue, on what is now MacDonald Drive (the home was condemned and demolished in 1960). McDonald lived in Edmonton until the early 1900s and then retired to Victoria.

MacDonald Drive may also have been named after the Hotel MacDonald, which was named for Sir John A. MacDonald (1815–1891), the first prime minister of Canada (1867–1873, 1878–1891). Situated on 100 Avenue and 100 Street, the Hotel MacDonald was built between 1912 and 1916 by the Grand Trunk Pacific Railway. It features an exterior of Indiana limestone and sheet-copper roofing. One of the most elegant hotels in Edmonton, it was restored in 1991 and designated a Municipal Historic Resource by the City of Edmonton.

Road   CU   C   7:C2 *

MacEwan

North of Ellerslie Road, west of 111 Street

John Walter Grant MacEwan (1902–2000) was a historian, author and politician. Born in Manitoba, he earned a Bachelor in Sciences from the Ontario Agricultural College in 1926 and then a master's degree from Iowa State University. MacEwan served as an alderman and mayor of Calgary, a member of the Legislative Assembly and was leader of the Alberta Liberal Party from 1958 to 1960. From 1966 to 1974 he was lieutenant-governor of

Lieutenant-Governor Grant MacEwan at the dedication of Edgar Millen Park, 1968. (CEA EA-20-29)

Alberta and resided in Edmonton. Over the course of his long life, MacEwan received several honorary doctorates of laws, including one from the University of Alberta in 1966. In 1975 he received the Order of Canada, and in 1982 the Alberta Order of Excellence. Grant MacEwan Community College opened in Edmonton in 1994.

Neighbourhood   2001   SW   2:D1

MacEwan Close

North of MacEwan Road

See MacEwan.

Road   2002   SW   2:D1 *

MacEwan Road

North of Ellerslie Road and west of 111 Street

See MacEwan.

Road   2002   SW   2:D1 *

Mackenzie and Mann Park

10431–113 Street

In 1899 Sir William Mackenzie (1849–1923) and Sir Donald Mann (1853–1934) founded the Canadian Northern Railway (CNoR). Over the next twenty years, the CNoR expanded into a transcontinental railway. During WWI the company experienced financial difficulties and sought the aid of the Canadian government. In return for providing assistance, the federal government took over the company. Four other railways—the Grand Trunk, Grand Trunk Pacific, Intercolonial and the National Transcontinental—also had trouble around this time. The government purchased all of them and merged the five companies to form the Canadian National Railways. The Mackenzie and Mann Park is in the Oliver neighbourhood and has an area of 0.4 ha.

Park   2001   C   7:B2 *

MacKenzie Drive

143 Street and 94 Avenue west to 147 Street and 95 Avenue

MacKenzie Drive runs along the north bank of McKenzie Ravine. *See* McKenzie Ravine.

Road   1960   SW   7:A2

MacKinnon Ravine

149 Street and Stony Plain Road east to the North Saskatchewan River

James A. MacKinnon (1881–1958) was a reporter, businessman and federal politician. He was born in Ontario and came to Edmonton as a school teacher in 1901. MacKinnon was a reporter for the *Edmonton Bulletin* and a prominent businessman before being elected as a Liberal member of parliament in 1935. He became a cabinet minister in 1939, was re-elected in 1940 and 1945, and was appointed to the Senate in 1949.

Ravine   CU   SW   7:A2

MacKinnon Ravine Bridge

Spanning the MacKinnon Ravine at 142 Street

This bridge was built over MacKinnon Ravine in 1961 and officially opened by Mayor Elmer E. Roper. *See* MacKinnon Ravine.

Bridge   1961   SW   7:A2

MacKinnon Ravine Park

Between 135 Street and 149 Street at 99 Avenue

The MacKinnon Ravine Park separates Crestwood from Grovenor and Glenora neighbourhoods and has an area of 19 ha. *See* MacKinnon Ravine.

Park   1984   SW   7:A2

Malcolm Groat Park

10760–132 Street

This park is located in the Westmount neighbourhood and has an area of 1.05 ha. *See* Groat Bridge *and* Groat Ravine.

Park   1984   NW   7:B2

Malcolm MacCrimmon Park

10403–29A Avenue

See feature story, page 206.

Park   1985   SW   4:C2

Malcolm Tweddle Park

2347 Millbourne Road West

This park has an area of 3.02 ha. in the Tweddle Place neighbourhood. *See* Tweddle Place.

Park   1985   SE   4:D2

Malcolm MacCrimmon Park

MALCOLM MACCRIMMON (1851–1928) was a railway builder who helped construct the first rail lines in western Canada. He was born in Ontario and left home at the age of 21 to work for the International Boundary Survey in Manitoba. For a time after this job, MacCrimmon used a team of mules to transport goods between the United States and Winnipeg.

It was in Winnipeg in 1881 that he became the partner of A. Quigley and received contracts to build roadbeds for the Canadian Pacific Railway, then pushing west. A year later he married Flora McArthur. She remained in Winnipeg while he worked on the rail route through Manitoba and Saskatchewan. MacCrimmon's road-building outfits included as many as 100 men. They lived in tent cities and used teams of horses and mules, fresnos, slush scrapers and wheel scrapers to complete the back-breaking work of building grades for ties and tracks.

In 1890 the family moved to the Calgary district; in 1901 the MacCrimmons moved to Edmonton, where housing shortages forced them to spend their first winter in a tent. MacCrimmon was awarded contracts to put down grade for the Edmonton, Yukon and Pacific Railway. In addition to horse and mule teams, MacCrimmon used scows on the North Saskatchewan River to transport supplies and equipment to work sites. He also graded Edmonton's first streetcar line, from the Low Level Bridge along 100 Street to 97 Avenue and 109 Street, and to 109 Street and Jasper Avenue.

In 1919, after nearly four decades of building railroads, MacCrimmon retired from railway work and established a sawmill operation with one of his sons.

The Malcolm MacCrimmon Park has an area of 0.74 ha. and is located in the Ermineskin neighbourhood.

Malcolm MacCrimmon, 1904. (CEA EA-10-669.111)

Malmo Plains

Whitemud Drive north to 51 Avenue, 111 Street to 122 Street

This area was once part of the University of Alberta Research Farm and was named for the soil found on the farm. Malmo soil, described as a loam, was first identified southeast of Wetaskiwin, Alberta, near the town of Malmo. The then dean of agriculture at the University of Alberta, C. Fred Bentley, suggested the name for the neighbourhood.

Neighbourhood   1962   SW   4:B2

Malmo Road

51 Avenue curving south to join 115 Street

See Malmo Plains.

Road   1962   SW   4:B2

Manning Drive

50 Street and 140 Avenue

Ernest C. Manning (1908–1996) was the premier of Alberta from 1943 to 1968, serving for a record seven terms. He was born in Saskatchewan and came to Alberta in 1927. In 1935 he was elected to the Legislative Assembly and appointed a cabinet minister in the Social Credit government led by William Aberhart. Following Aberhart's death in 1943, Manning became leader of the Social Credit Party and premier. After his retirement, Manning was appointed a senator. In 1981 Manning became the first recipient of the Alberta Order of Excellence and, that same year, received the Order of Canada. This road was originally named Manning Freeway.

Road   1988   NE   12:B2

Maple Downs Park

1615–66 Avenue

This park is in the Maple Ridge Mobile Home Park and has an area of 5.89 ha.

Park   1987   SE   5:B1

Premier Ernest Manning inspecting a power plant, 1962. (CEA A.97-52)

Maple Ridge Industrial

Whitemud Drive north to Sherwood Park Freeway, Meridian Street west to 17 Street

This neighbourhood was named after the nearby Maple Ridge Mobile Home Park. The area was annexed to the City of Edmonton on January 1, 1982.

Neighbourhood   CU   SE   5:B1

Marlboro Road

North of Westbrook Drive

The name of this road was suggested by the developers of the area, Westbrook Estates Ltd. Marl is a type of soil that consists of clay mixed with the

Mary Lobay, 1976. (CEA EA-338-46)

carbonate of lime. The hamlet of Marlboro, 25 km southwest of Edson, was named after local marl deposits.

Road 1963 SW 4:B2

Mary Burlie Park

10465–97 Street

Mary Burlie (1935–1996) was an outreach worker at the Boyle Street Cooperative. Born in Arkansas, Burlie came to Edmonton in 1969 with her Canadian husband, John Burlie, and their children. She soon began volunteer work at the Bissell Centre, an inner-city outreach facility. In 1972, she volunteered at the Boyle Street Community Service

Co-operative (founded in 1971) and in 1973 was hired as staff. The Boyle Street centre helps the city's poorest residents and is run by a non-profit charitable society. Although Burlie never completed high school, she was considered a highly skilled counsellor and was recognized with awards from the Canadian Council for Inner City Education (1986), the YMCA Tribute to Women (1989), and the National Black Coalition (1990). Burlie was president of the Black Women's Association of Alberta (1986–1991) and president of Change For Children (1984–1990). She died in 1996 at the age of 61 from cancer. The Mary Burlie Park is located in the Boyle Street neighbourhood and has an area of 0.18 ha.

Park 1999 C 7:C2 *

Mary Finlay Park

10150–80 Street

Mary A. Finlay (1884–1970) was superintendent of the Beulah Home for unmarried mothers from 1922 until her retirement in 1964. She was born in Ontario and came to Edmonton in 1909, where she helped start the Beulah Mission. From 1914 to 1922 Finlay took a leave of absence, but continued her evangelistic work. In 1962 the Junior Chamber of Commerce named her Citizen of the Year; in 1963 a scholarship for advanced study in social welfare and related fields was established in her name. The Mary Finlay Park is in the Forest Heights neighbourhood and has an area of 0.72 ha.

Park 1984 NE 7:D2

Mary Lobay Park

400 Reeves Crest

Alberta-born Mary Lobay (b. 1924) was a teacher and administrator who worked with many of the province's most influential groups and educational bodies. Among them were the Salvation Army,

Edmonton Historical Board, University of Alberta Board of Governors and Senate, Alberta Historical Resources Foundation Board and Edmonton Police Commission. Lobay graduated from the University of Alberta with Bachelor of Education and Master of Education degrees. She received the Order of Canada in 1988 and an honorary doctorate from the University of Alberta in 1992. The Mary Lobay Park is in the Rhatigan Ridge neighbourhood and has an area of 0.66 ha.

Park 1990 SW 4:A2

Maskepetoon Park

10915–29A Avenue

Chief Maskepetoon (c. 1810–1869) of the Cree nation tried to win peace with the Blackfoot nation by entering into a pact to end warfare between the two peoples. In about 1850 a peace treaty was concluded between the Cree and Blackfoot. A number of parks and neighbourhoods in this area are named for Aboriginal leaders. The Maskepetoon Park is in the Ermineskin neighbourhood and has an area of 0.6 ha.

Park 1983 SW 4:B2

Matheson Way

West of 50 Street, north of 149 Avenue

Douglas Matheson was appointed justice of the Court of Queen's Bench in 1985. Born in Edmonton, Matheson graduated from the University of Alberta in 1951 and was admitted to the Alberta Bar in 1952 and the Northwest Territories Bar in 1974. During WWII Matheson served with the Royal Canadian Air Force and was held as a prisoner of war from April 1944 to May 1945.

Road 1997 NE 11:A2

Matt Berry

153 Avenue to 167 Avenue, 59A Street to 66 Street

Massey "Matt" Berry (1889–1970) was a veteran of both world wars and an award-winning bush pilot who helped open northern Canada. Berry was born in Ontario and served in WWI with the Royal Flying Corps. Over the next decade, he continued his aerial training and flew throughout the Northwest Territories, joining Canadian Airways in 1931. He was awarded the McKee Trophy, Canada's oldest aviation honour in 1936 after captaining two difficult rescue flights. Berry served in WWII and retired from commercial flying in 1969. He was named to Canada's Aviation Hall of Fame in 1973.

Neighbourhood 1981 NE 11:A1

Matt Berry Park

15950–59A Street

This park is in the Matt Berry neighbourhood and has an area of 5.11 ha. *See* Matt Berry.

Park 1993 NE 10:D1

Maude Bell Park

7320–77 Avenue

Maude Bell (1875–1953) was a pioneer school teacher who served as principal of Rutherford Elementary School for 30 years. Bell was born in Ontario, and started teaching in 1898. In 1903 she came to Alberta to teach at a school near Olds. The following year she accepted a teaching position at Niblock Street School in the Town of Strathcona. In 1905 she started teaching at Grandin School. Bell was appointed principal of Rutherford Elementary School in 1911, remaining in this post until 1941. The Maude Bell Park is in the King Edward Park neighbourhood and has an area of 1.1 ha.

Park 1985 SE 5:A1

Wop May, circa 1934. (CEA EA-427-6)

Maurice Poirier Park

10816–67 Street

Maurice Poirier (1939–1991) was for 25 years an active and involved member of the Capilano community. He was born in Alberta and moved to Edmonton in 1966. Poirier volunteered as a coach and community league president in Capilano. The Maurice Poirier Park is in the Capilano neighbourhood and has an area of 0.54 ha.

Park   1994   NE   7:D1 *

Mayfield

107 Avenue to 111 Avenue, 156 Street west to Mayfield Road

Wilfrid R. "Wop" May (1896–1952) was a WWI fighter pilot and pioneer of Edmonton's civilian aviation scene. May earned his pilot's wings during WWI and was awarded the Distinguished Flying Cross in 1918 for his "keenness and disregard of personal danger." In 1919 May founded the first air service in Edmonton, and in 1928 established the Edmonton and Northern Alberta Aero Club. In 1929, he was awarded the McKee Trophy for his outstanding contribution to Canadian aviation as a result of his mid-winter mercy flight delivering diphtheria antiserum to Fort Vermilion. He was named to the Order of the British Empire in 1935 and inducted into Canada's Aviation Hall of Fame in 1973. The Mayfield name was chosen by the developers through a naming contest held in 1954.

Neighbourhood   1954   NW   8:D1

Mayfield Park

10945–161 Street

This park is in the Mayfield neighbourhood and has an area of 2.27 ha. *See* Mayfield.

Park   1982   NW   8:D1

Mayfield Road

Northeast off 170 Street from 102 Avenue, intersecting 111 Avenue

See Mayfield.

Road   1965   NW   8:C2

Mayliewan

153 Avenue to 167 Avenue, 72A Street to 82 Street

This neighbourhood is in the Lake District. The name Mayliewan is taken from the Cantonese word meaning "beautiful bay."

Ncighbourhood   1979   NE   10:C1

Mayliewan Close

North of 154 Avenue, west of 74 Street

See Mayliewan.

Road   1988   NE   10:C2 *

Mayliewan Place

Cul-de-sac between 74 Street and Mayliewan Close, off 154 Avenue

See Mayliewan.

Road   1988   NE   10:C2 *

McAllister Crescent

Off McAllister Loop, north of MacEwan Road and east of MacEwan Close

See Kathleen McAllister Park.

Road   2002   SW   2:D1 *

J.D. McArthur, circa 1925. (CEA EA–10–2254)

McAllister Loop

North of MacEwan Road, east of MacEwan Close

See Kathleen McAllister Park.

Road   2002   SW   2:D1 *

McArthur Industrial

127 Avenue to 137 Avenue, CNR railway tracks west to St. Albert Trail

McArthur Railway Terminal, which was located in the area near the McArthur Industrial neighbourhood, was likely named for J.D. McArthur (1854–1927), railway builder and president of the Edmonton, Dunvegan and British Columbia Railway. The railway, incorporated in Alberta in 1912, fell into debt and was taken over by the

Alberta government in 1920. Nine years later the government sold the railway to the Northern Alberta Railways Company. The McArthur Industrial area was annexed to Edmonton on January 1, 1982.

Neighbourhood   CU   NW   10:A2

McCauley

105 Avenue north to Norwood Boulevard, LRT tracks west to 101 Street

See feature story, page 213.

Neighbourhood   CU   C   7:C1

McConachie

North of 163 Avenue, 50 Street to 59A Street

George William Grant McConachie (1909–1965) was a barnstormer and bush pilot in Canada's north. He was born in Ontario and earned his pilot's licence in 1929. McConachie went on to found a number of airlines and throughout his career worked to improve Canada's international air services. He earned the McKee Trophy in 1945 and was named to Canada's Aviation Hall of Fame in 1973. Neighbourhoods in the Pilot Sound area are named in honour of Canadian pilots.

Neighbourhood   1981   NE   11:A1 *

McDougall Hill

100 Street and MacDonald Drive

Rev. George McDougall (1821–1876) came to Edmonton in 1871 and claimed land on the east side of the Hudson's Bay Reserve on behalf of the Methodist Church. Under his direction, a church was built at the top of this hill in 1873 (present-day 101 Street). Rev. McDougall left Edmonton in 1875; a new church was built on the original McDougall Hill site in 1893. In 1910 this church was replaced by the McDougall United Church. McDougall has been used as a road name since the early 1900s; the name was formalized in 1973.

Road   CU   C   7:C2 *

Steps up McDougall Hill, 1938. (CEA EA–160–1120)

McDougall Park

9976 McDougall Hill

This park is in the Downtown neighbourhood and has an area of 0.49 ha. *See* McDougall Hill.

Park   1981   C   7:C2

McIntyre Industrial

Whitemud Drive north to CP railway tracks, 75 Street to 91 Street

Dr. Wilbert McIntyre (1867–1909) was born in Ontario and received his education at the University of Toronto, graduating with a medical degree in 1901. McIntyre arrived in Edmonton in 1902 and started his medical practice. He soon entered local politics and in 1906 became

McCauley

Matthew McCauley (1850-1930), a pioneer liveryman and stagecoach operator, was the Town of Edmonton's first mayor. He was born in Ontario and came to Fort Saskatchewan in 1879. Two years later he moved to Edmonton where he established a livery stable and butcher shop. McCauley organized Edmonton's first public school in 1881 and was a founding member (and served for 18 years) of Edmonton's school board.

It was not until 1882 that a system of land titles and homestead grants was introduced in western Canada. Prior to this, in the absence of legal title, local residents led by McCauley protected their claims by force. McCauley was captain of what was known as "McCauley's Vigilantes," a group of local men who forcibly removed the property of newcomers who attempted to squat on land cleared by the area's first settlers. On at least two occasions, the shack of a claim-jumper who failed to heed warnings from the vigilantes was pushed over the banks of the North Saskatchewan River and the newcomer was driven out. In 1892, when the federal government sought to transfer the Land Titles Office from Edmonton to Strathcona, McCauley used his hastily gathered volunteers to stop the planned move.

When Edmonton was incorporated as a town in 1892, McCauley became mayor by acclamation and was re-elected in 1893 and 1894. In 1905, the year that Alberta became a province, he was elected to the first provincial legislature, representing Vegreville. He resigned after only a year to become warden of Edmonton's first federal prison, working there from 1906 to 1911. McCauley School (on McCauley Street, present-day 107A Avenue) was opened in this neighbourhood in 1912. McCauley lived in British Columbia from 1912 to 1925 and then moved to Sexsmith, Alberta. McCauley, the father of 12 children, lived to the age of 80 and died on his farm in the Peace Country.

Matt McCauley, and champion curling team, no date.
(CEA EA-10-2239)

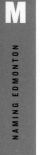

Area of McDougall Park, circa 1935. (CEA EA-495-53)

Strathcona's first elected representative in the Legislative Assembly of the new province of Alberta. In the 1908 federal election, he was elected to represent Strathcona in the House of Commons in Ottawa. *See* Dr. Wilbert McIntyre Park.

Neighbourhood 1973 SE 4:C1

McIntyre Road

53 Avenue and 86 Street

See McIntyre Industrial.

Road 1973 SE 4:D1

McKay Lane

North of Ellerslie Road, west of 119 Street

William Morrison MacKay (b. 1836), a surgeon for the Hudson's Bay Company (HBC), was the first medical doctor in northwest Canada. MacKay was born in Scotland and took his MD at the University of Edinburgh, graduating in 1858. He practised medicine in Edinburgh until 1864, when he decided to join the HBC. MacKay was the physician for a number of posts in the Mackenzie River and Peace River regions. In 1874 he married Jane

Flett (1857–1947), the daughter of an HBC factor. She acted as his interpreter and nurse until they retired to Edmonton in 1898. The Town of Edmonton honoured MacKay by naming McKay Avenue (now 99 Avenue) after him. Unfortunately, his name was incorrectly spelled. This error was perpetuated in the naming of the McKay Avenue School, and the familiar spelling is seen in this road as well.

Road 2001 SW 2:D1 *

McKenzie Ravine

From 148 Street east, along 93 Avenue to the North Saskatchewan River

Kenneth W. MacKenzie was an early Edmontonian and the city's first mayor. MacKenzie, a school teacher, arrived in Edmonton in 1895. He was elected mayor in 1900 and again in 1904, the first year of Edmonton's incorporation as a city. The official name of this ravine was misspelled, and has never been corrected. The McKenzie Ravine separates the Crestwood and Parkview neighbourhoods.

Ravine 1956 SW 7:A2

McKenzie Ravine Bridge

Spanning the McKenzie Ravine at 142 Street

A timber trestle bridge was built over the ravine in 1913. In 1966, the original bridge was replaced with a four-lane steel bridge. *See* McKenzie Ravine.

Bridge 1966 SW 7:A2

McKernan

72 Avenue north to University Avenue, 109 Street to 114 Street and 116 Street

See feature story, page 216.

Neighbourhood CU SW 4:B1

McKernan Park

7535–112 Street

This park is in the McKernan neighbourhood and has an area of 1.08 ha. *See* McKernan *feature story, page 216.*

Park 1956 SW 4:B1

McLean Court

Encircled by McLean Crescent, north of Ellerslie Road and east of 119 Street

Alexander "Dan" McLean (1896–1969) played an active role in the development of aviation in Alberta. He was born in Maxville, Ontario, but came to Innisfail in 1907 and attended school in Calgary. In 1917, he enlisted in the Royal Flying Corps and was transferred to England, where he was a flying instructor until the end of WWI. McLean returned to Alberta, attended the University of Alberta, and joined the Canadian Air Force Reserve in 1919. Ten years later he became Inspector of the Western Airways for the federal government, and organized the construction of the first airways system on the prairies. McLean also conducted an aerial survey of a Rocky Mountain flyway from Vancouver to Alberta via the Crowsnest Pass. In 1935, he began a survey of possible flight paths from northwest Canada to Alaska. McLean's knowledge and expertise became invaluable during WWII, when he participated in the British Commonwealth Air Training Plan. McLean advocated the construction of a chain of modern airports equipped with such features as night lighting on the runways, weather reporting and radio communication.

Road 2002 SW 2:D1 *

McLean Crescent

North of Ellerslie Road, east of 119 Street

See McLean Court.

Road 2002 SW 2:D1 *

McLeod

144 Avenue to 153 Avenue, 58 Street to 66 Street

Pioneer settler Murdoch McLeod (1844–1930) was born in Scotland and signed on with the Hudson's Bay Company (HBC) in 1861. He spent six years in the Arctic before leaving the HBC in 1868 and settling in Manitoba. In 1870, during the Riel Rebellion, Murdoch was held prisoner. He left Manitoba and came to Edmonton in 1879, where he farmed in the Belmont area. In 1907 Murdoch moved to British Columbia, but returned to Edmonton a short while later.

Neighbourhood 1962 NE 10:D2

McLeod Park

14503–59 Street

This park is in the McLeod neighbourhood and has an area of 1.01 ha. *See* McLeod.

Park 1987 NE 10:D2

McLeod Road

149 Avenue from 50 Street to 58 Street

See McLeod.

Road 1973 NE 10:D2

McKernan

THE MCKERNAN NEIGHBOURHOOD is part of the original land owned by Robert McKernan (1846–1908). He was born in Ontario and came west from Winnipeg in about 1877. He and his younger brother James worked on the erection of the first telegraph line from Red River to Hay Lakes. James had earlier served with the North West Mounted Police, as only the third man to enlist, before returning to Ontario and encouraging his brother to move west.

Robert and James took work with Dominion Telegraph and helped complete the line between Hay Lakes and Edmonton. They also were given the contract, in 1877, to maintain the telegraph line west of Battleford. In 1878 Robert settled south of the North Saskatchewan River, with his wife Sara. A large, two-storey farmhouse was built. It stood on the site of the present-day McKernan Elementary-Junior High School until the late 1940s, when it was demolished. Sara McKernan bore 11 children in the home, all but one of whom lived to adulthood.

In 1896 Robert McKernan left farming and became involved in real estate development. In 1903, McKernan built the Dominion Hotel; his son John went on to build the landmark Princess Theatre on Whyte Avenue in 1915. Complications from appendicitis claimed the life of Robert at the age of 62; Sara lived until the age of 91.

The lake lying just east of the McKernan property was known as McKernan Lake. Before the lake was drained in the 1940s, Edmontonians used it as a recreation area, picnicking there in the summer and skating in the winter.

Robert McKernan's farm, no date. (PAA B.220)

McMullen Green

Off MacEwan Road, north of Ellerslie Road and west of 111 Street

Archibald "Archie" Major McMullen (1906–1983) was part of Alberta's aviation industry for over 35 years. Born in Gilbert Plains, Manitoba, McMullen came to Alberta as a child. In 1927 he left his position as a mechanic with the McLaughlin Buick Company in Calgary to work for WWI flying ace F. R. McCall, also as a mechanic. McMullen, McCall, and three others formed the Great Western Airways company, based in Bowness, assembling and selling de Havilland aircraft, and running a flying school. Over the years that followed, McMullen was associated with a number of aviation companies, and gained a great deal of experience flying in Canada's north. He made the first airmail delivery to Fort Chipewyan. During WWII, McMullen participated in the British Commonwealth Air Training Plan by testing repaired aircraft intended for use in the training program. After the war, he flew northern routes for Canadian Pacific Airlines, and had a role in the construction of the Distant Early Warning (DEW) Line radar bases, completed in 1957, on the coast of the Arctic Ocean. In 1963, McMullen retired from the aviation industry.

Road 2002 SW 2:D1 *

McMullen Place

Off McMullen Green, north of Ellerslie Road and west of 111 Street

See McMullen Green.

Road 2002 SW 2:D1 *

McMullen Way

Off MacEwan Road and McMullen Green, north of Ellerslie Road and west of 111 Street

See McMullen Green.

Road 2002 SW 2:D1 *

McNamara Industrial

105 Avenue to 111 Avenue, 170 Street to 178 Street

William J. McNamara (1850–1930) was the mayor of Edmonton from 1913 to 1914. He was born in Canada West and came to Alberta in 1886. Before moving to Edmonton in 1911, McNamara taught school and was the mayor of Wetaskiwin. After leaving the Edmonton mayor's office, McNamara worked in real estate.

Neighbourhood 1976 NW 8:C1

McPhadden Close

South of McPhadden Way, west of 119 Street

John Riley McPhadden (1863–1945) was a pioneer farmer in the Edmonton area. Born in Ontario, McPhadden came west to Winnipeg in 1892. There, he became part of the McGrath survey party, traveling with them to Calgary. After working for a while freighting between Edmonton and Calgary, he found employ with John Walter, operating the ferry between Strathcona and Edmonton. During the Edmonton land boom, McPhadden purchased and farmed various properties throughout Edmonton and is most remembered for his farming contributions.

Road 2001 SW 2:D1 *

McPhadden Place

South of McPhadden Way, west of 119 Street

See McPhadden Close.

Road 2001 SW 2:D1 *

McPhadden Way

West of 119 Street, north of Ellerslie Road

See McPhadden Close.

Road 2001 SW 2:D1 *

Rev. D.G. McQueen, 1904. (CEA EA-10-669.13)

McQueen

107 Avenue to 111 Avenue, 142 Street to 149 Street

Rev. David George McQueen (1854–1930), born in Canada West, was a pioneer minister who came to Edmonton in 1887 to lead the Presbyterian congregation. In 1912 the landmark First Presbyterian Church (10025–105 Street) was opened and Rev. McQueen became moderator of the general assembly of the Presbyterian church. He was minister of the First Presbyterian Church for 43 years. This area was called Huff Estate and West Glenora before being named McQueen. In 1953 a mountain in Jasper National Park was named Mount McQueen.

Neighbourhood 1954 NW 7:A1

McQueen Park

10825 McQueen Road

This park is in the McQueen neighbourhood and has an area of 0.95 ha. *See* McQueen.

Park 1982 NW 8:D1

McQueen Road

107 Avenue and 144 Street

See McQueen.

Road 1955 NW 8:D1

Meadowlark Park

87 Avenue to 95 Avenue, 156 Street to 163 Street

This neighbourhood was once part of the Town of Jasper Place, which was annexed to the City of Edmonton in 1964. Development of the Meadowlark Park neighbourhood began in the late 1950s. The western meadowlark is common to central and southern Alberta during the summertime. The bird's distinctive song has been called "the voice of Alberta's grasslands."

Neighbourhood CU SW 8:D2

Meadowlark Park

15961–92 Avenue

This park is in the Meadowlark Park neighbourhood and has an area of 1.17 ha. *See* Meadowlark Park *neighbourhood.*

Park 1982 SW 8:D2

Meadowlark Road

Connecting 87 Avenue to 156 Street

See Meadowlark Park *neighbourhood.*

Road CU SW 8:D2

Meadows Industrial, The

34 Avenue north to Whitemud Drive, Meridian Street west to 17 Street

See The Meadows.

Neighbourhood   CU   SE   5:B2 *

Meadows, The

10 Avenue north to Whitemud Drive, Meridian Street west to 34 Street

This area was annexed to Edmonton in January 1982. It is named for the pioneers who established dairy farms in the area. These early settlers cleared the land to provide grazing for their cattle. The naming theme for neighbourhoods in The Meadows area uses names of Alberta wildflowers.

Area   1982   SE   5:B2 *

Menisa

10 Avenue north to Mill Woods Road, 66 Street to 80 Street

Menisa is a form of the Cree word *mînis* for berry.

Neighbourhood   1972   SE   1:B1

Menisa Park

943 Knottwood Road South

This park is in the Menisa neighbourhood and has an area of 3.05 ha. *See* Menisa.

Park   1984   SE   1:B1

Meridian Street

0 Street discontinuous between southern and northern city limits

This road is the north/south axis of Edmonton's quadrant address system. A meridian is a line of longitude.

Road   1981   NE   12:C2

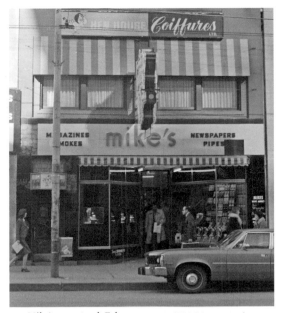

Mike's newsstand, February 1977. (CEA EA-245-205)

Meyokumin

Mill Woods Road South north to 23 Avenue, 50 Street to 66 Street

Meyokumin is said to be a form of the Cree word meaning "good water."

Neighbourhood   1974   SE   1:B1

Meyokumin Park

5811–19A Avenue

This park is in the Meyokumin neighbourhood and has an area of 4.52 ha. *See* Meyokumin.

Park   1987   SE   1:B1

Meyonohk

23 Avenue to 28 Avenue, Mill Woods Road west to 91 Street

This neighbourhood name comes from the Cree word *miyonohk*, which means "in a good spot."

Neighbourhood   1972   SE   4:C2

John Michaels, 1921. (CEA EA-25-23)

Meyonohk Park

1840 Lakewood Road South

This park is in the Meyonohk neighbourhood and has an area of 3.23 ha. *See* Meyonohk.

Park   1972   SE   4:C2

Michaels Park

38 Avenue north to Whitemud Drive, 66 Street to 76 Street

John "Mike" Michaels (1891–1962) was an active supporter of northern aviation and founded Mike's News and the Edmonton Newsboys' Band. He was born in New York and as a young man worked as a newsboy. Michaels came to Edmonton in 1912 and soon established Mike's News, a newspaper store located on Jasper Avenue. In 1913, in an effort to curb juvenile delinquency among newspaper boys, he founded the acclaimed Edmonton Newsboys' Band. The band toured the US and even played at the British Empire Exhibition at Wembley, England, in 1924. Michaels also sponsored airlines and air shows. In about 1930 he began a tradition of serving Christmas dinner to ex-servicemen. For

his efforts during both world wars he was awarded the Order of the British Empire. Michaels was also awarded the Medal of Freedom, a civilian honour, by the US government. He retired in 1957.

Neighbourhood   1972   SE   4:D2

Michaels Park

980 Millbourne Road East

This park is in the Michaels Park neighbourhood and has an area of 3.02 ha. *See* Michaels Park *neighbourhood.*

Park   1983   SE   4:D2

Mike Finland Park

7719–98A Avenue

Pioneer bush pilot and geologist George Harold "Mike" Finland (1901–1983) was inducted into the Canadian Aviation Hall of Fame in 1974. Born in Victoria, British Columbia, he played a crucial role in the early years of northern Canadian development, flying heavy equipment into isolated outposts and establishing new methods of aerial prospecting. In the 1930s, Finland carried out aerial mineral surveys and staked the Con Mine claims that led to the founding of Yellowknife and the creation of the mining industry in the Northwest Territories. The Mike Finland Park is in the Forest Heights neighbourhood and has an area of 2.34 ha.

Park 1982 SE 7:D2

Mill Creek

From eastern city limits south of 23 Avenue flows north-northeast into the North Saskatchewan River near 98 Avenue and 96A Street

From 1871 to 1874, William Bird ran a flour mill beside the creek that ran through his property (River Lot 19). This creek came to be known as Mill Creek. The course of Mill Creek is interrupted by city development between approximately 75 Street south of Wagner Road, and 83 Street at 69 Avenue.

Creek CU C 7:C2

Mill Creek Bridge

Spanning the Mill Creek Ravine at Whyte Avenue

Construction of the original Mill Creek Bridge began in 1910 and was finished in 1911. Strathcona Mayor A. Davies, city engineer A. S. McLean and W. Tipton were the first to cross the bridge in a motor car. According to news reports at the time, the bridge cost the City of Strathcona $40,000 and was 150 metres long and 21.3 metres above the water level. A new bridge, built to replace the 1911 one, was opened in 1961. It was 240 metres long and 17 metres wide and was built at a cost of an estimated $617,000. *See* Mill Creek.

Bridge CU SE 7:C2

Mill Creek Ravine

Along the course of Mill Creek

See Mill Creek.

Ravine CU SE 7:C2

Mill Creek, 1914. (CEA EA–184–33.)

Mill Creek Ravine Park

Mill Creek Ravine; Argyll Road north to Connors Road

This park has an area of 120.51 ha. *See* Mill Creek.

Park 1988 SE 7:C2

Mill Woods

10 Avenue north to Whitemud Drive, 34 Street to 91 Street

Mill Creek flows through the northeastern corner of the area, which was once woodland. This area was originally part of the Papaschase Indian Reserve. Many of the neighbourhood names in the Mill Woods area are Cree in origin and reflect the area's history. *See* Mill Creek.

Area 1970 SE 5:A2 *

Mill Woods Park

23 Avenue to 28 Avenue, 66 Street west to Mill Woods Road

This neighbourhood is composed entirely of school grounds and parks. It is named after the Mill Woods area in which it is located. *See* Mill Woods.

Neighbourhood   1980   SE   4:D2

Mill Woods Park

7004–23 Avenue

This 40.47-ha. park occupies most of the Mill Woods Park neighbourhood in which it is located, and after which it is named. *See* Mill Woods *and* Mill Woods Park *neighbourhood.*

Park   1980   SE   4:D2

Mill Woods Road

East of 91 Street off 39 Avenue, south to Mill Woods Road South

See Mill Woods.

Road   1973   SE   4:D2

Mill Woods Road East

East of 48A Street, south of 38 Avenue, intersecting with Mill Woods Road South at 16A Avenue

See Mill Woods.

Road   1973   SE   5:A2

Mill Woods Road South

South of 17 Avenue, joining Mill Woods Road and Mill Woods Road East

See Mill Woods.

Road   1973   SE   1:C1

Mill Woods Town Centre

23 Avenue to 28 Avenue, 50 Street to 66 Street

This commercial neighbourhood is located in the centre of Mill Woods. *See* Mill Woods.

Neighbourhood   1978   SE   5:A2

Millbourne

34 Avenue north to Whitemud Drive, 66 Street to 91 Street

The name is compatible with the overall naming pattern in the Mill Woods area. Subdivisions in this area have "mill" or "wood" as part of their name. *Bourne* is derived from an old French word that means "destination."

Subdivision   1971   SE   4:D2 *

Millbourne Road East

North of 36 Avenue, intersecting Millbourne Road West at 76 Street

See Millbourne.

Road   1972   SE   4:D2

Millbourne Road West

North of Mill Woods Road, intersecting Millbourne Road East at 76 Street

See Millbourne.

Road   1972   SE   4:D2

Miller

141 Avenue to 153 Avenue, 50 Street west to Manning Drive

Hungarian-born Abe William Miller (1897–1964) was a lawyer, politician and volunteer. He immigrated to Canada with his parents in 1899. Miller arrived in Edmonton in 1914 and graduated from the University of Alberta in 1925. He practised law for nearly 40 years and, from 1951 to 1957, served as an alderman on City Council. Miller was a member of the Alberta Legislature from 1955 to 1959, two years of which he also served as a city alderman. He was also a volunteer for organizations that help mentally disabled children.

Neighbourhood   1981   NE   11:A2

Miller Boulevard

North from Manning Drive at 144 Avenue

See Miller.

Road   1997   NE   11:A2

Millhurst

9 Avenue to 23 Avenue, 50 Street to 66 Street

"Mill" refers to Mill Creek, which runs through this area, while the Old English word "hurst" means "wood" or "grove." Subdivisions in the Mill Woods area share a common naming theme.

Subdivision   1973   SE   1:B1 *

Milton Jevning Park

10524 Lauderdale Road

This park honours Milton Jevning (b. 1920), a long-time resident of Lauderdale well known for helping his neighbours. The Milton Jevning Park is in the Lauderdale neighbourhood and has an area of 0.18 ha.

Park   1996   NW   10:C2 *

Minchau

34 Avenue north to Mill Creek Ravine, 34 Street to 50 Street

August Minchau (1862–1937) was an early settler of the area. He was born in Poland and immigrated to Canada with his wife, Caroline, and their children in 1894. Three generations of the Minchau family homesteaded this land for more than 80 years.

Neighbourhood   1978   SE   5:A2

Frederick J. Mitchell, 1952. (CEA EA-10-2611.8)

Minchau Park

3724 Mill Woods Road East

This park is in the Minchau neighbourhood and has an area of 2.66 ha. *See* Minchau.

Park   1985   SE   5:A2

Mistatim Industrial

CN railway tracks north to city limits, 149 Street and St. Albert Trail west to CN railway tracks

The literal translation of *mistatim* from the Cree language is "big dog," but it means "horse." From the 1870s, a lake in this area was called Horse Lake; the name was changed to Mistatim Lake in 1904. The name was officially rescinded in 1995 after the lake disappeared. A remnant of Mistatim Lake is now part of the Edcon Cement Plant.

Neighbourhood   1982   NW   9:C2

Mitchell Industrial

118 Avenue to 123 Avenue, 149 Street to 156 Street

Frederick J. Mitchell (1893–1979) was one of Edmonton's longest serving aldermen. He was born in Ontario and came to Edmonton in 1916. Mitchell was elected to City Council in 1940 and served for 24 years before retiring in 1964. He was also an avid tennis player and won several singles titles. Mitchell served as Edmonton's interim mayor for five weeks in 1959.

Neighbourhood   1965   NW   8:D1

Miwasin Park

12415–131A Avenue

The Cree word *miwasin* means "it is attractive" or "it looks very fine." A neighbourhood naming contest chose the word, said by its supporters to mean "quiet place," as the park name. Miwasin Park is in the Calder neighbourhood and has an area of 0.4 ha.

Park   1978   NW   10:B2

Monsignor Walter Fitzgerald Park

7120–180 Street

Monsignor Walter Patrick Fitzgerald (b. 1907) was ordained in 1942 and worked at St. Joseph's High School, and the Good Shepherd Convent and Atonement Home. In 1956 he was appointed director of religious education for Edmonton Catholic schools. He established and later won a provincial award for a pre-employment program. Fitzgerald was director of religious education for the Archdiocese of Edmonton and was appointed director of communications in 1972. His work in television production earned him a national award in 1983. Pope John Paul II gave him the title Right Reverend Monsignor in 1985. The Monsignor Walter Fitzgerald Park is in the Lymburn neighbourhood and has an area of 6.1 ha.

Park   1987   SW   3:C1

Montrose Elementary School, 1968. (CEA EA-20-5195)

Montrose

118 Avenue north to Yellowhead Trail, 58 Street west to CN railway tracks

The neighbourhood of Montrose was named after the Marquis of Montrose, a celebrated Scottish hero. James Graham, the 1st Marquis of Montrose, was born in 1612. In 1638 he signed a covenant that pledged him to defend the Presbyterian Kirk of Scotland against the attempts of King Charles I to impose Anglicanism upon the Scottish people. Between 1639 and 1640 he led Scottish troops against the English in the Bishops' Wars. In 1641 Montrose opposed forcing Presbyterianism on the English and joined King Charles I, promising to regain Scotland for the Royalists. He was defeated in battle in 1650 and, after being disavowed by King Charles II, was hanged. Edmonton's Montrose School opened in November 1951. City Council then decided that the neighbourhood should be named for the school.

Neighbourhood   CU   NE   7:D1

Montrose Park

5920–119 Avenue

This park is in the Montrose neighbourhood and has an area of 1.01 ha. *See* Montrose.

Park   1981   NE   7:D1

Muchias Park

JOHN "HENRY" COLLINS MATHIAS (1853-1939) was born at Lac Ste. Anne and worked at Fort Edmonton as a water hauler. Of Métis descent, Collins was known by the nickname Muchias. "Muchias" may have been an incorrect rendering of his actual name, Mathias. In the 1870s he settled across the North Saskatchewan River from Fort Edmonton, and worked first for Richard Hardisty, Hudson's Bay Company factor at Fort Edmonton. He later became a labourer and handyman for John Walter. Mathias, a dwarf, was a skilled archer and a strong swimmer.

His purpose-built house was across the road from the Walter home. The doors of Mathias' house were only four feet high and the furniture was built in miniature to accommodate its owner's small size. As reported in the original recommendation to the City Council for the naming of this park, Muchias' "life was spent beside the river, and each day he brought several barrels of water on his stone-boat to the families living in the Fort Edmonton stockade....He was a powerful swimmer and was reputed for swimming the river when it was in full flood. In his spare time he watched the children play, and one day saved an Indian child from drowning."

Mathias lived beside the North Saskatchewan River for more than 40 years. He died at the age of 86. His distinctive house was torn down in 1950. The Muchias Park is in the Bisset neighbourhood and has an area of 0.41 ha.

John Collins "Muchias" Mathias standing in front of his house, no date. (CEA EA-10-1514)

Morin Industrial

Stony Plain Road north to 105 Avenue, 178 Street to 184 Street

Alexis Morin (1870–1971) was chief of the Enoch Band Stony Plain Indian Reserve, in the Winterburn area, for 19 years and a band councillor for 25 years. Morin was born in Edmonton and was one of the first to move to the reserve near Winterburn.

Neighbourhood   1975   NW   8:C2

Morris Industrial

Sherwood Park Freeway north to CP railway tracks, 34 Street to 50 Street

Mr. and Mrs. Charles E. Morris operated the Morris Farm Dairy on land later included in this neighbourhood. The Morrises came to Edmonton in 1906 and ran the dairy until 1948.

Neighbourhood   1975   SE   5:B1

Morris Road

North of Whyte Avenue, west of 43 Street

See Morris Industrial.

Road   1975   SE   5:A1

Mount Lawn Road

75 Street and 121 Avenue

Mount Lawn was the former subdivision name of this area. The origin of the name Mount Lawn is not recorded.

Road   1958   NE   7:C1

Mount Pleasant Cemetery

5420–106 Street

Burials on this site, one of the highest land points in Edmonton, may date back to the 1880s. It was not until 1900, however, that the Strathcona Cemetery Company bought 2.83 ha. of land and incorporated it as Mount Pleasant Cemetery. In 1942 the City of Edmonton took over operation of the cemetery. Over the past century, the cemetery has been expanded several times. This cemetery is located in the Pleasantview neighbourhood and has an area of 7.70 ha.

Cemetery   CU   SW   4:C1

Mount Pleasant Park

5809–106 Street

This park is in the Pleasantview neighbourhood and has an area of 5.61 ha. *See* Mount Pleasant Cemetery.

Park   1988   SW   4:C1

Muchias Park

3524–25 Avenue

See feature story, page 225.

Park   1983   SE   1:C1

Canon Newton's hospital at the Hermitage, no date. (CEA EA–10–1794)

Namao Underpass

Carries 97 Street below the railway north of the Yellowhead Trail and south of 127 Avenue

97 Street was historically called Namayo Avenue and led to the hamlet of Namao, some 17 km north of Edmonton. The hamlet was named after the Cree word for sturgeon, *namao*, most likely because of the nearby Sturgeon River. Namao's first church was built in the early 1880s and its first post office opened in 1892.

Underpass   1958   NW   7:C1

Nellie McClung Park

9430 Scona Road

Nellie McClung (1873–1951) was a temperance reformer, suffragist, author and legislator. Born in Ontario and raised in Manitoba, McClung became a school teacher. In 1908 she published *Sowing Seeds in Danny*, the first of her 16 books. McClung moved to Edmonton in 1914 and was a lifelong activist for suffrage, prohibition and other legal reforms. She served as an MLA from 1921 to 1926. She was also a member of the "Famous Five," the group that campaigned for the right of women to sit in the Canadian Senate. This landmark case was won before the Privy Council of England in 1929. The Nellie McClung Park is located north of the Strathcona neighbourhood and has an area of 9.26 ha.

Park   1991   C   7:C2

Newton

118 Avenue north to Yellowhead Trail, 50 Street to 58 Street

Pioneer Anglican minister Canon William Newton came to Canada, from England, in 1840 and arrived at the Edmonton settlement in 1875. That same year he built a church, a home and a hospital ten kilometres east of Fort Edmonton, that he called Hermitage. The Rev. Newton continued to live there in his home for the next 25 years.

Neighbourhood   1954   NE   7:D1

Newton Park

5510–121 Avenue

This park is in the Newton neighbourhood and has an area of 0.55 ha. *See* Newton.

Park   1984   NE   7:D1

North Edmonton

A COLLECTION OF SHACKS and two hotels along Norton Street (present-day 66 Street) and Edmonton Avenue (present-day Fort Road) were incorporated as the Village of North Edmonton in 1910. The area was originally known as Packingtown, so-named because of the area's main employers, the J.Y. Griffin and the Burns meat packing plants. Two rail lines served the village: the Canadian Northern and the Grand Trunk Pacific.

The booming community, which boasted a four-room school and an emergency hospital, was annexed by the City of Edmonton in 1912, the same year that Edmonton and Strathcona were amalgamated. Meat packing continued to be the major economic activity in the area until the late 20th century. In 1986 the Gainers plant was the scene of violent labour strife. By the late 1990s, all the packing plants had closed down.

Remarkably, one of North Edmonton's first buildings, the Transit Hotel, at the corner of 66 Street and Fort Road, continues to serve customers. The three-storey, wood-frame hotel was built in 1909 at a cost of $50,000. It has been described as a perfect example of boomtown architecture. During times of rising land prices, commercial lots are often narrow and deep, increasing the number of commercial fronts open to the street; the Transit Hotel's street frontage is 9.8 metres (32 feet) wide and it extends back 24.4 metres (80 feet). The hotel was declared a historic site in 1980.

North Edmonton businesses, circa 1913. (CEA EA–267–74)

229

Looking west on Norwood Boulevard at 92 Street, 1958. (CEA EA–275–125)

Niska Trail

From Whitemud Drive at 173 Street,
paralleling 81 Avenue to 140 Street

The name of this trail reflects the theme of most of
Edmonton's walkways, which are named for prominent Aboriginal people or bear a relationship with
Aboriginal heritage. The name of this walkway was
originally recommended as Nisku Trail, taken from
the Cree word *nisku*, meaning a goose or a grey
goose. City Council, however, amended the name to
Niska Trail. Niska Trail is one of a number of trail
names approved between 1969 and 1971.

Walkway   1970   SW   3:C1 *

North Glenora

107 Avenue to 111 Avenue, Groat Road west to
142 Street

This area was formerly owned by Malcolm Groat.
The North Glenora neighbourhood was developed
in the 1950s. *See* Glenora.

Neighbourhood   CU   NW   7:A1

North Glenora Park

13535–109A Avenue

This park is in the North Glenora neighbourhood
and has an area of 2.36 ha. *See* Glenora *and* North
Glenora.

Park   1983   NW   7:A1

North Saskatchewan River

Flowing 1,223 km from the Columbia Icefield to
Hudson Bay; winding in a northeasterly direction
through Edmonton

See feature story, page 231.

River   CU   C   7:C2

North Sawle

North of 167 Avenue, 59A Street to 66 Street

The name of this neighbourhood is derived from
that of North Sawle (d. 1953), a pioneer of northern
aviation born in Athabasca Landing who lived in
Edmonton and flew for Canadian Pacific Airlines.
His father, trading post inspector A. L. Sawle,

North Saskatchewan River

THE NORTH SASKATCHEWAN RIVER, a tributary of the Saskatchewan River, takes its name from the Cree word, *kis-is-ska-tche-wan*, meaning "swift current." It flows from the Saskatchewan Glacier in the Columbia Icefield, some 500 km upstream from Edmonton, and has a total length of over 1,200 km. The North Saskatchewan River meets the South Saskatchewan River about 50 km east of Prince Albert, Saskatchewan, to form the Saskatchewan River.

The Blackfoot referred to it as the *Omaka-ty*, meaning "big river." French maps dating from the 1790s give it the name *Rivière Bourbon* after the French royal family. Alexander Mackenzie noted the Saskatchiwine River in 1793.

The North Saskatchewan River flows for 48 km in a northeasterly direction through Edmonton and forms the river valley, the largest stretch of urban parkland in North America. The river valley includes 22 parks, 150 km of trails and 14 ravines.

Both the Hudson's Bay Company and the North West Company saw the potential of the river in expanding trade and sited forts here in 1795. Using the river as a highway, Fort Edmonton soon became the centre of the western Canadian fur trade. Over the two centuries that followed, Edmonton grew to the northeast and southwest, following the course of the river valley.

The North Saskatchewan River divided the two earliest communities—Edmonton and Strathcona—until completion of the Low Level Bridge in 1900. Where once the river provided a means to connect the city with outlying regions, it was increasingly seen as a barrier to trade and communication between the still separate towns lying on the northern and southern banks of the North Saskatchewan. The two cities were amalgamated in 1912; a year later, the High Level Bridge was completed.

Postcard of the North Saskatchewan River at Edmonton, circa 1914. (CEA EA-270-06)

Saskatchewan River, Edmonton, Alta

named his son for "the North". During the 1930s, North Sawle worked for Mackenzie Air Services and later for Canadian Airways. In 1943 the veteran pilot made a record-breaking return flight from Edmonton to Fort Norman in the Northwest Territories. Sawle and his co-pilot, Captain Bud Poller, flew a heavily loaded Canadian Pacific Airline Lodestar there and back in only 10 hours and 20 minutes (4 hours and 45 minutes one way), traveling 3,717 km. Sawle died tragically in 1953 in Karachi, Pakistan, while testing a jetliner for Canadian Pacific Airlines.

Neighbourhood 1981 NE 11:A1 *

Northern Lights Cemetery

15203 Campbell Road

This north Edmonton cemetery was unofficially known as Sturgeon Cemetery before being named Sturgeon Heights Memorial Park in 1986. A year later, however, it was renamed Northern Lights Cemetery. The City of Edmonton purchased this land in 1972. This cemetery is located in the Rampart Industrial area and has an area of 29.80 ha.

Cemetery 1987 NW 9:D2 *

Northmount

137 Avenue to 144 Avenue, 82 Street to 97 Street

This neighbourhood is in the Dickinsfield subdivision and may be descriptive.

Neighbourhood 1967 NE 10:C2

Northmount Park

9204–140 Avenue

This park is in the Northmount neighbourhood and has an area of 5.14 ha. *See* Northmount.

Park 1981 NE 10:C2

Norwester Industrial

114 Avenue to 118 Avenue, 163 Street to 170 Street

This name recognizes fur traders of the North West Company (NWC), the sometimes bitter rival of the Hudson's Bay Company (HBC), which operated from the 1780s to 1821. Its agents were known as Nor'Westers. *The Nor'-Wester* was also the name of the first newspaper in the North-West Territories, published in the Red River settlement in 1859. The NWC amalgamated with the HBC in 1821. The Norwester Industrial neighbourhood is located in the northwest corner of Edmonton.

Neighbourhood 1973 NW 8:C1

Norwester Park

116 Avenue to 117 Avenue, 165 Street to 168 Street

This park is in the Norwester Industrial neighbourhood and has an area of 4.43 ha. *See* Norwester Industrial.

Park 1980 NW 8:C1

Norwood Boulevard

111 Avenue from 82 Street to 97 Street

This road name has existed since the early 1900s. It was so named because it formed the southern boundary of the Norwood subdivision. Alex Rowland was the first European to settle this land. In 1903 he sold his property to the McDougall & Secord real estate investment company. The company named the area Norwood and put lots up for sale the following year. In 1906 the first building was erected on Norwood Boulevard; in 1909 the Norwood School was opened. The origin of the name Norwood is not recorded.

Road CU NE 7:C1

Norwood Square

9516–114 Avenue

This park is in the Alberta Avenue neighbourhood and has an area of 0.91 ha. *See* Norwood Boulevard.

Park 1987 NE 7:C1

Oakes Gate

Joining Carter Crest Road to Oeming Road across Rabbit Hill Road

Ralph Oakes was a bush pilot who flew transport flights in northern Canada in the 1930s and 1940s. In the 1930s, Oakes flew with Yukon Southern Air Transport out of Edmonton to Grande Prairie, Whitehorse, the Yukon and other northern settlements. In 1939, a passenger and airmail service was added to his route. In 1941, Canadian Pacific Airlines bought Yukon Southern Air Transport. Oakes remained on staff until his retirement, and then moved to Vancouver. This road is in the Ogilvie Ridge neighbourhood.

Road 1981 SW 4:A2 *

Ockenden Place

South of Ogilvie Boulevard, east of Ower Place

Maj.-Gen. Gordon Ockenden (1923–1983) was a Canadian defence attaché to the United States. He was born in Alberta and joined the Royal Canadian Air Force as a pilot in 1941. Ockenden was awarded the Distinguished Flying Cross. During his career, he was stationed at several airforce bases in Canada and in the United States. In 1971 he was promoted to Brig.-Gen., and in 1976 to Maj.-Gen. It was at this time that he was posted in Washington, DC. Ockenden retired from the forces in 1978.

Road 1981 SW 4:A2

O'Connor Place

East of Rabbit Hill Road, north of Ogilvie Boulevard

George Bligh O'Connor (1883–1957) was a chief justice of the Alberta Supreme Court. Born and educated in Ontario, O'Connor came to Edmonton after being called to the bar in 1905. He joined an Edmonton law firm and was made King's Counsel in 1913. O'Connor became a member of the

George Bligh O'Connor, circa 1943.
(Photo courtesy of the Farnell family.)

Supreme Court in 1941. In 1944 he was named chairman of the Wartime Labour Relations Board and was later appointed chairman of the Canada Labour Relations Board. In 1950 he was named chief justice. O'Connor received an honorary degree from the University of Alberta in 1952.

Road 1984 SW 4:A2 *

Oeming Road

East of Rabbit Hill Road, south of Omand Drive

Albert F. Oeming was a WWII veteran, an Edmonton conservationist and a fellow of the prestigious London Zoological Society. He was born in Edmonton and graduated with a Bachelor's Degree and a Master's Degree in Zoology from the

University of Alberta. Oeming established an animal sanctuary, the Alberta Game Farm, in 1959 (it became the Polar Park in 1980). He was president of the Edmonton Zoological Society and was a recipient of the 1967 Everly Medal for excellence in animal conservation from the United States. In 1972 Oeming received an honorary degree from the University of Alberta. The Alberta Game Farm closed in thc 1990s after nearly 40 years of caring for his private collection of animals.

Road   1981   SW   4:A2 *

Ogilvie Boulevard

East of Rabbit Hill Road, south of Omand Drive

See Ogilvie Ridge.

Road   1985   SW   4:A2

Ogilvie Place

East of Rabbit Hill Road, north of Ogilvie Boulevard

See Ogilvie Ridge.

Road   1985   SW   4:A2 *

Ogilvie Ridge

29 Avenue north to Bulyea Road, Whitemud Park west to Rabbit Hill

James H. Ogilvie (1893–1977) was a WWI veteran, politician and, for 57 years, an Edmonton lawyer. Born in Nova Scotia, he came to Alberta in 1914 and enrolled at the University of Alberta that same year. After interrupting his studies to serve in the war, he was called to the bar in 1920. Ogilvie served as an alderman from 1932 to 1948, ran for mayor in 1934 and acted as deputy mayor in 1939. In 1947 he was appointed King's Counsel.

Neighbourhood   1979   SW   4:A2

J.H. Ogilvie, 1948. (CEA EA-267-529)

Ogilvie Ridge Park

951 Ogilvie Boulevard

This park is in the Ogilvie Ridge neighbourhood and has an area of 1.52 ha. *See* Ogilvie Ridge.

Park   1992   SW   4:A2

Oldman Creek

Flowing north into the North Saskatchewan River 21 km northeast of Edmonton city centre; north of 137 Avenue, west of 33 Street East

Oldman Creek, located within the city limits, is said to have been named after the local Old Man's Knoll, over which a historic trail passed from Edmonton to Fort Garry. The Oldman Creek Nursery is located in this area. The name of Oldman Creek was noted as early as 1882 by the Dominion Lands Survey.

Creek   CU   NE   11:C2

Oleskiw

River valley west to 170 Street, south of Wolf Willow Ravine

Joseph Oleskiw (1860–1903) was a Ukrainian academic who was instrumental in organizing Ukrainian immigration to western Canada. He visited Alberta in 1895 and, upon returning to Ukraine, wrote and distributed a pamphlet encouraging Ukrainians to immigrate to Canada. A year later, with Oleskiw's help, Ukrainians began arriving in Alberta. The neighbourhood's original name was Wolf Willow Farms. In 1972 the name was changed to Oleskiw.

Neighbourhood   1972   SW   3:C1

Oleskiw Park

203 Walker Road

This park is in the Oleskiw neighbourhood and has an area of 3.16 ha. *See* Oleskiw.

Park   1990   SW   3:C1

Oliver

River valley north to 104 Avenue, 109 Street to 124 Street

See feature story, page 237.

Neighbourhood   CU   C   7:B2

Oliver Park

10326–118 Street

This park is in the Oliver neighbourhood and has an area of 1.5 ha. *See* Oliver *feature story, page 237.*

Park   1983   C   7:B2

Olsen Close

North of Ogilvie Boulevard, west of Omand Drive

Imelda Olsen (1899–1975) was the organist at St. Joseph's Roman Catholic Cathedral for nearly 45 years. She was born in Quebec and moved to Edmonton in 1913. At the age of 15 she began playing the organ at the Immaculate Conception church, and from 1922 to 1925 was the organist at St. Joachim's church. Olsen was also a piano teacher, adjudicator and choral director of the Edmonton Civic Opera. From 1925 to 1933 she worked as the organist and choir director at St. Joseph's Cathedral. Olsen continued as a church organist until retiring in 1969.

Road   1984   SW   4:A2 *

Omand Drive

North of Ogilvie Boulevard, west of Osborne Crescent

Allan Omand (1857–1931) was one of Edmonton's first settlers, emigrating from the Orkney Islands to Canada in about 1880. He settled near Winnipeg before coming to Edmonton, where by 1883 he had purchased River Lot 3 (present-day Windsor Park neighbourhood). Omand worked as a riverman and boat builder. In the late 1890s he left Edmonton for the Klondike Gold Rush. He died in Vancouver.

Road   1981   SW   4:A2

Ormsby Close

Between Ormsby Road East and West at 189 Street

See Ormsby Place.

Road   1986   SW   3:C1 *

Ormsby Court

Between Ormsby Road East and West, west of 188 Street

See Ormsby Place.

Road   1986   SW   3:C1 *

Oliver

NEWSPAPERMAN AND POLITICIAN Frank Oliver (1853–1933) brought the first printing press to Edmonton and co-founded the *Edmonton Bulletin* in 1880. Oliver came to Edmonton in 1876 and went on to formulate much of the early legislation in the North-West Territories.

He was born in Ontario and attended high school in Brampton where he apprenticed at a local weekly newspaper. It was during this time that he dropped his original last name, Bowsfield, in favour of his mother's maiden name, Oliver. The name change apparently followed a disagreement between Oliver and his father over his plans to enter the printing trade. Oliver later worked in the composing room of the *Toronto Globe* before coming west in 1873, where he was employed at the *Manitoba Free Press* and the *Winnipeg Journal*. In 1876 he moved still further west to Edmonton, then only a small village controlled by the Hudson's Bay Company.

After a telegraph line to Edmonton was established, bringing regular news from the rest of the country,

Oliver went into partnership with the telegraph operator, Alex Taylor, and founded the *Edmonton Bulletin*. It was only the second newspaper on the prairies, the first being the *Herald* in Battleford, Saskatchewan. The first two-page edition of the *Bulletin* was published on December 6, 1880. In the paper's editorials, Oliver was an outspoken and sometimes fiery supporter of the west. He lobbied for elected representation, protection of settler land rights and the building of schools. Between 1883 and 1885 he was a member of the Regina-based North-West Territories Council; he was elected to the Legislative Assembly of the North-West Territories (which succeeded the council) and served from 1888 to 1896.

Under Liberal Prime Minister Sir Wilfrid Laurier, Oliver became the province of Alberta's first member of parliament in 1905. He sat in the House of Commons from 1896 to 1917, and was minister of the Interior and superintendent general of Indian Affairs from 1905 to 1911.

Frank Oliver giving a speech on the occasion of his appointment as Dominion Minister of the Interior, 1905. (CEA EA-10-2050)

Arthur W. Ormsby, Superintendent Electric Light Department, circa 1912–1913. (GAI NA-200-24)

Ormsby Crescent

East of Ormsby Road West, south of Ormsby Court

See Ormsby Place.

Road   1986   SW   3:C1 *

Ormsby Place

Callingwood Road north to 69 Avenue, 178 Street west to Ormsby Road West

Ontario-born Arthur W. Ormsby (1869–1961) was superintendent of the electric light department for 20 years. He came to Edmonton in 1892 and worked as a telephone repairman before joining the Electric Light and Power Company. From 1918 to 1920, Ormsby was a city commissioner. He later went into business and retired in 1953.

Neighbourhood   1972   SW   3:C1

Ormsby Road East

East of 188 Street, north of Callingwood Road

See Ormsby Place.

Road   1986   SW   3:C1

Ormsby Road West

West of 188 Street, north of Callingwood Road

See Ormsby Place.

Road   1986   SW   3:C1

Ormsby Wynd

Northwest of Ormsby Road West, south of 69 Avenue

See Ormsby Place.

Road   1986   SW   3:C1 *

Orval Allen Park

16055–127 Street

Orval W. Allen (1911–1982) was a photographer, part-time actor, and judge in the Court of Canadian Citizenship. He was born in Ontario and came west in 1938 to work for Canadian Kodak, selling photographic supplies in Alberta and Saskatchewan. Allen returned to Ontario during WWII, but moved back to Alberta in 1946. A year later he opened Progress Photo, a photo-finishing business, on 99 Street. In the early 1940s Allen moved his business to Whyte Avenue and started a second outlet, Allen's Studio. Before being appointed to the bench in 1960, Allen helped establish the Edmonton Citizenship Council. He was among the first laymen to be appointed to the bench. He retired in 1977. The Orval Allen Park is in the Dunluce neighbourhood and has an area of 2.52 ha.

Park   1984   NW   10:B1

Osborne Crescent

East of Omand Drive, north of Ogilvie Boulevard

Arsemous D. Osborne (1829–1917) was Edmonton's second postmaster. Born in Upper Canada, he came to Edmonton in about 1880 and was appointed postmaster in 1883. Osborne's participation in the 1892 scuffle over the government's decision to move the Land and Timber Office from the north side of the North Saskatchewan River to the south side (South Edmonton/Strathcona) cost him his position. As the land agent was attempting to leave Edmonton with the office documents, prominent citizens, including Osborne and Mayor Matt McCauley, surrounded the land agent's wagon. The agent was told that he could leave town but the contents of the office must stay. In the ensuing confrontation, amid threats of bloodshed, the North West Mounted Police intervened and restored order. In the end, the citizens of Edmonton were victorious and the office stayed in Edmonton. Osborne, however, was forced to resign because of his involvement in the protest. He then established a gold prospecting operation along the North Saskatchewan River.

Road 1989 SW 4:A2

Osborne Gate

Connecting Osborne Crescent with Ogilvie Boulevard

See Osborne Crescent.

Road 1989 SW 4:A2 *

Osland Close

South of Osland Drive, east of Osland Place

Major Andrew Osland (1920–1979) was an internationally accredited boxing official who was involved in Edmonton boxing for 40 years. Osland began boxing as an army recruit and in 1969 became the first president of the Canadian Amateur Boxing Association. He was an official at numerous boxing events, including the Canadian championships, the Pan-American Games and the Montreal Olympics. In 1974 and 1978 he chaired the boxing committee for the Commonwealth Games.

Road 1987 SW 4:A2 *

Osland Drive

East of Ogilvie Boulevard, north of Osland Place

See Osland Close.

Road 1987 SW 4:A2

Osland Place

East of Ogilvie Boulevard, south of Osland Drive

See Osland Close.

Road 1987 SW 4:A2 *

Ottewell

90 Avenue to 98 Avenue and Terrace Road, 50 Street to 75 Street

See feature story, page 240.

Neighbourhood 1957 SE 6:A2

Ottewell Park

6010–93A Avenue

This park is in the Ottewell neighbourhood and has an area of 2.36 ha. *See* Ottewell *feature story, page 240.*

Park 1967 SE 7:D2

Ottewell Road

90 Avenue at 69 Street to 98 Avenue at 71 Street

See Ottewell *feature story, page 240.*

Road 1959 SE 6:A2

Ottewell

RICHARD PHILLIP OTTEWELL (1848–1942) was an early pioneer who lived through the Riel Rebellion and was one of the first farmers to homestead in the Clover Bar area, in what is now eastern Edmonton. Ottewell emigrated from England to Ontario with his family in 1850, when he was still a small child.

In 1869, Ottewell travelled to Fort Garry (now Winnipeg) as part of a federal work party and, arriving amid the Métis rebellion, was imprisoned for six weeks by Louis Riel's provisional government. One of the party, Ottewell's cellmate Thomas Scott, was tried and executed by Riel's forces. Upon their release from prison, in March 1870, Ottewell walked for nine days in the dead of winter, the temperature falling as low as -40 °C, to reach the safety of Fort Abercrombie in the United States. Ottewell later returned to Ontario, where he married Frances Trevillion. In 1881, leaving his wife and family behind, he set off for the west once more. Ottewell was one of the first to stake his claim and homestead in what is today known as the Clover Bar area, then a distance of 16 kilometres east of Fort Edmonton. In 1883 his family, which would eventually number nine children, joined him. During the North-West Rebellion of 1885, the Ottewells took refuge in Fort Edmonton and Richard served in the home guard.

As Edmonton grew, the Ottewell farm shifted from grain to dairying. In 1904, Ottewell opened the Ottewell Coal Company and later founded Campbell & Ottewell Flour Mills. Ottewell continued to live on his homestead until shortly before his death at the age of 93 in 1942. The historic Ottewell farm, cut out of the bush in the 1880s, is today at the heart of Edmonton's heavy industrial area. Oil refineries and chemical plants now cover what was once considered among the best farmland in the region.

During the 1910s, part of the Ottewell subdivision (90 Avenue to Whyte Avenue and 50 Street to 67 Street) was known as East Glenora; to the north of this area, 90A Avenue to 95 Avenue was known as East Edmonton Park.

Ottewell family, April 10, 1905. (CEA EA-10-2050)

Otto Leslie Park

16304–110 Avenue

Otto Leslie (b. 1896) was an early pioneer remembered for his horse-drawn sleigh. Leslie was born and raised in Manitoba. After homesteading in Saskatchewan, he came to Edmonton in 1922 and settled on a farm west of the city. For many years he gave sleigh-rides to locals and church groups. After harvest, Leslie would hitch his horses to a hayrack, or a sleigh in the winter, and pick up streetcar passengers coming to the area's school socials and dances. The Otto Leslie Park is in the Mayfield neighbourhood and has an area of 0.39 ha.

Park 1982 NW 8:D1

Overlanders

CN railway tracks north to Kennedale Ravine, Victoria Trail west to 34 Street

In June 1862, 150 people, including one woman, left Winnipeg for the Cariboo Gold Fields in present-day British Columbia. They used Red River carts to transport their possessions and supplies westward across the prairies. Settlers who made this journey were called "Overlanders." They reached Fort Edmonton in July, traded their carts for pack horses and continued their journey with Aboriginal guides across the Rocky Mountains. Most reached their destination in October 1862 and settled in the vicinity of the Cariboo Gold Fields. The neighbourhood name of Overlanders is compatible with the naming theme of the Hermitage subdivision, which honours early settlers.

Neighbourhood 1981 NE 6:B1

Overlanders Park

1130 Hermitage Road

This park is in the Overlanders neighbourhood and has an area of 2.15 ha. *See* Overlanders.

Park 1999 NE 6:B1 *

Ower Place

West of Rabbit Hill Road, south of Ogilvie Boulevard

Dr. John J. Ower (1885–1962) was the first professor of pathology at the University of Alberta and went on to become dean of medicine. He was born in Ontario and studied and served his internship in Montreal. Ower did postgraduate studies in Glasgow, Berlin and Madrid. He served overseas during WWI with the Royal Canadian Army Medical Corps and returned as a lieutenant-colonel. In 1919, after the war, Ower joined the University of Alberta as a professor of pathology. He was acting dean of medicine from 1939 to 1944, dean from 1945 to 1948, and then retired in 1951. Ower was also a Boy Scout leader for two decades.

Road 1985 SW 4:A2 *

Oxford

127 Street to 135 Street, 153 Avenue to 163 Avenue

Oxford House was a Hudson's Bay Company post located at the northeast end of Oxford Lake in what is now southwest Manitoba, on the Hayes River route from Norway House and Lake Winnipeg to York Factory. Oxford House was the oldest post in the Keewatin District, operating continuously from 1798, and was of vital importance during the period when York boats were in operation. Neighbourhoods in The Palisades area are named after early fur trade forts and posts.

Neighbourhood 1984 NW 10:B1

Oxford Park

13040–155 Avenue

This park is in the Oxford neighbourhood and has an area of 5.41 ha. *See* Oxford.

Park 1995 NW 10:B1

Ozerna

153 Avenue to 167 Avenue, 66 Street to 74 Street

Ozerna is a Ukrainian word that means "lake area." This neighbourhood is in the Lake District area.

Neighbourhood 1979 NE 10:D1

Ozerna Park

7010–158 Avenue

This park is in the Ozerna neighbourhood and has an area of 2.45 ha. *See* Ozerna.

Park 1995 NE 10:D1

Ozerna Road

South of 165 Avenue, west of 67 Street

See Ozerna.

Road 1981 NE 10:D2

Palisades, The

*137 Avenue north to the proposed outer ring road,
127 Street to 142 Street*

The Palisades is a predominantly residential area
that covers 583.5 ha. The name recognizes the
contributions of the Hudson's Bay Company and
the North West Company to the settlement and
development of Edmonton and its hinterlands. A
palisade is a fence made of pales, pointed pieces of
wood, that sometimes served as fortifications at fur
trade posts.

Names used in The Palisades area are based on
early forts and posts that played an important part
in the historical development of western Canada.
The Palisades is part of the Northwest Area
Structure Plan, which is divided into a residential
and an industrial area. The Names Advisory
Committee decided that the names should relate to
each other and that the theme should complement
the already established Castle Downs area.

In 1912 the Summerland Park subdivision was
established in the northeast part of the area (north
of 137 Avenue and south of 167 Avenue, east of 149
Street and west of 127 Street). A subdivision called
Imperial Gardens, also established around 1912,
was located at what is now 142 Street and 162
Avenue. It was never formally developed. The
Palisades area was annexed to the City of
Edmonton in 1982.

Area 1984 NW 10:A2 *

Papaschase Industrial

*Whitemud Drive north to 51 Avenue, 91 Street
west to CP railway tracks*

See feature story, page 245.

Neighbourhood 1961 SW 4:C2

Pardee Bay

West of 199 Street, north of Potter Greens Drive

Marjorie Pardee (d. 1966) was the provincial
commissioner of the Girl Guides of Canada. Pardee
was born in Ontario and came to Edmonton in
1905. She was a Girl Guide leader for 13 years and
served as commissioner from 1933 to 1946. Pardee
died at the age of 82.

Road 1990 SW 3:B1 *

Park Drive

95 Avenue at 148 Street to 142 Street

This road was likely named for its location, above
McKenzie Ravine.

Road 1955 SW 7:A2 *

Parkallen

61 Avenue to 72 Avenue, 109 Street to 113 Street

The neighbourhood of Parkallen, formerly Beau
Park and Bridgeland, was developed after WWII.
The name of Parkallen, however, was already in
common usage. The Calgary Trail Community
League was renamed the Parkallen Community
League in 1945 and shops using the name of
Parkallen began to appear around 1949. The name
for Parkallen, bordered by the southside neigh-
bourhoods of McKernan and Allendale, was chosen
by local residents.

Neighbourhood 1951 SW 4:B1

Parkdale

*112 Avenue to 118 Avenue, LRT tracks west
to 89 Street*

Possibly a descriptive term, this name has been in
use since around 1907. In 1908, construction began
on a streetcar line along Alberta Avenue (118
Avenue), bordering the neighbourhood. By 1911,
land developers were selling lots in Parkdale.

Neighbourhood CU NE 7:C1

Papaschase Industrial

CHIEF PAPASCHASE (c. 1838–1918) was the leader
of the Papaschase Indian Reserve, located in what is
now southeast Edmonton. *Papaschase* is translated
from the Cree as "Big Woodpecker." He was also
known as *Pahs-pahs-chase*, *Passpasstayo* and *Passpasschase*,
while his English name was John Gladu-Smith.

Chief Papaschase signed the adhesion to Treaty No.
6 in Edmonton in 1877, one year after the treaty was
signed by the Plains and Wood Cree and the
Assiniboine of the North-West Territories. According
to the terms of the treaty, the band was to receive land,
but several years passed before Papaschase Indian
Reserve No. 136 was formed. It covered some 65
square kilometres comprising 42 sections of land.

The reserve encompassed the area now defined by
30 Avenue and 51 Avenue on the south and north, and
by 17 Street and 119 Street on the east and west.
European settlers already resident in the general area
opposed the creation of the reserve and the granting of
land to members of the Papaschase band.

When Treaty No. 6 was signed in 1876 there was no
recognized definition of the term Métis. By 1886,
however, the government had decided upon one and
offered scrip to anyone with Métis ancestry. About 194
of the 200 people on the reserve accepted the scrip
(either $240 or 240 acres of land); most of the Métis
chose the cash certificate. With so few people remaining
on the reserve, the government closed it and the band
members scattered, some joining other reserves,
including the Enoch band at Winterburn.

In 1888 the Papaschase Indian Reserve was surrendered to the federal government and in 1891 the rich
agricultural land was put up for sale at a public auction
held in Calgary; most of the quarter-section lots sold
went to speculators. A second auction was held in
Edmonton in 1893, this time with conditions placed
on the sales to encourage European settlers to purchase
the land. The Papaschase Indian Reserve was the first
reserve to be surrendered for immigrant settlement.

*Chief Papaschase, circa 1880s. (Although disputed, this photograph
has been identified as Chief Papaschase.) (CEA A96–140)*

Parkdale, looking west from the Canadian Northern Railway tracks on 115 Avenue at 79 Street, circa 1915. (CEA EA-10-1056)

Parkdale Park

8421–114 Avenue

This park is in the Parkdale neighbourhood and has an area of 0.55 ha. *See* Parkdale.

Park 1984 NE 7:C1

Parkview

87 Avenue north to McKenzie Ravine,
Valleyview Drive west to 149 Street

This neighbourhood enjoys scenic views of the river valley. That part of Parkview east of 142 Street was formerly the subdivision of Valleyview. Parkview also incorporates part of the former subdivision of Buena Vista. Parkview overlooks Buena Vista Park toward the east.

Neighbourhood 1956 SW 7:A2

Parkview Park

9135–146 Street

This park is located in the Parkview neighbourhood and has an area of 1.5 ha. *See* Parkview.

Park 1982 SW 7:A2

Parsons Industrial

23 Avenue to 34 Avenue, 91 Street west to
CP railway tracks

Sidney Parsons (1893–1955) was a WWI veteran and the mayor of Edmonton from 1950 to 1951. He was born in England and moved to New Jersey in the early 1900s. Parsons came to Edmonton in 1910 and worked as a bricklayer and contractor before serving as an alderman from 1937 to 1949.

Neighbourhood 1973 SE 4:C2

Parsons Road

South from 34 Avenue at 99 Street; also south from Ellerslie Road at 97 Street

See Parsons Industrial.

Road 1974 SE 4:C2

Patricia Crescent

77 Avenue between 165 Street and 167 Street

See Patricia Heights.

Road 1971 SW 3:C1 *

Patricia Drive

77 Avenue between 159 Street and 163 Street

See Patricia Heights.

Road 1971 SW 3:D1

Patricia Heights

Patricia Ravine north to Whitemud Drive, west of 156 Street

This area is named after Lady Patricia Ramsay and was annexed to Edmonton in 1964. *See* Princess Patricia Park.

Neighbourhood 1965 SW 3:D1

Patricia Place

158 Street and 76 Avenue

See Patricia Heights.

Road 1971 SW 3:D1 *

George McCulloch yard in Parkview, July 1961. (CEA EA-88-148)

Patricia Ravine

Separating the Patricia Heights and Westridge neighbourhoods; from the North Saskatchewan River northeast to Whitemud Drive

See Patricia Heights.

Ravine 1965 SW 3:C1

Patrick J. Ryan Park

15804–110 Avenue

Quebec-born Patrick J. Ryan (1913–1996) was a founding member of Alberta's co-operative and credit union movement. During the 1930s, Ryan travelled across Canada looking for work. In 1948, he settled in Edmonton and married Jacqueline Gamache. Ryan became involved in politics in the late 1950s, serving on the Jasper Place town council for two terms before its amalgamation with Edmonton in 1964. He was also a member of the Edmonton Social Planning Council, a public trustee of the Edmonton Public Library Board and a member of the New Democratic Party, running for both the federal and provincial parties. After helping to found the co-operative and credit union movement, he served as director of the Edmonton Savings and Credit Union (now Capital City Savings and Credit Union). The Patrick J. Ryan

Park is in the Mayfield neighbourhood and has an area of 0.75 ha.

Park 1999 NW 8:D1 *

Paul Kane Park

10220–121 Street

The painter and explorer Paul Kane (1810–1871) was born in Ireland and came to York (now Toronto) with his family before 1822. In 1845 he left Toronto to sketch Aboriginal peoples, travelling with Hudson's Bay Company traders westward to Fort Victoria (now Victoria, BC). Kane spent time in Fort Edmonton in 1846. He returned to Toronto in 1848 and in 1859 published an account of his travels. The main subjects of his paintings were Aboriginal people and western landscapes. He provided some of the earliest and most accurate images of the northwest and its people. The Paul Kane Park is in the Oliver neighbourhood and has an area of 0.78 ha.

Park 1976 C 7:B2

Pawson Cove

West of 199 Street, north of Potter Greens Drive

Harold "Hal" Pawson (1916–1981) was a WWII veteran, a journalist and the director of public relations for the City of Edmonton. Born in Saskatchewan, he came to Edmonton to work for the *Edmonton Journal* in 1941. Pawson served with the Royal Canadian Air Force in WWII and returned to the newspaper following the war, becoming sports editor in 1953. He worked as a public relations officer beginning in 1966 and from 1968 to 1976 was head of public relations for the City. In 1972 he played a major role in Edmonton's successful bid to host the 1978 Commonwealth Games. He went on to serve as the director of the Commonwealth Games Foundation.

Road 1990 SW 3:B1 *

Pearson Crescent

West of 199 Street, south of Potter Greens Drive

Manitoba-born Hugh E. Pearson (1887–1979) was a WWI veteran and a broadcasting pioneer. He came to Alberta in 1906 where he worked as a Dominion Land Surveyor. Pearson was awarded the Military Cross for his service in WWI. After the war, he co-founded the Radio Supply Company, later expanding his business to include automotive parts and broadcasting. Pearson retired in 1970 and was appointed to the Order of Canada in 1976.

Road 1990 SW 3:B1 *

Peggy Holmes Park

15803–109 Street

Author and artist Maud "Peggy" Holmes (1897–1997) described herself as "the oldest broadcaster in Canada." Holmes was born in England and came to Canada in 1919 as a war bride, settling in Edmonton in 1921. In 1974, when Holmes was in her seventies, she became a radio broadcaster, recounting stories over the airwaves of her experiences as a homesteader. Holmes published her memoirs *It Could Have Been Worse* in 1978 and authored two other books, *Never a Dull Moment* and *Still Soaring*. Holmes was awarded the Order of Canada in 1989. The Peggy Holmes Park is in the Beaumaris neighbourhood and has an area of 1.3 ha.

Park 1984 NW 10:B1

Pembina

137 Avenue north to Hudson Road, and 140 Avenue, 127 Street to 135 Street

The Pembina Post was established by the Hudson's Bay Company (HBC) on the Pembina River, along the Edmonton-Lesser Slave Lake Trail, in 1801. The post was also called Summerberry River Post. After being abandoned, the post was reestablished by the HBC and the North West Company in 1817.

Pembina Post was permanently closed around 1822. Pembina is a version of the Cree word *nîpiminân*, referring to the cranberry. Neighbourhoods in The Palisades area are named after early forts and posts.

Neighbourhood   1986   NW   10:A2

Peter Close

North of Potter Greens Drive, east of Phillips Row

Rosella "Babe" Dow (1896–1973) came to Edmonton in 1907 and married John C. Peter (1895–1968) in 1917. Babe Peter was a songwriter and composed songs for Klondike Days and the Edmonton Flyers hockey club. She was also a volunteer for the Catholic Women's League, the Duke of Edinburgh Chapter of the Imperial Order Daughters of the Empire, the University of Alberta Hospital and the Edmonton General Hospital. John Peter was born in Ontario and moved to Edmonton in 1910. He began working for Swift Canadian Co. meats in 1911; after 15 years in Edmonton, he became the manager of plants in British Columbia and Saskatchewan. John returned to Edmonton in 1946 and in 1953 was named a director of the firm. He retired in 1960. John was a volunteer with the Edmonton Exhibition Association, YMCA, the Edmonton Hospital Board and Rotary International.

Road   1990   SW   3:B1 *

Petrolia

34 Avenue north to Whitemud Drive, 111 Street west to Whitemud Creek

The name of this subdivision honours the history of the petrochemical industry in Canada. In 1857, oil was discovered in Canada West. Over the next decade, more than two dozen oil refineries were established in the town of Petrolia, Canada West.

Subdivision   1961   SW   4:B2 *

Phillips Row

North of Potter Greens Drive, east of Picard Drive

Dorothy Phillips (1914–1999) was the founder of Edmonton's Marian Centre. Phillips was born in Quebec and in 1950 joined the Madonna House Apostolate, a Roman Catholic lay order in Ontario. She came to Edmonton in 1955 and began raising funds for a shelter for the poor and needy. Phillips was named Edmonton's Citizen of the Year by the Junior Chamber of Commerce in 1965. In 1967, Phillips returned to the Madonna House Apostolate. Phillips Row is in the Potter Greens neighbourhood.

Road   1990   SW   3:B1 *

Phoebe McCullough Park

16316–107A Avenue

Phoebe Woodhouse McCullough (1896–1971) was a distinguished member of the Royal Purple, the women's auxiliary of the Elks Club. McCullough was born in Australia and, after a time living in England, came to Canada in 1913. She moved to Edmonton in 1936 and worked as a security officer and police matron. McCullough joined the Royal Purple in 1941 and served as national Supreme Honoured Royal Lady of the Order of the Royal Purple from 1951 to 1953. From 1964, she was a member of the Deaf Detection and Development Committee, which diagnosed and assisted children with hearing loss. The Phoebe McCullough Park is in the Mayfield neighbourhood and has an area of 0.83 ha.

Park   1990   SW   8:D1

Picard Drive

North of Potter Greens Drive, east of Proctor Wynd

J. Laurier Picard (1907–1983) was an educator with nearly 50 years of service to the separate school board. Picard was born in Edmonton and received his post-secondary education at the Edmonton

Pilot Cy Becker and his bush plane, circa 1927.
(CEA EA-10-3181-19-2)

campus of Laval University (present-day Faculté St-Jean). Beginning in 1924, he taught throughout Alberta. From 1930 to 1972 he was a teacher, assistant principal, principal and administrator for Edmonton's Catholic school system. Following his retirement, Picard was elected as a separate school trustee in 1974, and was reelected in 1977. Laurier's father, Joseph Henri, was the first chairman of the Edmonton separate school board and served on the board for 25 years. Picard Drive is in the Potter Greens neighbourhood.

Road   1991   SW   3:B1

Pilot Sound

153 Avenue north to proposed outer ring road, Manning Drive west to 66 Street

Neighbourhoods in this area are named after pioneer bush pilots: Brintnell, Cy Becker, Hollick-Kenyon, Matt Berry, McConachie and North Sawle. The Namao Airport is located nearby.

Area   1980   NE   11:A1 *

Place LaRue

100 Avenue north to Stony Plain Road, 170 Street west to Anthony Henday Drive

Stanislaus LaRue (b. 1860) was a surveyor, scout and pioneer businessman. Born in Canada East, LaRue came to Edmonton in 1883, where he worked as a surveyor and served as a scout during the North-West Rebellion (1885). In 1889, in partnership with J. H. Picard, he opened a general store. In 1907, after the store was closed, LaRue and Picard entered into the real estate business. Originally, the terrain of what would become the Place LaRue neighbourhood was marshland and peat moss, and residents in the area referred to it as Bog Meadows.

Neighbourhood   1980   SW   8:C2

Pleasantview

51 Avenue to 61 Avenue, Calgary Trail west to 111 Street

Until the 1950s, much of this neighbourhood was known as the Martin Estate, the name taken from pioneer David Martin, who settled on this land in 1899. Following WWII, the land was sold and developed for returning veterans and their families. The eastern portion had been annexed to Edmonton in 1914, while the western portion was annexed in 1947. The neighbourhood's name of Pleasantview is taken from its vantage point as one of the highest areas in Edmonton.

Neighbourhood   CU   SW   4:B1

Stanislaus LaRue, circa 1880. (CEA EA–10–689.25)

Pollard Meadows

Mill Woods Road South north to 23 Avenue, Mill Woods Road East west to 50 Street

Iowa-born Joseph Francis "Frank" Pollard (1872–1924) was a pioneer industrialist and politician who came to Edmonton before 1900. He and his brother owned a brick yard in the Walterdale subdivision. Pollard sat on Strathcona City Council from 1908 to 1912 and served in WWI.

Neighbourhood 1976 SE 1:C1

Pollard Meadows Park

1751–48 Street

This park is in the Pollard Meadows neighbourhood and has an area of 3.01 ha. *See* Pollard Meadows.

Park 1984 SE 1:C1

Porter Court

West of Picard Drive, connecting to Proctor Wynd

Vancouver-born Lois Porter (1918–1998) was a founding member of the Alberta Historical Resources Foundation board and an award-winning volunteer. In 1942, at the age of 24, Porter was widowed with a small child. Between 1943 and 1953 she worked and earned her private pilot's licence. In 1953 Porter moved to Edmonton to marry, but it was delayed until 1954 due to illness. In 1966, when her second child was ten years old, Porter returned to work outside the home. Retirement came in 1983.

Porter was involved in the Society for the Protection of Architectural Resources in Edmonton (SPARE), the Old Strathcona Foundation, the Historical Society of Alberta, Canada's Aviation Hall of Fame, the City of Edmonton Archives, the Alberta Historical Resources Foundation, the Alberta Museums' Association and the Friends of the Provincial Museum of Alberta. She received awards from the City of Edmonton, the Alberta Historical Resources Foundation, the Edmonton Historical Board and the Greater Edmonton Foundation.

Road 1991 SW 3:B1 *

Post Office Clock Tower

10135–100 Street

Construction of the Edmonton Post Office was completed in 1910. The four-faced clock tower on the southeast face of the building stood empty for nearly two years, until an English-made clock purchased at a cost of $1,000 was installed in 1912. In 1966 the new post office at 99 Street and 103A Avenue opened. The old post office was torn down in 1972, but the clock was preserved and now sits at the corner of 101A Avenue and 100 Street. The Post Office Clock Tower park marks the original location of the old post office. The park has an area of 0.26 ha. and is located in the Downtown neighbourhood.

Park 1981 C 7:C2

Potter Greens

North of Whitemud Drive, west of 199 Street

Sam Potter (1892–1984) was a pioneer who ran a dairy business in the Winterburn area. He was born in England and immigrated to Canada with his parents in 1902. In 1927 Potter moved to Edmonton and established a dairy. Two years later he settled in Winterburn and continued running his dairy business until 1948. In 1945 the family relocated to another property in the Winterburn area and Potter donated land for a new community church. The suffix "Greens" is used to indicate that a golf course is located in this area. Neighbourhoods in the Lewis Farms subdivision are named after the area's early pioneers.

Neighbourhood 1990 SW 3:B1

Potter Greens Drive

North of Whitemud Drive, west of 199 Street

See Potter Greens.

Road 1990 SW 3:B1

Poundmaker Industrial

105 Avenue to 109 Avenue, 184 Street west to Anthony Henday Drive

Cree Chief Pitikwahanapiwiyin "Poundmaker" (c.1842–1886) signed Treaty No. 6 in 1876 and became a chief two years later. During the North-West Rebellion in 1885, Poundmaker and his band held Fort Battleford and also caused the retreat of Lt. Col. W. D. Otter at the battle of Cut Knife Hill. For his participation in the rebellion, Poundmaker was convicted of treason and spent three years in prison. He became ill, and died shortly after being released from jail. The name of Poundmaker Industrial is compatible with nearby neighbourhoods in this area, Sunwapta Industrial and Morin Industrial.

Neighbourhood 1981 NW 8:C2

P.C.H. Primrose, circa 1935. (CEA EA-10-2247)

Primrose

Whitemud Drive north to 100 Avenue, 178 Street west to Anthony Henday Drive

Lt. Col. Philip C.H. Primrose (1864–1937) was a founding member of the North West Mounted Police (NWMP) and Alberta's fifth lieutenant-governor. He was born in Nova Scotia and educated at the Royal Military College in Kingston, Ontario. Primrose served as superintendent of the NWMP from 1885 to 1914. From 1915 to 1935, he was a police magistrate in Edmonton. Primrose was appointed lieutenant-governor in 1936.

Subdivision 1970 SW 8:C2 *

Primrose Park

8304–188 Street

In 1989, to celebrate the millennium year of Christianity in Ukraine, this park was named

Ukrainian Millennium Park. It was renamed, at the request of the community league, to Primrose Park. This park is in the Aldergrove neighbourhood and has an area of 2.06 ha. *See* Primrose.

Park   1989   SW   3:C1

Prince Charles

118 Avenue north to Yellowhead Trail, 122 Street to 127 Street

This neighbourhood was formerly known as North Inglewood. In 1953 an existing school was named Prince Charles Elementary School, in honour of Prince Charles (b. 1948), son of Queen Elizabeth II. The community league adopted the name and petitioned to have the neighbourhood renamed to Prince Charles.

Neighbourhood   1960   NW   7:B1

Prince Charles Park

12449–121 Avenue

This park is in the Prince Charles neighbourhood and has an area of 0.84 ha. *See* Prince Charles.

Park   1982   NW   7:B1

Prince Rupert

111 Avenue north to Kingsway, Kingsway west to 120 Street

The Prince Rupert Golf Course was run by the Hudson's Bay Company (HBC), on what was then the Hudson's Bay Reserve property, between 1930 and 1951. It was named for the first governor of the HBC, Prince Rupert, Duke of Cumberland and Earl of Holderness. In 1670, Prince Rupert, who was the nephew of King Charles II, was given a royal charter that allowed him (and his company) to trade furs in the territory traversed by rivers flowing into Hudson Bay. The Prince's trading area was known as Rupert's Land. The golf course closed in 1951, but the neighbourhood perpetuates the name.

Neighbourhood   1956   NW   7:B1

Prince Charles and Princess Diana at Fort Edmonton Park barbeque during royal visit to open Universiad, 1983. (CEA EA-340-1461)

Prince Rupert Park

11320–113 Avenue

This park is in the Prince Rupert neighbourhood and has an area of 0.41 ha. *See* Prince Rupert.

Park   1981   NW   7:B1

Princess Elizabeth Avenue

Northeast of Kingsway from 101 Street to 113 Street

In 1951, Portage Avenue was renamed Princess Elizabeth Avenue in honour of her royal visit to Edmonton. Princess Elizabeth (now the reigning sovereign, Queen Elizabeth II, b. 1926) and Prince Philip, Duke of Edinburgh, visited the city on October 27, 1951. This marked the second time that the road's name was changed because of a

Pylypow Industrial

IVAN PYLYPOW (1859–1936) was one of the first two Ukrainian settlers in Canada. He and his family lived in the village of Nebiliv in the Carpathian Mountains, in what were then the Hapsburg-ruled territories of modern-day western Ukraine. Pylypow was the eldest son of Hawrylo Pylypiwsky, a farmer.

Pylypow and a friend, Wasyl Eleniak (1859–1956), made a brief journey to the Fort Saskatchewan area in 1891, then returned to Ukraine to collect their families. Pylypow's reports of vast untilled land awaiting settlers in Canada sparked a rush for emigration by the impoverished residents of his home area. Quoted by local media on the opportunities available to new immigrants, Pylypow was arrested by the Ukrainian authorities and jailed for six months for promoting immigration to Canada.

He returned to Alberta with his family in 1893 and homesteaded in the Edna-Star district in east-central Alberta. Within a decade of his arrival, more than 1,500 homesteads in Alberta had been settled by Ukrainian immigrants. By WWI, an estimated 170,000 Ukrainians had settled in Canada.

Pylypow died in an accident in 1936 and was buried in the cemetery of the Church of the Transfiguration near the town of Chipman. The church served the first Ukrainian parish in Canada, founded in 1897 by, among others, Pylypow. His original farmhouse is now part of the permanent exhibition of the Ukrainian Cultural Heritage Village, east of Edmonton.

Ivan Pylypow, 1894. (PAA A.11151)

royal visit; in 1939, in honour of the royal visit of Princess Elizabeth's parents, the then-Portage Avenue switched names with Kingsway.

Road   1951   NW   7:B1

Princess Patricia Park

10440–108 Avenue

Princess Patricia of Connaught (1886–1974) lent her name to the Princess Patricia's Canadian Light Infantry. From 1914 until her death she was the honorary colonel-in-chief of the regiment. She was the daughter of the Duke of Connaught (the third son of Queen Victoria and the governor general of Canada from 1911 to 1916). After her marriage in 1919, she renounced the titles of Her Royal Highness and Princess and was known as Lady Patricia Ramsay. The Princess Patricia Park is in the Central McDougall neighbourhood and has an area of 0.69 ha.

Park   1995   C   7:C1 *

Proctor Wynd

West of Picard Drive, north of Potter Greens Drive

Katherine Allison Procter was a lifetime member of the Canadian Red Cross and held senior positions in both the Red Cross and the Victorian Order of Nurses. Procter served as vice-president of the Edmonton branch and vice-president of the Alberta division, president and secretary of the Victorian Order of Nurses, commissioner of the Girl Guides for northern Alberta and honorary president of the Junior Hospital League. In 1946 she became the second woman to receive an honorary doctorate from the University of Alberta. The road named in her honour—Proctor Wynd—was misspelled.

Road   1990   SW   3:B1 *

Pylypow Industrial

Whitemud Drive north to CN railway tracks, 34 Street to 50 Street

See feature story, page 254.

Neighbourhood   1974   SE   5:A1

Pylypow Road

58 Avenue and 47 Street to 34 Street and 67 Avenue

See Pylypow Industrial *feature story, page 254.*

Road   1974   SE   5:B1 *

Flower border at Queen Elizabeth Park, 1952. (CEA EA–10–1145)

Quadrant Avenue

North of 2 Avenue South, between 199 Street and 207 Street

This road shown on some maps as 0 Avenue, is one of the axes of Edmonton's quadrant addressing system. The original name recommended for this road was Central Avenue. If numbered, it would have been 1 Avenue South.

Road   1981   SW   2:A1

Queen Alexandra

70 Avenue north to Whyte Avenue, Calgary Trail west to 109 Street

Queen Alexandra (1844–1925) was born in Denmark and married Albert, Prince of Wales, in 1863. In 1901 he became King Edward VII (1841–1910) and she became the queen. In 1899 the northern portion of this neighbourhood was part of the Town of Strathcona. It may have been named in 1901, at the time of King Edward's accession when Alexandra became queen. Or, it is possible that the naming coincided with the renaming of the 1908 Duggan Street School to Queen Alexandra School in 1910.

Neighbourhood   CU   SW   4:B1

Queen Elizabeth Park

10350 Queen Elizabeth Park Road

The City of Strathcona bought land on this site in 1907 and named it Riverside Park. When Strathcona and Edmonton amalgamated in 1912, the land was transferred to the City of Edmonton. On June 2, 1939, King George VI and Queen Elizabeth (1900–2002), made a royal visit to Edmonton. In honour of the visit, the park's name was changed from Riverside Park to Queen Elizabeth Park. Queen Elizabeth Park is located north of the Strathcona neighbourhood and has an area of 31.5 ha.

Park   1939   C   7:C2

Queen Elizabeth Park Road

Connecting Walterdale Hill Road to Saskatchewan Drive at 102 Street

This road was built in 1952 and runs through Queen Elizabeth Park. *See* Queen Elizabeth Park.

Road   1952   C   7:C2 *

Queen Mary Park

105 Avenue to 111 Avenue, 109 Street to 120 Street

Mary of Teck (1867–1953) married the Duke of York in 1893. She became the queen when her husband became King George V in 1910. In 1953, just after the queen's death, the Queen Mary Park School opened. The community around the school took its name.

Neighbourhood   CU   C   7:B2

Queen Mary Park

11025–110 Street

This park is in the Queen Mary Park neighbourhood and has an area of 1.09 ha. *See* Queen Mary Park *neighbourhood.*

Park   1956   C   7:B1

Quesnell Bridge

Spanning the North Saskatchewan River at the Whitemud Drive

This bridge, located near Quesnell Heights, opened in 1968. *See* Quesnell Heights.

Bridge   1966   SW   3:D1

Quesnell Crescent

East of 149 Street, south of Whitemud Drive

See Quesnell Heights.

Road   1959   SW   3:D1

Queen Mary Park, circa 1968. (CEA EA–20–3743)

Quesnell Heights

River valley north to Whitemud Drive, east of 149 Street

Officially adopted in 1958, this neighbourhood name had existed since at least 1912. While the origin of the name is not recorded, there are several possibilities. Quesnell Heights may have been named after Dr. Philip Quesnel, a well-known physician, who moved to Edmonton in 1912, and later served in WWI. Another possibility is that it was named for J. B. Quesnelle, a prominent citizen of the Edmonton district in the 1880s. In 1885, J. B. Quesnelle was the director of the Agricultural Society; that same year he ended his part-ownership of a hotel in St. Albert and opened a saloon and billiard hall at the south end of the St. Albert Bridge. In 1888 he sold his claim on the St. Albert Trail and left for Victoria.

Another explanation is that the neighbourhood may have been named after Jules Maurice Quesnel. Jules Maurice (d. 1842) was a French-Canadian clerk with the North West Company who worked at Fort Augustus in 1804. He accompanied Simon Fraser, a fur trader and explorer, on his 1808 journey of exploration along the Fraser River. Quesnel River, Quesnel Lake and Quesnel City (originally a gold rush town that was established c. 1860) in British Columbia were all named for Jules Maurice Quesnel.

Neighbourhood   CU   SW   4:A1

Official opening of the Quesnell Bridge, 1968. (CEA ET-11-181)

Quesnell Park

39 Quesnell Crescent

This park is in the Quesnell Heights neighbourhood and has an area of 0.64 ha. *See* Quesnell Heights.

Park   1983   SW   4:A1 *

Quesnell Ravine

Separating the Quesnell Heights and Laurier Heights neighbourhoods, from 149 Street to the North Saskatchewan River

This ravine separates Laurier Heights from Quesnell Heights; Whitemud Drive is routed though the ravine to the Quesnell Bridge. *See* Quesnell Heights.

Ravine   CU   SW   3:D1 *

Quesnell Road

East of 149 Street, south of Whitemud Drive

See Quesnell Heights.

Road   1959   SW   3:D1

James Ramsey Ltd., no date. (CEA EA–160–148)

Rabbit Hill Road

From Terwillegar Park, southeast to 142 Street at 23 Avenue

Early settlers, dating from the end of the 19th century, named the road that runs through this area Rabbit Hill. There are prominent hills in the area and wild rabbits were abundant. The Rabbit Hill School District was established in 1895. The name became official in 1979.

Road   CU   SW   3:D2

Ralph Hopp Park

6802–130 Avenue

Ralph Hopp (1948–1976) was an Edmonton firefighter who died in the line of duty. He was born in Germany and immigrated to Canada in 1953. Hopp joined the Edmonton Fire Department in 1973 and played clarinet in the Fire Department band. He was also a member of the fire-truck crew that was present at all Edmonton Eskimos football games. Hopp and fellow firefighter Murray Clark were killed while fighting a blaze at a downtown nightclub, the JJ and Friends Discotheque, on August 15, 1976. The Edmonton Firefighters Memorial, Emergency Response Department, Community Services Department and the Hopp family were all involved in the building of the park. The Ralph Hopp Park is in the Balwin neighbourhood, where the Hopp family lived, and has an area of 0.19 ha.

Park   1992   NE   10:D2 *

Rampart Industrial

137 Avenue north to Campbell Road, 142 Street west to St. Albert Trail

A rampart is an embankment of earth surrounded by a parapet. Ramparts were used to protect forts from attack. This neighbourhood's name relates to the theme in The Palisades area, just to the east, that honours forts of the Hudson's Bay Company and the North West Company.

Neighbourhood 1984 NW 9:D2

Ramsay Crescent

Southwest of 43 Avenue, joining Whitemud Road

See Ramsay Heights.

Road 1976 SW 3:D2

Ramsay Heights

40 Avenue to 51 Avenue, Terwillegar Drive and Whitemud Drive west to Whitemud Road and 154 Street

Walter Ramsay (1870–1958) was Edmonton's first florist. Born in Ontario, Ramsay came to Edmonton in 1899 and was a teacher and school principal before establishing a floral business in 1906. Ramsay's greenhouses were located next to his home, at 111 Street and 100 Avenue. A replica of one his greenhouses was constructed at Fort Edmonton Park and is part of the permanent exhibition. He was chairman of the Edmonton School Board from 1912 to 1914.

Neighbourhood 1971 SW 3:D2

Ramsay Ravine Park

13105–102 Avenue

This park is probably named after the ravine in which it is located. The two names—Ramsay Ravine Park and Ramsey Ravine—are different because the Names Advisory Committee recommended an incorrectly spelled name and provided incorrect history for the ravine. The Ramsay Ravine Park is located in the Glenora neighbourhood. *See* Ramsey Ravine.

Park CU SW 7:B2 *

Ramsay Flowers staff, no date. (CEA EA–269–04)

Ramsay Road

Southwest of 43 Avenue, northwest of Ramsay Crescent

See Ramsay Heights.

Road 1976 SW 3:D2

Ramsey Ravine

South of 102 Avenue at 135 Street; separating St. George's Crescent from Tweedsmuir Crescent

This ravine was named for James Ramsey and Walter Ramsay. In the Names Advisory Committee recommendation, they were incorrectly referred to as brothers, whereas in fact they were unrelated. *See* Ramsay Ravine Park.

Ravine 1956 SW 7:B2 *

Rapperswil

167 Avenue north to the proposed outer ring road, Canossa west to 127 Street

The name of this neighbourhood is taken from an imposing Swiss castle founded in 1229 by the ruling counts of Rapperswil. The name of Rapperswil is compatible with the theme for the Castle Downs area, which names neighbourhoods for European castles. During the mid-1910s, part of this area was known as Edmonton Junction.

Neighbourhood 1982 NW 10:B1

The Rat Hole

FOR MORE THAN 70 YEARS, one of Edmonton's main north-south routes took drivers through a dimly lit, narrow underpass known as "the Rat Hole." Completed by 1928, the tunnel routed traffic on 109 Street beneath the Canadian National Railway yards and 104 Avenue. The 168-metre-long underpass was only 3.3 metres high and six metres wide. Before the underpass was built, northward traffic on 109 Street was blocked by 25 CN rail lines, restricting the city's north-south traffic to 101 Street and 116 Street.

Plagued by flooding and poor-quality building supplies, construction of the project ran over budget. The dispute between the contractor and the City eventually reached the Alberta Supreme Court, where the contractor was awarded compensation. When the underpass first opened, it was known as The Subway. It was not long, however, before the arched passageway was widely referred to as the Rat Hole.

Throughout the 72-year life of the underpass, flooding was an almost annual occurrence. Drainage was a constant problem because the tunnel's road level was below that of adjoining sewers. As well, on numerous occasions the drivers of trucks that exceeded the Rat Hole's height restriction attempted and failed to enter the passageway. Out-of-town drivers, unfamiliar with metric measurements and Edmonton's few north-south routes, were particularly prone to making the mistake.

In 2000, the 109 Street "Rat Hole" underpass was demolished and replaced with a six-lane intersection at 104 Avenue.

The Rat Hole under construction, 1927. (CEA EA–75–2)

Ravine Drive

*North of MacKinnon Ravine Park, south of
101 Avenue, east of 142 Street*

The name of this road, in the Glenora neighbourhood, is descriptive and has been in use since at
least 1942.

Road CU SW 7:A2

Ravine Point

*North of MacKinnon Ravine Park, south of
Stony Plain Road at 147 Street*

The name is descriptive of the road's location.

Road 1997 SW 7:A2 *

Reeves Crest

*South of Rhatigan Road East, east of
Riverbend Road*

English-born Gladys Reeves (1891–1974) was an
early Edmonton photographer. She arrived in
Edmonton in 1904 and within a year had begun
working for the prominent photographer Ernest
Brown. Between 1920 and 1950, she ran her own
photographic studio. Reeves and Brown were
responsible for taking many of the photographs of
early Edmonton and its pioneers. She was the first
woman to be appointed as the president of the
Edmonton Horticultural Society.

Road 1988 SW 3:D2

Reeves Gate

*East of Riverbend Road, joining Reeves Crescent
and Reeves Way*

See Reeves Crest.

Road 1988 SW 3:D2 *

Reeves Way

North of Rabbit Hill Road, east of Riverbend Road

See Reeves Crest.

Road 1988 SW 3:D2

Rehwinkel Close

*West of Terwillegar Drive, south of
Rehwinkel Road*

Alfred M. Rehwinkel (1887–1979) was the founder
of Edmonton's Concordia College. He was born in
Wisconsin and ordained as a Lutheran minister in
1910. Rehwinkel served as a missionary in western
Canada until 1914, when he accepted a post at
Edmonton's St. Peter's Church. Between 1916 and
1919, he obtained his BA, BD and MA degrees from
the University of Alberta. In 1921 he joined the
faculty at Concordia College, and remained there
until 1928. Rehwinkel helped establish the
Edmonton Zoo, then located in Borden Park, and
authored several books, including *The Wonders of
Creation: An Exploration of the Origin and Splendors of
the Universe* (1974), *The Flood: In the Light of the Bible,
Geology, and Archaeology* (c. 1957) and *Communism
and the Church* (1948).

Road 1988 SW 3:D2 *

Rehwinkel Road

West of Terwillegar Drive, south of Rhatigan Road

See Rehwinkel Close.

Road 1988 SW 3:D2

Reid Close

North of Rabbit Hill Road, east of Reid Place

Scottish-born Richard Gavin Reid (1879–1980) was
the premier of Alberta from 1934 to 1935. He was
appointed premier following the resignation of
John E. Brownlee. Reid was then defeated at the
provincial general election of 1935 by William
Aberhart's Social Credit Party. Reid came to

Canada from Scotland in 1903 and began home-steading in Alberta a year later. He was elected to the Alberta Legislature in 1921 and, over the next 13 years, held several portfolios for the United Farmers of Alberta party. During WWII, Reid worked for the mobilization board. At the age of 70, he became the librarian for Canadian Utilities. Reid served on the Edmonton Historical Board and was an honorary life member of the Edmonton Library Association. He did not retire until reaching the age of 95 and died at the age of 101.

Road   1986   SW   3:D2

Reid Place

North of Rabbit Hill Road, east of Riverbend Road

See Reid Close.

Road   1986   SW   3:D2

Reilly Park

14769–43 Avenue

This park is named in honour of the pilots John H. "Jack" Reilly (b. 1921) and Moretta F. B. "Molly" Reilly (1922–1980). Edmonton-born Jack Reilly earned his pilot's licence in 1938 and joined the Royal Canadian Air Force (RCAF) in 1940. By 1946 he had obtained the most advanced military instruction and earned the most senior pilot's licence. Jack was chief pilot at a commercial flying school and worked as chief pilot for several firms, flying all over the world.

Ontario-born Molly Reilly joined the RCAF as a photographer in 1942. She began flight training in 1944, earned her pilot's licence in 1945, her commercial licence and her instructor's rating in 1948. She also earned a class-1 instrument rating and an airline transport licence. The Reillys married in 1959 and moved to Edmonton in 1962. They were named to Canada's Aviation Hall of Fame in 1973. Reilly Park is in the Ramsay Heights neighbourhood and has an area of 0.59 ha.

Park   1984   SW   4:A2

Revell Crescent

North of Rabbit Hill Road, east of Reeves Way

Daniel G. Revell (1869–1954) was a professor at the University of Alberta and the provincial pathologist and bacteriologist. Born in Ontario, Revell came to Alberta in 1907. He aided police in solving crimes and lectured in anatomy at the University of Alberta until his retirement in 1938.

Road   1988   SW   3:D2

Revell Wynd

North of Rabbit Hill Road, west of Reeves Way

See Revell Crescent.

Road   1988   SW   3:D2 *

Rhatigan Ridge

Rabbit Hill Road north to Rice Road and 40 Avenue, Terwillegar Drive west to river valley

Edmonton native Tom Rhatigan (b. circa 1907) was an award-winning agriculturalist who began farming in the Rabbit Hill area in 1938. Rhatigan was named the World Oat King at the Royal Winter Fair in Toronto in 1953, 1966 and 1970. He won numerous ribbons at seed fairs and was instrumental in the testing of numerous varieties of grains. Rhatigan retired from farming in 1972.

Neighbourhood   1979   SW   3:D2

Rhatigan Road East

East of Riverbend Road, south of 40 Avenue

See Rhatigan Ridge.

Road   1979   SW   3:D2

Rhatigan Road West

West of Riverbend Road, south of Rice Road

See Rhatigan Ridge.

Road   1979   SW   3:D2

CFRN Radio Staff, G.R.A. Rice (left) and Frank Makepiece (right), 1933. (CEA EA-160-1482)

Rice Howard Way

101A Avenue from 100A Street to 101 Street

Located in the downtown neighbourhood, this pedestrian thoroughfare combines the two names of Rice Street and Howard Avenue, which have been in use since at least 1892. At that time, 100A Street was known as Howard Avenue and 100A Avenue was known as Rice Street. The origin of these names is not recorded. Howard Avenue, located on property that was once owned by the Methodist Mission, may have been named after Rev. J.H. Howard, a Methodist minister who arrived in Edmonton in 1884. In 1887, Howard received an appointment to minister in Prince Albert and left Edmonton.

The development of Rice Howard Way as a downtown pedestrian mall began in the mid-1960s, as part of the City of Edmonton's plan to improve and revitalize the downtown area. By about 1974, it was called Rice Howard Mall and in 1984 was renamed Rice Howard Way. Rice Howard Way includes a sculpture, a decorative brick roadway, trees and cafe-style restaurants.

Road 1984 C 7:C2 *

Rice Road

North of Rhatigan Road West, east of Riddell Street

G.R.A. "Dick" Rice (1900–1992) was a pioneer broadcaster who emigrated from England in 1919 and went on to found CFRN-TV. Rice broadcast CJCA's first program in 1922, co-founded the CFRN AM radio station in 1934 and introduced an FM station in 1947. His founding of CFRN-TV in 1954 was perhaps his most outstanding accomplishment. The station has been a major broadcasting presence in Alberta for half a century. Rice served on the

University of Alberta Senate and in 1966 received an honorary degree. In 1977 he was named Citizen of the Year by the Junior Chamber of Commerce. Rice was named to the Order of Canada in 1984 and received the Alberta Order of Excellence in 1985.

Road 1979 SW 3:D2

Richards Crescent

West of Riverbend Road, joining Rhatigan Road West

W. Clarence Richards (1897–1963) was a teacher at the Victoria Composite High School for 35 years. He was born in Ontario and moved to Alberta before WWI. After serving in the war, Richards founded the Edmonton Kinsmen Club in 1920. He graduated from the University of Alberta and joined the teaching staff at Victoria Composite High School in 1926. Richards established night school classes and correspondence courses and published teacher support materials. In 1951, he was named Citizen of the Year by the Junior Chamber of Commerce. Richards retired in 1961.

Road 1979 SW 3:D2

Richfield

34 Avenue north to Mill Woods Road, west to 91 Street east to Mill Woods Road

At the turn of the twentieth century, the land that this neighbourhood is located on was a flourishing farming community. The name probably indicates the productivity of the area when it was agricultural land.

Neighbourhood 1971 SE 4:C2

Richfield Park

7910–36 Avenue

This park is in the Richfield neighbourhood and has an area of 5.91 ha. *See* Richfield.

Park 1971 SE 4:D2

Richfield Road

West of 85 Street, south of 36 Avenue

See Richfield.

Road 1971 SE 4:C2

Richford

5 Avenue SW south to Ellerslie Road, 107 Street to 111 Street

The neighbourhood takes its name from the local designation for 5 Avenue SW—Richford Road (the road's name was officially changed to a number in 1982). Richford Estates, a rural residential property, was established in this area in the early 1980s. Historically, the name Richford was used to attract homesteaders, the suggestion being that an area was rich in fertile land.

Neighbourhood 1999 SW 1:A1

Riddell Street

West of Rice Road, north of Rhatigan Road West

Scottish-born Alex Riddell (1892–1971) served with the Edmonton Police Department for 44 years. He immigrated to Edmonton in 1914 and joined the police force, interrupting his service to fight in WWI. Over the course of his career, Riddell was a constable, detective, sergeant major, staff inspector, deputy chief and superintendent. He retired in 1958. This road was originally named Riddell Crescent.

Road 1979 SW 3:D2

Rideau Park

40 Avenue north to Whitemud Drive, Calgary Trail west to 111 Street

This neighbourhood may have been named in the early 1900s, and was most likely named after Rideau Hall, the Ottawa residence of Canada's governor general. Built in 1838, Rideau Hall overlooks the Ottawa and Rideau Rivers. The area in which the Rideau Park neighbourhood lies, from

Terwillegar Heights to Strathcona Industrial Park, was annexed by the City in 1959.

Neighbourhood 1967 SW 4:B2

Rideau Park

10605–42 Avenue

This park is in the Rideau Park neighbourhood and has an area of 3.04 ha. *See* Rideau Park *neighbourhood.*

Park 1984 SW 4:B2

Ridgewood

23 Avenue north to Mill Creek Ravine, 34 Street to 50 Street

This subdivision name conforms to the theme adopted for the Mill Woods area, incorporating the word "wood." The original boundaries of the Ridgewood subdivision were amended in 1978.

Subdivision 1975 SE 5:B2 *

Rio Park

7103–156 Street

This park is located south of the Rio Terrace neighbourhood. *Rio* is the Spanish word for river, thus, this is likely a descriptive name. Rio Park has an area of 0.94 ha.

Park 1965 SW 3:D1 *

Rio Park Road

East of 156 Street, south of Rio Terrace Road

This road leads to Rio Park. *See* Rio Park.

Road 1965 SW 3:D1 *

Rio Terrace

River valley north to Whitemud Drive, 149 Street to 156 Street

This neighbourhood was formerly part of the Town of Jasper Place, which was annexed to the City of Edmonton in 1964. It may have been named in 1958. Since *rio* is the Spanish word for river and a terrace is a raised level place, this name likely describes the neighbourhood's location.

Neighbourhood 1958 SW 3:D1

Rio Terrace Drive

73 Avenue between 149 Street and 156 Street

See Rio Terrace.

Road 1964 SW 3:D1

Rio Terrace Park

15504–76 Avenue

This park is in the Rio Terrace neighbourhood and has an area of 2.1 ha. *See* Rio Terrace.

Park 1983 SW 3:D1

Ritchie

72 Avenue north to Whyte Avenue, Mill Creek Ravine Park west to 100 Street and 102 Street

Robert Ritchie (1848–1932) arrived in Edmonton from Ontario in the early 1890s, just as development in South Edmonton was being spurred by the arrival of the Calgary and Edmonton Railway. In 1893 Ritchie and his brothers established the Edmonton Milling Company and built the Ritchie Mill. Ritchie went on to become mayor of the Town of Strathcona in 1901, and again in 1906; he was also an alderman and school trustee. He retired in 1920. Ritchie School, built in 1913, was named in his honour. The area, present-day Ritchie neighbourhood, was known as Richmond Park until the late 1950s. In 1959, the name Ritchie first appeared on a city map.

Neighbourhood CU SE 4:C1

Aerial view of Rossdale—River Valley Road can be seen on the right-hand side of the river between the Walterdale and High Level bridges and beyond, October 1932. (CEA EA–160–1318)

Ritchie Park

7727–98 Street

This park is in the Ritchie neighbourhood and has an area of 1.46 ha. *See* Ritchie.

Park 1980 SE 4:C1

River Heights Drive

East of 184 Street, north of 23 Avenue

This road overlooks the river valley and is in an area that was annexed by the City in 1972.

Road CU SW 3:C2 *

River Valley Road

Connecting 105 Street Bridge and Groat Bridge

This road follows the north bank of the North Saskatchewan River and was known as River Road before it was formally named.

Road 1958 C 7:B2

River View Way

South of Quadrant Avenue, west of 199 Street

This road was formerly known as River View Crescent. The name is descriptive.

Road 1982 SW 2:A1 *

Riverbend

45 Avenue north to the North Saskatchewan River, Whitemud Creek west to the North Saskatchewan River

The Riverbend subdivision takes its name from its location, bounded on the north and west by the North Saskatchewan River, which makes a sharp bend around the subdivision.

Subdivision 1961 SW 4:A1 *

Riverbend Road

West of Whitemud Drive at 149 Street, south of 62 Avenue

See Riverbend.

Road 1972 SW 4:A2

Riverdale

100 Avenue north to Rowland Road, 87 Street to 95 Street

In 1881, Richard Hardisty (1831–1889) and Daniel Robert Fraser (1851–1920) established a saw and a grist mill in this area, on the flats beside the river. In 1889 the name of the company was changed to D.R. Fraser & Company, and this district became known as Fraser Flats or Fraser's Flat. In 1910 residents of the area voted to change their community's name to Riverdale.

Neighbourhood CU NE 7:C2

Looking north across the North Saskatchewan River to Riverdale, 1938. (CEA EA–160–1110)

Riverdale Park

9231–100 Avenue

This park is in the unsubdivided portion of River Lot 18, in the Riverdale neighbourhood, and has an area of 2.62 ha. *See* Riverdale.

Park 1983 SE 7:C2

Riverside Crescent

95 Avenue and 141 Street

This road is in the Crestwood neighbourhood and runs along the river valley. It has existed since at least 1956.

Road CU SW 7:A2 *

Riverside Drive

95 Avenue to 98 Avenue and 140 Street

This road is in the Crestwood neighbourhood and runs along the bank of the North Saskatchewan River. Early maps, from 1909 and 1912, list this road as already being named Riverside Drive.

Road CU SW 7:A2

Robert Brett Park

13423–57 Street

Dr. Robert G. Brett (1851–1929) was the second lieutenant-governor of Alberta. He was born in Canada West and practised medicine there before moving first to Manitoba and then Banff, Alberta, where he established the Banff Sanatorium in 1886. He sat in the Legislative Assembly of the North-West Territories from 1888 to 1901, was a senator at the University of Alberta in 1908 and 1912, and was appointed lieutenant-governor of Alberta in 1915. Brett served two terms before retiring in 1925. The Robert Brett Park is in the Belvedere neighbourhood and has an area of 1.13 ha.

Park 1982 NE 10:D2

Robert Carter Park

1100 Carter Crest Road

This park is in the Carter Crest neighbourhood and has an area of 1.86 ha. *See* Carter Crest.

Park 1991 SW 4:A2 *

Robertson Close

South of Ellerslie Road, east of Robertson Way

Kenneth Robertson (1915–1992) was an active member of Edmonton's volunteer community for more than 45 years. From 1963 until 1992, he was vice-president of the Edmonton Opera company. In addition, he served on the board of EFFORT, an organization dedicated to supporting the arts in Edmonton, and on the Winspear Foundation, which contributed to such causes as a hot lunch program for underprivileged children and to providing inner city housing. For 30 years, Robertson was an employee of Edmonton Motors, retiring as general manager.

Road   2001   SW   2:D2 *

Robertson Place

West of Robertson Way

See Robertson Close.

Road   2001   SW   2:D2 *

Robertson Way

South of Rutherford Road, west of Robertson Close

See Robertson Close.

Road   2001   SW   2:D2 *

Roche Crescent

East of Rhatigan Road West, south of Richards Crescent

Henry J. Roche (1876–1968) was a pioneer printer and sportsman. He was born in Ontario and came to Edmonton in 1909. Roche was the owner of Commercial Printers, an early printing company, and publisher of the newspapers *Eastender* and *Edmonton Free Press*. In 1919 he was the manager of a baseball team and in 1933 secured tenancy for his team at Renfrew Park (present-day Telus Field), which had previously been used only for soccer and football. In 1934 he purchased the Edmonton Eskimos hockey team, an amateur and later professional team that existed from 1911 to 1939. This road was originally named Roche Drive.

Road   1979   SW   3:D2 *

Roe Crescent

North of Rhatigan Road West, west of Riverbend Road

Frank G. Roe (1878–1973) was a well-known author and historian. Born in England, he came to Alberta in 1894 and in 1909 began working for the Grand Trunk Pacific Railway. Roe was the author of *The Indian and the Horse* and *The North American Buffalo*. In 1951 he received an honorary degree from the University of Alberta. This road was originally named Roe Drive.

Road   1979   SW   3:D2 *

Rollie Miles Athletic Field

10503–74 Avenue

Roland "Rollie" E. Miles (1928–1995) was an outstanding football player and educator. Born in Washington, DC, Miles joined the Edmonton Eskimos football club in 1951. Over the course of his 11-year career with the Eskimos he won three MVP awards and was an eight-time Western All-Star. Miles graduated from the University of Alberta in 1956 and, after leaving the Eskimos, was a teacher and physical education supervisor until his retirement in 1986. He was inducted into the Alberta Sports Hall of Fame and the Canadian Football Hall of Fame in 1980. The Rollie Miles Athletic Field is in the Queen Alexandra neighbourhood and has an area of 5 ha.

Park   1995   SW   4:C1

Ronning Close

CHESTER ALVIN RONNING (1894–1985) was a veteran of both world wars, an educator, politician and diplomat. He was born in Fancheng, China, to Lutheran missionary parents, Halvor and Hannah. In 1899 the family left China on leave, missing the 1900 Boxer Rebellion, an uprising that targeted Christian missionaries. The Ronnings went to Norway and then to the United States. Deciding to return to China following the suppression of the unrest, the family travelled by train across Canada to the west coast. A chance meeting with other Norwegians in Calgary led Halvor Ronning to purchase land in Alberta. They continued to China but had created a tie to Canada.

Following the death of Hannah Ronning in China, the Ronning family came back to Canada in 1907, first to their farm at Bardo, near Tofield, and finally around 1913 to Valhalla in the Peace River Country. Chester Ronning became a teacher and taught in Edmonton schools. Later, he studied at the University of Minnesota. After serving in WWI, Chester Ronning went back to China to teach but returned to Alberta in 1927, when he became principal of Camrose Lutheran College, a position he held for 15 years. Ronning also served as a United Farmers of Alberta member of the Alberta legislature from 1932 to 1935. He was the leader of the Alberta Co-operative Commonwealth Federation from 1938 to 1943. In 1942, he joined the war effort in Ottawa, where he carried out intelligence work in the Royal Canadian Air Force.

He received his MA from the University of Alberta in 1942 and began his diplomatic career at the Canadian Embassy in Nanking, China, where he remained from 1945 to 1951, serving as first secretary and acting ambassador. From 1954 to 1956 he was ambassador to Norway and Iceland and from 1957 to 1964 served as high commissioner to India. Ronning was also the head of the Canadian delegation to the 1954 Geneva Conferences on Korea.

Although he retired in 1964, Ronning continued to carry out diplomatic missions, and was named special Canadian representative on peace missions to Hanoi to negotiate an end to the Vietnam War. He also wrote the book *A Memoir of China in Revolution: From the Boxer Rebellion to the People's Republic*. Ronning was named to the Order of Canada in 1972, and in 1974 became a member of the University of Alberta Senate. His life was the subject of a CBC film, *China Mission: The Chester Ronning Story*.

Chester Ronning, 1979.
(PAA J.4517)

Romaniuk Place

North of Romaniuk Road, west of Riddell Street

Edmonton-born Alex Romaniuk (1927–1988) was an internationally ranked wrestling judge, teacher and volunteer. He started competitive wrestling in 1939 and later coached at the University of Alberta. Romaniuk graduated from the university in 1951 and obtained his master's degree in 1964. He officiated at numerous wrestling championships around the world, and coached the Canadian team at the 1966 Commonwealth Games. For 25 years, Romaniuk was the principal of Lynnwood School, and continued to be an active volunteer. In recognition of his contributions to the community, Romaniuk received the Centennial Medal from the federal government in 1967.

Road   1979   SW   3:D2 *

Romaniuk Road

West of Riddell Street, south of Romaniuk Place

See Romaniuk Place.

Road   1983   SW   3:D2

Ronning Close

North of Rabbit Hill Road, west of Riverbend Road

See feature story, page 273.

Road   1986   SW   3:D2 *

Ronning Gate

Connecting Ronning Street to Rhatigan Road West

See Ronning Close *feature story, page 273.*

Road   1986   SW   3:D2 *

Ronning Street

South of Rooney Crescent, north of Roy Street

See Ronning Close *feature story, page 273.*

Road   1986   SW   3:D2

VW Body and Paint Shop in Rossdale, circa 1978.
(*Photo courtesy of Alan Brownoff*)

Ronning Street Neighbourhood Park

504 Ronning Street

This park is in the Rhatigan Ridge neighbourhood and has an area of 0.74 ha. *See* Ronning Close *feature story, page 273.*

Park   1996   SW   3:D2 *

Rooney Crescent

North of Rabbit Hill Road, west of Ronning Street

Dr. R.A. Rooney (1890–1961) was a WWII veteran and professor of dentistry at the University of Alberta. He was born in Ontario and came to Alberta in 1906. After completing his education in the United States, Rooney returned to Alberta, moving to Edmonton and entering private practice in 1911. During WWII, he helped form the Canadian Dental Corps. Rooney joined the University of Alberta in 1942, and taught there for 15 years. This road was originally named Rooney Street.

Road   1979   SW   3:D2

Roper Industrial

Whitemud Drive north to CN railway tracks, 50 Street to 75 Street

Elmer E. Roper (1893–1994) served two terms as mayor of Edmonton. Born in Nova Scotia, Roper came to Alberta in 1906 and in 1917 moved to Edmonton where he worked as a printer. He was elected to the Edmonton Public School Board and was a member of the Board of Governors of the University of Alberta. Roper was the provincial leader of the Co-operative Commonwealth Federation (CCF) party and was Alberta's first CCF Member of the Legislative Assembly from 1942 to 1955. In 1959 he received an honorary degree from the University of Alberta. Roper was elected mayor in 1959 and again in 1961.

Neighbourhood 1974 SE 4:D1

Roper Road

86 Street and 51 Avenue, east to 50 Street

See Roper Industrial.

Road 1973 SE 4:D1

Rosedale Industrial

CN railway tracks north to 63 Avenue, 91 Street to 100 Street

The Rosedale neighbourhood has existed since the early 1900s and was replotted in the early 1950s. As of March 1954, all the lots in the area were zoned for light industrial. The name may be descriptive.

Neighbourhood CU SE 4:C1

Rossdale

North Saskatchewan River north to 97 Avenue, Bellamy Hill, 99 Avenue and MacDonald Drive, west to 106 Street

Scottish-born Donald Ross (1840–1915) was one of the first to settle in this area and a founding member of Edmonton's public school board. After travelling through the United States and British Columbia, Ross came to Edmonton in 1872 and, the following year, bought land from a Hudson's Bay Company employee. In 1876 he established Edmonton's first hotel, the Edmonton Hotel. In 1881, Ross began to mine coal on this lot. Ross

Donald Ross, circa 1880. (CEA EA-10-689.30)

Flats, as the area was known, became the site of several industries, including a brewery, ice house and lumber yard. Rossdale is one of Edmonton's oldest neighbourhoods.

Neighbourhood CU C 7:C2

Rossdale Road

103 Street and 97 Avenue to the Low Level Bridge

This road runs through Rossdale neighbourhood. The name has existed since at least 1949. *See* Rossdale.

Road CU C 7:C2

Rosslyn

132 Avenue to 137 Avenue, 97 Street to 113A Street

The neighbourhood of Rosslyn dates to the early 1900s but was undeveloped until the late 1950s. It is possible that Rosslyn was named after Rosslyn Chapel, which is located in Roslin, Midlothian, Scotland. St. Clair founded the chapel in 1446. The

Mayor Hawrelak tries out the swings at the Rosslyn Park official opening, 1969. (CEA EA 20 888)

name is likely derived from the combination of "ross," a rock promontory, and "lyn," a waterfall.

Neighbourhood   1957   NW   10:B2

Rosslyn Park

11015–134 Avenue

This park is in the Rosslyn neighbourhood and has an area of 2.91 ha. *See* Rosslyn.

Park   1967   NW   10:B2

Routledge Road

Encircled by Rooney Crescent, west of Ronning Street

Alberta-born Robert Henry Routledge (1915–1970) was a WWII veteran and physical education teacher. From 1939 to 1941 he was a supervisor for the provincial health and recreation program. After serving in WWII, Routledge graduated from the University of Alberta with an education degree. In 1948 he began teaching at Victoria Composite High School and in 1954 was appointed coordinator of extracurricular sports for public schools in the Edmonton district. Routledge obtained his Master's Degree in Education in 1961 and in 1968 joined the University of Alberta.

Road   1979   SW   3:D2 *

Rowland Road

95 Street and 101A Avenue, crossing the Dawson Bridge

In July 1870, William Rowland (d. 1895) staked his claim on what became River Lot 18. James Rowland (d. 1897), William's brother, settled on the next lot to the west, River Lot 16 (the present-day site of the Alex Taylor school). Rowland Road traverses these two lots. James and William were the sons of a Hudson's Bay Company (HBC) employee and both worked for a time for the HBC. William was a founding member of Edmonton's public school board.

Road   CU   C   7:C2

Roy Gate

Joining Roy Street and Rabbit Hill Road, west of Ronning Street

Quebec-born Georges Roy (1846–1932) born in Canada East, was Edmonton's first federal civil servant. In 1867 Roy left Quebec for Ontario where he taught school and edited a newspaper. In 1870 he moved to Fort Garry, Manitoba, and worked for its provincial government. Roy was appointed registrar of the Edmonton-based North Alberta Land District in 1885. He came to Edmonton and worked in the land titles office for 26 years. After 40 years of service in government administration, Roy retired in 1911. The original name of this road was Roy Crescent.

Road   1986   SW   3:D2 *

Roy Street

South of Rooney Crescent, west of Ronning Street

See Roy Gate.

Road   1986   SW   3:D2

Rowland Road and Riverdale, circa 1965. (CEA EA-275-148)

Royal Gardens

40 Avenue north to Whitemud Drive, 111 Street to 119 Street

This neighbourhood in the Petrolia subdivision may have been named in honour of Joseph Royal (1837–1902), lieutenant-governor of the North-West Territories from 1888–1893. The name of Royal Gardens has existed in this area since 1912. It became official in 1962. A subdivision located directly to the south of Royal Gardens—Home Gardens—also carried the "garden" suffix, while other nearby subdivisions had names that follow a royal theme, including Victoria Park and Empire Park, the latter of which still exists as a neighbourhood.

Neighbourhood   1962   SW   4:B2

Royal Gardens Park

4030–117 Street

This park is in the Royal Gardens neighbourhood and has an area of 2.75 ha. *See* Royal Gardens.

Park   1982   SW   4:B2

Royal Road

Connecting 41 Avenue and 43 Avenue

See Royal Gardens.

Road   1967   SE   4:B2 *

Rue Hull

99 Street between Jasper Avenue and 103A Avenue

The City of Edmonton was twinned with the City of Hull, Quebec, in 1965. On May 27, 1986 City Council requested that the Names Advisory Committee recommend a road be named Hull Street in recognition of Edmonton's Canadian twin city.

Road   1986   C   7:C2 *

Rue Marie-Anne Gaboury

91 Street between Whyte Avenue and 88 Avenue

See feature story, page 278.

Road   1988   SE   4:C1 *

Rue Marie-Anne Gaboury

MARIE-ANNE GABOURY (1780–1875) was the first non-Aboriginal woman to live in western Canada and was the grandmother of Louis Riel. She was born in Maskinongé, Canada (Quebec), and married the voyageur and fur trader Jean-Baptiste Lagimodière (1778–1855) in 1806. Shortly after their marriage they travelled together to the west, first settling with a Métis community at Pembina (in present-day North Dakota) where their first child was born.

Marie-Anne and her husband arrived in Fort Edmonton in 1807 and remained there until 1811; she was the first non-indigenous woman to live in Fort Edmonton. The family later returned to Manitoba, where they settled at the confluence of the Red and Seine Rivers (present-day Winnipeg).

Marie-Anne and Jean-Baptiste had eight children, the sixth of whom, Julie (b. 1822), was the mother of Louis Riel (1844–1885). Riel was the leader of the Red River Rebellion in 1869–1870 and the North-West Rebellion of 1885. He was executed on November 16, 1885 after being found guilty of high treason. Today, Riel is celebrated as the father of Manitoba and the spiritual leader of his people, the Métis.

Using Fort Edmonton Park as a backdrop, the Edmonton-based filmmaker Fil Fraser chronicled Gaboury's remarkable life in the 1978 film *Marie Anne*.

Marriage of Marie-Anne Gaboury and Jean-Baptiste Lagimodière in 1806, no date. (GAI NA-3694-1)

Rundle Heights

102 Avenue to 118 Avenue, Rundle Park west to 34 Street and 36 Street

Rev. Robert Rundle (1811–1896) was the first Protestant missionary to serve at Fort Edmonton. He was, in fact, the first permanent missionary of any church to settle west of Manitoba. Rundle was born in England and was sent by the Methodist Missionary Society of England. In 1840 he came to Rupert's Land—the vast territory held by the Hudson's Bay Company (HBC)—at the request of the HBC. Later that year he came to Fort Edmonton. Rundle returned to England in 1848.

Neighbourhood 1963 NE 6:B1

Rundle Heights Playground

10915–34 Street

This park is in the Rundle Heights neighbourhood and has an area of 1.88 ha. *See* Rundle Heights.

Park 1972 NE 6:B1 *

Rundle Park

2529–118 Avenue

Rundle Golf Course is located within this park. Rundle Park is located east of Rundle Heights neighbourhood and has an area of 117.68 ha. *See* Rundle Heights.

Park 1970 NE 6:B1

Running Creek Lane

South of 9 Avenue, east of 111 Street

This road was named for the former neighbourhood of Running Creek, now part of the Twin Brooks neighbourhood. Running Creek is a descriptive name, relating to its location near Blackmud Creek.

Road 1990 SW 2:D1 *

Running Creek Point

Southeast of 110A Street, north of Running Creek Lane

See Running Creek Lane.

Road 1990 SW 2:D1 *

Running Creek Road

North of 12 Avenue, east of 111 Street

See Running Creek Lane.

Road 1990 SW 2:D1 *

Rutherford

South of Ellerslie Road, 111 Street to 127 Street

Alexander Cameron Rutherford (1857–1941) became the first premier of Alberta in 1905 upon the election of a majority Liberal government. He won a second election in 1909 but within a year had to resign because of a railway scandal. Rutherford was born in Canada West and educated in law at McGill University in Montréal. In 1895, he came to South Edmonton (now Strathcona) with his wife Mattie and their two children, Cecil and Hazel. After leaving politics, Rutherford resumed his law career. As premier, he was instrumental in ensuring that the University of Alberta was built in the City of Strathcona. Rutherford became a member of the university's senate in 1907 and was chancellor from 1927 until his death in 1941. Rutherford's two homes still exist: one was moved to Fort Edmonton Park, while the other is a provincial historic site and is located at the north end of the University of Alberta campus.

Neighbourhood 2001 SW 2:D2

Rutherford Close

South of Ellerslie Road, west of Rutherford Place

See Rutherford.

Road 2001 SW 2:D2 *

Alexander Rutherford, right, at reception for Lord Strathcona, left, 1909. (CEA EA-10-2505)

Rutherford Court

South of Rutherford Road

See Rutherford.

Road   2001   SW   2:D2 *

Rutherford Park

8406–91 Street

In 1907, then-Premier A.C. Rutherford donated a piece of his farmland to the City of Strathcona for a park. In light of Rutherford's generosity, Strathcona's mayor suggested that the park be named after the premier. The name remained in common usage and was approved by the Names Advisory Committee in 1967. Rutherford Park is in the Bonnie Doon neighbourhood and has an area of 3.84 ha. *See* Rutherford.

Park   CU   SE   7:C2 *

Rutherford Place

South of Ellerslie Road, west of 119 Street

See Rutherford.

Road   2001   SW   2:D2 *

Rutherford Point

North of Rutherford Road, west of Rutherford Close

See Rutherford.

Road   2001   SW   2:D2 *

Rutherford Road

South of Ellerslie Road, west of 119 Street

See Rutherford.

Road   2001   SW   2:D2

Ryan Place

North of Rabbit Hill Road, west of Terwillegar Drive

Edmonton-born Doreen McLeod Ryan (b. 1931) was an Olympic speed-skater and in 1965 was the first woman to be named to the Edmonton Sports Hall of Fame. Ryan won her first speed-skating title in 1947 and went on to compete at the 1960 and 1964 Winter Olympic Games. She set both Canadian and international speed-skating records. Ryan was national team manager for the Canadian national track-and-field team at the 1974 Commonwealth Games, the 1976 and 1980 Olympics and the 1979 Pan American Games. In 1978 Ryan was appointed to the board of directors for the Commonwealth Games in Edmonton and in 1983 was named vice-president of Canada's Commonwealth Games Association. She is the recipient of a Canadian Association for the Advancement of Women and Sport and Physical Activity award.

Road   1989   SW   3:D2

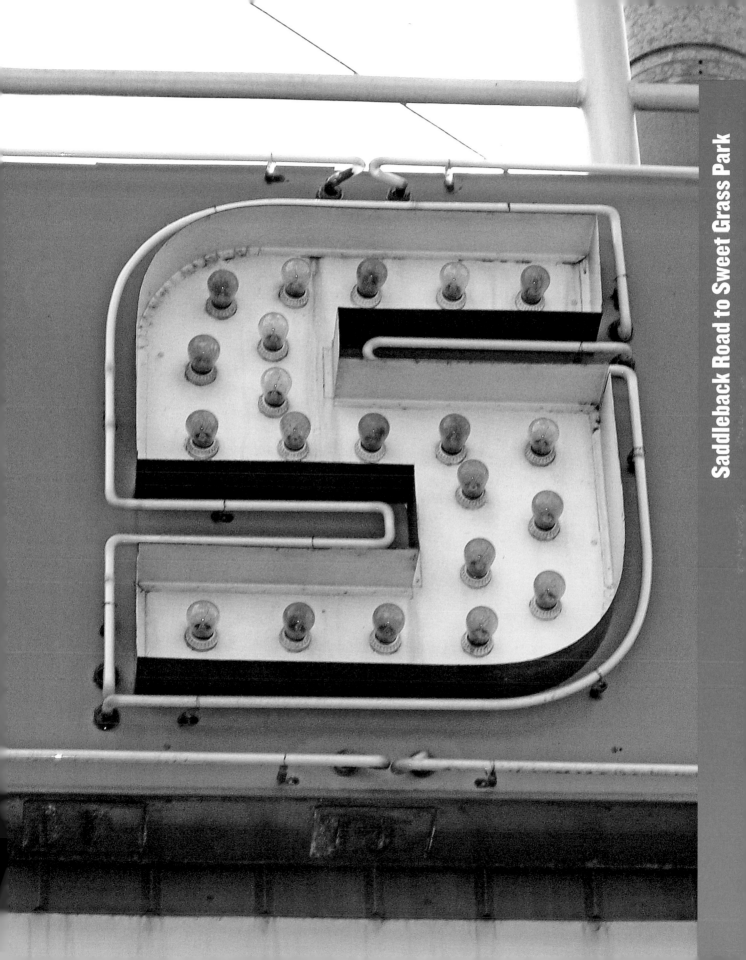

Saddleback Road

29 Avenue west of 111 Street

Joe Saddleback, an educator and a teacher of Cree traditions, was a chief of the Samson Band of Hobbema (80 km south of Edmonton). He was considered a living legend of the Western Cree.

Road   1974   SW   4:B2

St. Albert Trail

111 Avenue at 128 Street to 117 Avenue at 131 Street, 118 Avenue at 133 Street to the City of St. Albert

See feature story, page 283.

Road   CU   NW   7:B1

St. Anne Park

10208–153 Street

St. Anne's Roman Catholic Church, the first Catholic church in the Town of Jasper Place, was built on this site in 1952. It originally served a French-speaking congregation but later developed into a bilingual parish. In 1966 the church was destroyed by fire. The Canora Neighbourhood Improvement Association requested that the name of the church be perpetuated in the naming of the park. St. Anne Park is in the Canora neighbourhood and has an area of 0.24 ha.

Park   1976   NW   7:A2

St. Faith Park

11725–93 Street

St. Faith Park is named for the adjacent St. Faith Anglican Church. This is the second church on this site. The original St. Faith's Church was dedicated by the Bishop of Calgary in 1912. It was built as a direct result of an appeal by the Archbishops of Canterbury and York for English clergy to start mission churches in western Canada. The Rev.

W.G. Boyd was among the 17 clergymen who answered the call. He was head of the Edmonton mission in Norwood (now the Alberta Avenue neighbourhood), and named the church there after his home parish of St. Faith's in Stepney, London. In 1956, the original church was demolished and the present building erected. The St. Faith Park has an area of 0.21 ha.

Park   CU   NE   7:C1

St. Gabriel School Road

63 Street at 108 Avenue, south to 106 Avenue

St. Gabriel was chosen as the name for a separate school in the Hardisty subdivision in 1956. St. Gabriel's School, located on this road, was officially opened in 1958. In the Christian faith, St. Gabriel, the archangel, brought Mary the news that she was to be the mother of Jesus.

Road   1956   NE   7:D1

St. George's Crescent

South of 102 Avenue, east of 136 Street

The name St. George's Crescent first appears on a city map in 1912. Two years later, the first houses were built along this road. Nearby roadways, including Victoria Crescent (now part of St. George's Crescent) and Wellington Crescent, also reflected a British heritage. St. George's Crescent is named after St. George, the patron saint of England and symbol of the British Empire.

Road   CU   SW   7:B2

St. Olga Park

14704–87 Street

St. Olga (879–969) was a Ukrainian saint who was baptized in 957 AD and attempted to introduce Christianity to Ukraine. Her grandson, Prince Vladimir (d. 1015), began his reign in 980 AD and recognized Christianity as a state religion in 988.

St. Albert Trail

THE ST. ALBERT TRAIL is the main route between the City of Edmonton and the City of St. Albert, which abuts Edmonton's northwest boundary. It forms part of the Highway 2 route between the US border at Carway in the south, and through Grande Prairie in northern Alberta west into British Columbia. The continuation of the St. Albert Trail in St. Albert is called St. Albert Road.

The earliest trail past the site of what later became St. Albert was one created in 1824 under order of George Simpson, governor of the Hudson's Bay Company (HBC), that connected Fort Edmonton to Fort Assiniboine 120 km to the northwest. It was one of a network of trails branching out from Fort Edmonton.

Commencing at the fort, just below where the Alberta legislature is today located, the trail to St. Albert followed the edge of the river valley through the area that later became the HBC Reserve at 121 Street. It continued northwesterly past the east side of Mistatim Lakes, located between the current 156 Street and 170 Street. Once past these lakes, two thirds of the 14-kilometre distance from the fort to the St. Albert Settlement had been covered.

The importance of the trail northwest out of Edmonton increased after the establishment of the Roman Catholic mission in St. Albert in 1861 by Bishop Tâché. He named the mission in honour of the patron saint of his travelling companion, Father Albert Lacombe. An earlier mission had been established at Lac Ste. Anne in 1843. However, it was located in an area that was not suitable for farming, and was too far from a major provisioning centre. St. Albert was a more suitable spot. It became the operational centre of the Oblate Missionaries' work, first with the area's Cree and Métis people, and later with French-speaking Roman Catholic settlers.

An HBC post operated in St. Albert from 1866 to 1875. With its thriving agricultural community, St. Albert became a village in 1899, a town in 1904 and a city in 1977. Today, the St. Albert Trail is one of Edmonton's busiest thoroughfares.

Oiling St. Albert Trail, 1925. (CEA EA–75–389)

283

Saskatchewan Drive looking east, 1910. (CEA EA–364–4)

After his death, Prince Vladimir was declared a saint of the Orthodox Church. St. Olga Park is located in the Evansdale neighbourhood and has an area of 2.77 ha.

Park 1990 NE 10:C2 *

Sakaw

9 Avenue north to Mill Woods Road South, 50 Street to 66 Street

The Cree word *sakâw* means "wooded area." This neighbourhood is located in the Millhurst subdivision and was once part of the Papaschase Indian Reserve.

Neighbourhood 1974 SE 1:C1

Sakaw Park

5820–11A Avenue

This park is in the Sakaw neighbourhood and has an area of 3.73 ha. *See* Sakaw.

Park 1987 SE 1:C1

Samuel Dickson Rotary Park

10445–131 Street

Samuel A. Dickson (1876–1971) was a pioneer lawyer who moved to Edmonton from Ontario in 1909. In addition to practising law, Dickson was a charter member and the second president of the Rotary Club, which he helped establish in Edmonton in 1916. He was also a member of the Edmonton Public School Board, the Edmonton Historical Board and the Edmonton and District Historical Society. In 1970, at the age of 94, Dickson was named the first honorary mayor of Fort Edmonton Park. The Samuel Dickson Rotary Park is in the Glenora neighbourhood and has an area of 0.19 ha.

Park 1997 NW 7:B2

Santa Rosa Park

6725–121 Avenue

This park was named for the former subdivision of Santa Rosa. The Santa Rosa subdivision was subdivided and named around 1907. By 1909, lots in Santa Rosa were advertised as being for sale. Santa Rosa may have been named after St. Rose of Lima (or Santa Rosa de Lima), the patroness of Latin America, the Philippines, the New World and gardeners. Born in Lima, Peru, in 1586, St. Rose was the first saint born in the Americas. She died in 1617 and was canonized by the Vatican in 1671. This park is in the Montrose neighbourhood and has an area of 1.61 ha.

Park 1988 NE 7:D1

Saskatchewan Drive

Groat Road and 87 Avenue to 99 Street and 92 Avenue

Saskatchewan Drive follows the top of the south bank of the North Saskatchewan River and has existed since Strathcona (South Edmonton) was first developed. From the turn of the 20th century, the road was known as Saskatchewan Avenue. Between 1914 and 1915, however, the name was changed to Saskatchewan Drive.

Road CU C 7:B2

Satoo

9 Avenue to 23 Avenue, 80 Street and Mill Woods Road west to 91 Street

Chief Satoo of the Cree Nation was one of four brothers who were all chiefs between 1898 and 1922. The Cree word *satoo* is said to mean "jumping." Satoo forms part of the former Papaschase Indian Reserve, as does most of the Mill Woods area. Reserve lands encompassed the area from around 30 Avenue to 51 Avenue and 17 Street to 119 Street.

Road CU C 7:B2

Scona Road at Connors Road, no date.
(CEA EA–275–1166)

Satoo Park

445 Knottwood Road West

This park is located in the Satoo neighbourhood and has an area of 1.08 ha. *See* Satoo.

Park 1983 SE 1:B1

Schonsee

167 Avenue to 175 Avenue, 66 Street to 82 Street

This neighbourhood is located in the Lake District area and is named after the German word *schon*, meaning "beautiful," and *see*, meaning "lake." This neighbourhood has not yet been developed.

Neighbourhood 1979 NE 10:C1 *

Scona Road

99 Street and 92 Avenue north to the river valley

Scona Road runs through an area in the Strathcona neighbourhood that is informally known as Scona (a shortened form of Strathcona). The road has also been known as Strathcona Road. In 1973, the Names Advisory Committe recommended that Strathcona Road be renamed to Scona Road, since the posted road sign conformed with local usage by identifying the road as Scona Road. *See* Strathcona *feature story, page 295.*

Road 1973 C 7:C2

Sheffield Industrial

*111 Avenue to 114 Avenue, 156 Street to
163 Street*

Sheffield Industrial was annexed to Edmonton in
1964 when the Town of Jasper Place became part of
Edmonton. This neighbourhood was developed in
the late 1950s and its name predates the annexation. Sheffield, meaning an "open country on the
Sheaf," is also a place name in England, and may be
the origin of Sheffield Industrial.

Neighbourhood   CU   NW   8:D1

Sheppard Court

East of Parsons Road, south of Ellerslie Road

June Sheppard (circa 1920–2002) was a writer,
commentator and critic. Born in Edmonton,
Sheppard began her career in the media at the age
of 22 at the CJCA radio station. Later, she worked
for CBC television and in 1969 started writing a
regular column in the *Edmonton Journal*. Sheppard
was an early supporter of the feminist movement in
Alberta and in 1979 became the first honorary
member of the Alberta Status of Women Action
Committee. Sheppard was awarded the YWCA's
Tribute to Women in 1982.

Road   2000   SE   1:B1 *

Sheppard Park

2608–49 Street

William Henry Sheppard (1863–1944) was an
alderman and the mayor of Strathcona. He was
born in Canada West and came to Edmonton in
1894, where he managed a hotel and a brewery.
Sheppard was elected to Strathcona council in
1899, 1903 and 1908, and was mayor of Strathcona
in 1906. Sheppard Park is in the Weinlos neighbourhood and has an area of 0.61 ha.

Park   1983   SE   4:D2

Sherbrooke

*118 Avenue to 124 Avenue, 127 Street west to
St. Albert Trail*

This neighbourhood was subdivided using a grid
street pattern and named sometime around 1906. It
was annexed to Edmonton in 1913 but was not
really developed until after WWII. In the early
1950s the neighbourhood was replotted under the
direction of Noel Dant, Edmonton's first town
planner, becoming one of the first developments in
North America to be designed using the neighbourhood concept. The plan was based on a curvilinear
street pattern with limited access points; yards
were landscaped and houses arranged in a way to
discourage through traffic. Sherbrooke neighbourhood was likely named for the city of Sherbrooke in
Quebec, which was named after Sir John Coape
Sherbrooke (1764–1830), lieutenant-governor of
Nova Scotia in 1811 and governor-in-chief of
British North America in 1816.

Neighbourhood   CU   NW   7:B1

Sherbrooke Avenue

East of St. Albert Trail at 123 Avenue

This road does not appear on early subdivision
maps and was most likely constructed when the
area was replotted after WWII. *See* Sherbrooke.

Road   CU   SW   7:B1

Sherbrooke Park

12956–122 Avenue

This park is in the Sherbrooke neighbourhood and
has an area of 1.47 ha. *See* Sherbrooke.

Park   1982   SW   7:B1

Sheriff Robertson Park

8112–111 Avenue

Walter Scott Robertson (1841–1915) was the first
sheriff of Edmonton. The Robertson family moved

west from Ontario in the early 1880s and established their first residence overlooking the North Saskatchewan River, on the site of the Hotel Macdonald. Robertson also built Robertson Hall, one of Edmonton's first cultural venues. After being involved in business for several years, he became the first sheriff of Edmonton in 1905. While acting as sheriff, Robertson was also the manager of the Canada Life Assurance Company. In 1912, Robertson commissioned architect Alfred M. Calderon, who was responsible for the design of the landmark LeMarchand Mansion, 11523-100 Avenue, to design his retirement home in Cromdale. The Sheriff Robertson Park is in the Cromdale neighbourhood and has an area of 0.98 ha.

Park 2001 NE 7:C1 *

Sherin Road

58 Street north of 129 Avenue

This road name has been used since at least the early 1920s but was made official in 1974. Its origin is not recorded.

Road CU NE 11:A2

Sherwood

92 Avenue to 95 Avenue, 149 Street to 156 Street

This neighbourhood, developed in the 1950s, was formerly part of the Town of Jasper Place and was annexed to Edmonton in 1964. The name of Sherwood was chosen for its promotional value, its origin being the Sherwood Forest in Nottinghamshire, England. The forest is famous for its role in the legend of the outlaw Robin Hood.

Neighbourhood CU SW 8:D2

Sherwood Community Park

15430-93 Avenue

This park is in the Sherwood neighbourhood and has an area of 1.08 ha. *See* Sherwood.

Park 1982 SW 8:D2

Joe Shoctor, circa 1980. (CEA EA-340-1927)

Sherwood Park Freeway

North of 76 Avenue, east of 71 Street to the County of Strathcona

Sherwood Park Freeway connects the hamlet of Sherwood Park, east of Edmonton, to Whyte Avenue and Argyll Road. Officially opened in 1968, the expressway was originally known as Highway No. 14. In 1975 the Names Advisory Committee recommended that it be renamed Sherwood Park Expressway; the name was later amended to Sherwood Park Freeway.

Road 1977 SE 5:A1

Shoctor Alley

Portion of 101A Avenue east of 99 Street South of the Citadel Theatre

Joe Shoctor (1922–2001) was the executive producer and founder of the Citadel Theatre, a major regional theatre in Edmonton founded in the

1960s. Although Shoctor did not recommend that the road be named after himself, he did suggest the use of the word "alley," an allusion to Broadway and his earlier experiences as a producer at the Schubert Theatre on Schubert Alley in New York. Born in Edmonton, Shoctor graduated with a Bachelor of Arts/Bachelor of Laws from the University of Alberta and was admitted to the Bar in 1947. In 1960 he was appointed Queen's Counsel. Between 1965 and 1970, he was a producer on and off Broadway. Among the many honours he received were the Order of Canada (1986), the Alberta Order of Excellence (1990), the Great Canadian Award (1992) and an honorary Doctorate of Laws from the University of Alberta (1981).

Road 1998 C 7:C2 *

Sifton Park

Kennedale Ravine north to 137 Avenue, 40 Street to 50 Street

Arthur L. Sifton (1858-1921) was the premier of Alberta from 1910 to 1917. He was born in Canada West and practised law until he was elected under the Liberal Party banner to the territorial legislature for Banff in 1899. Sifton served on the Executive Council and was appointed territorial chief justice. In 1907 he became Alberta's first chief justice. In 1919, he resigned as premier and joined the federal Union government of Sir Robert Borden. Sifton held a number of portfolios, and in 1919 was part of the Canadian delegation at the Paris Peace Conference following WWI.

Neighbourhood 1972 NE 11:A2

Sifton Park

13317-47 Street

This park is in the Sifton Park neighbourhood and has an area of 2.1 ha. *See* Sifton Park *neighbourhood.*

Park 1981 NE 11:A2

Silver Berry

23 Avenue to 34 Avenue, 17 Street to 34 Street

This neighbourhood is in The Meadows area. The silver berry is a shrub that bears greyish-white berries.

Neighbourhood 1992 SE 5:B2

Silver Berry Road

East of 34 Street

See Silver Berry.

Road 2002 SE 5:B2 *

Silver Heights Park

8777–96 Avenue

This park is in the Strathearn neighbourhood and has an area of 1.03 ha. In the early 1900s this neighbourhood was known as Silver Heights. The origin of the name Silver Heights is not recorded.

Park 1984 SE 7:C2

Sir Wilfrid Laurier Park

13221 Buena Vista Road

In 1910 this park was named Laurier Park in honour of a visit by the then prime minister of Canada, Sir Wilfrid Laurier (1841–1919). It was officially re-named Sir Wilfrid Laurier Park in 1987. Laurier was born in Canada East and was elected to the Quebec legislature in 1871; in 1874 he was elected to the House of Commons. Laurier spent the next 45 years in federal politics, including four terms as prime minister from 1896 to 1911. He was leader of the Liberal Party from 1887 to 1919. In 1897 Laurier was knighted while attending Queen Victoria's jubilee celebrations as Canada's prime minister. Laurier was in Edmonton in 1905 to participate in the official proclamation of Alberta as a province. The Sir Wilfrid Laurier Park has an area of 53.23 ha. *See* Laurier Heights.

Park 1987 SW 4:A1

Sir Winston Churchill Square, the Civic Block, and Centennial (now Stanley A. Milner) Library, 1967. (CEA EA–408–7)

Sir Winston Churchill Square

10216–99 Street

Located in the heart of Edmonton, Sir Winston Churchill Square is adjacent to City Hall and the Stanley Milner Library. In 2003 renovations to the square were begun as a 2004 Legacy Project. City Council approved a $12.6 million renovation of the square, including construction of a public pavilion, an interpretive centre and an amphitheatre. Sir Winston Churchill Square is located in the Downtown neighbourhood and has an area of 0.85 ha. *See* Churchill Crescent.

Park 1965 C 7:C2

Skyrattler

Blackmud Creek north to 23 Avenue, 111 Street to 119 Street

Skyrattler was the Cree chief of the Winterburn Indian Reserve when Edmonton became a city in 1904. The Skyrattler neighbourhood is in the

Yellowbird subdivision. The naming theme established in the Kaskitayo area honours historical Aboriginal leaders.

Neighbourhood 1979 SW 2:D1

Smith Crossing

Spanning the Whitemud Creek at 23 Avenue

Robert (1870–1959) and Elizabeth (1886–1982) Smith were pioneers who came from North Dakota to the Rabbit Hill area in 1909. Their property encompassed the junction of Whitemud Creek and Blackmud Creek. The Smiths farmed areas to the west and east of Whitemud Creek for 34 years before moving to Edmonton in 1943. In support of the settler community, the Smiths donated some of their land for the building of a church.

Bridge 1996 SW 2:D1

Franklin K. Spragins, Chairman of the Board, Syncrude Canada, 1977. (CEA EA-340-427)

South Haven Cemetery

5004 Meridian Street

The City of Edmonton chose this site for a south-side cemetery in 1985. It was first named Northern Lights Memorial Park, then renamed to South Haven Cemetery because the name was considered more appropriate for a cemetery located on the south side of Edmonton. Located in the Maple Ridge Industrial neighbourhood, the 21.29-ha. cemetery was opened by the City of Edmonton in 1988.

Cemetery 1987 SE 5:C1 *

South Side Athletic Grounds

10425 University Avenue

This land was bought by the South Edmonton Agricultural Association in 1896. Queen Victoria's birthday was celebrated there on May 24, 1898. In 1910 the grounds were sold to the City of Edmonton and two years later, Strathcona and Edmonton were amalgamated. The grounds were used for annual celebrations like Dominion Day, as well as sporting events like horse racing and agricultural fairs. In 1953 construction began on Strathcona Composite High School, which is located on the south portion of the grounds. This park is located in the Queen Alexandra neighbourhood and has an area of 4.89 ha.

Park 1967 SW 4:C1

Southeast Industrial

Whitemud Drive north to Sherwood Park Freeway, 17 Street to 34 Street

This industrial area is located in southeast Edmonton. It was annexed to Edmonton in 1982.

Neighbourhood CU SE 5:B1

Southwood

10 Avenue to 23 Avenue, 34 Street to 50 Street

This subdivision is in the southern part of the Mill Woods area. The names of subdivisions in the Mill Woods area incorporate the words "mill" or "wood."

Subdivision 1975 SE 1:C1 *

Spartan Park

12649–66 Street

The Spartan Men's Club was formed in 1957 to promote sports in the northeast zone of Edmonton. It was part of the Amateur Athletic Union and supported hockey and baseball. From 1968 to 1981 the club participated in the *Edmonton Journal* Road Race, and from 1979 to 1994 sponsored an annual Sports Day held on the May long weekend. Spartan Park is in the Belvedere neighbourhood and has an area of 2.65 ha.

Park 1994 NE 7:D1

Spragins Sector

17 Avenue to 23 Avenue, 91 Street to 94 Street

Franklin K. Spragins was a consultant with the oil industry and a member of the Alberta Oil Sands Technology and Research Authority. Active in the Canadian oil industry for more than 35 years, Spragins was the first president of Syncrude Canada Ltd. This is the northeast portion of the Edmonton Research and Development Park.

Neighbourhood 1981 SE 1:B1 *

Springfield

North of Whitemud Drive, 170 Street to 178 Street

This name is likely descriptive.

Subdivision 1969 SW 3:C1 *

Aerial view northwest over the Spruce Avenue neighbourhood, showing the Royal Alexandra Hospital, 1927. (CEA EA-427-93)

Spruce Avenue

111 Avenue to 118 Avenue, 97 Street west to Princess Elizabeth Avenue and Kingsway

Spruce Avenue was originally named 114 Avenue-Spruce Avenue. In 1982 the name was shortened to 114 Avenue. The oldest portion of this area is along 97 Street (formerly Namayo Avenue) and 101 Street (First Street); these two streets were major thoroughfares leading to the downtown core. The road was likely named after the spruce tree, which was native to the area.

Neighbourhood CU NW 7:C1

Spruce Avenue Park

10240–115 Avenue

This park, adjacent to the Spruce Avenue Elementary and Junior High School, is in the Spruce Avenue neighbourhood and has an area of 1.33 ha. *See* Spruce Avenue.

Park 1984 NW 7:C1

Stadium Road

92 Street to 107A Avenue

This road was named for its proximity to Clarke Stadium, which was the home field of the Edmonton Eskimos until Commonwealth Stadium was built in 1978.

Road 1947 NE 7:C1

Star Blanket Park

2614–39 Street

Chief Ahchacoosahcootakoopit "Star Blanket" (b. 1840) was a member of the File Hills Crees, who lived northeast of Fort Qu'Appelle in the District of Saskatchewan. Star Blanket fought many battles with the Blackfoot and the Sioux and eventually became a chief. He reluctantly signed Treaty No. 4 at Fort Qu'Appelle on September 15, 1874, but refused to be confined on a reserve. In an attempt to retain his freedom, he and his followers made their way west to the Cypress Hills where they continued to live a traditional lifestyle. After four years, however, the dwindling supply of buffalo forced Star Blanket and his people to move on to the File Hills Reserve. To his dismay, reserve life provided little comfort and his people were still hungry.

Although sympathetic with the Riel uprising, Chief Star Blanket was determined to honour the peace agreement. He confronted Maj.-Gen. Middleton at Duck Lake and was assured that no harm would come to his people if they remained on the reserve. However, shortly after, a report to the contrary prompted Star Blanket and his band to set out for Fort Qu'Appelle, unaware that they were heading straight into the line of fire of Middleton's Canadian militia troops. In order to avoid a slaughter, the North West Mounted Police were requested to intervene, at which time they arrested Star Blanket and jailed him at Regina. He was released two weeks later. The Star Blanket Park is in the Bisset neighbourhood and has an area of 2.13 ha.

Park 1983 SE 1:C1

James Bond Steele, circa 1880. (CEA EA–10–2789)

Steele Crescent

53 Street to 54 Street and 143 Avenue

This road was named after two brothers, James Bond Steele and Sir Samuel Benfield Steele, who were born in Purbrook, Canada West (present-day Ontario), and came to Alberta in the latter part of the 19th century. James Bond Steele was one of the first teachers in the Edmonton area. His brother, Sam Steele (1849–1919), arrived in 1874. He was a member of the original North West Mounted Police (NWMP), formed in 1873. Steele, though only in his early twenties, was a veteran soldier, having served in the militia during the 1866 Fenian invasions and taken part in the Red River Expedition in 1870.

He was made a sergeant-major in the NWMP and five years later commissioned as an officer. From 1898 to 1899 Steele was superintendent of the NWMP in the Yukon. In 1900 he went overseas as commander of Lord Strathcona's Horse, a regiment formed to fight in the Boer War, and stayed on to serve with the South African Constabulary. Steele served as a major-general in WWI and was knighted in 1918. He retired at the end of the war and died only a few months later in London, England.

Road   1969   NE   11:A2

Steinhauer

30 Avenue to 34 Avenue, Calgary Trail west to 111 Street

Henry Bird Steinhauer (d. 1884), an Ojibway, was one of the first missionaries to live in Alberta. Rev. Steinhauer was born and educated in Upper Canada and came west to the Hudson's Bay territories as a Methodist missionary in 1840. He established a mission at Lac La Biche in 1850, but finding little success there, moved his mission to Whitefish Lake in 1858. Steinhauer remained at Whitefish Lake until his death in 1884.

Neighbourhood   1974   SW   4:B2

Steinhauer Park

10707–32A Avenue

This park is in the Steinhauer neighbourhood and has an area of 3.02 ha. *See* Steinhauer.

Park   1981   SW   4:C2

Steinhauer Trail

From 81 Avenue to 96 Avenue, west of 181 Street

The name of this trail, a major walkway in the Aldergrove neighbourhood, reflects the theme of most of Edmonton's walkways, which are named for prominent Aboriginal people or bear a relation-ship with Aboriginal heritage. Steinhauer Trail is one of a number of trail names approved between 1969 and 1971. *See* Steinhauer.

Walkway   1971   SW   3:C1 *

Stewart Crescent

South of Ellerslie Road, west of 91 Street

Charles Stewart (1868–1946) was premier of Alberta and served in the federal government for almost two decades. Before moving west in 1904, Stewart and his wife, Jane Russell Sneath, farmed in their home province of Ontario. In 1905, the family homesteaded on a farm in Killam, Alberta. Stewart also supported the family by working as a stonemason, bricklayer and real estate agent. In 1909 he took the Liberal Party nomination for the Sedgewick district and won the seat in the next two elections, in 1913 and 1917. After Premier Arthur L. Sifton resigned in 1917, Stewart was appointed premier. He held the position until his resignation in 1921 and then joined the federal government. From 1921 to 1926 he was minister of the Interior and Mines and general superintendent of Indian Affairs. Between 1921 and 1923, Stewart was also the acting minister of Immigration and Colonization.

In 1922, with the federal Liberal Party holding no seats in Alberta, Stewart was elected in a by-election as member of parliament for Argenteuil, Quebec. In 1926 and again in 1930 he won the House of Commons seat for Edmonton West. Stewart was defeated in the 1935 election when he ran as a Liberal candidate for Jasper-Edson. He continued to be active in the government, however, and in 1936 was appointed chairman of the Canadian Section of the International Joint Commission. In 1938 he was named chairman of the Canadian Section of the British Columbia-Yukon-Alaska Highway Commission.

Road   2000   SE   1:B1 *

Stirling

153 Avenue to 174 Avenue, 97 Street west to Castle Downs Road

The Stirling subdivision is named after a castle that played an important role in the history of Scotland from the 12th to the 18th centuries. The name follows the theme used by the developers of the Castle Downs area, who named subdivisions and neighbourhoods after famous castles.

Subdivision 1973 NW 10:B1 *

Stirling Road

North of 158 Avenue at 103 Street

See Stirling.

Road 1977 NW 10:C1 *

Stone Industrial

Stony Plain Road north to 105 Avenue, 170 Street to 178 Street

James Stone (1898–1965) was the first mayor of the Town of Jasper Place, serving from 1950 to 1957. Born in Ontario, Stone moved to Jasper Place in 1930 where he worked as a building contractor.

Neighbourhood 1976 NW 8:C2

Stony Plain Road

101 Avenue and 148 Street to 104 Avenue and 121 Street

Stony Plain Road has existed since at least 1912 and was the main street of the Town of Jasper Place, which was incorporated in 1951 and annexed by Edmonton in 1964. Stony Plain Road likely gained its name because it connects Edmonton with the town of Stony Plain, 34 km west of Edmonton. The precise origin of the name is not known. It likely derives from the Stoney people who lived in the area. The Stoney First Nation is culturally and linguistically related to the Plains Assiniboine and

historically lived along the foothills of the Rocky Mountains. The name may also have arisen from the abundance of boulders found in the area. In 1964, Stony Plain Road was extended from 121 Street and 104 Avenue on the east to 170 Street and 101 Avenue on the west. A further extension to 231 Street was made in 1982.

Road CU NW 8:C2

Strathcona

Whyte Avenue north to Saskatchewan Drive, Mill Creek Ravine Park west to 107 Street

See feature story, page 295.

Neighbourhood 1898 C 7:C2

Strathcona Industrial Park

34 Avenue north to Whitemud Drive, 91 Street west to CP railway tracks

See Strathcona *feature story, page 295.*

Neighbourhood 1973 SE 4:C2

Strathcona Park

10139–87 Avenue

This park is in the Strathcona neighbourhood and has an area of 1.61 ha. *See* Strathcona *feature story, page 295.*

Park 1983 C 7:C2

Strathearn

Connors Road north to Strathearn Crescent and Strathearn Drive, 85 Street west to Connors Road

This area was established on the plots of land originally identified as River Lots 21 and 23. George Donnell farmed River Lot 21 while James McKernan, Edmonton's first telegraph operator, owned the north half of River Lot 23. A.W. Bird, the builder of one of Edmonton's first water-driven

Strathcona

STRATHCONA was named for Sir Donald Alexander Smith, 1st Baron Strathcona and Mount Royal (1820–1914). He was born in Forres, near Inverness in northern Scotland, and apprenticed with the Hudson's Bay Company (HBC) in 1838. Fifty years later, in 1889, Smith became governor of the company.

In the 1870s, Smith was a politician and railroad financier who promoted the Canadian Pacific Railway (CPR). In 1896 he was appointed High Commissioner for Canada in the United Kingdom. Smith held this position, and the governorship of the HBC, until his death. Smith can be seen in one of Canada's most famous photographs: he is the white-haired, top-hatted gentleman driving the last spike for the CPR at Craigellachie, BC, in 1885.

In 1891 a town site was established when the Calgary and Edmonton (C&E) Railway reached the south side of the North Saskatchewan River. Rather than embark on the building of a bridge across the river, the C&E located its terminus on the south side. Its plan was to promote "South Edmonton" as the area's major commercial centre in competition with Edmonton, on the north bank of the river. To this end, C&E purchased land for the establishment of a town site in the spring of 1891. By the end of 1898, South Edmonton was renamed Strathcona (informally known as Scona).

The high hopes for Strathcona were never quite fulfilled, however, and by 1910 the CPR had undertaken to build the High Level Bridge across the North Saskatchewan River. Strathcona became a town in 1899 and a city in 1907. The City of Strathcona amalgamated with Edmonton in 1912.

The area now known as the Strathcona neighbourhood was originally part of River Lots 15 and 17. Whyte Avenue between 101 Street and 109 Street is Strathcona's traditional commercial area, and has gone through a number of transformations over the years. Through the efforts of the Old Strathcona Foundation and many others, much of the area's original historical character has survived.

Strathcona welcomes its namesake, Whyte Avenue at Gateway Boulevard, 1909. (CEA EA-10-3241)

grain mills in Mill Creek, owned the south half of River Lot 23. In the 1910s, part of River Lot 23 was known as Earnscliff. While Strathearn has existed as a name since 1914, the area remained largely undeveloped until the late 1940s. This neighbourhood was probably named after His Royal Highness Arthur William Patrick Albert, 1st Duke of Connaught and Strathearn (1850–1942). *See* Connaught Drive.

Neighbourhood CU   SE   7:C2

Strathearn Crescent

87 Street to north of 91 Avenue

Once called Strathearn Drive, the roadway's name was changed in 1952 so that there would not be two Strathearn Drives in Edmonton. *See* Strathearn.

Road   1952   SE   7:C2

Strathearn Drive

86 Street to 97 Avenue

This road was formerly called Saskatchewan Drive East but, because of confusion between this name and Saskatchewan Drive, was changed in 1952. The existing Strathearn Drive was renamed to Strathearn Crescent while Saskatchewan Drive East was renamed Strathearn Drive. *See* Strathearn.

Road   1952   SE   7:C2

Strathearn Park

8503–98 Avenue

This park is north of the Strathearn neighbourhood and has an area of 4.05 ha. *See* Strathearn.

Park   1960   SE   7:C2 *

Stutchbury Park

7707–112 Avenue

Howard Stutchbury (1873–1957) founded the Alberta Safety Council, a public body aimed at

Howard Stutchbury, no date. (CEA EA–10–2074)

encouraging the prevention of accidents, in 1946. He was also an active member of the community, participating in his church, the arts, veterans' affairs and industrial development. Stutchbury Park is in the Cromdale neighbourhood and has an area of 1.33 ha.

Park   1960   NE   7:C1 *

Suder Greens

87 Avenue to 89 Avenue, Lewis Estates Boulevard west to Winterburn Road

Ontario-born Joseph Suder (1869–1922) and his German-born wife, Kate (b. 1870), homesteaded in the Winterburn area in the 1890s. They came west shortly after their marriage in 1892. In 1902 the family purchased a second farm. In 1957 the farm was sold to one of the Suder children, Milton.

While Joseph died in 1922, Kate reached her 102nd birthday in 1972.

Neighbourhood 2001 SW 8:B2

Summerlea

90 Avenue to 95 Avenue, 170 Street to 178 Street

Summerlea, located directly north of West Edmonton Mall, is named for a summertime meadow. The neighbourhood has a large area of parkland. Development of the area began in the late 1970s; the majority of the residences were constructed in the 1980s.

Neighbourhood 1970 SW 8:C2

Summerside

Ellerslie Road south to 25 Avenue SW, 66 Street west to Parsons Road

Summerside is named for a city in Prince Edward Island and has an "East Coast Resort" naming theme. It is the first neighbourhood in Edmonton with a man-made lake that is not a stormwater collection facility. Rather, it is a functional lake that is 28 feet deep, has a surface area of 12.95 ha. and contains 680 million litres of water. Neighbourhood residents pay a maintenance fee and enjoy exclusive use of the lake, where they can swim, fish, or use non-motorized vehicles.

Neighbourhood 1999 SE 1:B2

Summerside Drive

East of Sheppard Court, south of Stewart Crescent

See Summerside.

Road 2000 SE 1:B2

Summerside Gate

Connecting Parsons Road with Summerside Drive

See Summerside.

Road 2000 SE 1:B2 *

Summit Drive

147 Street to 149 Street, south of Stony Plain Road

Originally called Summit Avenue, this roadway has existed since at least 1909. The name of Summit Drive appeared around 1922. In 1958, the Names Advisory Committee recommended that the name of Summit Drive be extended to a portion of 149 Street because residents were already using it in their addresses.

Road CU SW 7:A2

Summit Point

98 Avenue and 140 Street

This road is the no-exit continuation of 98 Avenue. Residents wanted a name that reflected their addresses, since most used Summit Avenue to access their street. The road was originally named Gardiner Point (but not listed on maps) after John B. Gardiner who established the subdivision of Capital Hill, now part of Crestwood and Glenora. Wanting to have Edmonton's finest house, Gardiner built his home where it would have the best view of the North Saskatchewan River—off the road currently named Summit Point. After Edmonton's land boom collapsed in 1914, he lost most of his wealth. A few years later Gardiner's house burned down, forcing him to move into his coach house. He then began growing cabbages that he sold to west-end stores. The Gardiner Estate remained mostly undeveloped until the 1950s.

Road 1958 SW 7:A2 *

Sunwapta

Stony Plain Road north to 105 Avenue, 184 Street west to Anthony Henday Drive

This name was selected because Sunwapta Broadcasting House lies within the neighbourhood's boundaries. There have been various interpretations of the Stoney word *sunwapta*. One interpretation is that the word means "turbulent

Sunwapta Broadcasting Company, CFRN Studios, circa 1960. (CEA EA–657–4)

river," and another is the meaning used by the Broadcasting House, "rippling or radiating waves." The latter meaning was told to the president of the company some years ago by one of the chiefs of the Stoney First Nation. Sunwapta Broadcasting Company was formed in 1934. It bought the radio station CFTP and changed the name to CFRN to reflect the owners' (George Rice and Hans Neilson) surnames. The company expanded into television and made its first televised broadcast in 1954.

Neighbourhood   1978   NW   8:C2

Sunwapta Trail

Between 184 Street and 105 Avenue

This roadway traverses the entire Sunwapta neighbourhood and continues through the Winterburn Area Structure Plan. *See* Sunwapta.

Road   1984   NW   8:C2 *

Sweet Grass

30 Avenue to 34 Avenue, 111 Street to 119 Street

Sweet Grass neighbourhood was named in honour of Chief Wikaskokiseyin "Sweetgrass," a Cree chief in the 1870s who is considered the first western conservationist. He was instrumental in gaining protection of the endangered buffalo or plains bison. Sweetgrass is said to have been murdered by his brother-in-law in protest of his signing of Treaty No. 6 in 1876. The area that includes Sweet Grass, in the subdivision of Blue Quill, was annexed to Edmonton in 1964 and development of the neighbourhood began in the 1970s.

Neighbourhood   1974   SW   4:B2

Sweet Grass Park

11351–31 Avenue

This park is in the Sweet Grass neighbourhood and has an area of 3 ha. *See* Sweet Grass.

Park   1987   SW   4:B2

H.E. Tanner, second from left, greeting the Toronto Blues football team, 1947. (CEA EA-600-434C)

Tanner Link

East of Tanner Wynd, north of Tomlinson Way

Harold E. Tanner was a city alderman from 1946 to 1955 and a Liberal MLA from 1952 to 1959. After serving with the 49th Battalion in WWI, Tanner worked as a principal at schools in Stettler and Wetaskiwin. During and following WWII, Tanner was president of the Canadian Legion and worked to establish housing and educational benefits for returning veterans. Until his retirement in 1958, he was a teacher and principal with the Edmonton Public School Board.

Road 1997 SW 2:C1 *

Tanner Wynd

East of Terwillegar Drive, south of 23 Avenue

See Tanner Link.

Road 1997 SW 2:C1

Tawa

28 Avenue to 34 Avenue, 50 Street to 66 Street

Tawa is said to be the Cree word meaning "You are welcome." This neighbourhood was once part of the Papaschase Reserve. Cree people led by Chief Papaschase lived in this part of the present-day Mill Woods area prior to its settlement by European immigrants. *See* Papaschase Industrial *feature story, page 245.*

Neighbourhood 1978 SE 5:A2

Tawa Road

North of 28 Avenue, connecting with 55 Street

See Tawa.

Road 1987 SE 5:A2 *

Taylor Close

Northeast of Towne Centre Boulevard

See Alex Taylor Road *feature story, page 6.*

Road 2001 SW 2:C1 *

Tegler Gate

Connecting 23 Avenue with Tory Road, west of 142 Street

Robert Tegler (1876–1921) was a prominent real estate broker and builder. Born and educated in Ontario, Tegler came to Edmonton in 1905, where he worked at the Alberta Hotel for two years before entering into a partnership with John Morris. Together they formed the real estate company of Tegler and Morris. In 1909, Tegler opened his own business as a realty and financial broker and in 1911 financed the building of the Tegler Block. It housed what was then the most prominent retail department store in Edmonton, Ramsey's, and was for years Edmonton's largest commercial block. The Tegler Block was demolished in 1982. The man who built it is remembered in the Robert Tegler Trust/Tegler Foundation, established in 1930. Created in Tegler's will, the trust was the first charitable trust in Alberta. It awards scholarships for postsecondary education and is involved in other worthy causes.

Road   1999   SW   2:C1 *

Tegler Green

South of 23 Avenue, west of Tegler Gate

See Tegler Gate.

Road   2002   SW   2:C1 *

Telus Field

10233 John Ducey Way

Telus Field is the home of the Edmonton Trappers, Edmonton's Triple A Baseball club, part of the Pacific Coast League and a major league "farm" team. It was originally called Renfrew Park after Edward, Prince of Wales (later, King Edward VIII) who, as heir apparent to the British throne, inherited the title of Baron Renfrew. The park was renamed John Ducey Park, after a local baseball promoter, in 1984. In 1995 the park was re-named for the second time, when the Telus Corporation paid for the privilege of having its name used. Telus Field is located in the Rossdale neighbourhood and has an area of 1.87 ha.

Park   1995   C   7:C2 *

Terra Losa

95 Avenue to 100 Avenue, 170 Street to 178 Street

Vittorio "Victor" Losa (1905–1987) was born in Italy and came to Edmonton in the 1920s as a professional watchmaker. He ran a jewellery store and trained people in the art of watchmaking. In 1931, Losa was nominated as a Royal Consul by the Italian monarchy and helped Italian immigrants settle in Edmonton. He held this position until 1939. Losa retired from the jewellery business in 1964.

Neighbourhood   1978   SW   8:C2

Terrace Heights

98 Avenue north to Fulton Creek, Terrace Road west to 75 Street

The name Terrace Heights was recommended because a small subdivision by the same name, dating to 1912, existed immediately north of the area. When the City redeveloped the neighbourhood in the 1950s, the original Terrace Heights area was extended. The Terrace Heights neighbourhood is located on land originally identified as River Lots 31 and 33 and includes a quarter section of land once owned by D. McLeod. McLeod was an employee of the Hudson's Bay Company, and later a saw mill operator. In 1883 he pioneered the weekly stage coach service between Edmonton and Calgary.

River Lot 31 was owned by Frank Oliver, co-founder of the *Edmonton Bulletin* newspaper and a member of parliament. Oliver sold the lot to the city in 1912 and it was renamed Terrace Heights.

Baseball game at Renfrew Park (now Telus Field) in 1943. (CEA EA-524-34)

Although subdivided, the area remained undeveloped until part of it, River Lots 31 and 33 and another portion north of 101 Avenue, was annexed by the city in 1954. The remaining land, the area south of 101 Avenue, was annexed in 1959.

Neighbourhood   1959   SE   7:D2

Terrace Road

Between 98 Avenue and 101 Avenue, 52 Street and 64 Street

See Terrace Heights.

Road   1965   SE   6:A2

Terwillegar Boulevard

South of Terwillegar Common, east of Thibault Way

See Terwillegar Heights.

Road   2002   SW   2:C1 *

Terwillegar Common

North of Terwillegar Boulevard, west of Towne Centre Boulevard

See Terwillegar Heights.

Road   2002   SW   2:C1 *

Terwillegar Drive

Commencing at Whitemud Drive east of 147 Street, passing southeast through the Riverbend and Terwillegar Heights subdivisions to 16 Avenue where it becomes 156 Street

See Terwillegar Heights.

Road   1972   SW   3:D2

Terwillegar Heights

16 Avenue to 45 Avenue, Whitemud Creek west to the North Saskatchewan River

Dr. Norman L. Terwillegar (1884–1948) was a pioneer surgeon and general practitioner who owned property in this area for a number of years. He practised in Edmonton from 1912 to 1947 and for over 35 years was on staff at the Royal Alexandra Hospital. Terwillegar served as president of the Edmonton Academy of Medicine and the Alberta Division of the Canadian Medical Association.

Subdivision 1971 SW 2:C1 *

Terwillegar Park

10 Rabbit Hill Road

Terwillegar Park, formerly Riverbend Park, lies in a bend of the North Saskatchewan River, west of Rhatigan Ridge neighbourhood. In the early 1900s this land was used for ranching and later, as a gravel pit. When the area was restructured as a park, the gravel pits were turned into ponds and trails. Over the years, the area was commonly identified by this name. The park's development plan calls for picnic and winter sports areas, an administration building, a nature centre, a boathouse and a number of trails that connect with existing river valley trails. Terwillegar Park is west of the Riverbend subdivision and has an area of 174.88 ha. *See* Terwillegar Heights.

Park 1981 SW 3:C2

Terwillegar Towne

16 Avenue to 23 Avenue, 142 Street to 156 Street

See Terwillegar Heights.

Neighbourhood 1995 SW 2:C1

Terwillegar Vista

Southeast of Tomlinson Common, west of Towne Centre Boulevard

See Terwillegar Heights.

Road 1999 SW 2:C1 *

Thibault Lane

Off Thibault Way, South of Tomlinson Common and west of Turner Square

Father Jean-Baptiste Thibault (1810–1879) was a Catholic priest and missionary to the Métis based in the North-West Territories from 1833 to 1868, and at Edmonton from 1842 to 1852. Father Thibault received his classical and theological education in Lower Canada (now Quebec), and came west to St. Boniface in 1833. As part of his mission to bring Christianity to the Métis by persuasion, he travelled to their meeting places across the west for 35 years. Ten of these were based at Fort Edmonton, from where he founded the mission at Lac Ste. Anne in 1844. Thibault returned to Quebec in 1868, but came back for a further two years in 1869, when he was part of an unsuccessful mission to negotiate with the Red River Métis led by Louis Riel. In 1872, Thibault returned to Quebec for the last time.

Road 2002 SW 2:C1 *

Thibault Way

South of Tomlinson Common, west of Turner Square

See Thibault Lane.

Road 2002 SW 2:C1 *

Thomas Rhatigan Park

270 Rhatigan Road East

This park is in the Rhatigan Ridge neighbourhood and has an area of 2.42 ha. *See* Rhatigan Ridge.

Park 1991 SW 4:A2

Thompson Court

West of Tory Road

Velva Thompson made history in 1943 when she refused to resign from her position as a teacher with the Edmonton Public School Board (EPSB) after marrying. During the 1920s, the EPSB established a policy of terminating the employment of any woman who married. Exceptions were made for women who could prove that they were the sole financial supporters of their family, but all others were expected to resign. Velva Thompson was the first who did not. Shortly after her marriage, Thompson wrote a letter to the EPSB, announcing her refusal to resign. She had been advised that, as the Alberta School Act did not allow discrimination between the sexes, the EPSB could not force her to leave. Thompson's decision met with disapproval and harassment from both men and women. Among those opposed to her stand was Mrs. W. J. Ross, a school trustee from 1935 to 1945, who maintained that women needed to stay home in order to retain control over their families and prevent juvenile delinquency. The EPSB requested a change in the Act to allow their policy to stand, but no changes were made. Velva Thompson stayed on for two more years, then took eleven years off to raise a family, and returned to teaching for a further nine years in 1956.

Road   2002   SW   2:C1 *

Thompson Place

North of Thorogood Lane and east of Tory Road

See Thompson Court.

Road   2002   SW   2:C1 *

Thorncliff

Whitemud Drive north to 87 Avenue, 170 Street to 178 Street

Thorncliff is a neighbourhood in the subdivision of Springfield. The name was suggested by the area developers.

Neighbourhood   1969   SW   3:C1

Thorncliff Park

8215–175 Street

This park is in the Thorncliff neighbourhood and has an area of 1.72 ha. *See* Thorncliff.

Park   1981   SW   3:C1

Thornton Court

South of Jasper Avenue at 99 Street

Sir Henry W. Thornton (1871–1933) was an American who went to Britain in 1914 as general manager of the Great Eastern Railway in London, England. Thornton began his career as an engineering draftsman with the Pennsylvania Railway in 1894, and in 1901 became the assistant president of the Long Island Railway. He was knighted in 1919 in recognition of his wartime service as director general of railways during WWI. In 1922 Thornton was named as president of the Canadian National Railway. Mayor Ken Blatchford requested that a road be named in Sir Henry's honour after meeting him in 1926. City Council approved the name Thornton Court that same year; the Names Advisory Committee officially designated the road decades later, in 1974.

Road   1974   C   7:C2 *

Thorogood Close

South of Thorogood Lane and east of Tory Road

John H. Thorogood (d. 1985), an employee of McLeary Manufacturing Northwest Utilities, was active in many facets of Edmonton's public life.

Tipton Park Playground summer program. Miss Kiefer and the Comic Strip Picnic, 1946. (CEA EA-20-6253)

Born around 1901, Thorogood arrived in Canada in 1919. During WWI he served in the Royal Flying Corps, and during WWII was the Commander of the South Edmonton Company. Thorogood was the secretary of the City of Edmonton Gas Approval Board, was a member of the Chamber of Commerce, and was a trustee of the Edmonton Public School Board, serving for three years as chairman. In addition, he was on the board of the United Way in Edmonton, was a member of the Cosmopolitan Club, and of the South Edmonton Business Association. Thorogood died in a fire that investigators suspected was the result of arson.

Road   2002   SW   2:C1 *

Thorogood Lane

North of Thorogood Close, east of Tory Road

See Thorogood Close.

Road   2002   SW   2:C1 *

Tipaskan

28 Avenue to 34 Avenue, Mill Woods Road west to 91 Street

Tipaskan is a variation of the Cree word that means "a reserve." The name Tipaskan was chosen because the Mill Woods area, where this neighbourhood is located, lies within the original boundaries of the Papaschase Indian Reserve No. 136. In 1889, the 103.3-square-kilometre reserve was allotted to Chief Papaschase and his band under Treaty No. 6.

Neighbourhood   1972   SE   4:C2

Tipaskan Park

1219 Lakewood Road North

This park is in the Tipaskan neighbourhood and has an area of 3.04 ha. *See* Tipaskan.

Park   1988   SE   4:C2

Tipton Park

10949–81 Avenue

Judge John G. Tipton (1849–1914) was a Strathcona lawyer, real estate investor and alderman. Born in Illinois and admitted to the bar of the United States Court in 1874, he immigrated to Edmonton in 1897. In 1904 Tipton was called to the Alberta Bar and from 1908 to 1911 served Strathcona as an alderman. When the park opened in 1924, it was called Gyro Park No. 3, the third park in the city to be named after the Gyro Club of Edmonton. The name, Tipton Park, however, was in common usage when it was officially adopted in 1967. Tipton Park is in the Queen Alexandra neighbourhood and has an area of 1.47 ha.

Park   1967   SW   4:B1

Toane Wynd

East of 156 Street, north of 16 Avenue

Clifford Toane (d. 1971) was a breeder of registered cattle. Toane's family came to southern Strathcona from Ontario in the early 1900s and established a dairy farm. After the death of his father, Clifford and his brother, Austin J. Toane, began to breed and show Holstein and Hereford cattle and Clydesdale horses. Clifford was a member of the Holstein-Friesian Association, the Clydesdale Horse Breeders Association and the local Old Timers' Association. He died at the age of 69 in 1971.

Road   1998   SW   2:C1 *

Todd Court

Southeast of Todd Landing

Frederick G. Todd (1876–1948) was a landscape architect whose 1907 report on Edmonton's park system had far-reaching effects on the City's parks policies. Todd was born in Concord, Massachusetts, and received his education in Andover and Amherst. From 1896 to 1900 he worked with the famous American landscape architect, Frederick Law Olmstead, the designer of Central Park, in New York. In 1900 Todd moved to Montreal, where he set up practice as a landscape architect, designing many prominent park schemes across Canada. *The Todd Report*, commissioned by the City of Edmonton, encouraged the extensive development of land for parks use, and especially advocated the preservation of the river valley and ravines for recreational purposes. He stated that "a crowded population, if they are to live in health and happiness, must have space for the enjoyment of that peaceful beauty of nature which because it is opposite of all that is sordid and artificial in our city lives, is so wonderfully refreshing to the tired souls of city dwellers."

Some of Todd's recommendations were adopted. In 1912 the City purchased the Hudson's Bay Company Flats, 62.73 ha. of land that became part of Victoria Park in 1916, and formed its first Parks Department, which was to manage, control, and embellish the parks and parkland in Edmonton. Unfortunately, the new department was abolished in the following year, due to lack of funds, and did not reappear as a separate entity for 33 years. Meanwhile, a commitment to parks did survive in a City regulation stipulating that all new subdivisions must contain park land, but development of river valley and ravine land was allowed to progress. It was not until the 1970s, when the City of Edmonton and the Government of Alberta spent $34 million to develop the Capital City Recreation Park, a 16-km swath of parkland along the North Saskatchewan River. Currently, Edmonton has 7,400 ha. of green space, including the river valley—the largest stretch of urban parkland in North America—and over 460 parks. Todd can be given credit as the originator of Edmonton's parks policies.

Road   2001   SW   2:C1 *

Todd Landing

West of Tory Road

See Todd Court.

Road   2001   SW   2:C1 *

Todd Link

East of Todd Landing

See Todd Court.

Road   2001   SW   2:C1 *

Tomahawk Trail

*From Arrowhead Trail west to Decoteau Trail,
north of 84 Avenue*

The name of this trail, a major walkway in the
Thorncliff neighbourhood, reflects the theme of
most of Edmonton's walkways, which are named
for prominent Aboriginal people or bear a relationship with Aboriginal heritage. Tomahawks are axes
that were traditionally used by Aboriginal peoples.
They were used as weapons, woodworking tools
and status symbols. Tomahawk Trail is one of a
number of trail names approved between 1969 and
1971.

Walkway   1969   SW   3:C1 *

Tomas Opalinski Park

1103–109 Street

Tomas Opalinski (1906–1990) was a Polish-born
miner and dairy farmer who owned the land in this
area. After immigrating to Alberta in 1928,
Opalinski worked at the Rabbit Hill coal mine. In
1936 he purchased Pine Creek Collieries and three
years later bought shares in Rabbit Hill Coal Mine
and a farm in south Edmonton. In 1947 Opalinski
established the Ellerslie Coal Company and the
Westwood Dairy Farm. The Tomas Opalinski Park
is in the Bearspaw neighbourhood and has an area
of 0.5 ha.

Park   1987   SW   1:A1

Tomlinson Common

*North of Terwillegar Vista, west of Towne Centre
Boulevard*

Aircraft mechanic Samuel Anthony Tomlinson
(1900–1973) was inducted into Canada's Aviation
Hall of Fame in recognition of his contributions to
aviation and aircraft maintenance during both
world wars. Trained as a machinist, Tomlinson
assembled and repaired aircraft during WWI. After
the war, he worked as an engineer with the Ontario
Provincial Air Service and later helped found the
Patricia Airways and Exploration Company. In
1926 he became chief mechanic with Western
Canada Airways, and in 1929 headed up the
company's prairie airmail division, serving
Manitoba, Saskatchewan and Alberta. During
WWII, Tomlinson commanded the engine test
bench and served on the Crash Investigation Board.
After the war, he worked as a chief mechanic until
his retirement in 1966. In 1973, in honour of his
remarkable contributions to Canadian aviation,
Tomlinson was inducted into Canada's Aviation
Hall of Fame.

Road   1997   SW   2:C1 *

Tomlinson Crescent

*East of Tomlinson Way, north of
Tomlinson Common*

See Tomlinson Common.

Road   1997   SW   2:C1 *

Tomlinson Green

East of Tanner Wynd, north of Tomlinson Square

See Tomlinson Common.

Road   1997   SW   2:C1 *

Henry Marshall Tory, circa 1918. (CEA EA–10–2800)

Tomlinson Square

West of Tomlinson Way, south of Tomlinson Green

See Tomlinson Common.

Road 1997 SW 2:C1 *

Tomlinson Way

North of Tomlinson Common, west of Towne Centre Boulevard

See Tomlinson Common.

Road 1997 SW 2:C1

Tommy Banks Way

102 Street and 86 Avenue

See feature story, page 309.

Road 1999 C 7:C2 *

Tompkins Place

North of Tompkins Way, east of Towne Centre Boulevard

Ottawa-born Peter Tompkins (1863–1940) moved to Winnipeg in 1879 and was employed by the federal Department of Indian Affairs. In 1885, he was captured by Louis Riel, but escaped with the help of Mary Dion, whom he later married. Tompkins later served as a witness at Louis Riel's trial. In 1907, he was transferred to Grouard and was appointed sub-agent for the Dominion Lands. From 1913 to 1923 Tompkins was an agricultural agent. He served as president of the Grouard Board of Trade and was an honorary member of l'Association des Métis and the Alberta and Saskatchewan League of Indians.

Road 1999 SW 2:C1 *

Tompkins Way

East of Terwillegar Vista, south of Tompkins Wynd

See Tompkins Place.

Road 1999 SW 2:C1 *

Tompkins Wynd

West of Towne Centre Boulevard, south of Tufford Way

See Tompkins Place.

Road 1999 SW 2:C1 *

Tory Crescent

North of Tory Road, west of Tory View

Henry Marshall Tory (1864–1947) was the first president of the University of Alberta. Born in Nova Scotia, Tory graduated from McGill University with an undergraduate degree in mathematics in 1890. In 1891 he was appointed lecturer in mathematics and continued with his education, earning a Master of Arts and, in 1903, a PhD in Science. In 1907, Premier A.C. Rutherford offered

Tommy Banks Way

TOMMY BANKS (b. 1936) is a legendary jazz band
leader, known both at home and internationally, and a
member of the Canadian Senate. Banks made his
professional debut in the early 1950s and has gone on
to receive a Juno award, a Gemini award and become
an officer of the Order of Canada. An accomplished
pianist, Banks has performed with a variety of jazz
groups and has appeared at such international venues
as the Montreux Jazz Festival in Switzerland. He has
also been a guest conductor for many of the major
professional orchestras in North America and worked
with such jazz greats as Aretha Franklin, Mel Torme
and Edmonton's own Clarence Horiatio "Big" Miller.
Banks' musical-direction credits include the 1978
Commonwealth Games, the 1983 World University
Games, Expo 1986 and the 1988 Olympic Winter
Games.

He was a founding member of the Alberta
Recording Arts Foundation, now the Alberta
Recording Industry Association, and the founding
chairman of the Alberta Foundation for the Performing
Arts from 1978 to 1986. Banks has served as a member
of the Board of Governors of Alberta College, chair of
the music program at Grant MacEwan Community
College and the Edmonton Concert Hall Foundation,
musical director for Edmonton Musical Theatre and
the Citadel Theatre, and was a member of the Canada
Council between 1989 and 1995. In 1993, Banks was
inducted into the Alberta Order of Excellence.

From 1968 to 1983 the Tommy Banks Big Band was
featured on *The Tommy Banks Show* on CBC Television
and ITV, and was syndicated internationally. In March
of 2003, Banks led his Big Band in its final concert in
Edmonton; Banks announced that he wanted to focus
on politics and the Senate and it was no longer possible
to juggle the responsibilities of managing his
Edmonton-based orchestra and his Senate job in
Ottawa. He and his wife Ida live in Edmonton. The
Yardbird Suite, home of the Edmonton Jazz Society, is
located on Tommy Banks Way.

Tommy Banks at the official opening of City Hall, 1992.
(CEA A.98–17 Envelope 2)

Kingsway at Tower Road, circa 1966. (CEA EA-275-200)

Tory the presidency of the University of Alberta, which was to open in 1908. He acted as president until 1916 when he left to take charge of the Khaki University (a university for Canadian soldiers who had served in WWI) in England. After it closed in 1919, Tory resumed his position at the University of Alberta. In 1923 he was named president of the newly founded Canadian National Research Council. Five years later he resigned from the University of Alberta and moved to Ottawa to devote more time to the council. He retired in 1935 and returned to academic work in 1942 when he became president of the newly established Carleton College. He held this position until his death in 1947.

Road   2000   SW   2:C1

Tory Road

North of 29 Avenue, south of Tegler Gate

See Tory Crescent.

Road   2000   SW   2:C1

Tory View

North of Tory Road, west of 142 Street

See Tory Crescent.

Road   2000   SW   2:C1 *

Touchdown Park

12845–125 Street

This park gained its name from the use of the area for football, the fact that the residents of the Calder neighbourhood felt that they had really scored in getting their parks upgraded through the Neighbourhood Improvement Program, and because of its proximity to the nearby Edmonton Municipal Airport, where planes regularly touched down. Touchdown Park is in the Calder neighbourhood and has an area of 0.49 ha.

Park   1978   NW   7:B1

Tower Road

Kingsway to 113 Avenue and 116 Street

Tower Road first appeared in *Henderson's Directory* in 1950. Its name derives from its proximity to the control tower of the Edmonton Municipal Airport.

Road   CU   NW   7:B1 *

Towne Centre Boulevard

South of Riverbend Road, north of Haddow Drive

The name was chosen by local developers because it was the main entrance roadway to the Terwillegar Towne neighbourhood and because the concept behind Terwillegar Towne was a neotraditional neighbourhood design, making the "towne centre" an important part of the development plan.

Road   1997   SW   2:C1

Tufford Way

Northeast of Tomlinson Common, southwest of Towne Centre Boulevard

C.R. Tufford helped establish the first school in the Town of Jasper Place. He was also one of the first town councillors in Jasper Place.

Road   1998   SW   2:C1

Tukquanow Park

3507–48 Street

Tukquanow is said to be a Woods Cree word referring to "peace, health, prosperity and friendship." Tukquanow Park is in the Minchau neighbourhood and has an area of 0.68 ha.

Park   1983   SE   5:A2

Turner Link

Links Turner Square with Terwillegar Vista

Herbert G. Turner (d. 1963) was a leading member of Edmonton's music community and was active in local labour organizations. He was born in Oxford,

England around 1883, and came to Edmonton in 1907. To begin with, Turner worked as a manual labourer for the city, but by 1913 he had won several awards for his singing, had opened a speech and singing studio, and was employed as chief clerk in the provincial secretary's department. Soon, Turner's involvement in labour organizations saw him become the secretary-manager of the Edmonton Musicians Protective Association, Local 390, a position he held from 1914 until 1963. Over the years he was also on the executive of the Edmonton and District Labour Council, the Edmonton Labour Temple, the Alberta Federation of Labour, and was president of the Alberta Registered Music Teachers' Association and its Edmonton chapter. Turner was active in the Alberta Music Festival early on, serving for many years as the event's secretary. In addition, he participated in many local choirs and musical societies (both singing and directing), produced hit musicals, and organized an orchestra. Among the other groups he actively participated in were the Edmonton Exhibition Association, and the John Howard Society. In 1953, Turner was selected by the Edmonton Junior Chamber of Commerce to receive their annual Citizen of the Year award.

Road   2001   SW   2:C1 *

Turner Square

North of Terwillegar Boulevard, east of Thibault Way

See Turner Link.

Road   2001   SW   2:C1 *

Turvey Bend

West of 156 Street, north of Toane Wynd

Scottish-born Helen Shirlaw Turvey was a prominent performer and creative artist. She came to Canada as a young girl and became an accomplished highland dancer. Turvey took part in dance competitions across the country and was a frequent

Aerial view of Twin Brooks neighbourhood, 1995. (CEA Line 9–191)

winner at the Banff Highland Gathering, a three-day competition attended by competitors from Canada and the United States. Turvey was the recipient of the Governor General's Trophy.

Road 1998 SW 2:C1

Tweddle Place

Mill Woods Road north to Whitemud Drive, 76 Street to 91 Street

Malcolm Tweddle (1906–1977) was a chartered accountant and city commissioner. Born in England, he came to Alberta with his parents in 1910. Tweddle joined the provincial audit department in 1934 and in 1935 moved to Edmonton.

From 1953 until his retirement in 1971, he was Edmonton's finance commissioner.

Neighbourhood 1972 SE 4:C2

Tweedsmuir Crescent

132 Street to 134 Street, south of 102 Avenue

John Buchan, 1st Baron Tweedsmuir (1875–1940), was a WWI veteran, a prolific author and, from 1935 to 1940, governor general of Canada. A member of the British parliament from 1927 to 1935, he came to Edmonton in 1936 to unveil a cenotaph dedicated to the memory of fallen servicemen. In the late 1930s, Buchan worked with Prime Minister Mackenzie King and US President

Roosevelt to promote peace. The name of
Tweedsmuir Crescent first appeared in the
Henderson's Directory in 1942.

Road   CU   SW   7:B2 *

Twin Brooks

*Between Whitemud Creek and Blackmud Creek,
north of 8 Avenue*

The Twin Brooks Area was annexed to the city in
1980. It consisted of the area between Whitemud
Creek and Blackmud Creek and north of the city
boundary. The name Twin Brooks was chosen
because the area lies between two creeks. Later, the
neighbourhoods of Hidden Brook and Running
Creek, formerly within the Twin Brooks Area, were
merged to form the neighbourhood of Twin
Brooks, and use of the name Twin Brooks Area was
discontinued.

Neighbourhood   1980   SW   2:D1

Twin Brooks Bay

Connecting with 115 Street, south of 12 Avenue

See Twin Brooks.

Road   1990   SW   2:D1 *

Twin Brooks Bend

East of 119 Street, north of 15 Avenue

See Twin Brooks.

Road   1990   SW   2:D1 *

Twin Brooks Close

West of 119 Street, south of Twin Brooks Point

See Twin Brooks.

Road   1990   SW   2:D1

Twin Brooks Court

Enclosed by Twin Brooks Close

See Twin Brooks.

Road   1990   SW   2:D1 *

Twin Brooks Cove

East of 116 Street, north of 10 Avenue

See Twin Brooks.

Road   1990   SW   2:D1 *

Twin Brooks Crescent

North of 12 Avenue, west of Twin Brooks Drive

See Twin Brooks.

Road   1990   SW   2:D1 *

Twin Brooks Drive

North of 12 Avenue, west of 111 Street

See Twin Brooks.

Road   1990   SW   2:D1

Twin Brooks Park

11323–12 Avenue

This park is in the Twin Brooks neighbourhood and
has an area of 2.6 ha. *See* Twin Brooks.

Park   1990   SW   2:D1

Twin Brooks Point

North of Twin Brooks Close, west of 119 Street

See Twin Brooks.

Road   1990   SW   2:D1 *

Twin Brooks Way

North of 15 Avenue, east of 119 Street

See Twin Brooks.

Road   1990   SW   2:D1 *

University Avenue, 1938. (CEA EA-88-124)

University Avenue

From Saskatchewan Drive at about 82 Avenue, southeast to Gateway Boulevard at 75 Avenue

At odds with the regular street layout, University Avenue follows the southern boundary of the old Edmonton Settlement, first surveyed in 1880. After passing the University Act of 1906, the Alberta government, led by Premier A.C. Rutherford, decided in 1907 to build the University of Alberta in Strathcona. That same year, the City of Strathcona renamed South Avenue and Hulbert Avenue, the roadways bordering the southerly end of the University of Alberta campus, to University Avenue.

Road 1907 C 4:B1

Uplands, The

Yellowhead Trail north to 137 Avenue, Anthony Henday Drive west to 231 Street

The topography of The Uplands is considered unique in the Edmonton area. The Uplands area sits above a pre-glacial channel of the North Saskatchewan River known as the Beverly Valley and is distinguished by elevated land formations.

Area 1990 NW 8:B1 *

Train at Storyland Valley Zoo, 1968. (CEA EA–20–6581)

Valley Zoo

13315 Buena Vista Road

Edmonton's first zoo opened in Borden Park (then East End Park) in 1909. The present-day Valley Zoo opened in 1959. The original name recommended was William Rowan Zoo, in honour of the former head of the Zoology Department at the University of Alberta. City Council, however, referred the name back to the Names Advisory Committee following its September 3, 1957 meeting, and a new name was chosen through a public contest. The winning name was the Storyland Valley Zoo, reflecting the nursery rhyme characters and exhibits planned for the zoo. In 1975, the word "Storyland" was removed from the zoo's name. The Valley Zoo is located south of the Laurier Heights neighbourhood and has an area of 28.33 ha.

Park 1975 SW 4:A1 *

Valleyview Crescent

South of 89A Avenue, east of 140 Street

This road was named after the former subdivision of Valleyview, which was named in 1956. The name is descriptive.

Road 1958 SW 7:A2

Valleyview Drive

142 Street, from 88 Avenue to 92 Avenue

See Valleyview Crescent.

Road 1958 SW 7:A2

Violet Archer Park

VIOLET BALESTRERI ARCHER (1913–2000) was a celebrated composer and educator. She was born in Quebec to immigrant Italian parents and graduated from McGill University with a bachelor of music degree in 1936 and a master's from Yale University in 1949. Archer performed with the Montreal Women's Orchestra and as a church organist until she began music studies in New York; from 1947 to 1962 she studied and taught in the United States. Among the artists she studied with were the French composer Claude Champagne at McGill University, the celebrated Hungarian composer Béla Bartók and, while at Yale University, the German composer and theorist Paul Hindemith. From 1962 until her retirement in 1978, Archer taught theory and composition at the University of Alberta.

Archer composed some 400 pieces for orchestra, chamber orchestra, piano, organ and voice. These include her *Scherzo Sinfonico*, first performed by the Montreal Symphony Orchestra in 1940; the *Britannia Overture*, performed by the BBC Symphony in Britain; the choral *Cantata Sacra* of 1966; and two one-act operas, *Sganarelle* and *The Meal*, both of which were premiered in Edmonton.

In recognition of Archer's accomplishments, McGill University awarded her an honorary Doctor of Music degree in 1971. In 1984 Archer became a member of the Order of Canada; that same year, she was named Composer of the Year by the Canadian Music Council. In 1985, the Violet Archer Festival was held in Edmonton. It was the first festival to honour a living Canadian composer. She continued to compose well into her eighties. In 1987 Archer was one of the first individuals to be inducted into Edmonton's Cultural Hall of Fame. The Violet Archer Park is in the Parkallen subdivision and has an area of 0.04 ha.

Violet Archer, circa 1950. (UAA 2001–58–99–6–3)

Victoria Park, folk dancing in celebration of Canada's 60th year in Confederation, 1927. (CEA EA-10-757)

Valleyview Point

South of 89A Avenue at Valleyview Drive

This road is the no-exit continuation of Valleyview Drive. *See* Valleyview Crescent.

Road   1958   SW   7:B2

Veterans' Park

10013–102 Street

This park, a triangular area of land at the top of Bellamy Hill road, commemorates Canadian veterans who lost their lives in the service of their country. Before the cenotaph was moved to City Hall in June 1978, Remembrance Day ceremonies were held at this location. Veterans' Park is in the Downtown neighbourhood and has an area of 0.1 ha.

Park   1981   C   7:C2

Victoria Cross Memorial Park

11111–108 Street

This park was previously named Portage Avenue Park. It honours all Alberta recipients of the Victoria Cross. Instituted by Queen Victoria in 1856, the Victoria Cross is the Commonwealth's premier military decoration for gallantry. The Victoria Cross Memorial Park is in the Prince Rupert neighbourhood and has an area of 0.5 ha.

Park   1989   C   7:B1

Victoria Park

12130 River Road

This park is named for Queen Victoria (1819–1901). The majority of this park land was acquired by the City of Edmonton in 1912, at which time it was known as Hudson's Bay Company Flats. Developed as one of Canada's first municipal golf courses, it was renamed to Victoria Park after local women's groups petitioned City Hall to identify the park with a famous woman. Victoria Park Golf Course (formerly known as the Municipal Golf Course) is located within the park. Victoria Park is located south of the Oliver neighbourhood and has an area of 111.67 ha.

Park 1916 C 7:B2

Victoria Park Road

116 Street at 100 Avenue, west to Groat Road

Victoria Park Road runs adjacent to the north side of Victoria Park. Maps dating from 1953 show a Victoria Park Road running parallel to the North Saskatchewan River on the south side. In 1958, however, this road was officially named River Park Road. By the 1960s the road leading down to the valley from 116 Street and 100 Avenue had been constructed, and was known as Victoria Park Road. *See* Victoria Park.

Road CU C 7:B2

Victoria Promenade

Portion of Heritage Trail on 100 Avenue, between 117 Street and 121 Street

This name was recommended for one of a series of promenades and lookouts built along the edge of the river valley. It overlooks Victoria Park. *See* Victoria Park.

Walkway 1989 C 7:B2 *

Victoria Trail

118 Avenue at 129 Street to 153 Avenue at 127 Street

The name Victoria Trail is a 1972 reinstatement of a historical name. This roadway led northeast from Fort Edmonton to the Victoria Settlement

(renamed Pakan, after the Cree chief), where the first mission site was established by the Methodist Rev. George McDougall in the 1860s.

Road CU NE 11:B2

Villa Avenue

South of 104 Avenue between 126 Street and 127 Street

Villa Avenue was developed around 1909. The land on which the roadway is located was originally owned by Malcolm Groat. In 1905 the land was sold to James Carruthers and subdivided. This road was named to appeal to wealthier Edmontonians; a villa is a country house.

Road CU NW 7:B2

Violet Archer Park

10920–70 Avenue

See feature story, page 319.

Park 1985 SW 4:B1

Virginia Park

Ada Boulevard and Kinnaird Ravine north to Borden Park Road, Wayne Gretzky Drive west to 79 Street

Developed during Edmonton's pre-WWI land boom, the Virginia Park neighbourhood includes Borden Park, Concordia College and part of Ada Boulevard. The former Virginia Park Greenhouse, established in 1912, was also located here, at 7534–110 Street. The greenhouse was bought by Marius Granstrom in 1928 and family members continued to run the business from its original location until 1981, when it was moved to Ellerslie Road and 111 Street.

Neighbourhood CU NE 7:D1

W.C. "Tubby" Bateman Park

9703–88 Avenue

Weldon C. "Tubby" Bateman (1906–1990) was the founder of the Bateman's stores in Edmonton. Born in Fredericton, New Brunswick, Bateman came to Edmonton with his family at the age of seven and settled in the vicinity of 99 Street and 91 Avenue. As a boy, Bateman supplemented the family income by delivering newspapers and groceries, raising chickens, rabbits and pigeons, and peddling eggs. At the age of 15 he dropped out of school to work as a delivery boy for a butcher shop. Bateman apprenticed in the trade, and in 1928 opened his own meat market in Edson. The business went bankrupt a year later and Bateman returned to Edmonton. In 1932 he started the Bateman Meat Market. Initially a modest shop, it eventually flourished to become the third-largest retail food chain in western Canada. Bateman was a member of several organizations, including the Rotary Club and the Chamber of Commerce. The W.C. "Tubby" Bateman Park is in the Strathcona neighbourhood and has an area of 0.18 ha.

Park   1987   SE   7:C2

W.E. Werner Park

11248–35 Avenue

William E. Werner (1877–1964) was an alderman and life-time member of the South Side Businessmen's Association. Ontario-born Werner was the brother of pioneer hardware merchant J.A. Werner and came to Edmonton in 1913. He established Werner's Hardware on the south side, which he ran until his retirement in 1945. Werner served as an alderman in 1925 and 1926 and was a president of the South Side Businessmen's Association and a life-time member of the Masonic Order. The W.E. Werner Park is directly east of J.A. Werner Park in the Greenfield neighbourhood and has an area of 0.66 ha.

Park   1984   SW   4:B2

W.P. Wagner Park

6204 Wagner Road

The W.P. Wagner Park is in the McIntyre Industrial neighbourhood and has an area of 3.06 ha. The park is adjacent to W.P. Wagner High School. *See* Wagner Road.

Park   1982   SE   4:D1

Wadhurst Road

West of 124 Street to 104 Avenue

This road first appears in the *Henderson's Directory* in 1912. Two of the first residences along the street were owned by Mr. and Mrs. Ben Hurst. The street is said to have been named after the Hursts' hometown of Wadhurst, England. Wadhurst, a village in Sussex, received its charter from King Henry III in 1253. The origin of the name Wadhurst, however, is much earlier as Wadhurst is a Saxon name, meaning "Wada's hurst" or "wood."

Road   CU   NW   7:B2 *

Wagner Road

Connecting 86 Street and 75 Street at 61 Avenue

William P. Wagner (1899–1986) was a veteran of both world wars, an educator and superintendent of the Edmonton Public School Board. Wagner began his teaching career in 1916 and left teaching during WWI to serve in the Royal Flying Corps. After the war, he was the principal of schools in the towns of Mannville, Provost and Viking. In 1929 Wagner took a teaching position at Strathcona High School. During the 1930s he took university courses while also teaching night school. In 1942 Wagner enlisted in the Canadian Army and served for four years. He returned to Edmonton and worked for the Edmonton Public School Board for the next 18 years, becoming superintendent in 1955. He retired in 1964.

Originally named Davies Road by the Names Advisory Committee, this road was renamed Wagner Road because it was adjacent to the W.P. Wagner Industrial Trade School (now called the W. P. Wagner High School). The roadway at 86 Street and 58 Avenue to Wagner Road was renamed Davies Road.

Road   1966   SE   4:D1

Wahstao Crescent

West of Wahstao Road, north of Walker Road

Wahstao is said to be the Cree word for "spiritual light." Wahstao, located northeast of Edmonton, was the site of one of the first Methodist schools in the area. From 1907 until 1957 there was a Wahstao post office, but over time the area depopulated and the name disappeared.

Road   1977   SW   3:C1 *

Wahstao Road

North of Walker Road, east of 170 Street

See Wahstao Crescent.

Road   1977   SW   3:C1 *

Wakina Road

Connecting with Wanyandi Road, south of Wolf Willow Road

Wakina is a variation of the Cree word meaning "to bend." Wakina Road is a scenic roadway that curves along the Wolf Willow Ravine.

Road   1977   SW   3:C1

Walker Road

Connecting with Wanyandi Road, east of 170 Street, south of Wolf Willow Road

Ella Mac Walker (1892–1960) was an author, musician and artist. Born in Minnesota, Walker was educated at the University of Saskatchewan and McGill University. In 1920 she and her husband, O. J. Walker, a professor of chemistry, moved to Edmonton. Over the next 40 years in Edmonton, Walker participated in a variety of women's clubs and music clubs. She was also interested in local history and wrote *Fortress North*, a historical novel set in Edmonton. Her paintings featured local and regional scenes, including the Edmonton Municipal Airport, Fort Edmonton, the John Walter House, a prairie fire, and settlers in Red River carts. Walker's paintings are in the permanent collections of the City of Edmonton Archives and the Edmonton Art Gallery.

Road   1977   SW   3:C1

Wallace (Wally) McSween Park

8703–75 Avenue

Wallace "Wally" McSween (1922–1996) was a WWII pilot, a lawyer and an actor. Born in Drumheller, McSween moved to Calgary in 1939. There he joined the Calgary Highlanders as a piper in the militia's band. In 1942, he enlisted in the Royal Canadian Air Force; he then spent the next two years as a pilot with Bomber Command. Following the war, he returned to Calgary, completed high school and moved to Edmonton to attend the University of Alberta. McSween completed an undergraduate degree in 1950 and a law degree in 1954; in 1955 he was admitted to the Alberta Bar. Although he was a successful lawyer, McSween eventually left the profession to become an actor. His stage work spanned four decades, including productions in Edmonton, Calgary and British Columbia. Throughout his career, McSween and his wife lived in the Avonmore neighbourhood where they had raised their three children. This park is located in the Avonmore neighbourhood and has an area of 0.17 ha.

Park   1999   SE   4:C1 *

Wallbridge Place

North of Wanyandi Road, east of Walker Road

James Emberly Wallbridge (1875–1945) was an early and prominent Edmonton lawyer. Born in Belleville, Ontario, Wallbridge attended the University of Toronto where he received his BA degree in 1897, and graduated in law from Osgoode Hall. In 1902, he came to Edmonton and was called to the bar of the North-West Territories. In 1913, Wallbridge was appointed King's Counsel, and later became a senior partner with the firm of Wallbridge, Cairns & Company.

Road   1984   SW   3:C1 *

Walsh Crescent

North of Wolf Willow Road, east of 170 Street

W. L. Walsh (1857–1938) was the lieutenant-governor of Alberta from 1931 to 1935. Walsh was born in Simcoe, Canada West, and practised law in Ontario for three years before moving to Dawson City, Yukon, in 1900. In 1904 Walsh moved to Calgary and became senior partner in the firm of Walsh, McCarthy & Carson. He was appointed King's Counsel in 1903 and as an Alberta Supreme Court judge in 1912.

Road   1981   SW   3:C1 *

Walter Polley Park

North of 89 Avenue, east of 101 Street

For 40 years, Walter Polley (1887–1993) lived in the King Edward Park neighbourhood and worked for the Edmonton City Dairy. Polley was born in England and immigrated to Edmonton in 1913. The Walter Polley Park is in the Strathcona neighbourhood and has an area of 0.15 ha.

Park   1994   C   7:C2 *

Walterdale Bridge

Spanning the North Saskatchewan River connecting 105 Street and Walterdale Hill Road

See feature story, page 327.

Bridge   1967   C   7:C2

Walterdale Hill Road

109 Street and Saskatchewan Drive, 106 Street and 90 Avenue

Walterdale Hill Road, running from the south end of Walterdale Bridge to 109 Street at 88 Avenue, was first paved in 1948. *See* Walterdale Bridge *feature story, page 327.*

Road   1975   C   7:B2

Wanyandi Road

Continuation of Callingwood Road east of 170 Street, north to Wolf Willow Road

The Wanyandi family was part of a group of Iroquois voyageurs who moved to Smoky River Country to trap furs for the North West Company and the Hudson's Bay Company in the 1820s. In 1910, Vincent Wanyandi was the last full-blooded Iroquois in Smoky River Country. Daniel Wanyandi (b. 1890) continued the family tradition of trapping and lived and worked in the area until his death in 1974.

Road   1989   SW   3:C1

Wanyandi Way

East of Wanyandi Road, north of Country Club Point

See Wanyandi Road.

Road   1989   SW   3:C1 *

Ward Crescent

West of 23 Street, north of 37B Avenue

Maxwell "Max" William Ward (b. 1921) is a WWII veteran, a well-known pilot and the founder of two charter airlines. He joined the Royal Canadian Air Force in 1940 and served as a commissioned flight instructor. After the war, Ward worked as a bush pilot in Yellowknife and started an airline, the Polaris Charter Company. In 1953, he founded a

Walterdale Bridge

THIS BRIDGE, completed in 1913, was originally named 105 Street Bridge. It was renamed in 1967 in honour of John Walter (1850–1920), an Edmonton businessman and pioneer who strung the first ferry cable across the North Saskatchewan River at Fort Edmonton, in the same area where the bridge is now located.

John Walter arrived in Fort Edmonton a penniless boat builder and went on to become one of the region's most successful entrepreneurs and the emerging city's first millionaire. Born in the Scottish Orkney Islands, Walter came to Edmonton in 1870 to work for the Hudson's Bay Company (HBC), building York boats for traffic on the North Saskatchewan River.

Under the terms of his employment, Walter was under contract to the HBC for a five-year period. At the end of that term, he left the HBC and went into business for himself. Walter settled on the south side of the North Saskatchewan River, across from Fort Edmonton, in what became known as Walterdale. He was the first settler to own property on the south bank. His simple log home would later house Edmonton's first telegraph office.

Walter set up many ventures, including carpentry and boat building, a sawmill and lumberyard and a cable ferry called *The Belle of Edmonton*, launched in 1882. Walter also built a sternwheeler, the *City of Edmonton*, launched in 1907, and a side-wheeler, the *City of Strathcona*, which was later converted to a stern-wheeler. His boat works constructed ferries and steamers used throughout the northwest. His many businesses, as well as his land holdings, made Walter a wealthy man; his worth at one time was estimated at $1 million.

Completion of the High Level Bridge in 1913, ending the need for regular ferry service across the river, had a dramatic impact on Walter's business. Two years later, in 1915, the North Saskatchewan River flooded and wiped out both of his sawmills, leaving him in financial ruin. At its height, Walter's sawmill operation cut 16 million board feet a year.

The name Walterdale has been in use since around 1907, was officially approved in 1969 and is no longer in use. At the turn of the 20th century the Walterdale district, bounded by 109 Street and the North Saskatchewan River, represented the heart of the region's industry. Hundreds of men were employed to work in the area's coal mine, sash and door plant, tannery and brickyard, as well as Walter's two sawmills. Walterdale's industries flourished until the flood of 1915. The riverside plants destroyed by the rising waters were never rebuilt.

Walterdale, looking north, circa 1912. (CEA EA-10-279)

Max Ward, 1978. (CEA EA-340-1947)

second airline, Wardair. By 1989, when Ward sold his Edmonton-based airline to Canadian Airlines International, it had become Wardair International. He was inducted into the Canadian Aviation Hall of Fame in 1974, was made an officer of the Order of Canada in 1975, and inducted into the Northern Alberta Business Hall of Fame in 1991.

Road   1999   SE   5:B2

Warwick

137 Avenue to 153 Avenue, Castle Downs Road west to 127 Street

The Warwick subdivision in the Castle Downs area is named after a castle in England. Warwick Castle was founded in 1068 by William I, the Conqueror, on the River Avon. Although the castle was Norman in origin, much of the present-day ruins were built in the 14th century. The subdivision's name reflects the theme of the Castle Downs area, with subdivisions and neighbourhoods being named after famous castles.

Subdivision   1972   NW   10:B2 *

Warwick Crescent

Connecting with Warwick Road; east of 127 Street, south of 167 Avenue

See Warwick.

Road   1978   NW   10:B1

Warwick Road

South of Dunluce Road, east of 127 Street, west of 116 Street

See Warwick.

Road   1983   NW   10:B1

Waygood Road

North of Wahstao Road, east of 170 Street

Barney Penry Waygood (d. 1999) was the fire chief of the Town of Jasper Place from 1958 to 1964. He was born in Swansea, South Wales, and graduated from the University of Edinburgh after studying fire engineering in 1938. Waygood enlisted in the British Army and served with the 13th Demi-Brigade French Foreign Legion at Dunkirk and in Abyssinia (Ethiopia), the Middle East, North Africa and Italy. He received several decorations, including the Médaille Militaire, the Croix de Guerre, Croix de la Résistance and Croix de Libération. After WWII, he returned to Swansea where he joined the National Fire Service, attaining the rank of district chief in 1954. In 1958 he immigrated to Edmonton and was appointed fire chief of Jasper Place. In 1964, when Jasper Place was amalgamated with Edmonton, Waygood was transferred to the City of Edmonton Fire Department. He served in various districts until retiring at the rank of district chief in 1977.

Road   1985   SW   3:C1 *

Wayne Gretzky, left, and Paul Coffey with the Stanley Cup, 1985. (Photo courtesy Edmonton Sun)

Wayne Gretzky Drive

South from Yellowhead Trail at Fort Road to 101 Avenue

Wayne Gretzky (b. 1961), known as "The Great One," is considered one of the most outstanding hockey players ever to play the game. After retiring from professional hockey in 1999, he was named executive director of Team Canada, the Canadian men's Olympic hockey team. Gretzky put together the players who went on to win a gold medal in the 2002 Winter Olympics in Salt Lake City, ending a 50-year drought in Canadian attempts to win the top prize in Olympic hockey. In July 2003, he was a member of the Vancouver Olympic bid team that

travelled to Prague to make a final presentation to the International Olympic Committee in support of the ultimately successful Canadian campaign to host the 2010 Winter Olympics.

From 1978 to 1988, Gretzky played for the Edmonton Oilers hockey team. During Gretzky's tenure with the Oilers, the team won four Stanley Cups, forever earning him a place in the hearts of Edmontonians. The trade of Gretzky—No. 99—to the Los Angeles Kings by Oilers' owner Peter Pocklington in 1988 was greeted with outrage by loyal Oilers fans. The draw of the hockey legend, then only 27 years old, in the United States, however, spurred National Hockey League expansion in warm-weather markets like Phoenix, Miami and Raleigh, North Carolina. Since his departure from Edmonton, he and his wife, Janet Jones, and their four children, have lived in the United States. During his 20-year career in the National Hockey League, Gretzky scored 894 goals and had 1,963 assists. He holds or shares 61 records listed in the NHL's Official Guide and Record Book. Gretzky received the Order of Canada in 1984 and was inducted into the Hockey Hall of Fame in 1998. Wayne Gretzky Drive was formerly known as Capilano Road (1967), Capilano Freeway (1974) and Capilano Drive (1995). The Capilano Bridge carries Wayne Gretzky Drive across the North Saskatchewan River.

Road 1999 NE 7:D1

Weaver Drive

East of Wedgewood Boulevard, south of 23 Avenue

Liverpool-born Col. Charles Yardley Weaver (1884–1930) came to Alberta in 1903 and went on to become a prominent lawyer and alderman. After working as a farm hand for two years, he claimed his own homestead near Mannville. Weaver later studied law at the University of Alberta and was called to the Alberta Bar in 1915. In 1909 he joined the 101st Edmonton Fusiliers (militia) as a private and quickly advanced through the ranks, becoming a major in the 49th Battalion (Edmonton Regiment), CEF, in 1914 and acting lieutenant-colonel in 1918. While serving overseas in WWI, Weaver was wounded three times and awarded the Distinguished Service Order in 1918. The following year he was made lieutenant-colonel of the 19th Alberta Dragoons and rose to the rank of colonel, commanding the 5th Mounted Brigade. Following the war, Weaver served as an alderman in 1921 and 1922.

Road 1988 SW 3:C2

Weaver Point

West of 184 Street, south of Weaver Drive

See Weaver Drive.

Road 1988 SW 3:C2 *

Webber Greens

Approximately 95 Avenue north to Stony Plain Road, 199 Street west to Winterburn Road

George Alfred Webber (d. 1929) and his family raised Hereford cattle and lived in the Winterburn district in the early 1900s. Webber became a councillor of the district in 1912. In 1918, the family moved to Edmonton and the land was rented. They returned to the area in 1922, buying a farm near the Splan School (established in 1898), of which Webber was a trustee for several years. After George's death in 1929, the family continued to live on the farm until 1932, when it was sold to E.R. Lewis. Neighbourhoods in the Lewis Farms area are named after early pioneers, while the word "Greens" reflects the area's association with a local golf course.

Neighbourhood 2000 SW 8:B2 *

Weber Close

South of 23 Avenue, west of 184 Street

L.A. Weber (b. 1887) and N. Roy Weber (1890–1936) were the founders of the real estate company Weber Brothers. They were born in Ontario and moved to Alberta in 1911, where both brothers opened real estate offices: L.A. Weber in Edmonton and N. Roy Weber in Calgary. In 1915, N. Roy joined his older brother in Edmonton and formed Weber Brothers. N. Roy later founded the Weber Brothers Agencies Ltd. and the Edmonton Credit Company, of which he was managing director and his brother, L.A. Weber, the manager.

Road 1988 SW 3:C2 *

Weber Gate

Southeast of Weber Way, northwest of Wedgewood Boulevard, west of 14 Street

See Weber Close.

Road   1988   SW   3:C2 *

Weber Place

West of Weber Close, north of Weber Way

See Weber Close.

Road   1988   SW   3:C2 *

Weber Way

South of 23 Avenue, west of 184 Street

See Weber Close.

Road   1988   SW   3:C2

Wedgewood Boulevard

South of Lessard Road, west of 184 Street

See Wedgewood Heights.

Road   1988   SW   3:C2

Wedgewood Crescent

131 Street and 102 Avenue

This roadway has existed since the 1960s but the name was made official in 1988. *See* Wedgewood Heights.

Road   1988   SW   3:C2

Wedgewood Heights

Wedgewood Ravine north to Lessard Road, and west to proposed outer ring road

Development of this neighbourhood in the Lessard subdivision began in the 1960s; most of the homes, however, were built in the 1980s. Wedgewood Ravine borders the Wedgewood Heights neighbourhood to the south and east. With the name Wedgewood Crescent already established through local usage, it was adopted as the neighbourhood name. Local roads in the Wedgewood Heights neighbourhood honour prominent Edmontonians whose surnames start with "We," including Dr. Robert B. Wells, Walter Roger Wells, William Alexander Wells and Col. Charles Yardley Weaver. The origin of the name Wedgewood Heights is not recorded.

Neighbourhood   1980   SW   3:C2

Wedgewood Heights Park

4304–184 Street

This park is in the Wedgewood Heights neighbourhood and has an area of 1.1 ha. *See* Wedgewood Heights.

Park   1990   SW   3:C2

Wedgewood Ravine

Separating the Wedgewood Heights and Donsdale neighbourhoods; east of 45 Avenue and 184 Street, and east of city limits at 23 Avenue

This name was in common usage for many years before its official adoption in 1980. *See* Wedgewood Heights.

Ravine   1980   SW   3:C2 *

Weinlos

23 Avenue to 34 Avenue, Mill Woods Road East west to 50 Street

Romanian-born Dr. Morris Weinlos (1902–1980) and Dr. Harry Weinlos (d. 1977) were prominent surgeons and active members of the Edmonton arts and humanitarian communities. The brothers immigrated to Canada in 1921. Harry practised medicine in Edmonton from 1932. Morris earned a BA from the University of Alberta in 1926 and a master's degree in surgery in Pennsylvania. In 1939 he became a member of the Royal College of

Police Commissioner's Board, Morris Weinlos, second from left, 1966. (CEA EA-10-2338)

Physicians and Surgeons. That same year, the brothers enlisted in WWII and served as majors in the medical corps.

Following the war, they returned to Edmonton and resumed their medical careers. Harry was senior surgeon at the Misericordia Hospital and the physician for the Home for Ex-Servicemen's Children. Morris founded, in 1957, the Weinlos Clinic; served as a clinical professor of surgery and pathology at the University of Alberta; and was chief of surgery and staff at Misericordia Hospital until his retirement in 1967. He also served on City Council for 11 years (1960–1971). Morris was on the boards of the Edmonton Exhibition Association, the Edmonton Symphony Society and the University of Alberta Hospital, and served as president of the John Howard Society, United Way and the Zionist Council of Edmonton. Harry was a member of the Junior Chamber of Commerce and the Alberta Red Cross, and on the boards of the United Way and Community Chest. In 1960, Harry received an Outstanding Citizenship Award.

Neighbourhood   1976   SE   5:A2

Weinlos Park

3103–48 Street

This park is in the Weinlos neighbourhood and has an area of 2.04 ha. Weinlos Park is adjacent to Weinlos Elementary School. *See* Weinlos.

Park   1987   SE   5:A2

Weir Industrial

CN railway tracks north to Sherwood Park Freeway, 34 Street to 50 Street

James White Weir was a pioneer boat builder, and has been credited as being the originator of the use of skis on light aircraft for winter landing conditions in remote areas. Weir's wooden boats were used on the North Saskatchewan River and helped open the north to trade and settlement. Northern bush pilots and the Royal Canadian Mounted Police used his skis and sleds to reach distant northern communities.

Neighbourhood   1974   SE   5:A1

Welbourn Cove

West of Wershof Road, south of Wellwood Way

George James Welbourn (1859–1942) and Annie Jean Welbourn (1860–1957) were pioneer residents in the Winterburn area. Annie Jean was born in Galt, Canada West, but in 1865 her family returned to their native Scotland. At the age of 16, Annie came back to Canada where she taught school in Oshawa, Ontario, until 1886. That year she resigned her post to marry a colleague, George Welbourn. Together they moved to Alberta in 1891 and established a Methodist mission at the Aboriginal reserve close to Winterburn; George served as superintendent of the reserve school. In 1893, however, the federal government decreed that all Aboriginal children living in the area were required to attend school in Regina, Saskatchewan, forcing the closure of the school in Winterburn.

George and Annie then moved to Edmonton where George became the principal of McKay Avenue School. During the same period, the Welbourns started a farm in the Winterburn area. In 1899 George resigned his teaching post to farm full time. The couple remained in Winterburn until 1942, when they retired and moved to Edmonton. George was a member of the Public School Board, a life member of the Northern Alberta Pioneers and Old Timers' Association, and was active in the Winterburn United Church. Annie was a Red Cross

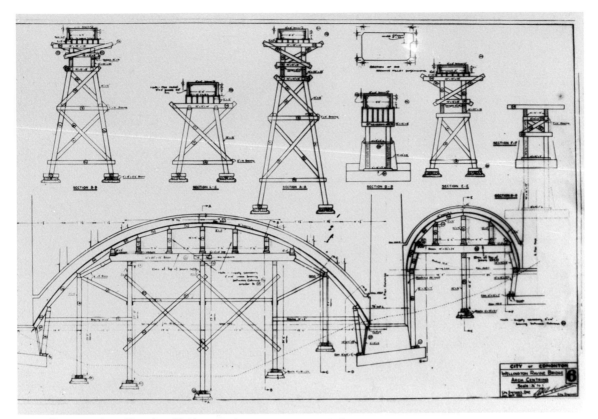

Wellington Ravine Bridge, plan of bridge centering, 1932. (CEA EA–75–838)

volunteer during both world wars and was a charter member and the first president of the Winterburn Women's Institute.

Road 1990 SW 3:C2 *

Welbourn Drive

West of Wershof Road, south of Wellwood Way

See Welbourn Cove.

Road 1990 SW 3:C2 *

Welbourn Lane

West of Wershof Road, south of Wellwood Way

See Welbourn Cove.

Road 1990 SW 3:C2 *

Wellington

132 Avenue to 137 Avenue, 127 Street to 142 Street

This area may take its name from Arthur Wellesley (1769–1852), 1st Duke of Wellington, who led the British victory over Napoleon at the Battle of Waterloo in 1814. Wellesley was knighted in 1805 and became the first Duke of Wellington in 1814. He served as prime minister from 1828 to 1839. Wellington Park, as the area was once called, has been named since at least 1910 and was annexed to Edmonton in 1913. However, much of the development in Wellington did not take place until the 1950s and 1960s. At the time of Wellington's naming, Wellington Park was one of the existing subdivision names in the area and the Edmonton

Public School Board was planning to use the name for a local school.

Neighbourhood 1956 NW 10:A2

Wellington Crescent

131 Street to 102 Avenue

Wellington Crescent, located in the Glenora neighbourhood, has existed since about 1912. It may have been named for Arthur Wellesley, 1st Duke of Wellington. Other road names in the neighbourhood follow a patriotic British theme, including St. George's Crescent and Connaught Drive. Originally, there was also a Victoria Crescent and a King's Road, but they no longer exist. *See* Wellington.

Road CU SW 7:B2

Wellington Park

13315–137 Street

This park is in the Wellington neighbourhood and has an area of 2.59 ha. *See* Wellington.

Park 1967 NW 10:A2

Wellington Ravine

South of 104 Avenue at 131 Street

This ravine was likely named for its proximity to Wellington Crescent. *See* Wellington Crescent.

Ravine CU SW 7:B2 *

Wellington Ravine Bridge

Spanning the Wellington Ravine at 102 Avenue

This reinforced concrete bridge was opened in 1932. *See* Wellington Ravine.

Bridge CU NW 7:B2

Wells Gate

Connecting Wells Wynd and Wedgewood Boulevard

Wells Gate is named in honour of Dr. Robert B. Wells, Walter Roger Wells and William A. Wells, three pioneers who contributed to the development of Edmonton. Dr. Robert B. Wells (b. 1867) was born in Ontario and received his medical degree from the University of Toronto in 1894. After completing postgraduate work in New York City, he opened an office in Delhi, Ontario, where he practised until 1906. That year he came to Edmonton where he specialized in eye, ear, nose and throat diseases. Robert was a member and vice-president of the Alberta Division of the Canadian Medical Association, a member of the Canadian Medical Association and a fellow of the American College of Surgeons.

Walter Roger Wells (1881–1949) was born in Nova Scotia and came to Edmonton prior to WWI. Some years after his arrival, he took over a butchers' supply firm and later expanded his business to include two meat stores and a cigar store. He retired in 1947. Walter was an ardent boxing and wrestling fan and played a major role in promoting professional boxing in Edmonton.

William Alexander Wells (b. 1884) was born in Nova Scotia and attended St. Francis Xavier University in Antigonish. He graduated in 1906 and came to Edmonton in 1908. After completing his law studies at the University of Alberta, he was admitted to the Alberta Bar in 1913 and was later associated with E. B. Cogswell, a crown prosecutor. In 1916 William enlisted as a private in the 218th Battalion, later becoming a lieutenant, and was sent overseas to serve in WWI in 1917. Following his return in 1919, William formed a partnership with John C. McDonald and A.G. McKay that lasted until 1927. He then left Edmonton to serve as a special supreme agent of the Knights of Columbus, a Roman Catholic fraternal service organization, lecturing throughout Canada and the United States.

Road 1989 SW 3:C2 *

Wells Wynd

South of 23 Avenue, west of Wedgewood Boulevard

See Wells Gate.

Road 1989 SW 3:C2

Wellwood Way

South of Wedgewood Boulevard, west of Wershof Road

Elleda Perley Wellwood (1879–1962) was a singer and music teacher and general secretary of the Young Women's Christian Association (YWCA) in Edmonton. Born and educated in Ontario, Wellwood began her music career after receiving her Associate of the Toronto Conservatory of Music in voice. In 1910, she married and moved west with her husband, who was a physician. After her husband's death in 1920, she came to Edmonton to teach voice and later took the position of music teacher and dean at a school for the children of missionaries. In 1930 she became general secretary of the YWCA in Edmonton. For the next 15 years, Wellwood assisted young women who came to Edmonton in search of employment. She also served as president of the Local and Provincial Council of Women, the Edmonton Soroptimist Club, the Women's Musical Club and the Women's Christian Temperance Union.

Road 1989 SW 3:C2 *

Wershof Road

South of Wedgewood Boulevard, east of Weaver Drive

Lithuanian-born Dr. Eli Wershof (1894–1973) was a veteran of WWI and Edmonton's first Jewish doctor. He came to Canada with his family in 1905 and in 1917 graduated from the University of Manitoba with a medical degree. In 1921, after serving in WWI, Wershof came to Edmonton and opened a medical practice. He was a member of the Edmonton Academy of Medicine and the St. John Ambulance Association, vice-president of the Zionist Organization of Canada and the first president of the Edmonton Zionist Council.

Road 1989 SW 3:C2

West Jasper Place

95 Avenue north to Stony Plain Road, 149 Street to 156 Street

This neighbourhood is located in what used to be the Town of Jasper Place. The area was homesteaded in 1876 by Henry Goodridge, a farmer and Edmonton town councillor in 1901–1902. The subdivision of West Jasper Place was developed and named around 1910 by Watson & Company, a real estate, loans and insurance firm. After becoming the village of West Jasper Place in December 1949, its name was changed to Jasper Place in March 1950. In November of that same year, the community was incorporated as the Town of Jasper Place, and in 1964 it was annexed by the City of Edmonton. The area previously encompassed by the town of Jasper Place became the neighbourhoods of Britannia Youngstown, Canora, Elmwood, Glenwood, High Park, High Park Industrial, Huff Bremner Estate Industrial, Lynnwood, Meadowlark Park, Rio Terrace, Sheffield Industrial, Sherwood, Stone Industrial, West Jasper Place, West Meadowlark Park, West Sheffield Industrial, Westlawn (now part of Glenwood) and Youngstown Industrial.

Neighbourhood CU SW 8:D2

West Meadowlark Park

87 Avenue to 95 Avenue, 163 Street to 170 Street

The West Meadowlark Park neighbourhood was originally part of the Town of Jasper Place and was annexed to Edmonton with the town in 1964. Development of West Meadowlark Park began in the 1960s. *See* Meadowlark Park *neighbourhood.*

Neighbourhood CU SW 8:C2

West Sheffield Industrial

109 Avenue to 114 Avenue, 163 Street to
170 Street

Once a neighbourhood located in the Town of
Jasper Place, West Sheffield Industrial was annexed
to Edmonton, along with the rest of Jasper Place, in
1964. The name of West Sheffield predates the
annexation. The area was zoned for industrial use
around 1963, and a development agreement
between Frances Development Ltd. and the Town
of Jasper Place was signed in February of 1964. It
was named West Sheffield Industrial because it is
located to the west of Sheffield Industrial. *See*
Sheffield Industrial.

Neighbourhood   CU   NW   8:C1

Westbrook Drive

119 Street to 30 Avenue

See Westbrook Estates.

Road   1962   SW   4:B2

Westbrook Estates

Westbrook Drive north to 39 Avenue, 119 Street
west to Whitemud Park

This neighbourhood was named Westbrook Estates
by developers because Whitemud Creek, which
could also be called a brook, meanders past to the
west of it. The word "Estates" was used because of
the area's large lots, some 0.2 ha. in size. The land
on which Westbrook Estates is located was annexed
to the City of Edmonton in 1960 and most of the
houses in the neighbourhood were built during the
1960s.

Neighbourhood   1962   SW   4:B2

Westbrook Park

12015–39A Avenue

This park is in the Aspen Gardens neighbourhood
and has an area of 3.33 ha. *See* Westbrook Estates.

Park   1983   SW   4:B2

Westclare Wynd

Manning Drive and 141 Avenue northeast to
144 Avenue and 43 Street

This winding roadway proceeds to the northeast
from Manning Drive to 144 Avenue. The origin of
the name Westclare Wynd is not recorded.

Road   1980   NE   11:A2 *

Westmount

Jasper Avenue north to 111 Avenue, 122 and
124 Streets west to Groat Road

Westmount, one of the oldest areas in Edmonton,
may have been named for a Montreal neighbourhood of the same name. Malcolm Groat settled here
in 1878. In the early 1900s, Groat sold his land and
Westmount was quickly developed. Most of the
area's homes were built around 1910. Marketed
towards young professionals, the Westmount
neighbourhood was a popular location because of
its proximity to downtown Edmonton. Beginning
in 1910, residents could easily travel to and from
downtown on the electric streetcar that ran from
Jasper Avenue to 110 Avenue via 124 Street. The
portion of Westmount located from 107 Avenue to
111 Avenue and 124 Street to 127 Street has also
been known as West Ingle; the first settlers here
were Malcolm Groat and John Norris.

Neighbourhood   CU   NW   7:B1

Westmount Park

10970–127 Street

This park is in the Westmount neighbourhood and has an area of 1.56 ha. The Westmount Community League building is located here. *See* Westmount.

Park 1982 NW 7:B1

Westridge

Wolf Willow Ravine north to Patricia Ravine, east of 170 Street

The neighbourhood of Westridge, developed in the 1970s, extends into the river valley. Prior to residential development, the area was home for 35 years to Wolf Willow Farm. Because of this, all street names in Westridge begin with the letter "W," many names beginning with the words "wolf" or "willow."

Neighbourhood 1969 SW 3:C1

Westridge Crescent

North and east of Westridge Road

See Westridge.

Road 1973 SW 3:C1 *

Westridge Park

505 Wolf Willow Road

This park is in the Westridge neighbourhood and has an area of 5.36 ha. *See* Westridge.

Park 1981 SW 3:C1

Westridge Road

Connecting with Wolf Willow Road, south of Whitemud Drive, east of 170 Street

See Westridge.

Road 1973 SW 3:C1

Westwood

118 Avenue north to Yellowhead Trail, 97 Street to 107 Street

The Westwood area was annexed by Edmonton in 1910 and remained largely rural until after WWII, when it underwent large-scale development. The northern portion of Westwood was once called Northcote.

Neighbourhood CU NW 7:C1

Westwood Park

12139–105 Street

The park is located within the Westwood neighbourhood and has an area of 0.35 ha. *See* Westwood.

Park 1983 NW 7:C1

Wheeler Place

East of Wheeler Road West, south of Wilkin Way

Dr. Benjamin M. Wheeler (1910–1963) was a WWII veteran and an Officer of the Order of the British Empire. He was born in Quebec and came to Edgerton, Alberta, with his parents in 1918. After graduating from the University of Alberta in 1935, he studied medicine in London, England, and then served in India with the Indian Medical Service. During WWII he was captured in Malaya and held prisoner in Formosa (Taiwan) by Japanese forces. He spent the next four years as a prisoner of war, serving as the doctor for a forced-labour mining camp. Following the war, Wheeler joined the Baker Clinic in Edmonton in 1946. In 1947 he was named an Officer of the Order of the British Empire. Wheeler was the founding president of the Alberta Society of Internists and an executive member of the Academy of Medicine. Wheeler's daughter is the filmmaker Anne Wheeler; she recreated his POW experiences in her film *A War Story*.

Road 1984 SW 3:C1 *

Wheeler Road West

East of 170 Street, south of Wanyandi Road

There is no Wheeler Road East. *See* Wheeler Place.

Road   1988   SW   3:C1

Whiston Bay

East of Whiston Road, south of Wanyandi Road

See Whiston Wynd.

Road   1988   SW   3:C1 *

Whiston Close

North of Whiston Road, east of Wheeler Road West

See Whiston Wynd.

Road   1988   SW   3:C1 *

Whiston Court

North of Whiston Road, west of Wanyandi Road

See Whiston Wynd.

Road   1988   SW   3:C1 *

Whiston Place

North of Whiston Road, west of Whiston Court

See Whiston Wynd.

Road   1988   SW   3:C1 *

Whiston Road

East of Wheeler Road West, south of Wanyandi Road

See Whiston Wynd.

Road   1988   SW   3:C1

Whiston Way

South of Whiston Road, east of Wheeler Road West

See Whiston Wynd.

Road   1988   SW   3:C1 *

Whiston Wynd

South of Whiston Road, west of Whiston Bay

Arthur K. Whiston was a pioneer resident and senior administrator for the City of Edmonton. Whiston was born in 1879 in Halifax, Nova Scotia. After graduating from business college, he worked as a clerk in a hardware firm for 13 years. Whiston moved to Edmonton in 1911 and worked as a businessman until 1915, when he was appointed special investigator for the City of Edmonton. He was credited with saving the city considerable sums of money as a result of his investigations and in 1916 was appointed municipal inspector. By 1918, Whiston was responsible for organizing, erecting and maintaining municipal hospitals throughout the province. He was later named as secretary and then supervisor of the Municipal Hospital Branch of the provincial Department of Public Health.

Road   1984   SW   3:C1 *

White Industrial

109 Avenue north to Yellowhead Trail, 184 Street west to Anthony Henday Drive

Alberta-born Henry White (1907–1991) was the first secretary of the City's Commission Board and held the position for 32 years. He was also the founder, in 1931, of the Maple Leaf Athletic Club. For many years, he played a prominent role in Boy Scout activities.

Neighbourhood   1981   NW   8:C1

Whitemud Creek, no date. (CEA EA–183–1)

Whitemud Creek

From the southern city limits east of 170 Street SW, flowing north into the North Saskatchewan River east of Whitemud Drive

The name of Whitemud Creek was noted in 1858 by Dr. James Hector of the Palliser Expedition. The white-coloured mud found along the creek's banks, and in the immediate vicinity, was used to white-wash the Hudson's Bay Company buildings.

Creek   CU   SW   2:D1

Whitemud Drive

Running east-west through south Edmonton; connecting Highway 14 with Anthony Henday Drive

Though named Whitemud Drive in 1968, the name was expected to be changed to Whitemud Freeway once the road was brought up to freeway standards. However, despite discussions in the Names Advisory Committee and City Council and popular use of the name Whitemud Freeway, the roadway continues to be called Whitemud Drive. *See* Whitemud Creek.

Road   1968   SW   3:D1

Whitemud Park

13204 Fox Drive

Whitemud Park includes all the parkland surrounding Whitemud Creek (over 162 ha.). The area has been used as a park since 1912, when Dr. L. L. Fuller offered the City of Edmonton 162 ha. of land in the Whitemud Creek Valley. Many of the footpaths still in use today were created in the 1930s. A second large donation was made by Thomas and Clara Fox, consisting of their Meadowview Ranch, fronting on the North Saskatchewan River west of Whitemud Creek. Part of the park was formerly known as the Rainbow Valley Park. *See* Whitemud Creek.

Park   1987   SW   4:A1

Whitemud Place

West of Whitemud Road at 57 Avenue

Whitemud Place is the name of the cul-de-sac appended to Whitemud Road on the west at 57 Avenue. The cul-de-sac is of a narrower road width than Whitemud Road and 57 Avenue, and was intended to create more privacy for the eight estate homes to be built there. *See* Whitemud Creek.

Road 1985 SW 3:D1 *

Whitemud Ravine

Along the course of Whitemud Creek

See Whitemud Creek.

Ravine CU SW 4:A2

Whitemud Ravine Nature Reserve

Encompassing the Blackmud Creek Ravine and Whitemud Ravine system

This park includes the entire Whitemud and Blackmud Creek Ravine system. The City constructed trails and creek crossings in the reserve to enable pedestrian recreation in the area while protecting the ravine from uncontrolled public use. *See* Whitemud Creek.

Park 1990 SW 4:A2

Whitemud Road

41 Avenue and 156 Street to 57 Avenue and 152 Street; westward extension of 58 Avenue

See Whitemud Creek.

Road 1962 SW 3:D1

Whyte Avenue

82 Avenue from 75 Street to 112 Street

See feature story, page 341.

Road 1961 C 7:C2

Wild Rose

35 Avenue to 38 Avenue, 17 Street to 34 Street

This neighbourhood is named for Alberta's wild rose (*Rosa acicularis*), the province's official flower since 1930. The neighbourhood is located in The Meadows area and follows the area's theme of naming neighbourhoods after flowers.

Neighbourhood 1982 SE 5:B2

Wild Rose Way

East of 23 Street

See Wild Rose.

Road 1999 SE 5:B1

Wilfred Webb Park

6411–187 Street

Windsor-born Wilfred Gilroy Webb (1888–1961) was an early homesteader who supported the provision of electricity to what is now the Willowdale subdivision. He first came to Edmonton in 1911, joining family members who had moved here earlier. With the outbreak of WWI, however, the family fell on hard times and left Edmonton, settling in Bluesky in the Peace River Country. After attempting to run a taxi business there, Webb returned to Edmonton in 1923 and farmed several plots of land. In 1934 he settled on property to the west of the city limits, then at 149 Street. He soon became a staunch supporter of community and school activities and played a key role in the building of the area's first power transmission lines. The Wilfred Webb Park is in the Ormsby neighbourhood and has an area of 1.82 ha.

Park 1983 SW 3:C1

Whyte Avenue

S<small>IR</small> W<small>ILLIAM</small> W<small>HYTE</small> (1843–1914) was born in Scotland and immigrated to Canada in 1863, where he worked for the Grand Trunk Railway. Over the next two decades he held a variety of railway jobs, including brakeman, freight clerk, yardmaster, conductor and station master, before becoming a senior member of management with the Canadian Pacific Railway (CPR).

In 1883 he was made superintendent of the Ontario and Quebec division of the CPR. From 1886 to 1897, Whyte was the general superintendent of the CPR's Winnipeg-based western division. By 1901 he was an assistant to the president, in 1903 was promoted to second vice-president, and in 1910 he became vice-president. Whyte was knighted following his retirement in 1911. He died in California in 1914.

The name Whyte Avenue has been in use since 1891, when the CPR-operated Calgary and Edmonton Railway surveyed and named the roadways in Strathcona. In return for siting its terminal in what would become South Edmonton, the CPR took ownership of half the building lots. The name Whyte Avenue was not, however, officially adopted until 1961.

Located in Edmonton's historic Strathcona neighbourhood, Whyte Avenue is considered a major arts and entertainment destination. Each summer, the avenue hosts a variety of events, including the Fringe Festival, one of the world's largest public theatre festivals.

Whyte Avenue at 102 Street looking west, circa 1930.
(CEA EA–275–908)

341

Wilkin Close

South of Wanyandi Road, west of Wilkin Road

William Lewis Wilkin (1876–1973) was a veteran of the Boer War and WWI, and an early Edmonton businessman. After emigrating from England to Strathcona, he first worked at his uncle's general store. Shortly before 1900, he left Canada to serve in the Boer War. Upon returning, Wilkin established a general store in Fort Saskatchewan. In 1907, Wilkin became a land speculator but soon found it unprofitable. In 1923, after serving in WWI, he started W. L. Wilkin Ltd., a real estate and insurance company. Wilkin retired in 1958 and left his business to his two sons. He died in 1973 at the age of 97.

Road 1988 SW 3:C1 *

Wilkin Place

West of Wilkin Road, south of Wilkin Close

See Wilkin Close.

Road 1988 SW 3:C1 *

Wilkin Road

South of Wanyandi Road, east of Wheeler Road West

See Wilkin Close.

Road 1988 SW 3:C1

Wilkin Way

West of Wilkin Road, south of Wilkin Place

See Wilkin Close.

Road 1988 SW 3:C1 *

Wilkin Wynd

East of Wilkin Road, south of Country Club Point

See Wilkin Close.

Road 1988 SW 3:C1 *

William Bramley-Moore Park

4711–144 Street

Dr. William Bramley-Moore (1906–1976) was registrar of the Alberta College of Physicians and Surgeons for 21 years. He was born on a homestead near Lloydminster and came to Edmonton in 1910. Bramley-Moore graduated from the University of Alberta in 1931. Following several years of general practice in Alberta and BC, he joined the Royal Canadian Medical Corps at the beginning of WWII and served in India, Burma and Europe. After the war, Bramley-Moore became registrar of the Alberta College of Physicians and Surgeons and held the post until 1967. He was the president of the Canadian Medical Council in 1965, an executive director and secretary-treasurer of the Alberta Division of the Canadian Medical Association, and lectured in medical economics at the University of Alberta. Bramley-Moore was a member of the boards of the Glenrose Hospital and the Edmonton Regional Hospital. The William Bramley-Moore Park is in the Brookside neighbourhood and has an area of 0.49 ha.

Park 1984 SW 4:A2

William Hawrelak Park

9330 Groat Road

William Hawrelak (1915–1975) was born in Wasel, Alberta, and moved to Edmonton in 1945. He served as mayor from 1951 to 1959, 1963 to 1965 and was re-elected in 1974. Hawrelak resigned in 1959 due to a provincial inquiry into land sales in which he was involved. The City sued Hawrelak for $266,000; he settled out of court, paying only $100,000 and his legal fees. The citizens re-elected him as mayor in 1963 but just two years later he was forced, once again, to resign after a Supreme Court of Alberta ruling on some of his real estate holdings and transactions.

Hawrelak was a 40 per cent owner of SunAlta Builders Ltd., and the transaction to sell land to the

Skating at Mayfair (now William Hawrelak) Park, 1968. (CEA EA-20-6485)

City of Edmonton was completed while he was in office. The City sued Hawrelak in a civil suit for $80,117. The Supreme Court of Canada, however, upheld an appeal filed by the mayor in March 1975. He was elected mayor for the final time in 1974 and died from a heart attack the following year. He was given a civic funeral, including a lying-in-state period in the City Council chambers. More than 10,000 people paid their respects to the late mayor who, despite his legal problems, had remained popular with Edmontonians.

In 1976 Mayfair Park was renamed in Hawrelak's honour. As mayor, he had campaigned for funding to develop what had been a gravel pit south of the Mayfair Golf Course into a park. William Hawrelak Park is located west of the Windsor Park neighbourhood, on the south side of the North Saskatchewan River, west of Groat Road, and has an area of 58.52 ha.

Park 1976 SW 7:B2

William Hustler Crescent

South of Hermitage Road, west of Victoria Trail

Dr. William Hustler (1886–1963) was a member of the University of Alberta's first medical class. After service in WWI, Hustler entered private practice in Edmonton. He retired in 1958 and died in 1963 at the age of 77.

Road 1975 NE 6:B1 *

William Short Road

East of Fort Road, north of 121 Avenue

William Short (1866–1926) served three terms as mayor of Edmonton. He was born in Canada West and came to Edmonton in 1894 to practise law. Mayor of the Town of Edmonton from 1902 to 1904, Short was one of the compilers of the Edmonton Charter, the enacting Territorial

Ordinance that created Edmonton as a city in 1904. In 1913 Short was again mayor, this time of the City of Edmonton.

Road 1975 NE 7:D1

Williams Court

West of 23 Street, south of 38 Avenue

US-born Leland "Lee" S. Williams (d. 1970) operated one of the largest livestock commission firms in Canada. Williams' father owned a small racing stable in New York State. In 1911, P.O. Dwyer, of Edmonton's Swift Canadian Co., purchased a horse from the stable and offered to help Lee Williams get a job at the plant. So, at the age of 19, Lee left the US and came to Edmonton where he began working at that company, first as a construction worker, then as a timekeeper and later as a livestock buyer. In 1916 he was transferred to Winnipeg and there joined the livestock commission agent firm of Wood, Weiller and McCarthy. In 1917, Henry Weiller and Lee Williams formed Weiller and Williams Ltd., which later became one of the largest livestock commission firms in the country. Williams served as president of the Edmonton Exhibition Association and was a well-known thoroughbred horse breeder.

Road 1999 SE 5:B1 *

Willow Way

East of Wolf Willow Crescent, south of Wolf Willow Road

This road, in the Westridge neighbourhood, is named, like a number of other roads in the area, for its location on land that was formerly the home of Wolf Willow Farms. *See* Wolf Willow Ravine.

Road 1973 SW 3:D1 *

H.C. Wilson, circa 1895. (CEA EA–10–2970)

Willowby Park

6315–184 Street

This park is in the Ormsby Place neighbourhood and has an area of 2.05 ha. The name is descriptive, alluding to the area's native willows.

Park 1998 SW 3:C1 *

Willowdale

Callingwood Drive north to Whitemud Drive, 178 Street west to Anthony Henday Drive

The name Willowdale is descriptive of the area; it was formerly known for its abundance of willows.

Subdivision 1970 SW 3:C1 *

Wilson Industrial

107 Avenue to 111 Avenue, 178 Street to 184 Street

Dr. Herbert Charles Wilson (1859–1909) became the first speaker of the first North-West Territories

Assembly in 1888. He came to Edmonton from Ontario in 1882 and opened up a drug store. Three years later, Wilson became the Edmonton and Fort Saskatchewan North West Mounted Police police surgeon. From 1895 to 1896, he served as mayor of Edmonton.

Neighbourhood   1975   NW   8:C2

Wilson Lane

North of Country Club Wynd, east of Wilkin Road

Ethel Cybil Wilson (1902–1983) was a union organizer, an alderman and a member of the provincial Social Credit government. Born in Sunnyside, Alberta, Wilson moved to Edmonton in 1925. After her husband died, Wilson took a seamstress position with Burns Meats Ltd. There she became involved in the activities of the United Packinghouse Workers Local 233 and served as secretary-treasurer of the Edmonton Labour Council.

Wilson was first elected to City Council in 1952 and went on to win each successive election until her retirement in 1966. She was elected to the provincial legislature as the Social Credit member for Edmonton North in 1959; in 1962 she was named minister without portfolio; and was twice re-elected, in 1963 and 1967, before the defeat of the Social Credit Party in 1971. Wilson helped develop a hostel for needy women, the provincial government's Women's Bureau, and the Alberta Girls' Parliament, and served as chair of the Royal Alexandra Hospital Board.

Road   1989   SW   3:D1 *

Windermere Crescent

West of 170 Street, north of 16 Avenue

Windermere Crescent is located in the neighbourhood of Windermere Estates. The name predates the annexation of this area by the City of Edmonton. *See* Windermere Estates.

Road   CU   SW   2:B1 *

Ethel Wilson, 1953. (CEA EA-267-502)

Windermere Drive

North of 9 Avenue, west of 170 Street

Windermere Drive was formerly known as Windermere Road. *See* Windermere Estates.

Road   1982   SW   2:B1

Windermere Estates

9 Avenue to 23 Avenue, 170 Street west to the river valley

Windermere Estates, located along the river valley, was developed in the 1960s as part of Strathcona County and was annexed to Edmonton in 1982. The name Windermere probably originates with the town of the same name, located in Cumbria, northwest England. It appears to have been formed from two words, "winder" and "mere." A "winder" is something that takes one's breath away, and "mere" has been defined as a boundary or land-

Picnicking on the site of the first house built in Windsor Park, 1912. (CEA EA–246–111)

mark. The word "estates" likely refers to the large lots on which the residential houses are built.

Neighbourhood   CU   SW   2:B1

Windross Crescent

North of 37A Avenue and west of 17 Street

Thomas Beswick Windross (d. 1963) was a journalist, newspaper publisher and poet. He was born in England in about 1875, but came to Canada as a young man to study theology. Windross ministered in Newfoundland, where he met and married Magdalene, a native Newfoundlander who had become a teacher after studying at the Boston Industrial Training School. The Windrosses soon moved to the United States, where Thomas was ordained in the Evangelistic Association in New England. After suffering a career-ending throat disability, Windross returned to Canada to take up

a career in journalism in Ottawa. In 1928 Windross moved his family to Calgary, and then on to Edmonton in 1929. Thereafter, he worked in the news department of the *Edmonton Journal* and later published a weekly newspaper, the *Spotlight*, which assisted the Independent Coalition of Liberals and Conservatives in the Alberta legislature. Windross authored two books of poetry: *Isle de la Demoiselle and other poems* (no date), and *Gates of Glory and other poems* (1949).

Road   2001   SE   5:B2 *

Windsor Park

University Avenue north to Saskatchewan Drive, 116 Street west to Saskatchewan Drive

The first owner of River Lot 3 (now partly Windsor Park) was Allan Omand, who first worked the land in 1882. In 1910, the area of Windsor Park was bought for residential development and named by an English syndicate. It remained largely undeveloped until after WWII. The neighbourhood's community league was founded in 1947 and a clubhouse built at 11814–87 Avenue in 1949.

This neighbourhood may have been named after Windsor, England, or after Windsor Castle which is found in Windsor. Windsor Castle is the largest castle in England and is the principal residence of Queen Elizabeth II. It is the only castle that has been continuously occupied by royalty since the Middle Ages.

Neighbourhood   CU   C   7:B2

Windsor Park

11840–87 Avenue

This park is in the Windsor Park neighbourhood and has an area of 1.57 ha. It was created when the neighbourhood was replotted after WWII. *See* Windsor Park *neighbourhood*.

Park   CU   C   7:B2

Windsor Road

East of Saskatchewan Drive near 91 Avenue, south to 89 Avenue

This road crosses Windsor Park neighbourhood. The name Windsor Road has been in use since the 1940s. *See* Windsor Park *neighbourhood*.

Road   CU   C   7:B2

Winterburn Industrial

Stony Plain Road north to 118A Avenue, 199 Street west to 231 Street

The name of Winterburn likely originates from old English, meaning "a stream dry except in winter." Local tradition, however, connects Winterburn with the burning off of muskeg in the winter. The Winterburn Industrial area was settled in the late 1800s; a post office was opened in 1904. The name

was established through local usage long before its formal adoption in 1982.

Area   CU   NW   8:B1

Winterburn Road

North-south road (215 Street), from the northern city limit at Big Lake, south to 9 Avenue SW

See Winterburn Industrial.

Road   1982   SW   2:A1

Wiseman Lane

East of 23 Street, north of and connecting to Wild Rose Way

David Wiseman (d. 1974) was one of Edmonton's longest-established fur traders. Educated at Alex Taylor Public School and Victoria Composite High School, Wiseman was engaged in fur trading for most of his life. He was secretary-treasurer of B'nai B'rith and an active member of Beth Israel Synagogue.

Road   1999   SE   5:B2

Wolf Crescent

East of Wolf Willow Road, north of Wolf Willow Crescent

See Wolf Willow Ravine.

Road   1973   SW   3:D1

Wolf Ridge Close

South of Wolf Ridge Way, west of Wolf Ridge Place

See Wolf Willow Ravine.

Road   1986   SW   3:D1 *

Winterburn, Alberta post office, 1922. (GAI NA-1644-155)

Wolf Ridge Place

South of Wolf Ridge Way, east of Wolf Ridge Close

See Wolf Willow Ravine.

Road   1986   SW   3:D1 *

Wolf Ridge Point

North of Wolf Ridge Way, west of Wolf Ridge Place

See Wolf Willow Ravine.

Road   1986   SW   3:D1 *

Wolf Ridge Way

East of Wanyandi Road, north of Wolf Ridge Close

Developers originally planned to build a bridge across Wolf Willow Ravine to connect the Westridge and Oleskiw neighbourhoods. The bridge was never built and the road remaining in Oleskiw was renamed Wolf Ridge Way. *See* Wolf Willow Ravine.

Road   1986   SW   3:D1 *

Wolf Willow Close

South of Wolf Willow Road, east of Wanyandi Road

See Wolf Willow Ravine.

Road   1985   SW   3:D1 *

Wolf Willow Crescent

North of Wolf Willow Point, east of Wolf Willow Road

This road is named after the nearby Wolf Willow Ravine. *See* Wolf Willow Ravine.

Road   1986   SW   3:D1

Wolf Willow Point

South of Wolf Willow Crescent

See Wolf Willow Ravine.

Road   1986   SW   3:D1 *

Wolf Willow Ravine

Separating the Westridge and Oleskiw neighbourhoods; east of 170 Street

The ravine is named for Wolf Willow Farm, which was located in the area from the mid-1930s to the early 1970s. The farm, covering 194 ha., was owned by Curtis and Edith Munson. Curtis Munson (d. 1980) was born in the United States, attended Yale University and served in the US Army during WWI before immigrating to Edmonton. In Edmonton, he formed Sterling Collieries and the Coal Valley Mining Company, which sold coal to the Canadian National Railway. Munson was also a part-owner of the *Edmonton Bulletin* newspaper. The farm likely took its name from the wolf willow, a locally abundant shrub. The flowers of the silvery-leafed bush are yellow and have a fragrant scent. The name Wolf Willow Ravine replaces the original name of Westridge Ravine. The ravine has also been called the Edith Ravine, after Edith Munson.

Ravine   1972   SW   3:D1 *

Wolf Willow Road

Continuation of 69 Avenue east of 170 Street

This road originally extended into Oleskiw but developers later changed their plans. The portion of Wolf Willow Road in Oleskiw was renamed Wolf Ridge Way. *See* Wolf Willow Ravine.

Road   1986   SW   3:C1

Woodbend Estates

South of 35 Avenue, east of 199 Street

Woodbend Estates takes its name from a post office that was once located in the area. The Woodbend post office was in operation from 1908 to 1953. This area was annexed to Edmonton in 1981.

Neighbourhood   CU   SW   3:B2 *

Woodbend Place

128 Street to 105 Avenue

Woodbend Place is a cul-de-sac in the Westmount neighbourhood. The road has existed since at least 1955 and may have been named after Sydney (or Sidney) B. Woods, an early Edmonton lawyer who owned the land on which Woodbend Place is located. Woods came to Edmonton in the early 1900s and lived at 12809 Stony Plain Road from 1913 to 1926. He began his career in Edmonton as deputy-attorney general and later joined a private firm.

Road   CU   NW   7:B2 *

Woodbend Wynd

199 Street and 33 Avenue

See Woodbend Estates.

Road   1983   SW   3:B2

Woodcroft

111 Avenue to 118 Avenue, Groat Road west to 142 Street

Woodcroft, considered a descriptive name, was first used around 1907. Real estate tycoon J. R. McIntosh, who had come to Edmonton in 1902, was responsible for the sale of the original lots. Although Woodcroft was established in the early 1900s, the majority of its development did not occur until the 1950s. The Westmount Shopping Centre, located in Woodcroft and constructed in 1955, was the first mall in Edmonton and, after renovations, one of the first enclosed malls in North America.

Neighbourhood   CU   NW   7:A1

Woodcroft Avenue

135 Street to 117 Avenue

The roadway has been in existence since 1954. *See* Woodcroft.

Road   CU   NW   7:A1

Woodvale

34 Avenue north to Whitemud Drive, 50 Street to 66 Street

This name was chosen because it was compatible with the naming theme of the Mill Woods area, which uses either the word "mill" or "wood" in area names.

Subdivision   1973   SE   4:D2 *

Woodvale Road East

South of 38 Avenue, connecting with Woodvale Road West at 58 Street

See Woodvale.

Road   1974   SE   5:A2

Woodvale Road West

South of 38 Avenue, connecting with Woodvale Road East at 58 Street

See Woodvale.

Road   1974   SE   5:A2

Wotherspoon Close

East of Wedgewood Boulevard, north of Weaver Drive

Catherine Wotherspoon (1909–1978) was a pioneer teacher and was said to have been the first child born in Beverly before it became a town. She taught school in the public system for nearly 35 years, starting first at a classroom located inside the Beverly Town Hall, then teaching at Beacon Heights and later at Lawton Junior High. Wotherspoon was well known for her artistic talent and in 1977 was named to the Alberta Society of Artists. The road was originally named "Weatherspoon" Close, a misspelling of Wotherspoon's name that was soon corrected.

Road   1989   SW   3:C2 *

Wyman Lane

East of 23 Street, south of Wild Rose Way

Brig. R.A. "Bob" Wyman (c. 1904–1967) was a decorated WWII veteran and a long-serving employee of Canadian National Railways (CNR). Born in Pennsylvania of Canadian parents, Wyman and his family moved west to Edmonton in 1914. In Edmonton, he attended Queen Alexandra, Strathcona and Victoria High schools. In 1918 Wyman went to work for the CNR. Three years later he enlisted with the 92nd Battery, and by the age of 25 was a battery commander. In 1939 he went overseas to serve as a lieutenant-colonel and commanded an artillery regiment. Wyman was promoted to brigadier in 1941 and became one of the youngest brigadiers in the Allied army.

During WWII he commanded the 1st Canadian Armoured Brigade in Sicily and Italy, and the 2nd Canadian Armoured Brigade at Normandy on D-Day. He was wounded at Falaise and retired from the army in 1945. For his service, Wyman was decorated by both the Canadian and the French governments, the latter awarding him the Chevalier of the Légion d'Honneur and the Croix de Guerre with Palm. Following the war, Wyman returned to the CNR where he worked as an industrial agent and later as superintendent of the CNR's Regina division. He died in 1967 at the age of 63.

Road   1999   SE   5:B1 *

Yellowbird

9 Avenue to 23 Avenue, Calgary Trail west to Blackmud Creek

Yellowbird was named in honour of a Cree chief and a First Nations band in Hobbema, south of Edmonton. Subdivisions and neighbourhoods in the Kaskitayo area have an Aboriginal naming theme.

Subdivision 1975 SE 1:A1 *

Yellowhead Corridor

Yellowhead Trail north to 127 Avenue, LRT tracks west to 127 Street

In 1995 the Canadian National and Canadian Pacific railway yards north of the Yellowhead Trail were amalgamated into one neighbourhood, the Yellowhead Corridor. *See* Yellowhead Trail *feature story, page 353.*

Neighbourhood 1995 NW 7:B1

Yellowhead Trail

Highway 16 running east to west through the city; 33 Street and 118 Avenue to 231 Street and 118 Avenue

See feature story, page 353.

Road CU NW 8:B1

York

137 Avenue to 144 Avenue, 50 Street to 66 Street

The York neighbourhood was named for Annie A. York Secord. Annie York was born in Ontario and came west to Alberta (then the North-West Territories) in 1889 to teach school at Poplar Lake and Namao. In 1891, she resigned from teaching to marry Richard Secord, an Edmonton businessman and later a member of the North-West Assembly from 1902 to 1904. Annie York Secord died in 1950.

Neighbourhood 1962 NE 10:D2

Annie York Secord, circa 1920. (CEA EA-9-25)

York Park

5825–140 Avenue

This park is in the York neighbourhood and has an area of 1.95 ha. *See* York.

Park 1983 NE 10:D2

Youngstown Industrial

103 Avenue to 107 Avenue, Mayfield Road west to 170 Street

Youngstown Industrial was developed by the Geneva Housing and Development Company and named around 1959. This neighbourhood was probably named after Ira L. Young, the owner and developer of the property. Young was also the presi-

Yellowhead Trail

THE YELLOWHEAD TRAIL, which passes through Edmonton, is part of the nearly 3,200-kilometre-long Yellowhead Highway that connects Winnipeg in the east to Massett on the Queen Charlotte Islands in the west. The highway is an amalgamation of many highways that originated as historic Aboriginal and fur trade routes. Before construction of the roads, the Canadian Northern Railway and the Grand Trunk Pacific forged their ways through the Yellowhead Pass between 1912 and 1914.

In the late 1910s and early 1920s the Edmonton Area Good Roads Association became involved in the first concerted effort to build automobile roads to the Rocky Mountains and beyond, and encouraged development of what would become a key section of the Yellowhead Highway. In 1947 the inaugural conference of the Trans Canada Highway System (Yellowhead Route) took place.

The Yellowhead Highway takes its name from Yellowhead Pass, the lowest crossing of the Continental Divide on the North American continent. The mountain pass was used for centuries by Aboriginal people and was first mentioned in European accounts around 1826. It was for many years the route used by fur traders travelling to the New Caledonia Department (an area beyond the Rocky Mountains in northern British Columbia) of the Hudson's Bay Company (HBC). HBC documents used the name Tête-Jaune, or Yellowhead, for Pierre Hatsinaton, sometimes called Pierre Bostonais, who was a Métis guide and trapper who worked in the area of the pass now known as Yellowhead.

Yellowhead Highway twinning ceremony, 1992.
(CEA A96–182 Box 3 F55)

Youville Drive East

YOUVILLE DRIVE East and West form a semicircular roadway that encompasses the Grey Nuns Hospital, located north of the Mill Woods Town Centre Mall. These "Grey Nuns"—so called because of the colour of their habits—are members of Les Sœurs de la Charité de l'Hôpital Général de Montréal. The order was founded in 1738 by Marguerite d'Youville (1701-1771), sister of the explorer Lavérendrye. The mother of two children, she was widowed at the age of 29. She dedicated the rest of her life to caring for the needy, the poor and the unwanted. Marguerite d'Youville was canonized in 1990.

The first nuns to settle in the northwest reached their destination, the Roman Catholic mission at Lac Ste. Anne, on September 24, 1859. The three Grey Nuns —Sisters Emery, Lamy and Alphonse —left their motherhouse in Montréal a year before, first stopping nine months in St. Boniface to acclimatize to the rigours of frontier life.

Writing in her journal that first day at Lac Ste. Anne, Sister Alphonse noted: "As we approached the goal where henceforth, our days would be spent…our pleasure abated and serious reflections replaced it. However, our trust in God soon dissipated the clouds which the future seemed to hold in store for us."

In 1861, when the Oblate priests decided to move their mission for the Métis closer to the large centre of trade at Fort Edmonton, the three sisters moved with them. Two years later, Father Lacombe's residence became the site of the settlement's first school, with Sisters Emery, Lamy and Alphonse as the teachers. In 1864 the Youville Asylum was opened and served as both convent and school. The asylum was later used as an orphanage and as the first hospital in central Alberta.

In 1894 Edmonton's rapidly growing population caused Drs. Wilson, McInnes, Royal, Tofield, Harrison and Braithwaite to petition Bishop Grandin to establish a hospital to be run by the Grey Nuns. The Grey Nuns purchased land from the Hudson's Bay Company facing Jasper Avenue, between present-day 111 Street and 112 Street, and the Edmonton General Hospital opened in 1895.

Ste-Marguerite d'Youville, no date. (ANQ 06M-P266-S4-P056)

354

dent and manager of Canadian Investments Ltd., a property management company. Youngstown Industrial was once part of the Town of Jasper Place and was annexed to Edmonton, along with the rest of Jasper Place, in 1964.

Neighbourhood 1959 NW 8:C2

Youville Drive East

North of 28 Avenue at 56 Street, meeting Youville Drive West at 58 Street

See feature story, page 354.

Road 1991 SE 5:A2

Youville Drive West

North of 28 Avenue at Hewes Way, meeting Youville Drive East at 58 Street

See Youville Drive East *feature story, page 354.*

Road 1991 SE 5:A2

Beverly Town Council at amalgamation, including Stephen Zaychuk, seated first from left, 1961. (CEA EA–16–2)

Zaychuk Road

167 Avenue to 40 Street

Polish-born Stephen Zaychuk (1908–1973) was a commercial vegetable and fruit farmer in the Beverly area. In 1935, after immigrating to Canada, he purchased land in the Beverly area. Zaychuk became the first grower in the district to produce commercial strawberry and raspberry crops for local markets. Through his dedication, the enterprise developed into one of the largest commercial vegetable and fruit farms in Alberta. In 1960 Zaychuk's holdings in Beverly were sold and a larger operation established at its current location at 24191–34 Street. From 1952 until 1961, when Beverly was amalgamated with Edmonton, Zaychuk served as a councillor on the Beverly Town Council. He was a member of the Edmonton Chamber of Commerce and the Alberta Fresh Vegetable Growers' Association. Zaychuk Road leads to the Zaychuk Nursery, Vegetable and Berry Farms.

Road   1982   NE   11:B1 *

Zoie Gardner Park

12710–70 Street

See feature story, page 359.

Park   1987   NE   10:D2

Zoie Gardner Park

VIOLET "ZOIE" GARDNER (1918–1998) cared for hundreds of homeless children, largely at her own expense, and was a member of the Order of Canada. Gardner was born in Manchester, England, and came to Canada with her parents when she was only a year old. The family homesteaded near Grande Prairie and later moved to Edmonton, where her father worked as a janitor at the legislative buildings. Gardner was the eldest of 11 children and left school after completing Grade 8 to work.

By the mid-1960s, Gardner was said to have a heart bigger than the 13-room house she called home in the Calder area of north Edmonton. It was here that she shared her life with handicapped and hard-to-place foster children. In the early years, Gardner supported herself and the children who lived with her by working as a dressmaker. At one point there were 24 children under her roof. Some stayed for only a few days while others remained with her for more than 20 years; the average stay was ten years.

For her contribution to Edmonton's children, Gardner was honoured as the Outstanding Citizen of 1961 by the Junior Chamber of Commerce. In 1966 the welfare department paid Gardner two dollars a day for each child under her care. While the sum was a marked increase from the sixteen cents a day she had received 25 years earlier, she told local media that she was struggling to make her monthly mortgage payments. In the late 1960s the Edmonton Rotary Club took over the mortgage and by the 1970s Gardner had taken on a second house.

In 1971 she received a citation from the Edmonton Foster Parents' Association recognizing her 30 years as a foster parent. Gardner, who loved opera, was also a long-serving volunteer for the Edmonton Opera Society, providing snacks for performers during rehearsals. The American singer Harry Belafonte was said to always ask for Gardner when he visited Edmonton.

Gardner died at the age of 80 in July of 1998, just three months after receiving the Order of Canada. The Zoie Gardner Park is in the Balwin neighbourhood and has an area of 0.85 ha.

Zoie Gardner on right, backstage with cast members, 1988. (CEA A99–152)

Appendix I: Lost Waterways

Groat Creek: The stream that once flowed down the road that now gets north-side residents across the river to the university was one of the most scenic of the city's river valleys.

By 1950, however, there were more than 80,000 car owners in Edmonton. More than 30,000 of them lived on the south side of town.

Responding to increasing complaints about traffic jams on the city's four bridges, city council started looking at its river ravines for new road routes. In the 1950s, Groat Creek was culverted, and then completely buried to make way for the new road.

Ramsay and MacKinnon Ravines: In the summer of 1965, a group of women vowed to lay down in front of a train of bulldozers to stop development of a freeway the city was proposing along the river valley through Ramsay, MacKinnon and Mackenzie ravines.

Led by artist/philanthropist Margaret Chappelle, the affluent group was not exactly your "Battle-in-Seattle" types. They would not, however, be denied. After 17 hard-fought years, and a great deal of support from the community and the media, they finally got the city to withdraw the plan and turn the land over to Parks and Recreation.

Some damage, however, had already been done. MacKinnon and Ramsay Creek were culverted, and the ravine filled in to create a suitable roadbed.

The river valley freeway concept, however, did not die. Five years ago, Coun. Larry Langley tried unsuccessfully to get city council to reconsider building MacKinnon Freeway.

Whitemud Creek: Hidden alongside one of the city's busiest transportation corridors in southwest Edmonton is a steeply walled ravine where mule and white-tailed deer, snowshoe hares and coyotes thrive. Whitemud Ravine is one of the best places in town to hear the call of cock pheasants, the knocking of pileated woodpeckers in springtime, or the hooting of a variety of owls.

The Cree called the stream that flows through the ravine "Flaming Spring." Legend has it that a mysterious upwelling of water in this notoriously dry area put out a grass fire that had been deliberately set by the Cree's arch enemy to kill a Cree princess.

Struck by the light-coloured mud that lines the banks of the creek, the Europeans gave Whitemud the name it is known by today. Had history taken a different course, Whitemud Ravine might have been filled in or turned into a sewer.

In 1912, Dr. L.L. Fuller ensured that the site would be saved from developers when he donated 200 acres of land to the city for the establishment of a park. Subsequent land donations by a number of other people, including Tommy Fox of Fox Drive fame, added to the size of the urban wildlife refuge.

The City of Edmonton nearly destroyed it all in 1973 when it proposed dumping the effluent from storm sewers in the Mill Woods subdivision into Whitemud Creek. Public protests forced the city to back down.

Drunken Lake: Located at 109th Avenue and 121st Street, it was here that Hudson's Bay Company employees routinely met with Aboriginal trappers to trade liquor for their furs. The lake was drained in the 1930s to make way for housing developments.

Alberta Legislature

Lendrum, First and Second Lake: The Lendrum lake system was a popular spot for picnicking, hiking and skating. First Lake was fenced in to keep out the dairy cattle on neighbouring farms. When the water level was high, paddlers could get their canoes from First Lake to McKernan's Lake without having to portage. Second Lake ran from 71st Avenue to 65th Avenue between 110th Street and 112th Street. The lakes were drained in the late 1940s with a series of irrigation ditches. The lakes still haunt hundreds of people who live in houses that were built on the drainage sites. When it rains very hard in summer, the basements of these houses routinely flood.

North Saskatchewan River

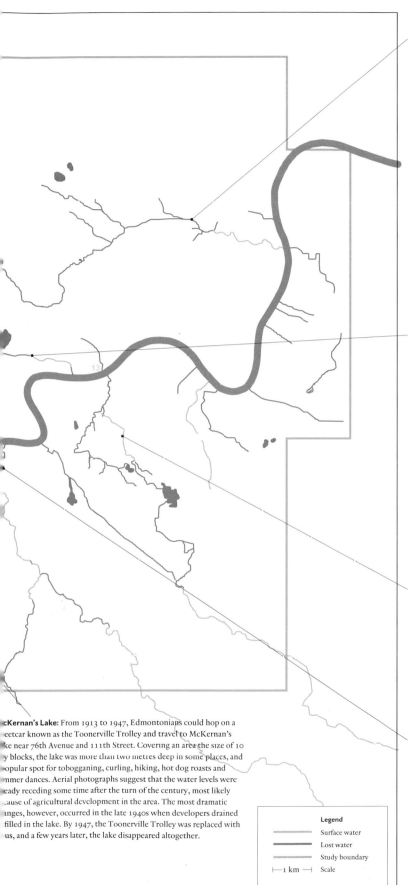

Kennedale Creek (also known as 2nd Rat Creek): Located at the east end of the city near 40th Street, Kennedale Creek was one of the city's longest streams. The sand and gravel deposits you see in the ravine today are ancient sediment beds that have been mined to build some of the city's taller buildings.

Archaeologists have discovered 14 prehistoric sites in the Hermitage Park/ Kennedale Ravine area. They are the remains of nomadic cultures that lived on the plains thousands of years ago.

The bone fragments found here suggest the nomads came to this site to hunt bison and other animals.

The ravine site was first settled in 1875 by Rev. Canon William Newton, who was forced to build his church and hospital on this site because he could not get along with officials at Fort Edmonton, 14 kilometres to the west.

The Anglican minister called it the Hermitage because of its remote location, and the name stuck. The lilac rows he planted can still be seen today.

The demise of the creek came early on when the city set up its first municipal dump along the banks of the stream.

Today, only a tiny section of the stream near the North Saskatchewan River still flows for part of the year.

Kinnaird Ravine (Rat Creek): Bordering the Cromdale residential area, Kinnaird Ravine was named in honour of George Johnston Kinnaird, one of Edmonton's first city commissioners. Kinnaird had come over from Scotland in the 1870s to apprentice with the Hudson's Bay Company before settling in Edmonton a decade later.

Rat Creek flowed out of the tail end of the ravine into the North Saskatchewan River. It was here that a division of Mounties camped in 1874 after an exhausting 1,500-kilometre horseback trip from southeast Saskatchewan.

"The trail grew worse, sloughs across it every hundred yards," wrote one of the Mounties.

"Men and animals struggled knee deep in black mud. Time and again, the wagons had to be unloaded and dragged out by hand. On every side were ponds covered with thin ice, which proved to be a menace."

The city acquired the land at the turn of the century, and turned the area into a park in 1967. Members of the Canadian Forces militia gravelled over part of the park to create a jogging trail. In 1979, Cromdale residents sodded part of the area.

Fulton Creek: In 1885, a 20-year-old Maritimer by the name of Daniel Fulton headed west to Edmonton and established a homestead on a hill overlooking a beautiful creek that now bears his name. Today, only small portions of that creek remain, and a western tributary has completely disappeared.

Flowing into the city from the southeast, the creek is culverted at Weir Industrial Park at 69th Avenue near 50th Street. It re-emerges at 98th Avenue and Terrace Road, and flows through a culvert for about three kilometres before passing through an undisturbed ravine and then going underground again at the Capilano Freeway.

McKernan's Lake: From 1913 to 1947, Edmontonians could hop on a streetcar known as the Toonerville Trolley and travel to McKernan's Lake near 76th Avenue and 111th Street. Covering an area the size of 10 city blocks, the lake was more than two metres deep in some places, and a popular spot for tobogganing, curling, hiking, hot dog roasts and summer dances. Aerial photographs suggest that the water levels were already receding some time after the turn of the century, most likely because of agricultural development in the area. The most dramatic changes, however, occurred in the late 1940s when developers drained and filled in the lake. By 1947, the Toonerville Trolley was replaced with a bus, and a few years later, the lake disappeared altogether.

Mill Creek: The creek got its name from a flour mill that was built near its confluence with the North Saskatchewan River in 1871. The river often overflowed its banks in spring-time before being reduced to a trickle in late summer. A huge section of the creek was filled in to make way for urban development in the 1950s. Today, what little water flows along the creek comes from snow melt and storm sewers. A plan to revitalize the creek and expand the ravine was put forward in 1971. It would have resulted in more than 400 homes being removed. The city eventually backed down, and in the end only 22 homes were acquired.

Legend

Surface water
Lost water
Study boundary
⊢ 1 km ⊣   Scale

Map created by University of Alberta researchers Kathryn Martell and Henry Dammeyer and published in the Edmonton Journal on May 5, 2002, page A1, with text by Ed Struzik. Used with permission.

Appendix II: Lost Names

IN EDMONTON before WWI, names were the rule rather than the exception on Edmonton street signs. Expansion was rapid and speculation rampant. Subdivision and street names proliferated, often with confusing results. In the wake of amalgamation with the City of Strathcona in 1912, it was decided that a rationalization of the naming system was in order. By the time a numbering system was decided upon and implemented in 1914, the young city's first development boom had gone bust.

The dust that settled over the defunct developments and the abandoned or re-numbered roadways obscured, but did not completely bury, the memory of Edmonton's early names. Years went by, the city started to grow again, boundaries were redrawn and roadways replotted. Despite the changes, some names carried on in popular usage—Norwood and Clover Bar Road are good examples of names that are not official but are still generally used. Others resurfaced in the same area in a different form, as was the case in 1958 with Gallagher Park in the Cloverdale neighbourhood, a part of town historically known as Gallagher Flats. Still others popped up in another part of town altogether, as did the name Fraser in 1979, when it was applied to a neighbourhood in the northeast, far from Riverdale where it was first used.

This list consists of names that either were but are are no longer in use in Edmonton, or that currently identify features other than those historically associated with them. Most of these lost names never passed through any official process, but rather were created by developers or came into being through common usage. Some cannot, through lack of information, be correlated with any current named feature. In this case, the word "Unknown" appears instead of "Current Name." Other names were attached to a known historic feature that no longer exists, such as a road that was redrawn, or a park that was abolished. The words "No longer exists" appear instead of "Current Name" under these circumstances. Some names on the list are plainly misspellings or typographical errors. These have been

included since they may have been perpetuated in other sources and can act as a reference back to the correct feature. It is not unusual to find the same name listed several times. These are differentiated by the addition of a number after the name, usually based on the date the name first appeared. On occasion, several different entries of a "Lost Name" may be connected with the same current name. This can often be explained by the fact that the feature (usually a road) was discontinuous, with different segments having been given different names. Or, a single feature may have had several different names sequentially over time. However, most, like Flanitz Avenue, have been lost from general recall, as have their origins.

Henderson's Directories from 1895, 1905, 1905/06, and 1907–1930 (except for 1918, when no volume was produced) were the main source of information for this list. In addition, the Lowe's Directory for 1899 was used. Maps from the collection of the City of Edmonton Archives were also extensively consulted, including survey maps, commercially produced street maps, and fire insurance maps. The earliest of these dates from 1892, and the most recent from 1970. A variety of other sources provided additional details.

In addition to the types of features that currently have official names, the list of Lost Names includes the following types: airport, ferry, flats, hill, point, square, town, tunnel and village. Additional information relating to all these names may be obtained by contacting the City of Edmonton Archives.

Lost Name

Current Name

Feature Type

---

105 Street Bridge

Walterdale Bridge

Bridge

2nd Rat Creek

Unnamed creek in Kennedale Ravine

Creek

Aberdeen Avenue

No longer exists

Road

Abernethy Avenue

111 Avenue

Road

Ackerman Street

71 Street

Road

Ada Avenue

109 Avenue

Road

Adamson Avenue

81 Street

Road

Adelaide Street

92 Avenue

Road

Adrian Avenue

115 Avenue

Road

Agnes Avenue (1)

115 Avenue

Road

Agnes Avenue (2)

128 Avenue

Road

Agnes Street (1)

128 Avenue

Road

Agnes Street (2)

78 Street/79 Street

Road

Agricultural Association Ground

Rollie Miles Athletic Grounds

Park

Agricultural Ground(s)

Rollie Miles Athletic Grounds

Park

Albany

110 Avenue

Road

Albany Avenue

110 Avenue

Road

Albany Street

No longer exists

Road

Albert Trail

St. Albert Trail

Road

Alberta Avenue

76 Avenue

Road

Alberta College Grounds

Gold Bar

Subdivision

Alberta Park (1)

Alberta Park Industrial/ Norwester Industrial

Subdivision

Alberta Park (2)

University of Alberta Farm

Subdivision

Alberta Park Addition

West Sheffield Industrial

Subdivision

Alberta Street

Unknown

Road

Alexandra Avenue (1)

No longer exists

Road

Alexandra Avenue (2)

135 Avenue

Road

Alexandra Park

Davies Industrial West

Subdivision

Alexandra Street

Unknown

Road

Alexandra Terrace

Unnamed

Park

Alexandria Street

Unknown

Road

Alexis Avenue

113 Avenue

Road

Algonquin Avenue

137 Avenue

Road

Alice Avenue

No longer exists

Road

Allansholm

Beaumaris

Subdivision

Allen Avenue

65 Avenue

Road

Allen Street

49 Street

Road

Allendale

Allendale/Pleasantview

Subdivision

Allendale Park

Mount Pleasant Park

Park

Allensholme

Beaumaris

Subdivision

Alloway Avenue

131 Avenue

Road

Anderson Addition

Unknown

Subdivision

Anderson Avenue

81 Avenue

Road

Anne Avenue

No longer exists

Road

Antony Street

109 Street

Road

Appelton Street

42 Street

Road

Armstrong Avenue

127 Avenue

Road

Ascot Park

Baranow/Caernarvon

Subdivision

Ash Street

154 Street

Road

Athabasca Avenue

102 Avenue

Road

Athabaska Avenue

102 Avenue

Road

Augier Avenue

No longer exists

Road

Austin Subdivision

Unknown

Subdivision

Avanmore

Avonmore

Subdivision

Avondale

Sifton Park

Subdivision

Aylmer Avenue

No longer exists

Road

Bailey Avenue

114 Avenue

Road

Bailey Drive

9 Avenue SW

Road

Bailey Way

Blackmore Court

Road

Balcan

Dechene

Subdivision

Balkan

Dechene

Subdivision

Balmoral

Glenwood/West Meadowlark Park

Subdivision

Balmoral Avenue

110 Avenue

Road

Banff Street (1)

No longer exists

Road

Banff Street (2)

No longer exists

Road

Barber Avenue

72 Avenue

Road

Barr Street

76 Street

Road

Barton

Baranow/Carlisle

Subdivision

Baseball Grounds

Diamond Park

Park

Baskerville Street

133 Street

Road

Beachmount Cemetery

Beechmount Cemetery

Cemetery

Beacon Heights Annex

Beacon Heights

Subdivision

Bean Park

McKernan/Parkallen

Subdivision

Beatrice Street

102 Avenue

Road

Beau Park

Belgravia/McKernan/
Parkallen/University of
Alberta Farm
Subdivision

Beau Park Crescent

No longer exists
Road

Beaver Avenue

135 Avenue
Road

Beech Avenue

117 Avenue
Road

Beech Street

117 Avenue
Road

Beechmont

Yellowhead Corridor
Subdivision

Beechmont Cemetery

Beechmount Cemetery
Cemetery

Beechmount

Beechmount Cemetery
Subdivision

Belesare Avenue

123 Avenue
Road

Bellamy Street

102A Avenue
Road

Belle Villa Gardens

Avonmore
Subdivision

Belleview

Bellevue
Subdivision

Bellevilla

Avonmore
Subdivision

Belleville Gardens

Avonmore
Subdivision

Belleville Street

73 Street/74 Street
Road

Bellevue Addition

Highlands
Subdivision

Belmont

Balwin/
Yellowhead Corridor
Subdivision

Belmont Gardens

Casselman
Subdivision

Belmont Heights

Casselman
Subdivision

Belmont Park

Yellowhead Corridor
Subdivision

Belmont View

York
Subdivision

Belvedere

Belvedere/Kennedale
Industrial
Subdivision

Bennet Avenue

80 Avenue
Road

Bennett Avenue

80 Avenue
Road

Beresford Avenue

No longer exists
Road

Berkley Avenue

No longer exists
Road

Bertha Avenue

130 Avenue
Road

Bertha Avenue

67A Avenue
Road

Beverley Street

131 Street
Road

Beverly

Abbottsfield/Beacon
Heights/Bergman/
Beverly Heights/
Rundle Heights
Town

Beverly Boulevard

38 Street
Road

Beverly Heights Annex

Beverly Heights
Subdivision

Beverly Jubilee Park

Jubilee Park
Park

Birch Street

149 Street
Road

Birmingham Street

21 Street
Road

Bishop Avenue

130 Avenue
Road

Bissel Street

77 Street

Road

Blackbird Street

No longer exists

Road

Bloor Street

No longer exists

Road

Bog Meadows

Place LaRue

Subdivision

Bolton Street

84 Street

Road

Borden Street

147 Street

Road

Boston Avenue

137 Avenue

Road

Boulevard Avenue

111 Avenue

Road

Boulevard Drive

No longer exists

Road

Boulevard Fraser's Flats

87 Street

Road

Boulevard Heights

Ottewell

Subdivision

Boulevard Norwood

111 Avenue

Road

Boulevard Street

87 Street

Road

Boundary Avenue

Unknown

Road

Bow Avenue

109 Avenue

Road

Boyle Street

103A Avenue

Road

Boyle Street Sports Fields

Unnamed

Park

Brackman Street

95A Street

Road

Brackman-Ker

Ritchie/Strathcona

Subdivision

Brackman-Kerr

Ritchie/Strathcona

Subdivision

Braemar

Ottewell/ Terrace Heights

Subdivision

Braemar Heights

Ottewell

Subdivision

Braemer Heights

Ottewell

Subdivision

Bramer Heights

Ottewell

Subdivision

Brandon Avenue

127 Avenue

Road

Brazeau Avenue

113 Avenue

Road

Bremner Estate

Garside Industrial/ Huff Bremner Estate Industrial

Subdivision

Bremner Road

No longer exists

Road

Brenton

78 Street

Road

Brewery Flats

Rossdale

Flats

Brewster Street

No longer exists

Road

Brickyard Road

No longer exists

Road

Bridge Road

Rossdale Road

Road

Bridge Road South

Rossdale Road

Road

Bridgeland

Parkallen/University of Alberta Farm

Subdivision

Brigham Street

71 Street

Road

Brighton

Forest Heights

Subdivision

Britannia

Britannia Youngstown

Subdivision

Britannia Park

Anthony Henday Drive

Subdivision

Brixton

Cloverdale

Subdivision

Broad Street

143 Street

Road

Broad Street

Unknown

Road

Broadview

Avonmore

Subdivision

Broadway

Riverside Crescent

Road

Bronx, The

Athlone/Hagmann Estate Industrial/ Sherbrooke

Subdivision

Brooklyn

Northmount

Subdivision

Brown Estate

Brown Industrial/ Hagmann Estate Industrial

Subdivision

Brown Street (1)

48 Street

Road

Brown Street (2)

68 Street

Road

Brown's Estate

Brown Industrial/ Hagmann Estate Industrial

Subdivision

Brown's Subdivision

Brown Industrial/ Hagmann Estate Industrial

Subdivision

Brunswick Street

No longer exists

Road

Buchanan Avenue

No longer exists

Road

Buckingham Avenue

108 Avenue

Road

Buckle Avenue

No longer exists

Road

Buena Vista

Laurier Heights/ Parkview

Subdivision

Buffalo Avenue

134 Avenue

Road

Burnaby Park

Dunluce

Subdivision

Burr Street

122 Street

Road

Burrows Court

Byrne Place

Road

Bury Industrial

Empire Park

Subdivision

C & E Trail

No longer exists

Road

C and E Trail

No longer exists

Road

Calder Estate

Aspen Gardens/ Whitemud Park

Subdivision

Calgary Avenue (1)

96 Avenue

Road

Calgary Avenue (2)

96 Avenue

Road

Calgary Trail (1)

109 Street

Road

Calgary Trail (2)

106 Street

Road

Calgary Trail (3)

No longer exists

Road

Calgary Trail (4)

Calgary Trail

Road

Calgary Trail East

Calgary Trail

Road

Calgary Trail North

Gateway Boulevard

Road

Calgary Trail Northbound
Gateway Boulevard
Road

Calgary Trail South
Gateway Boulevard
Road

Calgary Trail West
Gateway Boulevard
Road

Cambridge Boulevard
117 Street
Road

Cameron Avenue (1)
92 Street
Road

Cameron Avenue (2)
121A Avenue
Road

Cameron Street (1)
Cameron Avenue
Road

Cameron Street (2)
99 Street
Road

Campbell Street
61 Street
Road

Cape Breton Street
No longer exists
Road

Capilano
Parkdale
Subdivision

Capilano Drive (1)
No longer exists
Road

Capilano Drive (2)
Wayne Gretzky Drive
Road

Capilano Expresssway
Wayne Gretzky Drive
Road

Capilano Freeway
Wayne Gretzky Drive
Road

Capilano Road
Wayne Gretzky Drive
Road

Capital Hill
Crestwood/Glenora/
Grovenor
Subdivision

Capital Place
Roper Industrial
Subdivision

Capitol Hill
Crestwood/Glenora
Subdivision

Carey Avenue
78 Avenue
Road

Carey Street
94 Street
Road

Cariboo Avenue
133 Avenue
Road

Carle
76 Street
Road

Carleton Estate
Carleton Square
Industrial
Subdivision

Carleton Square
Carleton Square
Industrial
Subdivision

Carlton Square
Carleton Square
Industrial
Subdivision

Carlton Street
142 Street
Road

Carrol Street
76 Street
Road

Carter Avenue
137 Avenue
Road

Cascadden
No longer exists
Road

Casley
Belmont
Subdivision

Catherine
Unknown
Road

Cavan Street
88 Street
Road

Cenar
Gorman Industrial East
Subdivision

Cenar Park
Gorman Industrial East
Subdivision

Central Park
Strathcona High
School grounds
Park

Centre Road
No longer exists
Road

Chamberlain Avenue

110 Avenue

Road

Champion Street

40 Street

Road

Chaplin Street

40 Street

Road

Charles Street

77 Street

Road

Cherry Grove (1)

Mayliewan

Subdivision

Cherry Grove (2)

Belle Rive

Subdivision

Cherrydale

Belle Rive

Subdivision

Chestnut Street

151 Street

Road

Choren Street

No longer exists

Road

Chown Avenue

116 Avenue

Road

Christabell

101A Avenue

Road

Christibelle (Avenue)

101A Avenue

Road

Christibelle Street

101A Avenue

Road

Church

Unknown

Road

Churchill Avenue

108 Avenue

Road

City Gardens

Steinhauer

Subdivision

City Industrial Sites

Coronet Industrial/
Rosedale Industrial

Subdivision

City Park (1)

Strathcona High
School grounds

Park

City Park (2)

Coronation Park

Park

City Park (3)

No longer exists

Park

City Park (South Side)

Queen Elizabeth Park

Park

City Park and Nursery

Coronation Park

Park

City Park Annex

Montrose/Newton

Subdivision

City Park Annex Addition

Newton

Subdivision

City View

Lauderdale

Subdivision

City View Addition

Kilkenny

Subdivision

City View Drive

44 Avenue/
209 Street/
221 Street

Road

City View Heights

Davies Industrial East

Subdivision

Clair Street

106 Avenue

Road

Clara

103 Avenue

Road

Clara Avenue

103 Avenue

Road

Clara Street

103 Avenue

Road

Clara Street North

103 Avenue

Road

Clare Street

45 Street

Road

Clark Road

Karl Clark Road

Road

Clark Street

105 Avenue

Road

Cleave Avenue

119 Avenue

Road

Cleveland Avenue

No longer exists

Road

Cliff Street

100A Avenue

Road

Cliff Street South

Grierson Hill

Road

Cliffe Street

100A Avenue

Road

Clover Bar Avenue

No longer exists

Road

Clover Bar Road (1)

98 Avenue

Road

Clover Bar Road (2)

Connors Road

Road

Clover Bar Road (3)

95 Avenue

Road

Clover Bar Road (4)

101 Avenue

Road

Club Side

Westridge

Subdivision

Clyde Street

No longer exists

Road

CNR Heights

Cy Becker

Subdivision

CNR Industrial

Yellowhead Corridor

Subdivision

CNR Reserve

Cy Becker

Subdivision

Coal Fields

Beverly Heights/ Rundle Heights

Subdivision

Coal Street

93 Street

Road

Cobalt Street

148 Street

Road

Cochrane Avenue

No longer exists

Road

Coe Street

No longer exists

Road

Colbanks

Beverly Heights/ Rundle Heights

Subdivision

College Avenue

MacDonald Drive

Road

College Avenue Grounds

McDougall Park

Park

College Heights

Capilano/Fulton Place

Subdivision

College Park

Davies Industrial East

Subdivision

College Terrace

Gold Bar

Subdivision

College View

Eastgate Business Park

Subdivision

Columbia Avenue

105 Avenue

Road

Connaught Crescent

Connaught Drive

Road

Connaught Crescent

Rio Terrace

Subdivision

Connaught Driveway

Connaught Drive

Road

Connaught Heights

Rio Terrace

Subdivision

Conner Road

Connors Road

Road

Connor's Road

Connors Road

Road

Cook

Unknown

Road

Cooking Lake Trail (1)

Sherwood Park Freeway or 76 Avenue

Road

Cooking Lake Trail (2)

No longer exists

Road

Coot Avenue

108 Avenue

Road

Corby Avenue

No longer exists

Road

Cornell

102 Avenue

Road

Cornell Avenue
No longer exists
Road

Cotter Street
128 Street
Road

Couldhardt Avenue
No longer exists
Road

Covent Garden
Cloverdale
Subdivision

Coventry Street
24 Street NE
Road

Crafts Avenue
121 Avenue
Road

Craig Street
84 Street
Road

Crescent
No longer exists
Subdivision

Crescent Avenue
2 Avenue SW/
6 Avenue SW/
71 Street SW
Road

Crescent Heights
Pylypow Industrial/
Weir Industrial
Subdivision

Crescent Street
4 Avenue SW
Road

Crescent View
Capilano/Fulton Place
Subdivision

Crescentwood
No longer exists
Subdivision

Crescentwood Avenue
95 Avenue
Road

Cristabelle Street
101A Avenue
Road

Cromdale
Cromdale/Edmonton
Northlands/Parkdale
Subdivision

Cromdale Place
Cromdale
Subdivision

Crosby Street
No longer exists
Road

Curray
100 Street
Road

Currie Flats
Rossdale
Flats

Currie Street
100 Street
Road

Curry Avenue
100 Street
Road

Curry Street
100 Street
Road

Curzon Avenue
No longer exists
Road

D'Arcy Street
129 Street
Road

Daly Avenue
No longer exists
Road

Darroch Street
75 Street
Road

Darrock
75 Street
Road

David Street
No longer exists
Road

Davidson Avenue
112 Avenue
Road

Davidson Street
131 Street
Road

Davies Avenue
69 Avenue
Road

Davies Road
Wagner Road
Road

Day Avenue
124 Avenue
Road

Deasland
Bellevue
Subdivision

Delaware Avenue
96 Avenue
Road

Delesare Avenue
123 Avenue
Road

Deleware Avenue
96 Avenue
Road

Delton
Delton/Eastwood
Subdivision

Delton Addition
Balwin/
Elmwood Park/
Yellowhead Corridor
Subdivision

Delton Gardens
Evansdale/Northmount
Subdivision

Denman Street
No longer exists
Road

Denver Avenue (1)
97 Avenue
Road

Denver Avenue (2)
93 Avenue
Road

Denver Street
No longer exists
Road

Derriana
Unnamed
Subdivision

Detroit Avenue
No longer exists
Road

Divisional Street
101 Street
Road

Dominion
Dominion Industrial
Subdivision

Dominion Avenue
Unknown
Road

Dominion Park
Dominion Industrial/
Mitchell Industrial
Subdivision

Dominion Square
Milner Library
Square

Dominion Square
Unnamed
Subdivision

Donald Ross Flats
Rossdale
Flats

Donald Street
100A Street
Road

Dorval
Edmonton Municipal
Airport
Subdivision

Douglas
Abbottsfield
Subdivision

Douglas
Grandview Heights
Subdivision

Douglas Avenue
119 Avenue
Road

Douglas Street
78 Street
Road

Dover Avenue
No longer exists
Road

Dovercourt
Woodcroft
Subdivision

Dowler Hill Road
No longer exists
Road

Drunken Lake
No longer exists
Lake

Dublin Avenue
No longer exists
Road

Dubuc Park
Victoria Park
Park

Dufferin Avenue
No longer exists
Road

Dufferin Place
Glenwood/
Meadowlark Park
Subdivision

Dufferin Street
75A Street
Road

Duggan Street
106 Street
Road

Duluth Avenue
No longer exists
Road

Dundas
Unknown
Road

Duprau Street
68 Street
Road

Dupreau
68 Street
Road

Durdle's Ferry
No longer exists
Ferry

Dwyer

Yellowhead Corridor

Subdivision

Dwyer Addition

Belvedere

Subdivision

Dwyer Road

No longer exists

Road

Eagle Street

No longer exists

Road

Earl Street

67 Street

Road

Earle Street

76 Street

Road

Earnscliff

Strathearn

Subdivision

Earnscliffe

Cloverdale/Strathearn

Subdivision

East Avenue (1)

97 Street

Road

East Avenue (2)

No longer exists

Road

East Clover Bar Avenue

121 Avenue NE

Road

East Delton

Delwood

Subdivision

East Edmonton Gardens

Holyrood

Subdivision

East Edmonton Park

Ottewell

Subdivision

East Edward Park

Unknown

Subdivision

East Elm Park

Unknown

Subdivision

East End Bridge

Dawson Bridge

Bridge

East End Park

Borden Park

Park

East Glenora

Kenilworth/Ottewell

Subdivision

East Railway Street

102 Street

Road

East Street (1)

No longer exists

Road

East Street (2)

97 Street

Road

Eastbourn

*Industrial Heights/
Montrose*

Subdivision

Eastgate Industrial

Eastgate Business Park

Subdivision

Eastwood Addition

Eastwood

Subdivision

Eden

Davies Industrial East

Subdivision

Edith Cavell Square

Unnamed

Park

Edith Ravine

Wolf Willow Ravine

Ravine

Edmiston Street

110A Avenue

Road

Edmonton Avenue

Fort Road

Road

Edmonton City Heights

Argyll

Subdivision

Edmonton Country Club

*Edmonton Country
Club & Golf Course/
Oleskiw*

Subdivision

Edmonton Heights

Edmiston Industrial

Subdivision

**Edmonton Industrial
Airport**

*Edmonton Municipal
Airport*

Airport

**Edmonton Industrial
Exhibition Grounds**

Telus Field

Park

**Edmonton Industrial
Research Park**

*Edmonton Research and
Development Park*

Subdivision

Edmonton Junction

Rapperswil

Subdivision

Edmonton Market Gardens
Kiniski Gardens
Subdivision

Edmonton Place
Steinhauer
Subdivision

Edmonton South
Strathcona
Subdivision

Edmonton South Cemetery
Mount Pleasant Cemetery
Cemetery

Edmonton Street
Unknown
Road

Edward Street
124 Street
Road

Elgin Street
75 Street
Road

Elisabeth Avenue
64 Avenue
Road

Elizabeth Street
102 Avenue
Road

Elliot Street
81 Street
Road

Elm Avenue
113 Avenue
Road

Elm Park
Calder
Subdivision

Elm Street
113 Avenue
Road

Elmwood Park
John Devoldere Memorial Park
Park

Elsie Street
No longer exists
Road

Elysian Fields
Tawa
Subdivision

Emma Avenue
No longer exists
Road

Empire Park
Pleasantview
Subdivision

Erwin Street
63 Street
Road

Eureka
La Perle
Subdivision

Evanston
Edmonton Municipal Airport
Subdivision

Exhibition Grounds
Edmonton Northlands
Park

Exhibition Park
Edmonton Northlands
Park

Fabre Avenue
88 Avenue
Road

Fair Grounds
Rollie Miles Athletic Grounds
Park

Fairfield Street
No longer exists
Road

Fairhaven
Pylypow Industrial
Subdivision

Fairholme
Southeast Industrial
Subdivision

Fairmont
Ozerna
Subdivision

Fairmount
Mayliewan/Ozerna
Subdivision

Fairview
Alberta Avenue
Subdivision

Ferndale
Unknown
Subdivision

Fernwood
Oxford
Subdivision

Ferry Street
No longer exists
Road

Fifth Street Bridge
Walterdale Bridge
Bridge

Findlay Street
87 Street
Road

Fir Avenue
No longer exists
Road

Fir Street

No longer exists

Road

Fisher Road

No longer exists

Road

Flanitz Avenue

123 Avenue

Road

Flint Crescent

Unknown

Road

Foley Avenue

No longer exists

Road

Forbes Avenue

70 Avenue/

No longer exists

Road

Ford Park

Hollick-Kenyon

Subdivision

Forrest Avenue

No longer exists

Road

Fort Saskatchewan Road

Fort Road

Road

Fort Saskatchewan Trail

Fort Road

Road

Fort Trail

Fort Road

Road

Fox Street

89 Street

Road

Franitz Avenue

No longer exists

Road

Franklin Avenue

105 Avenue

Road

Fraser Avenue

98 Street

Road

Fraser Boulevard

87 Street

Road

Fraser Flats

Riverdale

Flats

Fraser Street

98 Street

Road

Fraser's Boulevard

87 Street

Road

Fraser's Flat

Riverdale

Flats

Fraser's Flats

Riverdale

Flats

Fraser's Lane

73 Street

Road

Frasers Flats

Riverdale

Flats

Frazer Avenue

98 Street

Road

Frederick Street

No longer exists

Road

Fredericton (1)

Industrial Heights

Subdivision

Fredericton (2)

Dovercourt

Subdivision

Furz

No longer exists

Road

Galbraith Road

No longer exists

Road

Gallagher

Cloverdale

Subdivision

Gallagher Estate

Cloverdale

Subdivision

Gallagher Flats

Cloverdale

Flats

Gallagher Road

98 Avenue

Road

Gallagher Street

109A Avenue

Road

Garden Park

Brookside/

Ramsay Heights

Subdivision

Garden Street

No longer exists

Road

Gardiner Point

Summit Point

Point

Gardiner Point

Summit Point

Road

Garneau Estate

Garneau

Subdivision

Garneau Street

111 Street

Road

Garnett Crescent

Galland Close

Road

Garth Street

133 Street

Road

George Avenue

No longer exists

Road

George Street

56 Street

Road

Gerald Street

89 Street

Road

Gertrude Avenue

66 Avenue

Road

Gibbard Street

57 Street

Road

Gibbon Avenue

111 Avenue

Road

Gibson Avenue

111 Avenue

Road

Gibson Place

Unnamed

Subdivision

Girard Place

Davies Industrial East/
Girard Industrial

Subdivision

Gladys Lane

No longer exists

Road

Glamorgan Crescent

49 Avenue/159 Street

Road

Glamorgan Heights

Ramsay Heights

Subdivision

Glen Eden

Whitemud Park

Subdivision

Glencoe Road

137 Avenue

Road

Glengarry Street

92 Street

Road

Glengary Street

92 Street

Road

Glenlyon

Pembina

Subdivision

Glenora

Glenora/North
Glenora/Westmount

Subdivision

Glenora Crescent

Wellington Crescent

Road

Glenyon

Pembina

Subdivision

Gold Bar Farm

Gold Bar

Subdivision

Gold Street

Unknown

Road

Gordon Drive

Strathearn Crescent

Road

Gordon Park

North Sawle

Subdivision

Gordon Street

72 Street

Road

Gould Street

No longer exists

Road

Government Avenue

92 Street

Road

Government Extension

92 Avenue

Road

Government Grounds

No longer exists/
Boyle Street

Park

Government Reserve

No longer exists/
Boyle Street

Park

Government Road (1)

92 Street

Road

Government Road (2)

95 Street

Road

Government Road (3)

137 Avenue

Road

Government Street

92 Street

Road

Grace Street

62 Street

Road

Gracey Avenue

109 Avenue

Road

Gracey Street

109 Avenue

Road

Graham Street

70 Street

Road

Grand Trunk Annex

Kensington

Subdivision

Grandin Street

100 Street

Road

Granville Street (1)

Unknown

Road

Granville Street (2)

No longer exists

Road

Grassy Hill Park

Gallagher Park

Park

Gray Street

58 Street

Road

Green Avenue

109 Avenue

Road

Greenbach

105A Avenue

Road

Greesbach

105A Avenue

Road

Grey Avenue

No longer exists

Road

Grierson

Delton/Elmwood Park

Subdivision

Grierson Avenue

*101 Avenue/
Grierson Hill*

Road

Grierson Estate

Delton/Elmwood Park

Subdivision

Grierson Hill Road

Grierson Hill

Road

Grierson Street

*101 Avenue/
Grierson Hill*

Road

Griesbach Avenue

85 Avenue

Road

Griesbach Street (1)

105A Avenue

Road

Griesbach Street (2)

85 Avenue

Road

Griesback Street

105A Avenue

Road

Groat Estate

Oliver/Westmount

Subdivision

Groat Flats

Victoria Park

Flats

Groat Road South

Groat Road

Road

Groat Street

126 Street

Road

Groat's Flats

Victoria Park

Flats

Grosdale

Malmo Plains

Subdivision

Grossdale

Malmo Plains

Subdivision

Grosvenor

Southeast Industrial

Subdivision

Grove Park

*Coronet Addition
Industrial/Davies
Industrial West*

Subdivision

Grove Park

W.P. Wagner Park

Park

GTP Addition

Carlisle

Subdivision

GTP Annex

Kensington

Subdivision

Guthrie Drive

5 Avenue SW

Road

Gyro Park

Kitchener Park

Park

Gyro Park No. 3

Tipton Park

Park

Hagmann

*Edmonton Municipal
Airport*

Subdivision

Hagmann Estate

*Hagmann Estate
Industrial/Sherbrooke*

Subdivision

Hamilton Avenue

90 Street

Road

Hamilton Street (1)

90 Street

Road

Hamilton Street (2)

130 Street

Road

Hampton Heights

*Davies Industrial/
McIntyre Industrial*

Subdivision

Hardisty Avenue (1)

98 Avenue

Road

Hardisty Avenue (2)

98 Avenue

Road

Hardisty Park

No longer exists

Park

Hardisty Street

101 Street

Road

Harriet Avenue

124 Avenue

Road

Harris Avenue

No longer exists

Road

Harrison Street

78 Street

Road

Harroun Street

No longer exists

Road

Hart Street

71A Street

Road

Harvard Avenue

No longer exists

Road

Harvey Street

84 Street

Road

Hastings Street (1)

87 Street

Road

Hastings Street (2)

Unknown

Road

Hastings Street (3)

No longer exists

Road

Hay Hill

No longer exists

Road

Hay Lakes Trail

23 Avenue/66 Street

Road

Hazeldene

*Hazeldean/
Rosedale Industrial*

Subdivision

HBR Industrial

Prince Rupert

Subdivision

Heiminck Street

107 Avenue

Road

Helena Avenue

132 Avenue

Road

Hemlock Street

156 Street

Road

Hempriggs

Inglewood

Subdivision

Henderson Street

36 Street

Road

Henry Street (1)

44 Street

Road

Henry Street (2)

91 Street

Road

Hereford Park

Canossa

Subdivision

Hidden Brook

Twin Brooks

Subdivision

Higgins Street

Unknown

Road

High Park

High Park Industrial

Subdivision

Highland Park
Bonnie Doon/
Strathearn
Subdivision

Highland Park Addition
Bonnie Doon
Subdivision

Highland Road
No longer exists
Road

Highland Street
95 Street
Road

Highlands Road
No longer exists
Road

Hill
No longer exists
Road

Hill Street
No longer exists
Road

Hillcrest
Brander Gardens
Subdivision

Hillcrest Crescent
Hillside Crescent
Road

Hillhurst Street
50 Street
Road

Hillock Avenue
68 Avenue
Road

Hillsboro
104 Avenue
Road

Hillside Avenue (1)
No longer exists
Road

Hillside Avenue (2)
No longer exists
Road

Hillview Drive
197 Avenue
Road

Hillview Road
231 Street
Road

Hirsh Avenue
No longer exists
Road

Hirst Road
No longer exists
Road

Holgate Avenue
No longer exists
Road

Holgate Street
No longer exists
Road

Hollywood
Capilano/Gold Bar
Subdivision

Home Gardens
Greenfield
Subdivision

Horse Hill Creek
Horsehills Creek
Creek

Horse Lake
Mistalim Lake
Lake

Horse Lake #1
No longer exists
Lake

Horse Lake #2
Mistatim Lake
Lake

Houston Street
64 Street
Road

Houston Street
64 Street
Road

Howard Avenue
100A Street
Road

Howard Street
100A Street
Road

Hudson's Bay Co.'s
Reserve
Central McDougall/
Downtown/Edmonton
Municipal Airport/
Oliver/Queen Mary
Park/Spruce Avenue
Subdivision

Hudson's Bay Company
Flats
Victoria Park
Flats

Hudson's Bay Park
Victoria Golf Course/
Victoria Park
Park

Huff Estate
Huff Bremner Estate
Industrial/McQueen
Subdivision

Hulbert Avenue
University Avenue
Road

Hulberts
Belgravia/McKernan
Subdivision

Hulberts Addition
Belgravia/McKernan
Subdivision

Humberstone

Abbottsfield/
Overlanders

Subdivision

Huron Avenue

No longer exists

Road

Huron Street (1)

No longer exists

Road

Huron Street (2)

No longer exists

Road

Huston Street

64 Street

Road

Hutton Avenue

92 Avenue

Road

Hyde Park

Edmonton Country
Club & Golf Course/
Oleskiw

Subdivision

Imperial Avenue

No longer exists

Road

Imperial Gardens

The Palisades

Subdivision

Imperial Square

No longer exists

Square

Industrial Centre

Delwood

Subdivision

Industrial Heights

Industrial Heights/
Newton

Subdivision

Industrial Park

Delwood

Subdivision

Industrial Park

Kirkness

Subdivision

Industrial Place

Hairsine

Subdivision

Industrial View

Bergman/Homesteader

Subdivision

Inkerman Avenue

126 Avenue

Road

International Park

Kirkness

Subdivision

Ira Street

No longer exists

Road

Irene Avenue

73 Avenue

Road

Iriquois Avenue

No longer exists

Road

Iron Bridge

Groat Ravine Bridge

Bridge

Irvine (CPR)

CPR Irvine/
Hazeldean/Ritchie

Subdivision

Irvine Estate

CPR Irvine/
Hazeldean/Ritchie

Subdivision

Irving Estate

CPR Irvine/Ritchie

Subdivision

Irvington

Gariepy

Subdivision

Irwin Estate

Homesteader/
Sifton Park

Subdivision

Irwin Estate Addition

Belmont/Homesteader/
Overlanders

Subdivision

Irwin Street

63 Street

Road

Isabella Street

104 Avenue

Road

Jackson Place

81 Street

Road

Jackson Place

Athlone

Subdivision

James Street

123 Street

Road

James Street

81 Street

Road

Jamha Crescent

Jamha Road

Road

Jarvis Street

No longer exists

Road

Jasper Avenue (1)

101 Avenue/
111 Avenue/
113 Avenue (Beverly)/
Ada Boulevard/
Jasper Avenue
Road

Jasper Avenue (2)

101 Avenue
Road

Jasper Avenue (3)

Stony Plain Road
Road

Jasper Avenue East

Jasper Avenue
Road

Jasper Avenue West

Jasper Avenue
Road

Jasper Extension

Jasper Avenue
Road

Jasper Park Addition

Unknown
Subdivision

Jasper Place

Britannia Youngstown/
Canora/Elmwood/
Glenwood/High
Park/High Park
Industrial/Huff
Bremner Estate
Industrial/Jasper

Park/Lynnwood/
Meadowlark Park/
Rio Terrace/Sheffield
Industrial/Sherwood/
Stone Industrial/West
Jasper Place/West
Meadowlark Park/
West Sheffield
Industrial/Youngstown
Industrial
Town

Jasper Place

Crestwood/Sherwood/
West Jasper Place
Subdivision

Jellett Crescent

Jellett Way
Road

Jenner Road

Jenner Cove
Road

Jennings Crescent

Jennings Bay
Road

Jewish Cemetery

Edmonton Jewish
Cemetery
Cemetery

John Ducey Park

Telus Field
Park

John Street

80 Street
Road

Johnson Road

244 Avenue
Road

Johnson Street

83 Street
Road

Johnston Estate

Caernarvon
Subdivision

Johnston Street (1)

83 Street
Road

Johnston Street (2)

62 Street
Road

Johnstone Estate

Caernarvon
Subdivision

Johnstone Street

62 Street
Road

Joseph Avenue

No longer exists
Road

Joyce Street

Joyce Crescent
Road

Julia Street

94 Street
Road

Julian

Unknown
Road

Kakiteeo

Kaskitayo
Subdivision

Kaskiteeo

Kaskitayo
Subdivision

Kathleen Street

No longer exists
Road

Kelley Avenue

124 Avenue
Road

Kemp Street

83 Street
Road

Kennedale

Kennedale Industrial
Subdivision

Kennedale Park

No longer exists
Park

Kennedy Addition

Kennedale Industrial
Subdivision

Kennedy Drive
No longer exists
Road

Kennedy Street
93 Street
Road

Kenora Street
No longer exists
Road

Kensington
Rosslyn
Subdivision

Kent Street
58 Street
Road

Kenward Drive
130 Avenue
Road

Kenyon Street
94 Street
Road

King Edward
Strathcona
Subdivision

King Edward Addition
Gainer Industrial/
King Edward Park
Subdivision

King Edward Park Addition
Gainer Industrial
Subdivision

King George Park
Kenilworth
Subdivision

King George Park
No longer exists
Park

King Powell Estate
Unknown
Subdivision

King Street (1)
No longer exists
Road

King Street (2)
86 Street
Road

King Street (3)
108A Street
Road

King's Circle
No longer exists
Road

King's Road (1)
Unknown
Road

King's Road (2)
130 Street
Road

Kingston Avenue
No longer exists
Road

Kingsway (1)
Princess Elizabeth
Avenue
Road

Kingsway (2)
No longer exists
Road

Kingsway Avenue
Princess Elizabeth
Avenue
Road

Kinistino Avenue
96 Street
Road

Kinnaird Ravine
Kinnaird
Park

Kinnaird Street
82 Street
Road

Kinross-Kerr Park
Ronning Street
Neighbourhood Park
Park

Kirkness Street
95 Street
Road

Kitchener Square
Kitchener Park
Park

Kitto Avenue
94A Street
Road

Kitts Avenue
94A Street
Road

Knob Hill
Bonnie Doon
Subdivision

Knox Avenue
112 Avenue
Road

Kootenay Avenue
90 Avenue
Road

Lake Street
60 Street
Road

Lambton Park
Lambton Industrial
Subdivision

Lambton Street
105 Avenue
Road

Landon Avenue

94 Avenue

Road

Lang Street

129 Street

Road

Laurelhurst

Argyll

Subdivision

Laurier Park (1)

Laurier Heights

Subdivision

Laurier Park (2)

Sir Wilfrid Laurier Park

Park

Laurier Street

145 Street

Road

Lavigne

Strathcona

Subdivision

Le Roy Avenue

No longer exists

Road

Lee Street

85 Street

Road

Legal Avenue

89 Avenue

Road

Legget Street

87 Street

Road

Leggett Street

87 Street

Road

Lenora

Armstrong Industrial

Subdivision

Leonard Street (1)

No longer exists

Road

Leonard Street (2)

No longer exists

Road

Lincoln Avenue

No longer exists

Road

Lola Street

83 Street

Road

Long Lake

Kinokamau Lake

Lake

Lorne Avenue (1)

No longer exists

Road

Lorne Avenue (2)

No longer exists

Road

Lorne Park

Britannia Youngstown/ Youngstown Industrial

Subdivision

Lorne Street

92 Street

Road

Lornedale

Aldergrove/ Anthony Henday Drive

Subdivision

Lumsden Avenue

84 Avenue

Road

Lysle Street

105 Avenue

Road

M'Kay Avenue

99 Avenue

Road

Mable Street

58 Street

Road

MacCauley Street

Unknown

Road

Macdonald Drive

MacDonald Drive

Road

MACDONALD DRIVE

MacDonald Drive

Road

MacDonald Fraser's Flats

88 Street

Road

MacDonald Frasers Flats

88 Street

Road

Macdonald Street

47 Street

Road

Macdonald Terrace

McDougall Park

Park

Mackenzie Avenue

104 Avenue

Road

MacKenzie Heights

Hollick-Kenyon

Subdivision

Macleod Street

No longer exists

Road

Madison Avenue

No longer exists

Road

Magrath Avenue

113 Avenue

Road

Magrath Holgate Subdivision

Beacon Heights/ Bergman/Homesteader

Subdivision

Main Street

104 Street

Road

Makenzie Avenue

104 Avenue

Road

Mamie Street

Unknown

Road

Manchester

Papaschase Industrial/ Strathcona Industrial Park

Subdivision

Manhattan Park

CFB Griesbach

Subdivision

Manhatton Avenue

No longer exists

Road

Manhatton Park

CFB Griesbach

Subdivision

Manitoba Avenue

93 Avenue

Road

Manning Freeway

Manning Drive

Road

Manning Industrial Area

Possibly Ebbers Industrial

Subdivision

Maple Street

150 Street

Road

Margery Street

Rowland Road

Road

Marjorie Street (1)

Rowland Road

Road

Marjorie Street (2)

No longer exists

Road

Marjory Street

Rowland Road

Road

Market Square

No longer exists

Square

Markham Street

134 Street

Road

Marlborough Heights

Roper Industrial

Subdivision

Marten Street

88 Street

Road

Martin Estate

Allendale/Pleasantview

Subdivision

Martin Street

88 Street

Road

Mary Avenue

No longer exists

Road

Mary Road

No longer exists

Road

May Avenue

No longer exists

Road

May Street

102A Avenue

Road

Mayfair

Mayfair Golf & Country Club/William Hawrelak Park

Subdivision

Mayfair Avenue

No longer exists

Road

Mayfair Drive

No longer exists

Road

Mayfair Park

Mayfair Golf & Country Club/William Hawrelak Park

Park

Mayo Street

Unknown

Road

Mays Avenue

No longer exists

Road

McCauley Street

107A Avenue

Road

McDonald Avenue (1)

83 Avenue

Road

McDonald Avenue (2)

88 Street

Road

McDonald Avenue (3)

76 Avenue

Road

McDonald Drive

MacDonald Drive

Road

McDonald Fraser's Flats

88 Street

Road

McDonald's Flat

Riverdale

Flats

McDougal Street

100 Street

Road

McDougall Avenue

100 Street

Road

McDougall Drive

MacDonald Drive

Road

McDougall Extension

100 Street

Road

McDougall Park

Unnamed

Park

McDougall Street (1)

Rossdale Road

Road

McDougall Street (2)

100 Street

Road

McDougall Street South

Rossdale Road

Road

McGill Boulevard

118 Street

Road

McKay Avenue (1)

99 Avenue

Road

McKay Avenue (2)

99 Avenue

Road

McKenzie Avenue

104 Avenue

Road

McKenzie Heights

Hollick-Kenyon

Subdivision

McKenzie Ravine

MacKenzie Ravine

Ravine

McKernan Estate

*Belgravia/University of
Alberta Farm*

Subdivision

McKernan Lake

No longer exists

Lake

McKinley Street

78 Street

Road

McKye Avenue

99 Avenue

Road

McLeod Avenue (1)

93 Avenue

Road

McLeod Avenue (2)

95 Avenue

Road

McLeod Avenue (3)

95 Avenue

Road

McMurray Street

No longer exists

Road

McNamara Estate

Greenfield

Subdivision

McPherson Street

No longer exists

Road

McRae Street

134 Street

Road

Meadow

Place LaRue

Subdivision

Meadow Brook

Glastonbury

Subdivision

Meadowlark Drive

Meadowlark Road

Road

Meadows

Place Larue

Subdivision

Mee Yah Noh

Killarney

Subdivision

Meeyahnoh

Killarney

Subdivision

Meeyanoh

Killarney

Subdivision

Mekan

Unknown

Subdivision

Memorial Walk

No longer exists

Road

Merton Street

Unknown

Road

Michigan Avenue

Unknown

Road

Michigan Street

No longer exists

Road

Mill Avenue

79 Avenue

Road

Miller Avenue

129 Avenue

Road

Minto Avenue

No longer exists

Road

Mohawk Avenue

No longer exists

Road

Montana Street

205 Street NW

Road

Montgomery Street

55 Street

Road

Moore Avenue

62 Avenue

Road

Moore Park

Hollick-Kenyon

Subdivision

Moreau

90 Street

Road

Morgan Avenue

Yellowhead Trail

Road

Morris Street

106A Avenue

Road

Moser Street

65 Street

Road

Mount Avenue

No longer exists

Road

Mount Lawn

Montrose

Subdivision

Mount Pleasant

Forest Heights/
Holyrood

Subdivision

Mount Royal

Highlands

Subdivision

Mount Royal Park

Edmonton Municipal
Airport

Park

Mount Royal Park

Highlands

Subdivision

Mount View Street

43 Street

Road

Muir Avenue

No longer exists

Road

Mulmer Park

Eastgate Business Park

Subdivision

Mulmur Park

Eastgate Business Park

Subdivision

Municipal Golf Course

Victoria Golf Course

Park

Municipal Golf Links

Victoria Golf Course

Park

Murray Street

73 Street

Road

Muskoka Avenue

111 Avenue

Road

Namao Avenue

97 Street

Road

Namayo Avenue (1)

97 Street

Road

Namayo Avenue (2)

100 Street

Road

Namayo Crescent

Klarvatten/Lago Lindo

Subdivision

Namayo Park

Glengarry

Subdivision

Namayo Street

97 Street

Road

Namayo View

Lorelei

Subdivision

Nellie Street

Unknown

Road

Nelson Avenue

107 Avenue

Road

Nelson Street (1)

63 Street

Road

Nelson Street (2)

No longer exists

Road

Neraclam

Bonnie Doon

Subdivision

Neralcam

Bonnie Doon

Subdivision

Neralgam

Bonnie Doon

Subdivision

New Delton

Balwin

Subdivision

New Delton Addition

Balwin

Subdivision

New Hagmann

*Edmonton Municipal
Airport*

Subdivision

New Haymann

*Edmonton Municipal
Airport*

Subdivision

New Inglewood (1)

Kensington

Subdivision

New Inglewood (2)

*Edmonton Municipal
Airport*

Subdivision

Niblock Street

105 Street

Road

Nipigon Avenue

112 Avenue

Road

Nob Hill

Connors Hill

Hill

Norfolk Avenue

No longer exists

Road

Normandale Avenue

117 Avenue

Road

North Belvedere

York

Subdivision

North Belvidere

York

Subdivision

North Delton

Glengarry/Killarney

Subdivision

North Eastwood

Elmwood Park

Subdivision

North Edmonton

*Balwin/Belvedere/
Eastwood/
Kennedale Industrial*

Village

North Inglewood

Prince Charles

Subdivision

North Jasper Place

Canora/High Park

Subdivision

North Railway Avenue

130 Avenue

Road

North Railway Road

130 Avenue

Road

Northcote

Westwood

Subdivision

**Northern Lights
Memorial Park**

South Haven Cemetery

Cemetery

Northview Park

Ozerna

Subdivision

Norton Street

66 Street

Road

Norwood

Alberta Avenue

Subdivision

Norwood Extension

Westwood

Subdivision

Norwood Park

Norwood Square

Park

Notre Dame Street

122 Street

Road

Notre Dame Street

Unknown

Road

O'Connell Road

98 Avenue

Road

Oak Avenue

116 Avenue

Road

Oak Crescent

No longer exists

Road

Oakland Avenue

No longer exists

Road

Okanagan Avenue

115 Avenue

Road

Okanagon Avenue

115 Avenue

Road

Old Car Barns Site

Giovanni Caboto Park

Park

Old City Hospital

Unnamed

Park

Old Exhibition Grounds

Telus Field

Park

Old Fort Hill Road

106A Street/Fort Hill

Road

Old Golf Links

Victoria Park

Park

Old School Grounds

Kitchener Park

Park

Oliver Avenue

86 Avenue

Road

Oliver Gardens

Unnamed

Subdivision

Oliver Street

144 Street

Road

Onion Park

Grand Trunk Park

Park

Ontario Street

No longer exists

Road

Ottawa Avenue

93 Street

Road

Ottawa Fort Trail

Unknown

Road

Ottawa Fraser Flats

Unknown

Road

Ottawa Street

93 Street

Road

Otter Street

90 Street

Road

Oxford Avenue

130 Avenue

Road

Oxford Street (1)

No longer exists

Road

Oxford Street (2)

No longer exists

Road

Pace Street

113A Street

Road

Pacific Avenue

Unknown

Road

Packingtown

Belvedere/Kennedale Industrial

Village

Pardale

Allendale/ Queen Alexandra

Subdivision

Park Drive

No longer exists

Road

Park Road

No longer exists

Road

Park Street (1)

103A Street

Road

Park Street (2)

103A Street/ Calgary Trail

Road

Park Street (3)

127 Street

Road

Park Street (4)

78 Street

Road

Parkdale

Allendale/ Queen Alexandra

Subdivision

Parkdale North

Parkdale

Subdivision

Parkdale South

Allendale/ Queen Alexandra

Subdivision

Parkfield

CFB Griesbach

Subdivision

Parkville

Carlisle

Subdivision

Patricia Park

Giovanni Caboto Park

Park

Patricia Square

Giovanni Caboto Park

Park

Paul Avenue

129 Avenue

Road

Paul Street

80 Street

Road

Peace Avenue

103 Avenue

Road

Pearce Avenue

No longer exists

Road

Pearce Street

No longer exists

Road

Pelican Street

No longer exists

Road

Pembina Avenue

117 Avenue

Road

Pembroke

103 Avenue

Road

Percey Avenue

89 Avenue

Road

Percy Avenue

Unknown

Road

Phillips Avenue

120 Avenue

Road

Phillips Street

76 Street

Road

Phoenix Avenue

132 Avenue

Road

Phoenix Street

96 Street

Road

Picard Street

108 Avenue

Road

Piccadilly Avenue

131 Avenue

Road

Pickering Street

79 Street

Subdivision

Pine Avenue

112 Avenue

Road

Pine Place

112 Avenue

Road

Pine Street

No longer exists

Road

Pittsburg

Clareview Campus

Subdivision

Pleasant Hill

MacIntyre Industrial

Subdivision

Pole Street

No longer exists

Road

Pollard's Flat

Walterdale

Flats

Poplar Avenue

75 Avenue

Road

Poplar Lake

Unknown

Lake

Poplar Street

155 Street

Road

Portage Avenue

Kingsway Avenue

Road

Portage Avenue Park

*Victoria Cross
Memorial Park*

Park

Portage Road

Kingsway

Road

Portage Road

Kingsway Avenue

Road

Portland Street

No longer exists

Road

Poundmaker

*Edmonton Research and
Development Park*

Subdivision

Powell Estate (1)

Unknown

Subdivision

Powell Estate (2)

CFB Griesbach

Subdivision

Prescott Avenue

94 Avenue

Road

Presidio Heights

Eastgate Business Park

Subdivision

Primrose Place

Forest Heights

Subdivision

Prince Avenue

No longer exists

Road

Prince Rupert Golf Links

No longer exists

Park

Princes Street

No longer exists

Road

Princess Street

76 Street

Road

Princeton

Ottewell

Subdivision

Prospect Point

Unknown

Road

Quebec Street

No longer exists

Road

Queen

106A Street

Road

Queen Avenue

No longer exists

Road

Queen Mary Park

Kensington

Subdivision

Queen Mary Park

No longer exists

Park

Queen's Avenue

99 Street

Road

Queen's Drive

No longer exists

Road

Queen's Park

Delwood

Subdivision

Queen's Park Estate

Delwood

Subdivision

Queens Avenue (1)

99 Street

Road

Queens Avenue (2)

No longer exists

Road

Queens Crescent

No longer exists

Road

Queens Park

Delwood

Subdivision

Quesnel

Quesnel Heights

Subdivision

Race

38 Street

Road

Radial Park

Bonaventure/ McArthur Industrial

Subdivision

Railway Road

No longer exists

Road

Rainbow Valley Park

Whitemud Park

Park

Randolph Avenue

No longer exists

Road

Rat Creek

No longer exists

Creek

Rat Creek Canyon

Kinnaird Park

Park

Rat Creek Park

Kinnaird Park

Park

Rat Creek Ravine

Kinnaird Ravine

Ravine

Rat Hole (The)

No longer exists

Tunnel

Raven Street

No longer exists

Road

Ravine Court

5 Avenue SW

Road

Ravine Drive

Guthrie Point

Road

Ravine Park

Kinnaird Park

Park

Raymer Avenue

79 Street

Road

Raymer Street

81 Street

Road

Raymond Avenue

111 Avenue

Road

Rayner Street

81 Street

Road

Reese Avenue

No longer exists

Road

Regent Avenue

129 Avenue

Road

Regents Park

Roper Industrial

Subdivision

Regina Street

No longer exists

Road

Renfrew Ball Park

Telus Field

Park

Renfrew Park

Telus Field

Park

Reppert Crescent

28 Avenue SW

Road

Research Centre Loop

Karl Clark Road

Road

Rice Howard Mall

Rice Howard Way

Road

Rice Street (1)

101A Avenue

Road

Rice Street (2)

38 Street

Road

Richard Avenue

89 Street

Road

Richard Avenue Frasers Flats

89 Street

Road

Richard Fraser Flats

89 Street

Road

Richard Fraser's Flats

89 Street

Road

Richards

89 Street

Road

Richards Fraser Flats

89 Street

Road

Richford Road

5 Avenue SW/
107 Street SW

Road

Richmond Heights

No longer exists

Subdivision

Richmond Park

Hazeldean/Ritchie

Subdivision

Riddell Crescent

Riddell Street

Road

Ridgeway Park

Capilano/Fulton Place

Subdivision

Riggs Street

72 Street

Road

Ring Road

119 Avenue/
120 Avenue/
226 Street

Road

Riot Street

99 Street

Road

Rist Street

99 Street

Road

River Avenue

No longer exists

Road

River Bank

100B Street

Road

River Boulevard

87 Street

Road

River Bridge

Low Level Bridge

Bridge

River Front Fraser's Flats

Riverdale

Flats

River Heights

Bonnie Doon/
Strathearn

Subdivision

River Heights Addition

Bonnie Doon

Subdivision

River Road Drive

River Valley Road

Road

River Street

94 Street

Road

River Valley Street

Grandisle Road

Road

River View Avenue

95 Avenue

Road

River View Crescent

River View Way

Road

River View Heights

Belgravia/University of
Alberta Farm

Subdivision

Riverbend Park

Terwillegar Park

Park

Riverdale Boulevard

87 Street

Road

Riverdale Park

Unknown

Park

Riverside Avenue (1)

No longer exists

Road

Riverside Avenue (2)

No longer exists

Road

Riverside Drive

No longer exists

Road

Riverside Park

Queen Elizabeth Park

Park

Riverview

Cromdale

Subdivision

Riverview Avenue

110 Avenue

Road

Riverview Crescent

Grandisle Point

Road

Riverview Heights

*University of Alberta
Farm*

Subdivision

Roberts Street

94 Avenue

Road

Robertson Avenue (1)

90 Avenue

Road

Robertson Avenue (2)

122 Avenue

Road

Robertson Street

73 Street

Road

Robin Street

No longer exists

Road

Robins Avenue

76 Street

Road

Roche Drive

Roche Crescent

Road

Roe Drive

Roe Crescent

Road

Roland Road

Rowland Road

Road

**Roman Catholic
Cemetery**

St. Joachim Cemetery

Cemetery

Ronald Avenue

Strathearn Drive

Road

Rooney Street

Rooney Crescent

Road

Roosevelt Street

113A Street

Road

Rosedale

Rosedale Industrial

Subdivision

Rosedale Addition S.

Unknown

Subdivision

Roseglen

Brookside

Subdivision

Roslyn

Rosslyn

Subdivision

Roslyn Street

135 Street

Road

Ross Avenue (1)

121 Avenue

Road

Ross Avenue (2)

No longer exists

Road

Ross Flats

Rossdale

Flats

Ross Road

Scona Road

Road

Ross Street (1)

108A Avenue

Road

Ross Street (2)

No longer exists

Road

Ross' Flats

Rossdale

Flats

Ross' Hill

Bellamy Hill

Hill

Ross' Point

Unnamed

Point

Rouleau Avenue

80 Avenue

Road

Rowand Park

No longer exists

Park

Rowland Addition

Boyle Street/McCauley

Subdivision

Rowland Estate

McCauley

Subdivision

Rowland Street

Rowland Road

Road

Roxboro

Brander Gardens/
Brookside

Subdivision

Roxborough

Brander Gardens/
Brookside

Subdivision

Roy Avenue

77 Avenue

Road

Roy Crescent

Roy Gate

Road

Royal Avenue

87 Avenue

Road

Royal Heights

Clareview Campus

Subdivision

Royal Park

Stone Industrial

Subdivision

Running Creek

Twin Brooks

Subdivision

Rupert Street (1)

105A Street

Road

Rupert Street (2)

105B Street

Road

Rutherford

Bonnie Doon/
King Edward Park

Subdivision

Rutherford Avenue

90 Street/92 Street

Road

Rutherford Park

Mill Creek Ravine Park

Park

Ryder Street

64 Street

Road

S'cona Brae

Bonnie Doon

Subdivision

Sache Avenue

88 Avenue

Road

Sage Street

46 Street

Road

Salter

Unknown

Road

Samson Drive

111 Avenue

Road

Sanderson Estate

Unknown

Subdivision

Sandison Place

No longer exists

Road

Santa Rosa

Industrial Heights/
Montrose/
Yellowhead Corridor

Subdivision

Santa Rosa Road

Yellowhead Trail

Road

Saskatchewan Avenue (1)

Saskatchewan Drive

Road

Saskatchewan Avenue (2)

97 Avenue

Road

Saskatchewan Avenue (3)

No longer exists

Road

Saskatchewan Avenue (4)

No longer exists

Road

Saskatchewan Avenue (5)

97 Avenue

Road

Saskatchewan Avenue (6)

Fort Road

Road

Saskatchewan Avenue (7)

Saskatchewan Drive

Road

Saskatchewan Avenue (8)

No longer exists

Road

Saskatchewan Drive East

Strathearn Drive

Road

Saskatchewan River
North Saskatchewan River
River

Saskatoon Street
No longer exists
Road

Saunders Avenue
86 Street
Road

Saunders Street
86 Street
Road

School Avenue
No longer exists
Road

Scona Brae
Bonnie Doon
Subdivision

Scona Square
No longer exists
Park

Scotia Avenue
No longer exists
Road

Scott Street
69 Street
Road

Seager Street
No longer exists
Road

Semered Avenue
No longer exists
Road

Severn Avenue
110A Avenue
Road

Shaftsbury Avenue
111 Avenue
Road

Shand Avenue
111 Avenue
Road

Shand Street
111 Avenue
Road

Sharp Street
37 Street
Road

Sharpe
37 Street
Road

Shaughnessy Heights
Duggan/Rideau Park
Subdivision

Shelbourne
Bonnie Doon
Subdivision

Shelburne
Bonnie Doon
Subdivision

Sherrif Addition
King Edward Park
Subdivision

Sheriff's Addition
King Edward Park
Subdivision

Sherriff Addition
King Edward Park
Subdivision

Sherwood Park Expressway
Sherwood Park Freeway
Road

Shields Avenue
128 Avenue
Road

Short Avenue (1)
107 Avenue
Road

Short Avenue (2)
Unknown
Road

Short Street
109 Avenue
Road

Silver Heights
Strathearn
Subdivision

Simpson Street
70 Street
Road

Sinclair Avenue
95A Street
Road

Sinclair Street
95A Street
Road

Skunk Hollow
Lavigne
Subdivision

Slocan Avenue
90 Avenue
Road

Slogan Avenue
92 Avenue
Road

Smith Avenue
No longer exists
Road

Smith Street
No longer exists
Road

Soulien Avenue
No longer exists
Road

Soulier

No longer exists

Road

Soullier

No longer exists

Road

South Avenue

University Avenue

Road

South Edmonton

Strathcona

Town

South Groat Road

Groat Road

Road

South Jasper Place

Elmwood/Lynnwood

Subdivision

South Park

Strathcona Industrial

Park

Subdivision

South Railway Avenue

129 Avenue

Road

South Railway Road

129 Avenue

Road

South Side Park

Queen Elizabeth Park

Park

South Side Park and

Bathing Pool

Queen Elizabeth Park

Park

South Strathcona

Pleasantview

Subdivision

South Street

No longer exists

Road

South Valley View Drive

Valleyview Crescent

Road

Spadina Avenue (1)

120 Avenue

Road

Spadina Avenue (2)

No longer exists

Road

Sparling Street

69 Street

Road

Sparrow Street

No longer exists

Road

Speedway

Coronet Industrial

Subdivision

Speedways

Coronet Industrial

Subdivision

Sprag Street

No longer exists

Road

Spruce Avenue

Unknown

Subdivision

Spruce Avenue (1)

No longer exists

Road

Spruce Avenue (2)

114 Avenue

Road

Spruce Street

No longer exists

Road

St. Albert Avenue

St. Albert Trail

Road

St. Albert Road

St. Albert Trail

Road

St. Albert Street

110 Street

Road

St. Catherine Street (1)

No longer exists

Road

St. Catherine Street (2)

125 Street

Road

St. Catherines Street

125 Street

Road

St. Elmo Park

Poundmaker Industrial/

Sunwapta Industrial

Subdivision

St. George Street

74 Street

Road

St. George's Street

74 Street

Road

St. Germaine Avenue

109 Avenue

Road

St. James Street (1)

123 Street

Road

St. James Street (2)

No longer exists

Road

St. John Street
No longer exists
Road

St. Lawrence
109A Avenue
Road

St. Leon Avenue
No longer exists
Road

St. Leon Boulevard
No longer exists
Road

St. Paul Street (1)
90 Avenue
Road

St. Paul Street (2)
No longer exists
Road

St. Placide Street
91 Avenue
Road

Stanford Avenue
No longer exists
Road

Stanley Avenue (1)
Unknown
Road

Stanley Avenue (2)
87 Avenue
Road

Stanley Park
Belmont/Kernohan
Subdivision

Steel Bridge
Groat Ravine Bridge
Bridge

Stephen Avenue
106 Avenue
Road

Stephens Avenue
106 Avenue
Road

Stewart Street
101A Avenue
Road

Stikeen Avenue
114 Avenue
Road

Stikine Avenue
114 Avenue
Road

Stoney Plain Road (1)
Stony Plain Road
Road

Stoney Plain Road (2)
Stony Plain Road
Road

Storyland Valley Zoo
Valley Zoo
Park

Strathcona Athletic Grounds
Rollie Miles Athletic Grounds
Park

Strathcona Athletic Park
Rollie Miles Athletic Grounds
Park

Strathcona Cemetery
Mount Pleasant Cemetery
Cemetery

Strathcona Fairgrounds
Rollie Miles Athletic Grounds
Park

Strathcona Heights
Greenview/Hillview
Subdivision

Strathcona Hill
Possibly Connors Hill
Hill

Strathcona Place
Garneau/McKernan
Subdivision

Strathcona Recreation Grounds
Rollie Miles Athletic Grounds
Park

Strathcona Road
99 Street/Scona Road
Road

Strathcona-Edmonton Viaduct
High Level Bridge
Bridge

Strathearn Drive
Strathearn Crescent
Road

Strathspey
Strathcona
Subdivision

Sturgeon Cemetery
Northern Lights Cemetery
Cemetery

Sturgeon Heights Memorial Park
Northern Lights Cemetery
Cemetery

Summer Gardens
Keheewin
Subdivision

Summerland Park
Cumberland
Subdivision

Summerville
Evansdale
Subdivision

Summerwilde

Edmonton Municipal Airport

Subdivision

Summit Avenue

Summit Drive

Road

Sunalta

Glengarry

Subdivision

Sunny Brook

Callingwood North

Subdivision

Sunnyslope Gardens

Southeast Industrial

Subdivision

Sunset Park

Dovercourt

Subdivision

Sunset Park

Dovercourt Park

Park

Sutherland Park

Morris Industrial/ Weir Industrial

Subdivision

Sutherland Street

106 Avenue

Road

Swallow Street

No longer exists

Road

Swamey Avenue

94 Street

Road

Swansea Street

94 Street

Road

Sydney Street

No longer exists

Road

Syndicate Avenue

95 Street

Road

Tarbolton Road

No longer exists

Road

Tarbolton Street

No longer exists

Road

Taylor Avenue

77 Street

Road

Taylor Street

146 Street

Road

Teddington Avenue

No longer exists

Road

The Braids

Belvedere

Subdivision

The Country Club Road

No longer exists

Road

The Heighlands

Highlands

Subdivision

The Highlands Park

The Highlands Golf Course

Park

Thistle Street

No longer exists

Road

Thomas Avenue

No longer exists

Road

Thomas Street

91 Avenue

Road

Thompson Avenue

110 Avenue

Road

Thompson Crescent

No longer exists

Road

Thornton Street

77 Street

Road

Threadneedle Avenue

128 Avenue

Road

Threadneedle Street

128 Avenue

Road

Tipton Avenue

51 Avenue

Road

Tipton Crescent

No longer exists

Road

Tipton Park

Queen Elizabeth Park

Park

Tipton Square

No longer exists

Park

Todd Street

73 Street

Road

Toronto Avenue

No longer exists

Road

Travis-Barker Park

Unnamed

Park

Trethaway
105 Avenue
Road

Tretheway Avenue
105 Avenue
Road

Trethewey Avenue
105 Avenue
Road

Tupper Street
41 Street
Road

Tuxedo Heights
University of Alberta Farm
Subdivision

Tuxedo Park
Eastgate Business Park
Subdivision

Ukrainian Millennium Park
Primrose Park
Park

Uneeda Place
Davies Industrial East/ Girard Industrial
Subdivision

University City
Strathcona
City

University Drive
University Avenue
Road

University Park
Lendrum Place
Subdivision

University Place
Belgravia/McKernan
Subdivision

University Place Addition
Belgravia
Subdivision

Uplands
LaPerle
Subdivision

Valley Avenue
No longer exists
Road

Valley View Crescent
Valleyview Crescent
Road

Valley View Drive
Valleyview Drive
Road

Valley View Point
Valleyview Point
Road

Valleyview
Parkview
Subdivision

Vancouver Street
62 Street
Road

Vermilion Avenue
106 Avenue
Road

Vermillion Avenue
106 Avenue
Road

Vermillion Street
106 Avenue
Road

Vernan Street
No longer exists
Road

Vernon Street
No longer exists
Road

Victoria Avenue (1)
100 Avenue
Road

Victoria Avenue (2)
No longer exists
Road

Victoria Avenue (3)
100 Avenue/ Ravine Drive
Road

Victoria Avenue (4)
No longer exists
Road

Victoria Crescent (1)
No longer exists
Road

Victoria Crescent (2)
St. George's Crescent
Road

Victoria Park
Papaschase Industrial/ Strathcona Industrial Park
Subdivision

Victoria Park Road
River Valley Road
Road

Victoria Place
113 Avenue
Road

Victoria Place
Montrose
Subdivision

Victoria Street (1)
60 Street
Road

Victoria Street (2)
No longer exists
Road

View Point

Cromdale

Subdivision

View Point Boulevard

111 Avenue

Road

View Point Crescent

111 Avenue

Road

View Street

No longer exists

Road

Viking Road

Unknown

Road

Vogel

Bonnie Doon

Subdivision

Vogel Estate

Bonnie Doon

Subdivision

Vogel Street

No longer exists

Road

Wadhurst Park

Westmount

Subdivision

Wadleigh Street

67 Street

Road

Waldemere

Eaux Claires

Subdivision

Waldermere

Eaux Claires

Subdivision

Waldmere

Eaux Claires

Subdivision

Walkers Flats

Unnamed

Flats

Wall Street

94 Avenue

Road

Wallace

74 Street

Road

Walnut Street

152 Street

Road

Walsh Avenue (1)

94 Avenue

Road

Walsh Avenue (2)

94 Avenue

Road

Walter Flats

Walterdale

Flats

Walter Street

108 Street

Road

Walter's Ferry

No longer exists

Ferry

Walterdale

No longer exists

Subdivision

Walterdale Flats

Walterdale

Flats

Wankel Street

77 Street

Road

Ward Drive

28 Avenue SW

Road

Washington Avenue (1)

133 Avenue

Road

Washington Avenue (2)

No longer exists

Road

Washington Avenue (3)

107 Avenue

Road

Water Avenue

100 Avenue

Road

Water Front

100 Avenue

Road

Water Street (1)

100 Avenue

Road

Water Street (2)

83 Street

Road

Waterloo Avenue

125 Avenue

Road

Watt Street

83 Street

Road

Weatherspoon Close

Wotherspoon Close

Road

Webb Road

28 Street NE

Road

Wedgewood

Eastwood

Subdivision

Wedgewood

Parkdale

Subdivision

Wellington Park

Wellington

Subdivision

Wellington Park Addition
Pembina
Subdivision

Wellington Terrace
Louise McKinney Park
Park

Wentworth Street
66 Street
Road

Wernerville
Ellerslie
Subdivision

West Capilano
Forest Heights
Subdivision

West Crescent Avenue
2 Avenue SW/
4 Avenue SW/
28 Street SW
Road

West Delton
Alberta Avenue
Subdivision

West Edmonton
Calder
Village

West End
Unknown
Park

West End Gardens
Unnamed
Subdivision

West Glenora
Grovenor/McQueen
Subdivision

West Grove
Grovenor
Subdivision

West Ingle
Westmount
Subdivision

West Jasper Place
Morin Industrial/
Poundmaker Industrial/
Sunwapta Industrial
Subdivision

West Jasper Place Park
Callingwood Park
Park

West Lawn
Glenwood
Subdivision

West Lynnwood
Elmwood
Subdivision

West Lynwood
Elmwood
Subdivision

West Railway Street
103 Street
Road

West Street
107 Street
Road

Westgrove
Grovenor
Subdivision

Westlawn
Glenwood
Subdivision

Westminster Avenue
121 Avenue
Road

Westmount
Inglewood/Westmount/
Woodcroft
Subdivision

Westmount Park
Coronation Park
Park

Westpoint Road
4 Avenue SW/
7 Avenue SW/
8 Avenue SW/
181 Street SW
Road

Westpoint Wynd
Wolf Willow Close
Road

Westridge Ravine
Wolf Willow Ravine
Ravine

White Avenue
Whyte Avenue
Road

White Street
132 Street
Road

Whitemud Creek
Whitemud Park
Subdivision

Whyte Avenue
No longer exists
Road

Wilkin Avenue
No longer exists
Road

William Avenue
No longer exists
Road

Williard Street
94 Street
Road

Willow Avenue
115 Avenue
Road

Willow Street
190 Street
Road

Wilmot Street

Unknown

Road

Wilson Avenue

87 Street

Road

Wilson Street (1)

110 Avenue

Road

Wilson Street (2)

39 Street

Road

Wilton Street

65 Street

Road

Windermere Road

Windermere Drive

Road

Windham Street

132 Street

Road

Windsor Park Road

116 Street

Road

Windsor Terrace

William Hawrelak Park

Subdivision

Winnipeg Street

No longer exists

Road

Wolf Willow

Oleskiw

Subdivision

Wolf Willow Farms

Oleskiw

Subdivision

Woodland (1)

Delton

Subdivision

Woodland (2)

Alberta Avenue

Subdivision

Woodland Addition

Delton

Subdivision

Woodland Avenue

121 Avenue

Road

Woodland Industrial

Delton

Subdivision

Woodlands Estate

Delton

Subdivision

Woodsworth Street

105A Avenue

Road

Woodward Avenue

122 Avenue

Road

Woodworth

Delton

Subdivision

Wrangle Street

77 Street

Road

Wright Street (1)

59 Street

Road

Wright Street (2)

No longer exists

Road

Wye Road

76 Avenue

Road

Y Road

*82 Avenue/Sherwood
Park Freeway*

Road

Yale Avenue (1)

No longer exists

Road

Yale Avenue (2)

No longer exists

Road

Yonge Avenue

No longer exists

Road

Yonge Street (1)

85 Street

Road

Yonge Street (2)

No longer exists

Road

York Avenue

96 Street

Road

York Street (1)

61 Street

Road

York Street (2)

No longer exists

Road

Young Street

98 Street

Road

Youngstown

Britannia Youngstown

Subdivision

Yukon Avenue

116 Avenue

Road

Sources

Akrigg, G.P.V. and Helen B. Akrigg. *1001 British Columbia Place Names*. Vancouver, British Columbia: Discovery Press, 1973.

Alberta Family Histories Society and the Alberta Genealogical Society. *Alberta Cemetery Records and Other Sources*. Calgary, Alberta: Alberta Family Histories Society, 1995.

Alberta Genealogical Society. *1901 Census: Alberta District (No. 202)*. http://www.agsedm.edmonton.ab.ca/1901_census_202_online.html.

Andreae, Christopher. *Lines of Country: An Atlas of Railway and Waterway History in Canada*. Erin, Ontario: Boston Mills Press, 1997.

Babcock, Douglas R. *A Gentleman of Strathcona: Alexander Cameron Rutherford*. Historic Sites Occasional Paper No. 8. Edmonton, Alberta: Alberta Culture Historical Resources Division. March 1980.

Blue, John. *Alberta, Past and Present, Historical and Biographical*. Chicago, Illinois: Pioneer History Publishing Company, 1924.

Bowler, Vaughn and Michael Wanchuk. *Volunteers: Edmonton Federation of Community Leagues, A History of the Largest Volunteer Organization in North America*. Edmonton, Alberta: Lone Pine Publishing, 1986.

Canadian Parliamentary Guide. Guide Parlementaire Canadien. Place of publication and publishers vary, 1905–.

Cashman, A.W. *The Edmonton Story*. Edmonton, Alberta: The Institute of Applied Art Ltd., 1956.

———. *More Edmonton Stories*. Edmonton, Alberta: The Institute of Applied Art Ltd., 1958.

Copley, George J. *English Place Names and Their Origins*. New York, New York: A.M. Kelley, 1968.

Dictionary of Canadianisms Based on Historical Principles. Toronto, Ontario: Gage Publishing, 1967.

Ellis, Frank. *Canada's Flying Heritage*. Toronto, Ontario: University of Toronto Press, 1954.

Faries, R., ed. *A Dictionary of the Cree Language*. Toronto: Church of England, 1865.

Farnell, Peggy O'Connor. *Old Glenora*. Edmonton, Alberta: Old Glenora Historical Society, 1984.

Federation of Saskatchewan Indian Nations. "Sweetgrass: Negotiator and Patriot." *Saskatchewan Indian* (fall 1987): 17. http://collections.ic.gc.ca/indian/a87fal17.htm.

Field, Dorothy. *Edmonton Historical Walking and Driving Tour: The Highlands*. Edmonton, Alberta: The Highlands Historical Foundation and Alberta Community Development, n.d.

Fisher, Chris and John Acorn. *Birds of Alberta*. Edmonton, Alberta: Lone Pine Publishing, 1998.

Geographic Board of Canada. *Place-Names of Alberta*. Ottawa, Ontario: Department of the Interior, 1928.

Gilpin, John F. "The City of Strathcona, 1891–1912: 'We see just ahead the glory of the sun in his might.'" Unpublished MA thesis, University of Alberta, 1978.

———. *Edmonton, Gateway to the North*. Windsor, Ontario: S.n., 1989.

Henderson's Edmonton, Alberta, City Directory. Vancouver, British Columbia: S.n., 1904–1987.

Holtslander, Dale. "School Districts of Alberta." Unpublished manuscript, 1979.

Hooper, A.B. and T. Kearney. *Canadian National Railways: Synoptical History*. Montreal, Quebec: Canadian National Railways, 1962.

Kostek, M.A. *A Century and Ten: The History of Edmonton Public Schools*. Edmonton, Alberta: Edmonton Public Schools, 1992.

LeClaire, Nancy and George Cardinal. *Alberta Elders' Cree Dictionary: alperta ohci kehtehayak nehiyaw otwestamâkewasinahikan*. Edmonton, Alberta: The University of Alberta Press, 1998.

Little, William, H.W. Fowler and J. Coulson. *The Shorter Oxford English Dictionary on Historical Principles*. London and Glasgow, United Kingdom: Oxford University Press, 1964.

Lowe, Shirley and Lori Yanish. *Edmonton's West Side Story: The History of the Original West End of Edmonton From 1870*. Edmonton, Alberta: 124th Street and Area Business Association, 1991.

Macdonald, J. S. *A History of the Dominion Telegraph*. Battleford, Saskatchewan: Canadian Northwest Historical Society, 1930.

MacGregor, J. G. *Edmonton, Alberta: A History*. Edmonton, Alberta: Hurtig Publishers, 1975.

MacMillian Dictionary of Canadian Biography. New York, New York: MacMillan, 1963.

Magnusson, Magnus, ed. *Chambers Biographical Dictionary*. Edinburgh, Scotland: Chambers, 1993.

Marsh, James H., ed. *Canadian Encyclopedia*. 3 vols. Edmonton, Alberta: Hurtig Publishers, 1985.

Martin, Chester. *Dominion Lands Policy*. Toronto, Ontario: Macmillan, 1938.

Myles, Eugenie Louise. *Airborne From Edmonton*. Toronto, Ontario: Ryerson Press, 1959.

Patrick, David, ed. *Chamber's Concise Gazetteer of the World*. Edinburgh, Scotland: W. & R. Chambers Ltd., 1906.

Place Names of Alberta. 4 vols. Edmonton, Alberta: Alberta Community Development and Friends of Geographical Names of Alberta Society and the University of Calgary Press, 1991–1996.

Porter, Darwin and Danforth Prince. *Frommer's 99: London*. London, United Kingdom: Millian, 1998.

Powell, Karen L. *A History of Name Changes of Alberta Government Departments and Agencies, 1905–1971*. Edmonton, Alberta: Legislature Library, 1971.

Ream, Peter. *The Fort on the Saskatchewan*. Fort Saskatchewan, Alberta: Metropolitan Printing, 1974.

Reaney, P. H. *Origins of English Place Names*. London, United Kingdom: Routledge and Kegan Paul, 1961.

Rich, E. E. *Hudson's Bay Company, 1670–1870*. Vol. 3, *1821–1870*. Toronto, Ontario: McClelland and Stewart, 1960.

Room, Adrian. *A Dictionary of Irish Place-Names*. Belfast, Ireland: Appletree Press Ltd., 1986.

Rowswell-Schroeder, Alyce. *Early Pioneers: They Came in 1879: The Origins and Chronicles of the Rowswell/Hutchings Families of Poplar Lake*. S.l.: Michael Haynes and Sheila Adams, 1990.

Schneider, Ena. *Ribbons of Steel: The Story of the Northern Alberta Railways*. Calgary, Alberta: Detselig Enterprises, 1989.

Smythe, Terry. "Thematic Study of the Fur Trade in the Canadian West, 1670–1870." Unpublished manuscript prepared for the Historic Sites and Monuments Board of Canada, 1968.

South Edmonton, Papaschase Historical Society. *South Edmonton Saga*. Edmonton, Alberta: South Edmonton, Papaschase Historical Society, 1984.

Stanley, G. F. G. *Louis Riel*. Toronto, Ontario: Ryerson Press, 1963.

Strathearn, Gloria. *Alberta Newspapers, 1880–1982: An Historical Directory*. Edmonton, Alberta: The University of Alberta Press, 1988.

University of Alberta Archives. *From the Past to the Future: A Guide to the Holdings of the University of Alberta Archives*. Edmonton, Alberta: University of Alberta Archives, 1992.

Winterburn W. I. *Memory Trails of Winterburn*. Winterburn, Alberta: Winterburn Women's Institute, 1977.

Women of Unifarm. *Cherished Memories*. Ardrossan, Alberta: Ardrossan Unifarm, 1973.

Wood, Nicola. *Scottish Place Names*. Edinburgh, Scotland: Chambers, 1989.

Archives

City of Edmonton Archives. (In particular manuscripts, map, newspaper clippings, and city government records groups were used. The most useful government records were the meeting minutes of the City Council, Names Advisory Committee, and Planning Departments.)

National Archives of Canada. (Notably the on-line finding aids for Western Land Grants, Post Offices and Postmasters, and the Diaries of Mackenzie King.)

National Library of Canada

University of Alberta Archives
University of Saskatchewan Library

Newspapers
Edmonton Bulletin
Edmonton Journal

Web sites consulted
"Abbey ruins." http://www.glastonbury.co.uk/
Alberta. Legislative Assembly.
    http://www.assembly.ab.ca/lao/library/
Alberta. Lieutenant-Governor.
    http://www.lieutenantgovernor.ab.ca/
Alberta Sports Hall of Fame. http://www.cahf.ca/
"Alexandra Oldenbury (Queen Alexandra)."
    http://www.camelotinl.com/heritage/alexand.html
"Beaumaris." http://www.beaumaris.com/
"Braemar Castle, Royal Deeside, Scotland."
    http://www.royal-deeside.org.uk/braecas.htm.
*British Civil Wars, Commonwealth and Protectorate,
    1638-60.* http://www.british-civil-wars.co.uk/
British Columbia Archives, Online Death Registration
    Index. http://www.bcarchives.gov.bc.ca/index.htm
"Caernarfon Castle."
    http://www.castlewales.com/caernarf.html
Canada. Governor General. http://www.gg.ca
Canadian Aviation Hall of Fame. http://www.cahf.ca/
Canadian Police Officers Memorial Association.
    http://www.cacp.ca/english/memoriam/
    honour.asp
"Capilano Suspension Bridge: Park History."
    http://www.capbridge.com/parkhistory.html
"The Cariboo Gold Rush."
    http://www.tbc.gov.bc.ca/culture/schoolnet/
    cariboo/place.htm
"Castles." http://www.castles.org/castles/
"Catholic Online Saints: St. Rose of Lima."
    http://saints.catholic.org/saints/roselima.html
"Chief Joseph Capilano."
    http://www.robirda.com/pauline.html
City of Edmonton. http://www.edmonton.ca/
    (In particular the information on parks, council

minutes, biographies of councillors and mayors
    were used.)
"Cumbria." http://www.reivers.com/cumbria.htm
Dictionary of Canadian Biography.
    http://www.biographi.ca/EN/
"Dunluce."
    http://www.irelandseye.com/visit/IC/dunluce.html
"The Early History of Scotland—Place-Names
    Appearing On the Map."
    http://www.gwp.enta.net/scothist.htm#clans
Edmonton Public Library. "Elections in Edmonton
    (1892-2001)."
    http://www.epl.ca/Elections/EPLIndex.cfm
Edmonton Public Schools Archives and Museum.
    http://archives.epsb.net/
Edmonton Sports Hall of Fame.
    http://www.edmontonsport.com/
"Fort Edmonton Park: The Five Sites of Fort
    Edmonton." http://www.gov.edmonton.ab.ca/
    comm_services/city_op_attractions/
"Genuki: Caithness County—Contents Page."
    http://www.frayston.demon.co.uk/genuki/cai/
"Her Majesty Queen Elizabeth II."
    http://www.canada.gc.ca/howgoc/queen/qubio.e.
    html
Heritage Community Foundation. *Adventurous
    Albertans.* http://collections.ic.gc.ca/
    pasttopresent/settlement/.
"History of Caledon: Inglewood."
    http://homc.col.ca/~ske/library/community/
    history/history2.html
Histor!ca. *Canadian Encyclopedia.*
    http://www.thecanadianencyclopedia.com/
Home Sweet Heritage Home: Biographies of Famous
    Calgarians and Their Homes. "Sam Livingstone."
    http://collections.ic.gc.ca/calgary/res48.htm.
Indian and Northern Affairs Canada. First Nations
    Lands Registry System.
    http://pse-esd.ainc-inac.gc.ca/
"Inglewood."
    http://www.glenbow.org/histcal/inglewood.html
"Lambton County.com." http://www.lambton-
    county.com.

"London Place Names."
http://www.krysstal.com/londname.html#n

"North Central Kentucky Place Names: Clifton."
http://home.netcom.com/~jog1/nckyplacenames.html

"North East England History Pages: Place Names and their Meanings—Kaldecoates to Owton Manor."
http://www.thenortheast.fsnet.co.uk/Place%20Name%20Meanings%20K%20to%20O.htm.

"Our Patron Saint George."
http://www.vaxxine.com/stgeorge/saint/

Stonechild, A. Blair. "The Indian View of the 1885 Uprising."
http://www.smokylake.com/history/native/indianview.htm

"Winston Churchill."
http://www.time.com/time/time100/leaders/profile/churchill.html

Index by Surnames of Entries

MANY OFFICIAL NAMES in Edmonton were derived from people's names. This is an alphabetical list by surname, except for Aboriginal names or titled persons, of those individuals, indicating the places named for them. The entries in the book are arranged alphabetically, word by word, as they are officially listed in the public record. Many places are listed under the first name or title of the person the place is named after, for example, Queen Alexandra can be found in the Q section and Orval W. Allen is in the O section.

Naming Edmonton Letters

Pembina Hall, University of Alberta, 9101–114 Street

Strathcona Furniture, 8226–103 Street

Java Jive, SUB, University of Alberta, 8900–114 Street

Garneau Theatre, 8712–109 Street

106 Street and 103 Avenue

Commercial Hotel, 10329 Whyte Avenue

Birks Building, 10354 Jasper Avenue

Lillo's Music, 10848 Whyte Avenue

Francis Winspear Centre for Music, #4 Sir Winston Churchill Square (99 Street and 102 Avenue)

Julio's Barrio Mexican Restaurant, 10450 Whyte Avenue

Metals Building,
10190–104th Street

Pembina Hall, University of
Alberta, 9101–114 Street

Sadler Insurance window,
10808–82 Avenue

Strathcona Hotel,
10302 Whyte Avenue

Paramount Theatre,
10233 Jasper Avenue

Southpark Pontiac Buick Cadillac
GMC Ltd., 10615 Whyte Avenue

Great West Saddlery Building,
10137–104 Street

Strathcona Furniture Exchange,
8226–103 Street

Metals Building,
10190–104th Street

HUB Cigar & Newstand,
10345 Whyte Avenue

Coast Mountain Sports,
124 Edmonton City Centre
(west of 100 Street and north of
102 Avenue)

Great West Saddlery Building,
10137–104 Street

 Pembina Hall, University of
Alberta, 9101–114 Street

 Pharo's Pizza and Spaghetti House,
8708–109 Street

 Avadh Bhatia Physics Laboratory,
University of Alberta,
11239 Saskatchewan Drive